Black British | White British

Black British | White British

DILIP HIRO

REVISED EDITION

MONTHLY REVIEW PRESS
NEW YORK AND LONDON

To Beverly

First published by Eyre & Spottiswoode, 1971
Revised edition published by Monthly Review Press, 1973

Library of Congress Cataloging in Publication Data

Hiro, Dilip
  Black British, white British.

  (Pelican books)
  Bibliography: p.
    1. England—Foreign population. 2. England—
Race question. 3. Race discrimination—England.
I. Title.
DA125.A1H53 1973   301. 45′1′0941   72-92026
ISBN 0-85345-270-9

First Printing

Monthly Review Press
116 West 14th Street, New York, N.Y. 10011
33/37 Moreland Street, London, E.C. 1

Manufactured in the United States of America

CONTENTS

PREFACE

I have updated and slightly trimmed the hardback edition of *Black British*, *White British* without substantially altering the basic structure of the book. This version, like its hardback predecessor, is in three parts, with each part written respectively from the West Indian, Asian and white British viewpoint. In the last case I have attempted to subdue my *emotional* antipathy towards the illiberal British viewpoint to meet the demand of objectivity. The result may appear ambivalent to some readers, particularly those who identify themselves totally with the illiberal or liberal camp, and those who are specialists. But then my book is not addressed to specialists or policy-makers but to the general reader.

I am well aware of the current debate regarding the use of the words 'coloured' and 'black'. The British generally call anybody who is not white and caucasoid 'coloured'. Many West Indians nowadays, especially the young, prefer 'black' to 'coloured'. There is no popular term for 'coloured' in Urdu or Punjabi or Bengali, although *rangdaar* (meaning 'coloured') is increasingly being used by the official and quasi-official agencies in Britain. The terms in common use among the Asian immigrants are *kala* (black) and *gora*, *chita* or *shadha* (white). Under the circumstances I have used the words 'coloured' and 'black' interchangeably, and feel that, for all practical purposes, it is correct to call the West Indian and Asian settlers in Britain 'Black British'.

Next, the term West Indian. It is true that West Indian society is multi-racial: it has Africans (negroids), East Indians (brown caucasoids), Chinese (mongoloids), Europeans (white caucasoids) and various combinations of these. But most of the West Indian settlers in Britain are from Jamaica and Barbados where the population is overwhelmingly of African stock. Hence, in this context, the term West Indian is to be regarded as a synonym of Afro-Caribbean.

By the same token, the Asian should be considered to mean Indian/Pakistani/Bangla Deshi from the Indian sub-continent or East Africa. It does *not* include the Chinese, either from Hong Kong, Singapore or Malaysia.

Unlike many other authors on this subject I have not concerned myself with influencing government policies. Hence I have not submitted a neat package of conclusions and recommendations at the end. My aim is general, and modest: to create a better understanding of the problem by highlighting the historical perspective and providing some previously unknown information and fresh insight. If at the end of the book the reader feels that he is able to see the wood instead of the trees, the purpose of the book will have been amply served.

London, 1 May 1972   DILIP HIRO

INTRODUCTION:
A HISTORICAL VIEW

*Self-knowledge, for a nation as well as an
individual, begins with history.*
ARTHUR M. SCHLESINGER JR[1]

*I think that the past is all that makes the
present coherent, and further, that the past
will remain horrible for exactly as long
as we refuse to assess it honestly.*
JAMES BALDWIN[2]

*Slavery was not born out of racism: rather,
racism was the consequence of slavery.*
ERIC WILLIAMS[3]

*Of all the colonialists, the British have been
the least willing to mingle with their subject
races.*
PETER GRIFFITHS[4]

The first major contact of the (Anglo-Saxon) English with
coloured people occurred during 193–211 A.D. when Septimius
Severus, a north African, ruled England as the Roman Emperor.
He once remarked that the English made 'bad slaves'. The English
later came into contact with coloured people in the Middle East
during the Second Crusade (1189–91) and the Ninth Crusade
(1271–2). These Crusades, however, failed to release the Holy
City of Jerusalem from the hands of the 'infidel' Muslims.

Later still, contact developed through trade, by sea, with West
Africa and Asia. In 1554, John Locke, an English trader, brought
slaves from West Africa to England, and sold them as household
servants. By then Spain and Portugal had established extensive
colonies in the New World, and were developing them as producers of cotton, sugar-cane and tobacco for export to Europe as
fast as the supply of labour – consisting of native Indian tribes,

1. *Crisis of Confidence*, André Deutsch, 1969, p. 10.
2. *Notes of a Native Son*, Michael Joseph, 1964, p. 14.
3. *Capitalism and Slavery*, André Deutsch, 1964 p. 7.
4. *A Question of Colour?*, Leslie Frewin, 1966, p. 19.

poor whites and African slaves - would allow. As the supply of American Indians and poor whites began to dwindle, the Iberians began to lean more heavily on the expediency of securing slave labour from Africa.[5]

It was the lucrative prospect of supplying the Iberian colonies with African labour that tempted Sir John Hawkins to engage in the slave trade. He transported the first 'cargo' of five hundred slaves from West Africa to the New World in 1562. Later, during the early 1600s, as England established her own plantation colonies on the north American mainland and Barbados, her economic and political interests in the slave trade and slavery increased. In 1655 Oliver Cromwell gave further boost to this development by seizing Jamaica from Spain.

Under the treaty of Utrecht in 1713, Britain acquired, from France, the contract to supply African slaves to the Spanish colonies from her Caribbean territories. The result was that within fifty years Britain became the leading slave-trading nation in the world, the foremost 'slave carrier' for other European nations, and the centre of the Triangular Trade. Her ships carried manufactured goods to West Africa, transported slaves to the New World, and brought back sugar, tobacco and cotton to Britain. In 1757, in the month of July alone, 175 ships with cargo worth £2m. (equivalent to £35m. today) docked in British ports.[6]

As British involvement in, and the profits from, slavery and the slave trade increased, the concept of the African slave as a commodity or, at best, a workhorse, began to emerge. Aboard ship the African captive was considered an item of cargo. This seemed to be the legal position as was illustrated by the case of the slave-ship *Zong*. During a rough crossing of the Atlantic by this ship, 130 slaves were thrown overboard. When the case went to the court, the issue was not the deliberate drowning of 130 human

5. 'Both Indian slavery and white servitude were to go down before the blackman's superior endurance, docility, and labour capacity,' wrote J. S. Bassett. *Slavery and Servitude in the Colony of North Carolina*, p. 77.

6. Liverpool's first slave-ship sailed for Africa in 1709. By 1771, one-third of *all* its ships were slave-traders. By 1792, Liverpool had forty-two per cent of the total European slave trade. Eric Williams, *Capitalism and Slavery*, p. 34.

beings, but whether throwing slaves overboard was 'an act of jettison', for which the insurance company was obliged to pay, or 'an act of fraud' which released the insurance company of its obligation.[7] On plantations, African slaves were catalogued along with livestock and treated as work-animals, to be worked to the maximum at the minimum cost of maintenance.

A similar view of slaves as property was taken by the courts in England where, by the mid-eighteenth century, thousands of households of English aristocrats and retired planters[8] used African slaves, often wearing padlocked copper or silver collars around their necks,[9] as serving-boys and menservants. Some Englishmen, who deplored this inhuman treatment of Africans challenged the system of slavery, in the English courts, by providing legal aid to runaway slaves. But they lost their cases. Twice, in 1720 and 1749, courts ruled that a runaway slave in England could be recovered. Until 1771, Lord Mansfield, the Lord Chief Justice, was unwilling to face the consequences of the masters losing 'their property by bringing slaves to England'. He hoped the proposition would never be finally discussed.[10]

However, a year later, Lord Mansfield was obliged to give judgement in the case of James Somersett, an escaped slave who had been recaptured and put aboard a ship sailing for Jamaica. The point under dispute was the master's right to remove his slave from England to the sphere of colonial law. Lord Mansfield concluded his verdict with the statement that, 'The state of slavery is ... so odious that nothing can support it but positive law ... I cannot say that this case is allowed or approved by the law of England and therefore the Black must be discharged.'[11]

7. A. Chater, *Race Relations in Britain*, Lawrence and Wishart, 1966, p. 12.

8. By 1770, in London alone, there were 18,000 black slaves, forming nearly three per cent of an estimated population of 650,000. (The first recorded population of London, in 1801, was 959,000.)

9. An advertisement in the *London Advertiser* in 1756 read, 'Matthew Dyer intimates to the public that he makes silver padlocks for Blacks or Dogs; collars etc.'

10. Bob Hepple, *Race, Jobs and the Law in Britain*, Allen Lane The Penguin Press, 1968, pp. 39–40.

11. Edward Fiddes, 'Lord Mansfield and the Somersett Case', *Law Quarterly Review* 50 (1934), pp. 499–511.

This judgement is popularly construed to mean that thereafter the slaves in England were set free, and that slavery became illegal. Nothing of the sort happened. '[Lord Mansfield's] decision freed no slaves,' writes Michael Banton; 'it declared that, until Parliament enacted legislation explicitly covering the question, the power in dispute [regarding shipping a slave from England to the colonies] could not legally be exercised.'[12] Indeed, by then, there was a strong vested interest in England, committed to the continuance of slavery and the slave trade, which had learnt to rationalize these practices.

To counter the criticism from liberal, humane quarters, the slave masters and merchants argued that the African slaves were 'an equivocal race, between man and monkey', and that they were only 'half human'.[13] In other words, in order essentially to justify their economic greed, while simultaneously exorcizing themselves of any guilt they might have felt, the slave masters and merchants argued that the slave was sub-human and received the treatment he (naturally) deserved. Was it 'inhuman', for instance, indiscriminately to whip a recalcitrant horse or donkey? The fact that the slave was of a different race, and black, led the British masters and traders to apply their beliefs to the whole race.[14] They ceased to call the slave African and, instead, referred

12. *Race Relations*, Tavistock, 1967, p. 23. Slaves continued to be bought and sold after 1772 as shown by the following advertisement which appeared in a Liverpool newspaper in October 1779: 'To be sold by auction at George Dunbar's office, on Thursday next, the 21st inst., at one o'clock a black boy, aged about 14 years old, and a large Mountain Tiger Cat.' Bob Hepple points out that the courts in England 'continued far into the nineteenth century to countenance slavery'. *Race, Jobs and the Law in Britain*, p. 41. However, Lord Mansfield's judgement in 1772 gave an impetus to the anti-slavery movement and encouraged liberally inclined masters to free their slaves. But then the freed slaves found it impossible to find work and became residents of the common lodging houses for destitutes in the St Giles area of London. This earned them the nickname of 'St Giles Blackbirds'.

13. Halliday, *The West Indies*, p. 56. 'Blacks are monkeys to be trampled upon', was one of the remarks made by the dockers protesting outside Parliament in 1968. The *Observer*, 28 April 1968.

14. 'The effect of the slave trade was that all Africans were considered present or potential slaves,' wrote K. L. Little. *Negroes in Britain*, Kegan Paul, 1947, p. 214.

to him by his racial label – negro. Generalizations about negroes proliferated, and became part of the popular beliefs and myths of Britain.

At the intellectual level, religious and cultural justifications were often advanced to establish the inherent inferiority of negroes as a race. It was argued that the negroes were the descendants of Ham, the black son of Noah. As such they were *natural* slaves, condemned for ever to remain 'hewers of wood and drawers of water'. Besides, they were not only physically black, the colour of Satan, but also morally black. They were, in short, savage creatures, who jumped from tree to tree in the steamy jungles of Africa, and ate one another with relish. To transport these sub-human, biologically inferior, mentally retarded creatures from the hell of African jungles to the tranquillity and order of the plantations in the New World, where they were assured of a protected existence, was almost an act of Christian charity.

David Hume, the historian and philosopher, arrived at the conclusion of inherent negro inferiority from another, wider perspective. In his essay, 'Of National Characters', published in 1753, he stated:

I am apt to suspect the Negroes to be naturally inferior to the Whites. There scarcely ever was a civilized nation of that complexion, nor ever any individual, eminent either in action or speculation. No ingenious manufacturers among them, no arts, no sciences. On the other hand, the most rude and barbarous of the Whites such as the Germans, the present Tartars, still have some thing eminent about them in their valour, form of government or some particular. Such a uniform and constant difference could not happen in so many countries and ages, if Nature had not made an original distribution between these breeds of men.[15]

Since this 'original distribution' of intelligence and ingenuity by Nature was everlasting and unalterable, any negro manifesting mental agility could only be considered a freak or a hoax. Referring to one negro – Francis Williams, in Jamaica – reported to be 'a man of learning', David Hume wrote that 'it is likely that

15. Cited in Wilfred Wood and John Downing, *Vicious Circle*, SPCK, 1968, p. 30.

he is admired for his slender accomplishments, like a parrot who speaks a few words plainly'. A similar argument was advanced by another British historian, Edward Long. In his *History of Jamaica*, published in 1774, he wrote:

We cannot pronounce them unsusceptible of civilization since even apes have been taught to eat, drink, repose and dress like men. But of all the human species hitherto discovered, their natural baseness of mind seems to afford least hope of their being (except by miraculous interposition of Divine Providence) so refined as to think as well as act like men. I do not think that an orang-outang husband would be any dishonour to an Hottentot female.[16]

By the late eighteenth century this type of racism had become so ingrained in social thinking at all levels of British society that the abolition of the slave trade in 1807, and of slavery in 1834, seemed to leave the basic attitudes essentially unaltered. Now the efforts of the freed negroes to 'civilize' themselves became a subject for mockery. Following his visit to Jamaica in 1859–60, Anthony Trollope wrote of the negro:

He burns to be regarded as a scholar, puzzles himself with fine words, addicts himself to religion for the sake of appearance, and delights in aping the little graces of civilization ... If you want to win his heart for an hour, call him a gentleman; but if you want to reduce him to despairing obedience, tell him that he is a filthy nigger, assure him that his father and mother had tails like monkeys, and forbid him to think that he can have a soul like a white man.[17]

It was in the British plantation colonies in the western hemisphere that race relations emerged in their clearest form: the whites, as masters, were the superior race; the blacks, as slaves, were the inferior race. A basically similar model of race relations also emerged in the eastern hemisphere once the British had consolidated their hold over the Indian sub-continent. This was ironic. Because the British, like the pioneering Portuguese, had ventured to India as a result of the reports of India's riches, originating with Marco Polo's descriptions, in 1298, of the coun-

16. Cited in A. Chater, *Race Relations in Britain*, Lawrence and Wishart, 1966, pp. 15–16.
17. *The West Indies and the Spanish Main*, 1860. Cited in Wilfred Wood and John Downing, op. cit., pp. 30–31.

tries of the East, which had excited the imagination of many European traders and rulers.

Of the king and three brothers of Maabar (Malabar), a part of the Greater India, 'being the noblest and richest country in the world', Marco Polo wrote, 'they import as many as five thousand [horses] at a time and for each pay five hundred saggi of gold which is equal to one hundred marks of silver [about $1,000].'[18] He described Zeilan (Ceylon) as the island which 'produces more beautiful and valuable rubies than are found in any other parts of the world and likewise sapphires, topazes, amethysts, garnets and many other precious stones'.[19]

The *sole* purpose of the Latin European exploration of the high seas which began in earnest in the mid-fifteenth century was to find a sea route to India, since the land route continued to be blocked by the generally hostile Muslim rulers in the Middle East. It was this exploration which brought the Portuguese to the deltas of the Niger and Senegal rivers on the West African coast and led, in due course, to the trading of African slaves.

Christopher Columbus in 1492 thought he had discovered 'The Indies', and hence he called the islands' inhabitants Indians. It was seven years later that Vasco da Gama, a Portuguese sailor, finally succeeded in reaching the real India via what was later to be called the Cape of 'Good Hope'. He was captivated by the country and by its inhabitants. British ambassadors and traders who followed the Portuguese, and other Europeans too, evinced great interest in, and fascination for, Indian people and their religions, philosophy and languages.

But as British trading interests became allied to territorial ambitions, and as the British, by virtue of their successive military victories over rulers of the fragmented parts of the sub-continent, began to acquire self-confidence, they grew less and less interested in the Indian people and culture. With the loss of the American colonies in 1783, the centre of the Empire shifted to India; and, with it, the distance of the ruling British from the subjugated Indians grew even further. 'As the occupation of India proceeded,'

18. Milton Rugoff, edr., *The Travels of Marco Polo*. New York. 1961. p. 249.
19. ibid., p. 244.

writes V. G. Kiernan, 'English masters were no longer in a humour to admire anything Indian.'[20]

By 1792 Charles Grant, a British historian, was calling the Indian people 'a race of men lamentably degenerate and base, retaining but a feeble sense of moral obligation . . . governed by a malevolent and licentious passion . . .' And this 'race of men' was, by then, commonly referred to by the British as 'blacks'. In his autobiography William Thackeray mentioned travelling to England from India (in 1817) as a child in care of a 'black servant' from Calcutta. 'Englishmen were already prone to this racialism as a result of long involvement with African slavery,' writes V. G. Kiernan, 'and there was some coming and going between the East and West Indies.'[21] Another term, originating from African slavery – 'nigger' – was also freely applied to Indians. By the 1850s, Indians had been described as 'the wild barbarians, indifferent to human life . . . yet free, simple as children, brave, faithful to their masters' by the historian Herbert Edwardes. This could well have been a general description of African slaves by their white masters.[22]

'Europeans lord it over the conquered natives [in India] with a high hand,' observed E. J. Trelawney in 1831. 'Every outrage may be committed almost with impunity.'[23] And yet the British reacted to the Mutiny by Indian soldiers in 1857 with an unprecedented savagery. 'History shudders at the recollection of the terrible "Spanish fury" which desolated Antwerp in the days of William the Silent,' wrote G. O. Trevelyan, 'but the "English fury" was more terrible still.'[24] The degree of the 'English fury' was described, in a single line, in a letter to a London newspaper by an Englishman in India: 'Every nigger we meet [we] either string up or shoot'. While the British reacted to the Mutiny in openly racialist terms the basic reason for the Mutiny itself lay in their racialist attitudes. Discussing the major cause that led to the

20. *The Lords of Human Kind*, Weidenfeld and Nicholson, 1969, p. 21.
21. ibid., p. 34.
22. Two generations later, Rudyard Kipling was to describe the negro as 'a big, black vain baby and a man rolled in one'. Cited in Roi Ottley, *No Green Pastures*, John Murray, 1952, p. 22.
23. *The Adventures of a Younger Son*, p. 57.
24. *Competition Wallah*, London, 1866, pp. 244–5.

Mutiny, a correspondent to *The Times* wrote, 'The most scrubby mean little representative of *la race blanche* . . . regards himself as infinitely superior to the Rajpoot with a genealogy of a thousand years'.[25]

Following the Mutiny, India was formally annexed to Britain. With that began the century of imperialism proper.[26] The British in India evolved an elaborate code of behaviour for dealing with the natives resting on 'the cherished conviction of every Englishman in India, from the highest to the lowest . . . that he belongs to a race whom God has destined to govern and subdue' [as Seton Kerr, once Foreign Secretary of the Government, put it].[27] This policy of racial apartheid was effective in uniting the upper and lower echelons of the British in India: they all considered themselves as belonging to an inherently superior race. 'As a white man,' writes V. G. Kiernan, 'he [the indispensable Tommy Atkins] had the privilege . . . of seeing all Indians from Highness to sweeper officially regarded as inferior.'[28] The situation was almost identical with that prevalent then in the Southern states of America. On the eve of the Civil War in 1861, Jefferson Davis, the Southern leader who later became the President of the Confederacy, said:

One of the reconciling features of the existence [of negro slavery] is the fact that it raises white men to the same general level, that it dignifies and exalts every white man by the presence of a lower race.[29]

Charles Darwin's theories of evolution and the 'survival of the fittest', enunciated in his *Origin of Species*, first published in 1859, led most white people to believe that they were in a dominant position throughout the world because of their *inherent* superiority. 'It is this consciousness of the inherent superiority of the Europeans which has won for us India,' declared Lord Kitchener, Commander-in-Chief in India from 1902–9. He then illustrated

25. Cited in K. L. Little, *Negroes in Britain*, p. 211.

26. It is interesting to note that 1857, more or less, marks the beginning of what Michael Banton feels might be called, by future historians, the 'century of racism' – 1850–1950. *Race Relations*, p. 164.

27. Cited in E. Thompson and G. T. Garrett, *Rise and Fulfilment of British Rule in India*, London, 1934, p. 536.

28. V. G. Kiernan. *The Lords of Human Kind*, p. 58.

29. Cited in Michael Banton, *Race Relations*, p. 117.

the doctrine of 'inherent inequality' thus: 'However well-educated and clever a native may be, and however brave he may have proved himself, I believe that no rank we can bestow on him would cause him to be considered an equal of the British officer.'[30]

However, once the doctrine of superiority and its evidence – power of arms and efficient organization – had been established, the imperial father-figure could well afford to show a paternalistic concern for the 'native' child-figure without, in any way, undermining his own dominant position. It was this attitude of superiority blended with a paternalistic concern that underlay the actions of those who administered the Empire. And it was this attitude that Rudyard Kipling conveyed, in 1899, in his much celebrated poem 'The White Man's Burden':

> Take up the White Man's burden –
> Send forth the best you breed –
> Go bind your sons to exile
> To serve your captives' need;
> To wait in heavy harness,
> On fluttered folk and wild –
> Your new-caught, sullen peoples,
> Half-devil and half-child.[31]

In practice, the policy of sending forth 'the best you breed' by the British was complemented with receiving, in Britain, the best among the black natives to educate them in British theology, law, literature and medicine. Hence, from about 1875 onwards, students from the coloured colonies began arriving in Britain to study at the universities. But the British public could not be expected to make an exception of these selected few from among the 'fluttered folk and wild'. In *The Anglo-Fanti*, Kobina Sekyi noted that 'Coloured students studying social welfare or methods of teaching in the poorer quarters of London and other cities still complain fairly frequently of attitudes of "superiority" as well as curiosity towards them on the part of even some of the down-at-heel and decrepit inhabitants of the districts concerned.'[32]

30. Cited in K. M. Panikkar, *Asia and Western Dominance*, Allen and Unwin, 1959, p. 116.
31. *Rudyard Kipling's Verse, 1885–1926*, London, 1928, p. 320.
32. K. L. Little, *Negroes in Britain*, p. 218.

Even British university and college students often showed prejudice and antipathy towards coloured fellow-students. 'In England it appears as if the negro students were left to live their lives apart, even from the student class, and some, it seems, sought companionships and consolation in less desirable directions,' wrote K. L. Little. 'In some universities – Cambridge is cited as a case – prejudice against them was shown; although in this respect Indians were apparently even less popular. In London they were regarded with tolerance, but also with apathy.'[33] The situation was so unsatisfactory that a special meeting of those interested in the welfare of colonial students was called in 1913.

Then came the First World War. It created an unprecedented shortage of manpower and materials. The government requisitioned ships trading with Africa and Asia for troop transport and, with the ships, their black crews. Labour gangs were drafted in many coloured ports of the Empire and brought to England. Black colonials were employed in ordnance factories. Others were recruited as merchant seamen to replace the white seamen transferred to the Royal Navy. Several thousands of coloured workers were involved.[34]

But once the war was over, almost all of them were dispatched to 'where they belonged': they had served the interests of the metropolitan country and were of no more use to it. The few thousands who did not return to their countries of origin took to seafaring, the only avenue of employment open to them in peacetime, and settled in the dockside areas of London, Liverpool, Bristol, Manchester, Glasgow, Swansea, Cardiff and South Shields.

Racialist feeling in Britain was so strong then that even this insignificant number proved too much for the British public to bear. The result was a series of race riots in many of the port towns of Britain, when coloured settlers became targets of violence. The general attitude of the British public was summed up by an editorial in a Cardiff newspaper which said, 'The

33. ibid., p. 193. In his autobiography, *This Your England*, D. F. Karaka, the first Indian ever to be elected the President of the Oxford Union, in the 1930s, describes his experiences of racial discrimination in England.

34. K. L. Little, *Negroes in Britain*, p. 195.

government ought to declare it to be part of the national policy that this country is not to be regarded as an emigration field, that no more immigrants (as distinguished from visitors) can be admitted – and that immigrants must return to whence they came from'. That this demand had to do with racialist considerations rather than immigrants *per se* became evident when the newspaper added, 'This must apply to black men from the British West Indies as well as from the United States.'[35]

In 1920 there was a series of articles in the *Spectator* which established, beyond doubt, that a colour bar existed in Britain. This was also the conclusion of R. T. Lapière, a French sociologist, who after long research during the post-war period, published his results in 1928 in America. For example, of the twenty hotels in England he visited, only four were open to coloured guests.[36]

'It was usually found at the hotels and boarding houses where they [coloured people] were refused accommodation,' wrote an Indian correspondent to the *Spectator* in March 1931, 'that the "objectors" were white lodgers who had been in the East and "had seen the native in his den".'[37] It was particularly galling for the Briton who had enjoyed the 'white man boss' position[38] in the coloured colonies to treat the dark 'natives' as equals in the metropolitan country. He found it hard to reconcile the practice of racial apartheid in the coloured colonies with the concept of racial equality for all those resident in Britain.[39] He considered it subversive to cast Paul Robeson, an American negro, as Othello to play opposite Peggy Ashcroft as Desdemona, as happened in the West End in the 1930s, and joined the chorus of protest that arose. 'How then is it possible to maintain the stern creed in the policy of the Empire, the eternal supremacy of the white over the black?' asked one protestor in his letter to a London newspaper.[40]

35. Cited in K. L. Little, *Negroes in Britain*, p. 59.

36. 'Race Prejudice: France and England', *Social Forces*, Vol. VII, 1928, p. 106.

37. Cited in K. L. Little, op, cit., p. 217.

38. Sheila Patterson, *Dark Strangers*, Penguin Books, 1965, p. 212.

39. 'Whatever may have been the exhortations of Winston Churchill as Colonial Secretary, *Civis Britannicus sum* could never be the boast of any Indian or African,' wrote Hugh Tinker. *New Society*, 29 February 1968.

40. Cited in Roi Ottley, *No Green Pastures*, p. 26.

A quarter of a century later, in her field research in South London, Sheila Patterson found that, 'The only people, apart from a pathologically prejudiced handful, who displayed uncompromising verbal hostility towards the coloured newcomers seemed to be those who had had ... first-hand contacts with coloured people overseas during the war. This "wog complex" ... was reasonably widespread, and of course tended to influence the views of others to some extent.'[41]

To be fair, racialist views were not the monopoly of the British public: they were reflected in some of the actions of post-war British governments. The vetoing of Seretse Khama's plan to return to his native Basutoland after he had married a white girl in London, illustrates this. In Roi Ottley's view the reasons for this action by the government were rooted in 'race-sex-colonial policies'.[42] As a resident American journalist in Britain he came into frequent contact with government authorities and discovered that stereotypes regarding Africans existed in the highest circles.

I asked the Secretary of State for the Colonies if he envisioned eventual self-government for the African people. He was frankly shocked by the question. 'You must remember,' he countered, 'the Africans are savages, still eating each other up in places like Nigeria.'[43]

That was in 1950 when three major coloured colonies – India, Burma and Ceylon – had been freed from British domination. Apparently liquidating the coloured Empire did not mean discarding the notions and beliefs that had grown during the centuries of imperial experience. But nor did the abolition of slavery dispel the belief in the inherent inferiority of the negro. Had the freed slaves in the Caribbean then migrated to Britain, instead of to the Central American republics and other islands in the Caribbean, as they did, they would have realized this, as would have most British people. But they did not do so. In the 1950s, however, the situation developed differently and ironically: the liquidation of the coloured Empire was accompanied by the growing presence of coloured colonials in Britain.

41. *Dark Strangers*, p. 212.
42. ibid. p. 26
43. ibid, p. 55.

This development brought into relief the dichotomy between the British practice of racial apartheid in the coloured colonies, and the general British regard for 'human dignity' and a belief in 'the equality of all British subjects'. This conflict had always existed, but because the coloured colonies were overseas, in far-flung parts of the world, most Britons had still been able to consider themselves racially liberal and fair-minded, censorious of the white American and South African mistreatment of the blacks. But as the presence of blacks in Britain itself became more and more noticeable the situation changed: the contradiction between the moral attitudes of most British and their socio-historical attitudes became apparent. The constant interplay between these contradictory attitudes keeps race relations in Britain (as well as in America) in a dynamic state.

PART I: WEST INDIANS

1　THE NEW JERUSALEM

*I remember a Christmas pantomime in
Barbados where everyone departed for
England. That was the happy ending of the
plot.*
CLIFFORD CHASE, a West Indian settler
in Birmingham.

The people of the West Indies are now where they are because
they were transported in large numbers from Africa and Asia,
involuntarily or voluntarily, as part of the colonial policies of
European powers. From 1680 to 1786, for instance, more than
two million slaves were carried across the Atlantic,[1] a third of
them for the specific purpose of developing Jamaica, then a
British colony, into a lucrative sugarcane island.

This was done because the major source of labour supply
initiated by Charles II after his restoration in 1660 – banishment
of English felons, criminals, rioters and indentured servants to
the Caribbean – proved inadequate and unsuitable to meet the
ever-expanding demand of the planters. Population statistics
illustrate this change-over to the policy of an almost total reliance
on the African labour. In 1673, the black and white populations
in Jamaica were nearly equal: almost 10,000 of each. Fifty
years later, slaves outnumbered whites by ten to one: 74,000
blacks to 7,500 whites. Jamaica was fast becoming the leading
sugar producer in the world, a position she occupied for more
than a century, and which brought unprecedented prosperity to
British planters. In contrast, irreparable damage was done to the
economic interests of Jamaica herself.

By inundating Jamaica with a population out of all proportion
to her inherent resources, the seed of an insoluble problem was
implanted. This fact, and this alone, is the root cause of the
economic troubles that have plagued the island since then, and
which became uncomfortably apparent as soon as sugar cane
ceased to be a prized crop and slavery was abolished. Following

1. Eric Williams, *Capitalism and Slavery*, p. 33.

the Emancipation in 1834, Africans left plantations *en masse*, eager to explore the environment on their own, as free men and women.

What did they discover? Between the forty per cent mountainous non-arable land and the English plantations, there was very little fertile land left for them to develop. So they cleared the mountains here and there, and eked out a hazardous living. One of the few means of relieving their poverty was to leave the island altogether – to migrate.

By the 1860s migration had become a part of the island's life. Jamaicans went to Panama to build railways, and then to assist in survey work and construction of the Canal. At one time or another 68,000 Jamaicans participated in these projects. Jamaican labour was engaged to boost sugar production in Cuba after America had dislodged Spain as the imperial power in 1898. Later, Jamaicans were recruited to develop coffee and banana plantations in Honduras and Costa Rica. For its oil exploration Venezuela tapped this source of labour supply. But despite these temporary and permanent migrations, and a severe epidemic of cholera, the Jamaican population leapt from 320,000 in 1834 to 832,000 in 1910. The pressure to migrate kept rising.

Latterly, migration and seasonal work in America became popular. Before 1920, America was an 'open' country, a haven for immigrants. It was also English-speaking. Migration to America grew. Before America introduced literacy tests and visas for immigrants in 1924, more than 200,000 British West Indians had settled there.[2] But the immigration restrictions and the economic depression in America reduced the West Indian intake dramatically. In turn, this led to economic and political unrest in the British West Indies. A rash of strikes and serious rioting broke out in Jamaica, Trinidad and St Kitts during the late 1930s.

The situation would have grown worse had not the Second World War broken out. The war provided opportunities for employment *and* adventure to the unemployed and the young. Thousands of West Indians joined the British (and later,

2. Michael Kraus estimates immigration from the West Indies to America at 300,000 during the period of 1900–1930. *Immigration, The American Mosaic*, Van Nostrand, 1966, p. 97.

American) Armed Forces and war industries.[3] Others joined as 'Overseas Volunteer Workers' to man British ordnance factories.

There was little, if any, overt racial discrimination in the highly structured armed forces. Outside the barracks, too, the British people, in the midst of war, noticed more the uniform than the colour of the wearer. Indeed some black servicemen, on being demobbed, decided to settle in Britain, especially when they had married English girls.

The vast majority, however, returned home, but were soon disillusioned. The economic prospect was bleak. They also had considerable psychological difficulty in readjusting to civilian life in the West Indies: it was twice removed from war conditions in Britain. This was particularly true of those West Indians who had joined the forces straight from school.

Roy Terrelonge was one such person. Born in Jamaica, he joined the Royal Air Force after he left school. He served for six years. When demobbed he returned to Jamaica, but found 'not enough jobs, bad pay, tough conditions'. So he left for England, in June 1948, aboard the SS *Empire Windrush*. So did 491 other Jamaicans with similar backgrounds, and at least half of them had jobs or friends waiting for them in England.

Much to the British authorities' relief, this shipload of the West Indians did *not* prove to be the first wave of 'an unarmed invasion'. Despite the widely known labour shortage in Britain, no more than a thousand West Indians arrived each year – until 1952. Why? Because the West Indian migrant vastly preferred America to Britain. It was nearer; it was richer; it already had a large, established West Indian community. And, once the West Indian passed the literacy test and medical examination, it was easy to gain entry. The American law-makers had included the British West Indies in their immigration quota for Britain – a generous (and never fully subscribed) 65,000 a year. But, after the war, as the West Indian migration to America rose the American legislators, out of racial considerations, modified the law.

3. 'During the war more than 100,000 workers from the British West Indies were recruited for agricultural and industrial work in the United States.' James Wickenden, *Colour in Britain*, Oxford University Press, 1958, p. 5.

The resulting McCarran–Walter Act, in 1952, detached the British West Indies from Britain, and allotted a separate, meagre quota of eight hundred to the area: one hundred to Jamaica, one hundred to Trinidad, and so on. This amounted to a virtual ban on West Indian migration to America and caused much resentment among the islanders and the authorities.

Having been deprived of the American outlet the West Indians were compelled to explore other avenues for migration. And imperial Britain with its 'open-door' policy seemed a natural choice. Consequently there was a sudden upsurge in West Indian migration to Britain. Nearly 11,000 West Indians came to Britain in 1954. The following year the figure more than doubled. After that, the number stabilized at about 17,000 a year until rumours of impending restrictions on Commonwealth immigrants created the 'beat the ban' rush. The peak was reached in the first half of 1962 when more than 34,000 West Indians arrived in Britain as immigrants. The current rate is about 7,000 a year, consisting mainly of dependants of immigrants already here. In contrast, almost 15,000 Jamaicans left for America in 1968.[4]

Clearly the McCarran Act boosted West Indian migration to Britain. Before the Act, for every West Indian migrating to Britain, at least nine went to America. After the Act, the ratio was reversed. The West Indians were obliged to look at Britain as their country of settlement, a prospect they had not seriously considered before. In any case, the idea of permanent migration is never contemplated lightly. As long as the native island offers some prospect of reasonable life, the chances are that the islanders will stay rather than leave. The wide variance in the migration rates for different islands in the Caribbean proves this.

Trinidad, the richest of the islands, is a net importer of labour, drawing people from the smaller and poorer neighbouring islands. The comparatively poorer and the more populous island, Jamaica, drives out its native sons and daughters in thousands.[5]

4. 'The US Embassy [in Kingston, Jamaica] is the second busiest visa-issuing post in the world,' wrote Colin McGlashan in the *Observer* 23 November 1969.

5. With over two million people Jamaica accounts for more than half the population of the (British Commonwealth) West Indies.

Its population density is three times that of its neighbour, Cuba. Its birth rate is high – 4·3 per cent; and so is unemployment, which fluctuates between twenty per cent and thirty-five per cent.

The most thickly inhabited island in the Caribbean, however, is Barbados. A quarter of a million people must manage to survive in an area of twenty miles by eight miles. At that density Great Britain would have a population of 135 millions. No wonder then that the Barbadian government was the first (and the only) authority in the Caribbean to inaugurate an *official* emigration scheme. That happened in 1950. They sent twenty orderlies to British hospitals. Within a decade, nearly four thousand Barbadians had been processed and sent to work for London Transport, British Railways, hotels and hospitals. But for every 'sponsored' Barbadian emigrant there were three who left on their own initiative.

Elsewhere migration was unprocessed and, given the funds, simple to undertake: inter-island passports were valid for travel to England. Though the legal and financial aspects of migration to Britain did not change between 1948 and 1962, the profile of the 'typical' West Indian migrant did. During the earlier phase – from 1948 to 1955 – the migrant was generally skilled or semi-skilled, and was often motivated (sub-consciously) by a desire to acquire the social graces of the West Indian middle class by travelling to England, which was considered the historico-cultural navel of the West Indian society. During the latter phase – from 1955 to 1962 – the 'typical' migrant was unskilled or semi-skilled with a rural or semi-rural background of poverty.

Two categories of West Indians pioneered the trail to Britain. Firstly, there were those already familiar with Britain, having served during the war, and their relatives and friends. Secondly, there were those professionals and skilled workers who, being well-informed about the manpower needs of post-war Britain, were willing to migrate in order to earn more money and to find a social niche in a society which had moulded their thinking and attitudes. Above all, they were the only ones who could afford the fare. Subsequently, however, their enthusiasm began to ebb. Positive and negative forces came into play to bring about this change.

On the negative side were the reports of difficulties encountered in securing suitable jobs in Britain, the general prejudice against coloured people, and the high cost of living. On the positive side was the growth of manufacturing, service and tourist industries during the 1950s in the West Indies. The number of tourists to Jamaica, for instance, increased from 74 in 1950 to 226,000 in 1960.[6] During the period 1954–60, the overall contribution made by industry towards the gross national product of Jamaica rose by seventy-five per cent.[7] The bauxite industry opened up opportunities for skilled and professional people, offering wages almost equal to those in Britain. The prosperity of the oil industry in Trinidad did the same for the islanders. However, the comparative decline in the rate of migration of skilled West Indians was more than offset by a rise in the migration of unskilled workers, which became substantial during the latter period (from 1955 to 1962).

Previously, the rural, unskilled labourer had been deterred from migration by lack of information and, more importantly, funds, since it cost six months' wages to undertake the journey to Britain. In time, both these hurdles were lowered. Friends and relatives already in Britain provided information as well as money. An extraneous element also entered the picture: travel agents, many of whom painted a glowing portrait of Britain, and in some cases even arranged loans for travel. Nearly two-thirds of the West Indian male migrants to Britain in 1960–61 were found to have received monetary help from one or other source to come to Britain.[8]

Throughout, the island governments maintained a posture of benevolent neutrality: they neither encouraged nor discouraged the prospective emigrant. Their reasons were economic. Emigration relieved, albeit partially, the increase in population and the consistently high unemployment.[9] The moneys remitted by the expatriates were beneficial to the West Indian economy. (Between

6. R. B. Davison, *West Indian Migrants*, Oxford University Press, 1962, p. 63.

7. ibid., p. 63.

8. ibid., p. 32.

9. R. B. Davison estimated that if there had been no migration, every year Jamaica would have had 47,000 more people to feed. op. cit., p. 40.

1955 and 1960, Jamaicans in Britain sent home £16,500,000.)[10] It was also believed that the West Indians werè performing a useful function within the British economy by taking up the jobs that were least popular with the indigenous people.

In the final analysis, the pull of the British labour market was what mattered. The rest was peripheral. As Hugh Gaitskell, the Labour Party leader, pointed out in 1961, there was 'an almost precise correlation between the movement in the numbers of unfilled vacancies [in Britain] ... and the immigration figures.'[11] This correlation held until late 1960 when it was distorted by political controversy on immigration control, which led travel agents in the West Indies to fill all available space on ships and aeroplanes to help the prospective migrants to 'beat the ban'.

But whatever reasons prompted West Indians to leave home – economic necessity, joining relatives, a spirit of adventure, academic or professional ambition – most of them visualized their migration as an interlude during which they intended to earn a lot of money and/or acquire skills to ensure a future in their home countries. This was borne out by the composition of the immigrant inflow. Initially the newcomers were predominantly male and young. But even when, by the early 1960s, the male/female ratio had nearly balanced, most of the children were left behind.[12] This was an unmistakable indication that most immigrants had no definite plans for permanent settlement. As late as 1961 the *Economist* Intelligence Unit survey of Commonwealth immigrants showed that, in London, only a third of them intended to stay permanently.

Indeed, a few years earlier, some West Indian leaders·from the

10. ibid., p. 64.

11. Cited in Paul Foot, *Immigration and Race in British Politics*, Penguin Books, 1965, p. 187. 'The migration [from the West Indies] rose and fell according to the demand for labour [in Britain] from year to year 'wrote Ceri Peach. 'When demand fell away, as it did between 1957 and 1959, there was a corresponding decrease in West Indian immigration.' *West Indian Migration to Britain*, Oxford University Press, 1968, p. 93.

12. R. B. Davison's study of West Indian immigrants in Britain, conducted after the 1962 Commonwealth Immigrants Act, showed that ninety-eight per cent of the children had been left behind. *Black British*, Oxford University Press, 1966, p. 114.

Midlands had suggested to the Colonial Office that West Indians be allowed to enter Britain on a contractual basis, for a limited number of years. This suggestion was rejected by the Colonial Office because it argued that, 'The people living in the British colonies are British subjects; and there can be no restrictions, whatsoever, on their movement into or out of Britain.'

The British authorities were apparently taking a legalistic stand which was applicable to *all* British colonies. Nevertheless, there was a special factor about the West Indian colonies: apart from their experience of European colonialism, the modern West Indian had no history. The original inhabitants, the Indian tribes, with their own history and culture, had become extinct as a result of bloody conflicts with, and subsequent servitude and over-work under European colonizers. The territories had then been populated with slaves from Africa (and, later, indentured labour from India) at the express wish of the British planters. Having been forcibly denied the practice of their own languages and religions, African slaves grew up under the cultural shadow of their British masters, a development that the British authorities, in the post-Emancipation era, had actively encouraged. Thus there had developed a correlation between the length of British rule over a territory and the extent of anglicization of its (imported) inhabitants.

2 CHILDREN OF SLAVERY: THE ANGLICIZED AFRO-CARIBBEANS

Twenty million Africans made the middle passage, and scarcely an African name remains in the New World.
V. S. NAIPAUL[1]

I remember, in my school in Jamaica, our teacher would ask: 'What's your mother country?' And we children would shout, 'England!'
PATRICIA FULLWOOD, a West Indian housewife in Wolverhampton.

Barbados, the oldest British possession in the Caribbean, shows the strongest symptom of anglophilia, and is considered one of the most anglicized parts of the world outside England. So too is Jamaica. (These two islands account for nearly three-quarters of the total West Indian immigration to Britain.) The three counties in Jamaica are called Cornwall, Middlesex and Surrey. Trafalgar Square and the Nelson's column in Bridgetown, Barbados, are much older than London's. Lord Nelson is closely associated with the island of Antigua. It is not surprising therefore to realize that to most West Indians the names of places and people in Britain often convey images of places and people in the Caribbean.

However, anglicization did not stop with names: it went further, deeper. It was induced by the authorities, religious and secular, through the church and school. It began early – with nursery rhymes:

> Mary had a little lamb,
> Its fleece was white as snow ...
>
> Old King Cole was a merry old soul,
> And a merry old soul was he ...

It did not matter that there were no lambs or snow on the island, or whether King Cole had any historical significance to the

1. *The Middle Passage*, André Deutsch, 1962, p. 66.

islanders. Simply because these were English nursery rhymes they were going to be sung in the West Indies as well.

Children saluted the Union Jack before starting their classes in school. Textbooks written before the Second World War were still in use in the mid 1950s. They extolled the 'crusading' Wilberforce and the benign British Parliament which outlawed the slave trade, a clever distinction having thus been made between the 'baddie' white planters and the 'goodie' British statesmen. On the whole the emphasis was on the history and life of Britain, the West Indies being treated as a rather insignificant freak.[2]

In the West Indies the impact of this traditional indoctrination can still be felt. For instance, when asked in 1960 to name 'People most important in West Indian history', senior school students in Jamaica chose Wilberforce, Queen Victoria and Captain Henry Morgan (who was once a pirate) – in that order. Ralph Abercrombie and Sir Walter Raleigh topped the list in Trinidad.[3] There was no mention whatsoever of Cristoforo Colombo, an Italian, who *discovered* the islands during the period 1492–8, or of Deacon Paul Bogle who led the Morant Bay rebellion in Jamaica, or Marcus Garvey, the father of the 'Black is beautiful' movement. No wonder then that these same children in the cinema yelled for Tarzan to beat the hell out of the tribal Africans. They had, after all, grown up memorizing Kipling's 'White Man's Burden'.

Eulogizing Queen Victoria as the 'good' queen who set the slaves free has left a deep imprint on the West Indian psyche. Even Marcus Garvey, the Jamaican leader denounced by the authorities as an extremist, could not desist, in his speech in London in 1928, from referring to 'a woman by the name of

2. 'The philosophy underlying curricula at all levels and motivating government action is that the West Indies are an appendage of Europe,' writes Neville Maxwell, *The Power of Negro Action*, p. 48. Recalling her school days Patricia Fullwood, a Jamaican, said, 'I knew more about Britain than about Jamaica. Knew all the kings and queens, and coal mines and copper industry and fishing industry in England more than I knew where Port Royal (the former Jamaican capital) was, and the importance of Port Royal to Jamaica.'

3. The *West Indian Gazette*, London, May 1961.

Victoria the Good'.[4] In the West Indies the Queen's Birthday and Empire Day were the most celebrated events of the years – days of rejoicing, flag waving and parades. During the last war, particularly, the air would ring with

> We'll never let the old flag fall,
> For we love it best of all.

> We don't want fight just to show our might,
> But when we start we will fight, fight, fight.

> In peace or war you'll hear us sing
> God save Britannia, God save the King.

Identification with Britain and her monarchy could not have been more total. The sinking of HMS *Hood* during the last war brought tears to many West Indian eyes. Generally speaking, conscious and subconscious attachment to English values was more prevalent among the middle class, the educated. The rest tended to take their cue from this minority.

Formal education in the West Indies meant a thorough grounding in the concept of Britain as the mother country, the land of hope and glory; and imbibing of Victorian social values – church marriage, marital fidelity, dressing up for dinner, chivalry to the 'ladies', social snobbery, and formality in conduct. West Indian teachers, the recipients and propagators of these Victorian middle-class values, were especially notable for their role. They and other middle-class West Indians prided in naming their children after British ststesmen and soldiers: Vernon Lancelot Barron Hammond, Ivanhoe Constantine Gladstone Hemmings, Raeburn Hume Hogarth Miles *et al*. The pinnacle of educational achievement by such children was to win a British university scholarship. For others, being able one day to play cricket at Lord's was their most cherished dream.[5]

The education system in the Caribbean stressed standard English and encouraged the West Indians to disown the com-

4. Nearly two generations later, a West Indian speaker at a CARD (Campaign Against Racial Discrimination) meeting suggested, in all seriousness, that the Queen should adopt a black baby 'to improve race relations in Britain'.

5. It is worth noting that cricket, and not football, is the most popular game in the West Indies.

monly spoken creole English. This is not a dialect or 'broken English' (as many non-West Indians seem to think) but a fully-fledged language with its own vocabulary, syntax, grammar, imagery and folklore.[6]

The evolution of the creole language was related directly to the mechanics of slavery: African slaves from different tribes were systematically banded together in work gangs to prevent communication among them. Teaching English to slaves was strictly forbidden. Work had nevertheless to be done on the plantation, and some communication was therefore essential. So the slaves were instructed to imitate the lip movement of their masters and their (white) assistants. Thus they were able to accumulate a limited vocabulary of distorted and mispronounced English words. On this foundation, in time, a whole language was built.

The emergence of a new, common language created just the situation that the master had dreaded. The slaves could now communicate with one another without the master understanding what they were saying. Often the slaves used this language in their speech and song – spirituals, as they were then, and even now, called – to deride the master, to express their dissatisfaction, and to forge plans for rebellion. However, it remained the slave's language – inferior – a fact so deeply instilled among its users that even today most West Indians will not speak it in the white man's presence, and will sometimes deny that they know it.[7]

The intermixing of tribes had another deleterious effect on the slaves. It dramatically ruptured the continuity of their social order, and destroyed their communal way of life. It also tended to encourage a 'go-it-alone' attitude among the slaves, though the cruelty of the system periodically brought them together to

6. Many of the words and phrases in use in the Jamaican creole (English) are not immediately intelligible to the speakers of standard English. Some of the examples are: *bangarang* (which means 'trouble'); *back, back* (meaning 'reverse'); and *rebameko* (which is a derivative of 'carry, go, come' and means 'carry it, and bring it back'.) As early as in 1869, J. J. Thomas, a negro teacher in Trinidad, published *The Theory and Practice of Creole Grammar*, a book that was reprinted recently, in 1966.

7. This was one of the reasons why it took a long time for many British teachers to discover the existence of creole English in the West Indian homes in Britain.

revolt. Extreme individualism remains one of the noteworthy characteristics of the modern Afro-Caribbean.[8]

Indeed, every important facet of the contemporary Afro-Caribbean way of life – family relationship, sexual morals, social class, colour-caste system, religious beliefs and practices, language, music and literature – as well as personality traits and behaviour, is rooted in the historical experience of slavery. A slave existence for centuries, for instance, undermined the African's self-confidence and destroyed his spirit of adventure and enterprise. The result is that in the West Indies, as well as black America, business concerns are mostly in the hands of non-Africans.[9]

The cruelty of slavery bred into the slaves a deep hatred and distrust of the white man. But since open expression of dislike or disobedience was summarily and barbarously punished, the slaves devised subtle means of expressing their feelings. They lied; they played dumb; they deliberately, and yet undefiantly, slowed their movements and thus reduced their work output. They perfected circumlocution as a fine art. In short, they developed repression of their real feelings and 'playing it cool' as defence mechanisms against the system.[10] Unable to fathom the slave's real feelings, the white masters dubbed them as 'devious, shifty and habitual liars', the traits which are still today, to a certain extent, associated with negroes by many whites.

8. The West Indian community in modern times manifests similar tendencies in a different context. In normal times, individualism among West Indians, and the absence of the tradition of following a recognized leader – tribal, communal, or caste – which occurs in the settled societies of Asia and Africa, make it difficult to organize the community for the purpose of pursuing such positive objectives as, say, establishing community centres. However, when faced with a common threat of violence against them, the West Indians close ranks – temporarily.

9. Compared with the business establishments of Asians and Cypriots in Britain today, the number of West Indian enterprises is insignificant.

10. When asked to complete a story about a coloured man which ran 'He finds English people discriminate against him because he is coloured and so what he does is . . .' more than half of the sample of 207 West Indian youths in North London in 1969–70 said, in effect, 'He comes to hate white people although he doesn't let them know it.' Though this survey was directed by two white market researchers – Dennis Stevenson and Peter Wallis – the actual interviews were conducted by trained West Indian youths.

The slave also learned to expend his frustration and misery into humour and laughter – often at himself, sometimes at his fellow-slaves. For him, laughter became a safety valve. Post-Emancipation literature in the West Indies is full of self-derisive humour. But sometimes the slave's defence mechanism and diversionary tactics would collapse. Suddenly, unable to bear the misery of life any longer, he would go wild. Here then is the historico-cultural origin of the mercurial change of mood of many West Indians – from being sulky and withdrawn to being emotional and outspoken – to which frequent reference is made by many British employers, social workers and teachers.

A system which by virtue of its instant reward and punishment bred informers and lackeys among the slaves made the slave conduct his life with a certain wariness. To drop suspicion was to become vulnerable. A general distrust of all, except a few chosen friends, was essential for his personal safety and survival. Distrust of all 'outsiders', particularly the whites, by most West Indians continues. This is coupled with a general reluctance to express themselves, fully and truly, in front of whites. It is salutary to discover the gap that lies between what a black tells the white man and what he *really* thinks, particularly concerning white people.[11] Memories of all persecuted people, unlike their persecutors, are long. And blacks in the Western world, being the most and longest persecuted people of all, nurse, in their subconscious, the deepest memories of the past.[12]

They survived three centuries of servitude by undergoing a

11. At the end of a year-long survey of West Indian youths in North London in 1969–70, Dennis Stevenson and Peter Wallis concluded that 'many coloured people, while being restrained from overt militancy by the desire to accumulate enough money to meet certain social and economic pressures emanating from home ties in the West Indies, are nonetheless extremely hostile to white people'.

12. The following incident illustrates the point. 'I recently was able to take a black American singer down the Goree (in Liverpool), the old slave market in the merchant quarter, and (having read a book on the subject) to give a knowledgeable account of the millions of Africans shipped into slavery via Liverpool,' wrote Stanley Reynolds. 'The black girl burst into tears thinking that the odds were pretty good that her ancestors stood naked and under the hammer at the Goree.' *New Statesman*, 16 January 1970.

psychological transformation which enabled them to hold themselves together. It was essential for them to accept their station in life with resignation, which came as they concurred, however subconsciously, with the masters that they were *inherently* inferior to whites. Racial and colour differences provided the visual foundation on which they were made to base their belief. Unable to release themselves from their blackness and negroid features they gradually began despising themselves. Proverbs such as 'Every Jim Crow think him pickney white, and every jackass think him cubby race horse' (which means, 'Every black man thinks of himself as a child of a white man just as every jackass thinks of himself as a child of a race horse') grew among the slaves. Legal emancipation from slavery did not bring about the psychological liberation of the Afro-Caribbean. Despite generations of 'free' existence he continues to suffer from self-contempt. This affects his behaviour towards the white man. He tends either to evade the white man or be aggressive and truculent towards him. Both stem from an inner feeling of inferiority and are symptomatic of neurosis regarding colour, a legacy of the slavery which gave rise to the colour-caste system based on varying degrees of pigmentation: white, fusty, musty, dusty, tea, coffee, cocoa, light-black, black and dark-black.

This happened as a consequence of the sexual exploitation of subject women by white masters which often led to the birth of mulatto children. As a rule, white masters were partial towards their mulatto children. They made them house slaves, promoted them as overseers, or even set them free. The mulattoes (also called coloured) reciprocated by proving themselves loyal supporters of the system, often acting as lackeys and informers faithfully reporting to the 'massa' what they had seen or heard in the field.[13] Many freed mulattoes became slave masters. They

13. In modern times 'moderate' black leaders in America and Britain are known to be in the habit of briefing the white authorities on what they have seen or heard in the black districts, a service for which they are duly rewarded. In the old times the house-slaves used to be rewarded with the master's left-over food and clothes for similar services. 'The inherited slave complex of telling the master what was happening on the plantations dies hard with some of us,' writes Amy Garvey, the widow of Marcus Garvey. *Garvey and Garveyism*, Collier-Macmillan, New York, 1970, p. 13.

hated the 'niggers' even more than the whites, and bitterly opposed the abolition of slavery.[14] The attitude underlying this colour-caste system is well summed up by the rhyme:

> If you're white, you're right;
> If you're brown, hang around;
> If you're black, get back.

This rhyme is heard, even today, throughout the black districts of the Western world, be it Kingston, Jamaica, or Harlem, America, or Brixton, England.[15]

This attitude is still well entrenched in the Caribbean as well as among West Indian settlers in Britain. 'Commercial photographers [in Jamaica] know the secret of success is to make portraits look several shades lighter,' writes Colin McGlashan. '"God, man, why you make me so *black*?" exclaimed a Government Minister furiously when he saw his official photograph.'[16] Air Jamaica advertisements for stewardesses stipulate 'good complexion, good hair'. The word 'good' here implies 'fair' or 'straight'. 'In a Birmingham school only two West Indian mothers ordered school photographs,' writes a correspondent of *The Times*. 'When asked they said that the children's faces were "too dark". The mothers' idea of a good picture is one in which their child is shown to be almost white. They prefer obvious deception to reality.'[17]

Nothing illustrates the effect of the past on the present better than the contemporary family structure and sexual mores among Afro-Caribbeans and Afro-Americans. Under slavery, marriage was meaningless because the 'husband' could not protect his 'wife' from the sexual demands of other men. Any attempt to protect his 'wife' from being ravished by the white master meant stiff punishment. By law, the slave had no rights; nor could a free

14. On the eve of Emancipation mulattoes in Jamaica owned fifty thousand slaves.

15. One of the bitter disappointments of early West Indian migrants was the discovery that the British made no distinction between different pigmentation hues. To them, you were either white or coloured/black.

16. The *Observer*, 29 December 1969.

17. 4 November 1963.

man plead for him. Subject women were the exclusive 'property' of the master for whom they performed three major functions: labour; the breeding of slaves; and his sexual gratification.

There was a popular notion among the masters that a slave woman would breed more and better if she were mated with different men. The male slave's function, therefore, began and ended with being a sexual inseminator. As the slave children too were the master's property and could be separated from their mothers at his whim, there was no such thing as a 'slave family'. The end-result was the total destruction of the conventional family system.

After Emancipation the slaves tried to emulate their ex-masters' model of the stable, patriarchial family system, but they were only partially successful. The previous anarchy of family life was replaced by the custom of a man and woman co-habiting together without necessarily going through the formal, legalistic ritual of a 'wedding'. This practice continues. The census of Jamaica in 1953 showed that only one-third of the mothers were 'legally' married.

Under the circumstances there is a more frequent change of partners than is the case with societies where legal marriage is the norm. It is customary for the mother to assume the responsibility of bringing up the children, a function in which she is aided by her own mother and aunts. The man has remained, in some ways, dispensable to the family. His impermanence, and the frequent presence of children born out of union with different men in a given family, have inhibited him from exercising his traditional role of disciplining the children. Instead, the disciplinarian role has generally been assumed by the mother. Over the generations, like her Afro-American 'soul sister', the Afro-Caribbean woman has emerged as an energetic, hard-working and resourceful person. combining within herself the dual roles of mother and father.[18]

18. Present evidence suggests that migration to Britain tends to lower the incidence of 'common law' marriage, and accelerates the emergence of patriarchial families. However, the overall situation, summed up by Valerie Knox, is that, 'With West Indians ... the dominant figure is usually the woman, who may be married to the father, co-habiting with him on a fairly settled basis or even with a number of men in succession. The mother

She has become the central arch of the Afro-Caribbean family.[19]

In the Caribbean the matriarchal family nucleus exists within an extended family system which developed in the post-Emancipation period and which, seen in historical context, is a variant of the communal way of life that many African tribes lead. The extended family system, wherein young children are brought up by older female members, thus releasing young mothers to earn, proved especially suitable as more and more West Indian males were compelled to migrate in search of work. The migrant male worked abroad for a few years and then returned to co-habit with his previous woman or established a new liaison; or he settled in the new country and then sent for his spouse first, and then their children.

Migration to Britain during the 1950s and 1960s generally followed the latter pattern.

is usually a tough disciplinarian, who will beat her child if she thinks he deserves it.' *The Times*, 22 March 1968.

19. The main reason for a matriarchal family system evolving in the Caribbean (and black America) was the fact that the woman, with her historical experience of being a productive slave in her own right, was not economically dependent on the man.

3   EVERYWHERE THE COLD SHOULDER

*We get the job the white man does not want,
the room the white man does not want to live
in, the woman he throws out.*
JONATHAN CLARKE, a West Indian settler
in Birmingham.

*Brotherly love was always at a premium, and
the more obvious the differences between
brothers, the less the loving.*
E. R. BRAITHWAITE [1]

The primary reason for the West Indian leaving his native land was economic.[2] It seemed logical therefore that, once in Britain, he should give top priority to securing a job. He tried to get one on his own initiative or, if that failed or proved too cumbersome, through the British Caribbean Welfare Service.[3]

In the beginning, while both his enthusiasm and hopes were high, the newcomer attempted to find a job he considered commensurate with his skills and experience. But as application after application ended in failure, he became desperately anxious and willing to take whatever was offered. A study of West Indians in London by Ruth Glass in 1958–9 showed that fifty-five per cent of them had undergone job down-grading due to migration. The

---

1. *Paid Servant*, Bodley Head, 1962, p. 100.

2. 'All the persons interviewed during the sample survey [of West Indian migrants in 1961] were asked whether they were going to Britain (a) to seek employment; (b) to join relatives; (c) to study; (d) for any other reason. They answered almost unanimously "to seek employment".' R. B. Davison, *West Indian Migrants*, p. 36.

3. This agency was set up in 1956 (with the backing of the Jamaican government) to meet the West Indian immigrants at their points of arrival, to help them adjust to the new environment, and to direct them to the national agencies or departments which could help them with jobs and social welfare. Later, in 1958, this Welfare Service was incorporated into the Migrant Service Division of the Federation of the West Indies.

professional and clerical West Indian male suffered most. His chance of finding a similar job was one in four.[4]

Recalling his early days in London a West Indian welder said,

> It didn't take me long to realize that I couldn't get a job in that trade ... So I start' to ask for anything which take me off the dole ... When I start' riding the buses looking for job, I would jump off wherever I saw a chimney ... At last I went to Lyons, and get a job there as a porter.[5]

A police sergeant from Barbados became a bus conductor in London. Not that it was always easy, in the early 1950s, for a black immigrant to be recruited as a busman. Until 1954, jobs on the Birmingham buses, for instance, were the exclusive domain of the white people, whether they be native or immigrant.

For the coloured immigrant, a job was the first economic necessity; but shelter was the prime physical necessity. Having a place to live was a *sine qua non* of his search for work. He could hardly afford to live in a hotel, even if he could find one that would take him in, and go job-hunting from there. He discovered a frustrating situation prevalent in Britain: jobs were available precisely in those conurbations where the housing shortage was most acute. No doubt all newcomers to these areas faced problems in finding suitable accommodation, but the West Indian immigrant faced something extra – because of his colour. Discrimination by private landlords against him was widely practised.

John Darragh, a British journalist, found through a private poll in 1956 that only fifteen out of a thousand white Brummies were willing to rent accommodation to coloured people.[6] The situation in the preceding years was no better.

When, in 1953, Stanley Bryan arrived in Wolverhampton from Jamaica he could find no place to live, not even a room for the night. Finally he arrived at a West Indian's house which was 'like a satchel filled with human beings: there were men sleeping under the stairs'. But at least this was better than the fate of a pioneering West Indian group which arrived in High Wycombe

4. Ruth Glass, *Newcomers*, Allen and Unwin, 1960, p. 31.
5. Donald Hinds, *Journey to an Illusion* Heinemann, 1966, pp. 71–2.
6. Cited in A. Chater, *Race Relations in Britain*, p. 7.

in 1953, on a summer evening, and had to pass the night, talking and napping, at a bus shelter, because no hotel or lodging house would accommodate them. Friendless new arrivals in London from the West Indies were often forced to pass the night in trains, under bridges, in telephone kiosks, and sometimes in public lavatories.

Describing the difficulties encountered by early West Indian migrants, Donal Hinds wrote,

A twenty-year-old Jamaican girl who went to Birmingham had to share a room with four [West Indian] men ... The young lady said that the men were very 'gallant' about it. They would give her time to put up her screen and get into bed before they came in ... Another West Indian lived in a large room converted from the hall of an old people's centre. There were fifteen beds in it ...[7]

No wonder then that trail-blazing was not popular. Instead, the preference was for following the footsteps of those already here, to arrive in England with a few addresses of early settlers. Besides, personal contacts were crucial in securing jobs and were used extensively for this purpose. R. B. Davison discovered that eighty per cent of the West Indians had found employment through friends or chance application.[8]

Accident and tradition had placed the pioneering West Indians where they were to be found in the early 1950s. The contingent from the *Empire Windrush* was sent to Clapham simply because an empty air-raid shelter was available there. Later, the Brixton Labour Employment Exchange assisted them in finding jobs. So they tried, and gradually managed, to find accommodation in Brixton. Some West Indian ex-servicemen settled in Nottingham because, during the last war, they had been posted at one of the three Royal Air Force stations in its vicinity, and had thus become familiar with the city. It was the same with Birmingham and Wolverhampton. Since Greater London and the West Midlands also had jobs to offer, latter-day West Indian migrants generally headed for these areas.[9]

7. *Journey to an Illusion*, p. 59.   8. *Black British*, p. 77.
9. Willesden is a case in point. Present-day West Indian settlement there is directly attributable to employment opportunities–at its two large hospitals, railway workshop and station, and the nearby industrial estate.

Tradition played its role. Newcomers to London tend to settle, in the first stage, near railway termini, such as Euston and Paddington. Black immigrants followed the same pattern, but with one difference: they had much less choice. As only one in six white landlords was willing to let rooms to blacks, they were restricted to smaller districts within these areas. They also had to pay premiums on rent.[10] As a rule, newcomers to London put up with a bed-sitter as a stop-gap arrangement. But with many black settlers a single room with shared facilities for cooking, washing and personal hygiene became the norm.

A study of coloured immigrants in Notting Hill in 1963 by Pearl Jephcott showed that nearly three-fifths of households had the sole use of one room only.[11] Describing a 'typical [black] family' of 'a couple with three little girls', she wrote:

The father is a factory worker in his early 30s. The mother came to this country in 1956. They have lived at five different addresses since 1960, all local. The present one, a single room with a minute stairhead for the gas-oven and sink (at £3. 10s. a week) is tidy, clean and grossly inadequate, especially since this mother, tied to the house by her own children, acts as a minder to other children too.[12]

Earlier, the situation in Brixton had been summed up by the authors of *Immigrants In London* thus:

Most West Indians in Brixton have evolved their own short-term solution to the housing shortage by living in single-room units, usually in one of the several hundred houses now owned by West Indian landlords.[13]

10. Over the years the situation has hardly changed. The *Notting Hill Housing Survey*, published in July 1969, for instance, stated: 'Ninety-seven per cent of the less-than-£1-per-week rent and almost eighty per cent of the less-than-£2-per-week rent categories of households have U K-born heads of families. By comparison, thirty-one per cent of the £6-£7-per-week rent category have West Indian-born heads of households, who represent only sixteen per cent of the total households in the Survey district. West Indians clearly pay, on average, a much higher rent than U K households.' pp. 38–9.

11. Pearl Jephcott, *A Troubled Area*, Faber and Faber, 1964, p. 83.

12. ibid., p. 82.

13. The London Council of Social Service, *Immigrants in London*, 1963, p. 8.

The several hundred landlords among an estimated eleven thousand West Indians then in Brixton had not emerged overnight. It had taken fourteen years for this to happen. In the provinces, however, this period was greatly reduced, because rented accommodation was more or less barred to black immigrants. This happened against their will and inclination. They were generally undecided whether to settle permanently or to return home after a few years' stint. Also, they could not afford to buy houses. But they had no other choice.

Since one man's savings were seldom enough joint pools had to be organized. Thus 'pardner' groups emerged. Five to fifteen 'pardners' – immigrants from the same parish or island – would pool their weekly savings and quickly build up a substantial fund.

However, at this point, other obstacles appeared. Very few estate agents were prepared to do business with West Indians; and fewer still white vendors. But a blockade could not be maintained *ad infinitum*. Demand from among the blacks was rising, and supply was bound, however niggardly and reluctantly, to follow. Some small, fledgling estate agents, wishing to establish themselves in business, were tempted to help the eager blacks with cash on hand 'on certain terms'. These were: extra commission for the agent, in cash, under the table, sometimes called 'an initial fee';[14] and fifty per cent or more cash to be paid for the house obtainable at a certain premium to overcome the white vendor's resistance. To the vendor such an offer was doubly attractive: higher price and more cash, and a quick sale of old property in slum areas which was least in demand among white buyers.

How much premium was paid by black buyers? According to the *Birmingham Post*, 'It [a house] costs £300–£400 more [to coloured people] than the market price of £1,000–£1,200'.[15] It can therefore be claimed that by paying premiums coloured immigrants have been subsidizing Britain's housing development

14. A West Indian in Birmingham was asked by his estate agent to pay an 'initial fee' of £65. His enquiries at a building society revealed that there was no such thing as an initial fee. Richard Hooper, edr, *Colour in Britain*, BBC, 1965, p. 62.
15. 28 November 1961.

plans. A building firm manager in Wolverhampton told Elizabeth Burney that immigrants had 'indirectly done the business a good turn by helping to boost demand for new houses from white people fleeing from the older areas'.[16]

Formation of partner groups compelled black buyers to purchase large houses, preferably with vacant possession, so that three or more families, sharing common facilities, could be accommodated. That was why in Wolverhampton, for example, large boarding houses on Waterloo and Newhampton Roads came into West Indian possession in the mid 1950s.

However, these houses were soon overcrowded. The reasons were economic and psychological. There was a steady stream of black newcomers. Families were reunited. Relatives and friends came. Children were born. But there was no corresponding growth in the overall accommodation available to black people. Consequently there was continual pressure to make intensive use of space already available to the black immigrants; and to buy more property even if it was dilapidated *and* costly.

By the late 1950s, various factors were simultaneously at work to keep the black newcomers together in concentrated knots. Racial discrimination in housing was widespread, and was known and accepted by blacks. This made them rely solely on mutual help and support.

The tendency to 'stick together' is common to immigrants throughout the world, and is the result of the unfamiliarity and the insecurity that they feel on arrival in a new country. The West Indians proved no exception to this pattern. In their case also the general unfamiliarity was compounded by the racial alienation that they felt from white society. In addition, there was a contrast between their temperament and that of the English. They were exuberant, gregarious, expressive and full of zest; quite antithetical to most of the English. All these elements tended to hold the West Indians together – and apart from British society.

Above all, there were practical advantages in staying together in the same household or street. Socialization and friendship with fellow-islanders were guaranteed. Child-minding under the same

16. Elizabeth Burney, *Housing on Trial*, Oxford University Press, 1967 p. 214.

roof or in the same street by fellow West Indians was easy to arrange, thus enabling mothers to work. In times of unemployment, ill-health or personal calamity, help and human warmth were close at hand.

A close examination of present West Indian settlements proves the seminal importance of these considerations. Since the contingent from the *Empire Windrush* was Jamaican, their place of settlement, Brixton, attracted their relatives and friends from Jamaica. The result is that eighty per cent of the West Indians now in Brixton are Jamaicans. In Notting Hill and Paddington, on the other hand, the majority of the West Indians are from the smaller islands. 'Relations and people from the same island tend to live in the same house', writes Pearl Jephcott, describing the coloured community in Notting Hill. 'A case in point is a house with seven sets of tenants (nineteen persons) all of whom are related and come from one of the smaller West Indian islands.'[17]

Because the first group of migrants from St Vincent were directed to High Wycombe by the Colonial Office's Welfare Officer in 1953, the St Vincentians now comprise eight-five per cent of all West Indians settled there. Similarly, most of the West Indians in Leeds are from St Kitts; and Slough has a large colony of Anguillans.

In time, as savings grew and the urge to re-unite with the family mounted, the single West Indian tenant began to consider buying a house. It seemed natural for him to want to buy one in a familiar neighbourhood where, somehow, houses seemed to be available for sale more frequently than before. A slow, but definite, exodus by whites had begun, and the neighbourhood was becoming increasingly black. Unknown to him, his road had been nicknamed 'Banana Row' by the native residents of the town and considered 'undesirable'. At this point, in Wolverhampton for example, more and more of the smaller houses in side streets between Waterloo Road and Newhampton Road were being sold to blacks. Geneva–Somerleyton Roads in Brixton were commonly known as 'Little Jamaica'.

Rejection, or at best avoidance, of black immigrants was not limited to housing: it included other spheres such as pubs, clubs

17. *A Troubled Area*, p. 82.

and dance-halls. Even the churches generally failed them. This was the most galling discovery for the West Indian who, after Emancipation, had adopted Christianity with the zeal of a new convert.

During slavery, knowledge of Christianity was systematically withheld from the slaves, although one of the earliest justifications for embarking upon the slave trade and slavery given by Europeans in general, and Sir John Hawkins in particular, was to 'Christianize the Africans'.[18] But, with the development of plantation economy in the West Indies, the planters considered it imperative to deprive the slaves of any knowledge that might lead to their 'enlightenment', and possible disobedience. And that included knowledge of Christian doctrine.[19] Furthermore, by intermingling slaves from different tribes to form work gangs, and banning the practice of their respective religious rituals and languages, the masters ensured the decline of African religions. The slaves were thus made to lead a barren life, in the religious sense. But gradually the situation changed.

Over generations, a class of 'house slaves' developed: they worked in the master's mansion, and were allowed to stand in at the rear of the church on Sundays. Through them, and through periodic, distant observation of the white masters at church, a garbled version of Christian ritual and doctrine percolated down to the 'field slaves'. The result was an amalgam of orthodox Christianity and African beliefs in withcraft, spirits and the supernatural. The masters in Jamaica considered this development disturbing, and attempted to formalize it by importing, in 1745, Moravian missionaries from America 'properly' to instruct the slaves. They allowed religious meetings to be addressed by the missionaries. Later they let in Baptist ministers from America and England to preach the gospel. By the time Emancipation came in 1834, almost all slaves in Jamaica had been

18. The first ship that Sir John Hawkins used as a slave carrier was named *Jesus*.
19. 'Even in the little time I was in Grenada,' wrote Ottobah Cugoano, an educated ex-slave, in 1787, 'I saw a slave receive twenty-four lashes of whip for being seen in a church on a Sunday instead of going to work.' Cited in James Pope-Hennessy, *Sins Of The Fathers*, Weidenfeld and Nicholson, 1967, p. 132.

exposed to Christian doctrine in one form or another. After Emancipation, the freed slaves adopted Christianity with the gusto of men long deprived.

The Biblical story of Moses leading the 'herd' back to Israel aroused strong emotions among slaves who had been dragged from Africa. The cry 'Jesus Saves' had an irresistible appeal to the African, caught inextricably in the wrench of lifelong slavery. The present was unbearable as well as unchangeable. Only the future, promising the miracle of a messiah, held out hope. Deliverance would come, but only from above. Thus the African belief in the supernatural was blended with the Christian concept of Jesus the Saviour, producing an irresistible compound. Out of the marriage of Baptist fundamentalist gospel and African belief in the supernatural grew the 'native Baptist', or Pentecostal, school of Christian doctrine which, in the post-Emancipation period, attracted thousands of ex-slaves, and which today claims the allegiance of about twenty or twenty-five per cent of the Jamaican population.

The participatory approach to service at a Pentecostal church – consisting of congregate singing, richly interspersed with responses of 'True!', 'Amen!', 'Praise the Lord!', 'Thank you, Jesus!' and 'Hallelujah!', and incorporating the spiritualist practices of trances, spirit possession and 'speaking in tongues' – has proved particularly popular with the rural and/or poor Jamaicans. Consequently the influence of this church on its members is high, and does not diminish with their migration to Britain. Among the rest of the island community, conventional churches such as Anglican, Baptist and Methodist are popular. More than half of the Jamaican population belongs to the first two churches;[20] and the membership of the Anglican church in Barbados, the most anglicized island, is high.

On the other hand, in Trinidad, St Vincent and St Lucia, initial colonization by the Spanish and French left a deep Roman Catholic mark, which remains entrenched despite the later British take-over of the islands. The Roman Catholic church, for instance, had, and still has, a grip over schools; and Catholicism,

20. Malcolm J. C. Calley, *God's People*, Oxford University Press, 1965, p. 121.

in a wider sense, remains an important part of the Afro-Caribbean life there.

Similar trends manifested themselves in Jamaica and Barbados, the islands held longest by the British. That is, religion and religious service acquired profound meaning. Much potential leadership has been channelled into religious institutions, a development that preceded the Emancipation. Church has become an open, warm and lively place, an integral part of the community, where people gather every Sunday, dressed at their best, to sing and engage in a participatory ritual. Church attendance on Sundays in the West Indies is high: almost seventy per cent of the total population are regular church-goers.[21] Even the smallest parish gives religious instruction to children. Larger, richer churches often maintain schools.

It is against this blackcloth that we have to examine the arrival of West Indian migrants in the Britain of the mid-1950s. To their utter bewilderment and disappointment, they found the British, the harbingers of Christianity in the West Indies, mostly indifferent to religion. Ralph Barry, a young West Indian in North London, for instance, was appalled to count only nineteen people in his Anglican church 'during Christmas season'.

But by far the most disturbing aspect was the reception accorded to the individual West Indian by the congregation. It was frosty. Nobody said 'Hello!'. Nobody smiled. Even worse, often English people would sit apart from the West Indian, or would walk away from the pew where he took his seat. This behaviour, although deplorable, should not have been unexpected because, as the authors of *Colour and Citizenship* point out, 'Research, both here and in the United States, has shown that regular churchgoers are no less inclined than the population at large to display rejecting attitudes towards coloured peoples.'[22]

An open demonstration of white hostility against coloured people (in a religious context) occurred in Liverpool in July 1969. When a sculpture of Christ was unveiled at the Methodist church

21. Clifford S. Hill, *West Indian Migrants and the London Churches*, Oxford University Press, 1963, p. 22.
22. E. J.B. Rose and Associates, *Colour and Citizenship*, Oxford University Press, 1969, p. 374.

in Liverpool's Princes Park, many white Liverpudlians were incensed. The minister-in-charge was threatened with murder and the burning down of his church. This violent reaction was due to the colour used for Christ's body – a blend of brown, orange, pink and white to represent the skin colours of West Indians, American-Indians and Europeans.

The generally monolithic Roman Catholic church seems to have fared no better. Most Catholic Trinidadians felt no nearer to the Anglo-Catholics or the Irish than did the Anglican Barbadians to their English counterparts. 'It's surprising to see how the *same* doctrine has one meaning for some people and another meaning for others,' said Rose Lipton, a Trinidadian nurse living in Paddington. 'As a Roman Catholic I don't feel any nearer to white Roman Catholics, nor they to me. You're white or black first, and a Roman Catholic afterwards.'[23] Apparently colour, the divider, has proved weightier than Catholicism, the unifier. 'In Sparkbrook, Birmingham,' wrote Robert Hughes, 'there is evidence that West Indian Roman Catholics felt themselves squeezed out of the church to which they belong because of Irish influence there.'[24]

Rose Lipton still calls herself a Catholic, but attending Mass *every* Sunday seems to belong to a 'very distant past'. In this she is typical of the vast majority of the West Indian settlers, for according to the researches of Clifford S. Hill, only four per cent of the West Indians in London regularly attend church on Sundays.[25]

It was not only the conventional British churches that were written off by the West Indians as 'cold, dreary, unreceptive places' but also the (white) Pentecostal churches. Of the six Pentecostal churches in Wolverhampton and the surrounding district, for example, only one managed to retain a substantial number of West Indians. Having been disillusioned with the established churches they decided, after much soul-searching, to strike out on their own.

As early as 1954, West Indians in Wolverhampton started

23. *New Society*, 22 February 1968.
24. *Alta*, Winter 1967, pp. 217–18.
25. Clifford S. Hill, *West Indian Migrants and the London Churches*, p. 22.

meeting in their homes for Pentecostal services on Sunday. Out of this evolved a Church of God of Prophecy, a New Testament Church of God, and a Church of God in Christ, the first two of which now have their own buildings. Of the estimated one thousand *regular* church-going West Indians in Wolverhampton, some seven hundred to eight hundred attend these Pentecostal churches and the Seventh Day Adventist church. By the late 1950s, eight halls were being hired in London every Sunday for Pentecostal services. Now there are at least that many Pentecostal churches with their own buildings. The number of Pentecostal congregations was estimated in 1962 at seventy-seven.[26] Since then the number has increased, and most of these congregations have become part of the three major national Pentecostal churches. One such national church alone has thirty-five ministers and owns twenty-two buildings throughout the country. Each Sunday these churches overflow with black worshippers who actively participate in the mid-week activities as well. Indeed, the Pentecostal church is the only purely West Indian institution in Britain that has its own identity, and is functional.

The only established church which showed some warmth toward black settlers – the Seventh Day Adventists – proved so popular with them that by 1963 they constituted a third of its national membership.[27] In areas of coloured settlement the West Indian proportion became almost overwhelming – eighty-three per cent in Luton, seventy-five per cent in Huddersfield, seventy per cent in London and sixty per cent in Birmingham.[28] However, one of the reasons for this was the white members' propensity to leave as West Indians joined in numbers.[29] In Brixton for instance, within a few years a Seventh Day Adventist church changed from being all white to being almost exclusively West Indian.

Summing up the overall situation in the country the Rev. Clifford S. Hill, an English minister and a student of race rela-

26. Malcolm J. C. Calley, *God's People*, p. 39.
27. ibid., p. 118.   28. ibid., p. 118.
29. 'A study of churches [in Birmingham] by Robert Moore showed that . . . the Seventh Day Adventist church loses white membership where blacks come in.' The *Birmingham Post*, 4 October 1965.

tions, wrote in *Race: A Christian Symposium* that, in 1967, 'it was estimated that at least fifty per cent of the West Indian immigrants who were regular church-goers attended churches run by and mainly or exclusively attended by coloured people.'

But, in any case, church was, and still is, of marginal importance to life in Britain. No more than seven to twelve per cent of the British population aged fifteen and over in the large conurbations attends church regularly.[30] So, even if the West Indian had been accepted as a 'Brother in Christ', it would have made little difference to the *general* acceptance which he, as an anglophile, was anxiously seeking.

Positive acceptance and friendliness were expected to flow from contact in a social context; and no place in Britain is better suited for that than the pub. Knowing this, the West Indian hoped to make English friends in the pub – provided, of course, he was allowed in and served, which was not always the case. One refusal to serve, one statement 'We don't serve the coloured here' was enough to make the West Indian feel generally unwelcome and rejected and, more importantly, implant in his mind the seed of doubt, making him wonder every time he went to a new pub whether or not he would be served – hardly a state of mind conducive to striking up friendships with the English.

To be fair, not *all* pubs erected a colour barrier, but there were enough, especially in the incipient black settlements, for the newcomer to be exposed, by his peers, to the idea that a colour bar existed in the country and that it was based, as many publicans claimed, 'on their [white] customers' objections'.[31] The West Indian had no legal or even moral redress since the publican had the right, by law and custom, to refuse service to whomsoever he pleased.

Managements of clubs and dance-halls too had a similar right, and often used it against coloured customers. As private and formal institutions, many clubs kept out West Indians without any difficulty or fuss. There was little that the black settlers could do, except set up their own clubs. Which they did. At one time there

30. E. J. B. Rose and Associates, *Colour and Citizenship*, p. 372.
31. The *Birmingham Planet*, 12 December 1963.

were fifty basement clubs in south London managed and/or owned by West Indians. However, they could not establish public dance-halls of their own.

As a predominantly single, male group, black immigrants had all the greater need for female companionship. Hence, to be barred from local dance-halls was all the more galling to them. When this happened, the West Indians complained. Sometimes their protest was echoed in the metropolitan press. In 1954, for instance, it became known that a Sheffield dance-hall had imposed a colour bar. Liberal circles were enraged. Questions were asked in Parliament where an M.P. from Sheffield openly defended the dance-hall management in the name of 'freedom of choice'. There the matter rested. The black settlers, locally and nationally, accepted the situation with the same degree of resignation they had shown with regard to oral and physical violence perpetrated against them in pubs and dance-halls which allowed them entry.

The earlier phase of the West Indian immigration – from the late 1940s to the mid 1950s – was littered with violent incidents which, as a rule, went unreported or were, at most, accorded small headlines in local papers. Instances of rejection and refusals at hotels, pubs, restaurants and barber-shops were too numerous and were generally considered too trivial by the mass media to be reported. Robert Hamilton, a West Indian bus cleaner in Birmingham, summed up the life of most West Indian immigrants, in the mid 1950s, thus: 'Bad accommodation, lack of social amenities, and hurtful taunts.'

None of this, however, changed the economic facts of life. The pressure on the West Indian to emigrate, or to languish in the West Indies, was high. The British economy, on the other hand, surging ahead, needed as much labour as it could get. Birmingham alone had forty-eight thousand job vacancies in 1955.[32] The West Indians were willing to fill these even if it meant travelling five thousand miles and accepting the social restrictions imposed by the whites.

But many Britons took a totally different view. They considered the West Indians as indolent blacks, draining the National

32. In contrast, unemployment in the West Indian islands varied between fifteen to thirty per cent.

Assistance funds while simultaneously living off the immoral earnings of white women. By 1958, this image of the West Indian was past the stage of grapevine, pub talk, occasional newspaper headline or readers' letters. It was echoed at the highest level of government. Commenting that the newcomers were a 'headache', a junior minister at the Home Office in 1958 said, 'They come in by air and at once begin to draw National Assistance'.[33] But there was little, or no, evidence to support such statements.

The image of the 'lazy black man' is as old as the slave trade; and, being a part of the British subconscious, was easy to revive, notwithstanding the contrary evidence that the prime reason for the West Indian's presence was his search for *work*. When this image was compounded with sexual relationships between black men and white women, a very old taboo, the result was bound to disgust and infuriate many whites. Here again the facts were to the contrary. The incidence of pimping and soliciting in Birmingham, for instance, was low. In 1954 there were only 212 cases of prostitutes being charged in Birmingham, a city with a population of over one million, of whom eleven thousand were black and single.[34] Hardly a cause for concern.

Nevertheless, the stereotype of the black pimp, ostentatiously dressed and driving a flashy car, was becoming a fixture of popular mythology. This development happened to coincide with the emergence of Teddy Boys, white youths dressed in Edwardian style. They were often aggressive and in the social milieu of the times, they found in the black man their perfect target. He was 'highly visible'; he was in a hopeless minority and he aroused antipathy among the white majority. Attacks on black people, especially when alone, became frequent.

33. *Daily Herald*, 8 May 1958.
34. The *Birmingham Post*, 15 April 1956.

4 RACE RIOTS

This is a white man's country, and I want it to remain so.
SIR CYRIL OSBORNE[1]

Now with the veil crudely torn from the bland face of prejudice, they [black settlers] were being terrorized, even in their very homes.
E. R. BRAITHWATE[2]

Always 'the black man' was the quarry, and whenever one was rooted out, the mob rushed upon him.
K. L. LITTLE[3]

It is often argued nowadays in Britain that white people's hostility towards blacks is related to the size of the black population. 'How many black immigrants must come before I become a racialist?' asked a liberal character in *The Enoch Show* at the Royal Court Theatre in 1969. It is not the dislike of black people *per se*, but the psychological threat of blacks 'flooding the country' that creates anxiety and leads to aggression. So the argument runs. But the racial history of Britain does not provide evidence to support this argument.

The first race riot in Britain took place in 1919, in Cardiff, and was soon followed by similar riots in almost all the dock areas in the country where coloured people then lived – Manchester, Glasgow, Hull, Liverpool and London. There could not have been more than thirty thousand coloured settlers in Britain then.

The rioting consisted chiefly of whites attacking the persons and property of blacks, and the terrified blacks trying to defend themselves as best as they could, a pattern that has been repeated over and over again, most recently in Leeds in 1969.

A scuffle between a few white and black men on the evening of

1. Cited in Paul Foot, *Immigration and Race in British Politics*, p. 129.
2. Citing the race riot in Notting Hill in 1958, *Paid Servant*, p. 157.
3. Describing the race riot in Cardiff in 1919, *Negroes in Britain*, p. 59.

10 June 1919, in Bute Town, Cardiff, led to a riot when a mob of white men, 2,500 strong, went on a rampage, assaulting blacks and destroying a lodging house where coloured seamen lived. Pistol shots were fired; and one coloured seaman was killed.

A more elaborate 'nigger-hunting' occurred the following evening. At one point, a house with coloured residents was attacked by a white mob led by two uniformed soldiers firing pistols. The scene was later described by a local paper as 'reminiscent of the French Revolution'.

As a result of the race riot, black residents of Bute Town were too scared to leave their barred and boarded houses for the following few days. During the race riot in Liverpool at about the same time, seven hundred blacks were removed to a jail for their own safety.

It was in Liverpool again, nearly thirty years later, that violence against coloured people broke out. A fight outside an Indian restaurant led to a race riot that lasted two nights and resulted in scores of arrests.

One might rationalize the outbreaks of racial violence against the blacks in 1919 as being a result of unemployment among seamen. But how is one to explain the Liverpool riot in 1948 when jobs were going begging?

The following summer, in 1949, there was a series of fights between blacks and whites in Deptford, London, which culminated in a siege of a black men's hostel by a white mob. Frustrated by the police cordon around the place, the mob finally attacked the police. The number of blacks in Deptford was insignificant, as was also the case in Camden Town, five years later. There, in assaulting the blacks, whites used bottles and axes – and finally a petrol bomb, which burned out a building where blacks lived.

However, none of these events registered on the popular mind nationally, for they received no, or little, publicity, The official attitude was that these confrontations were between two groups of 'citizens', and that colour had nothing to do with them. But this façade could not be maintained when major riots broke out four years later, in 1958, first in Nottingham and then in Notting Hill. The extent of violence; the type of slogans used – 'We'll get the blacks', 'Down with niggers', 'We'll kill the blacks'; and the number of arrests made (177 in London, 25 in Nottingham) underlined the racial nature and seriousness of the rioting.[4]

The popularly held view that time, familiarization and a small coloured community would help engender racial tolerance among the British is *not* upheld by the case of Nottingham in 1958. The citizens of Nottingham became familiar with black faces during the early 1940s when many West Indian servicemen posted at nearby R A F stations used the city's Y M C A for 'rest and recreation'. On demobbing, some of the West Indians and West Africans, married to local girls, settled thére. From that base, gradually, the number of West Indians and Africans grew to 2,500 by 1958, and that of Asians to 600. Put together the Afro-Asian-Caribbean community formed a mere one per cent of the total population. In short, the coloured community was small and the local people had had ample time to get used to black faces.

And yet this did not immunize many Nottingham citizens from believing the worst of the blacks. The West Indians were thought to be 'slow in their movements [at work]' and were liable 'to fall asleep on the job'.[5] Those out of work were widely believed to be living off white prostitutes, wearing expensive suits, and sporting flashy cars – even houses, where they held parties at which eighty to ninety people sang and danced through the night. Also they were thought to be carrying knives and jumping queues at the Labour Exchange.

The blacks' experiences were altogether different. They were often turned down for jobs which continued to be advertised. The Labour Exchange had started treating blacks and whites separately. This had exacerbated mutual antagonism, already high. When the whites saw a black leave the counter with a card they presumed he had been offered a job whereas, in point of fact, the card was only for an interview.

At work, blacks were often objects of racial abuse. The young among them retaliated in kind. The resultant ill-feeling was

4. 149 of those arrested were whites and 53 blacks.
5. James Wickenden, *Colour in Britain*. p. 24.

carried over outside the factory gates. It poisoned the atmosphere of the St Ann's, where most blacks lived. As elsewhere in the country, in this slum of Nottingham there were certain pubs popular with the blacks and which, by a law of nature, attracted (white) prostitutes. In the atmosphere of rising tension, the sight of black men with white women became an irritant to many whites.

Some teddy boys had been capitalizing on this hostility, assaulting and robbing black men with impunity. During the few weeks preceding the final flare-up, at least a dozen black men had been beaten up and robbed. The police seemed to show little interest or concern, however.[6] For instance, in the summer of 1958, a West Indian complained that he had been attacked and his suit torn off. He was merely asked, 'Haven't you got another suit? Go home and put it on.' Descriptions of such incidents circulated rapidly in the black community and heightened the sense of frustration and helplessness.

An eruption of feelings seemed imminent; and, finally, it was triggered off by a minor incident. During an argument in a pub a West Indian hit his white woman friend. And that led to a scuffle: the few blacks present in the pub were badly beaten by the many whites.

The West Indians felt they had had enough. They decided to retaliate. The next evening, a Saturday, a group of them returned to the pub bearing knives and razors. At closing time they attacked, injuring six whites. The word spread quickly. A mob of 1,500 whites launched a counter-attack with razors, knives, palings and bottles. Eight people, including policemen, were hospitalized.

This flare-up made national radio and newspaper headlines, and had an immediate effect in North Kensington where trouble had been brewing for some time. Some right-wing organizations, with their headquarters in the area, had been active, distributing leaflets, scrawling slogans, holding indoor and outdoor meetings – generally inciting the white people to 'ACT NOW' to 'KEEP

6. During the spring of 1970, when attacks by Skinheads (white youths with short hair) on Asians became frequent, Asian leaders often complained that the attitude of the police was cavalier.

BRITAIN WHITE'. Sporadic attacks on blacks, when alone, had become commonplace. In July a gang of white youths had wrecked a West Indian-owned café in the Shepherds Bush area. They had returned a fortnight later and smashed up the place again. Three weeks later a black man's house in the Notting Hill area had been besieged and stoned by white youths. Day by day the tension in the area had been mounting.

The news of the Nottingham race riot acted as the final detonator. Within hours of the news, a gang of teddy boys went 'nigger-hunting' with iron pipes, rods, table legs and knives. They stopped any blacks seen alone or in pairs. Some blacks were able to escape, but at least five had been severely assaulted and left unconscious on the pavement before the police arrested some of the white assailants.

The following Saturday, 30 August, more violence erupted in Nottingham and Notting Hill. A crowd of three or four thousand whites gathered at the junction of St Ann's Well Road, Pease Hill Road and Pym Street in Nottingham. No blacks were to be seen in the streets: they were following their leader's advice to stay indoors 'from Friday evening until Monday morning'. Frustrated, the mob attacked the police for 'having protected the blacks on the previous Saturday'.

The same evening more widespread and vicious violence against black people and property broke out in Notting Hill. Shortly before midnight, a crowd of two hundred whites attacked coloureds' houses near Bramley Road. One house was set alight and two others were pelted with bricks and milk-bottles. Another house had a bicycle thrown through its window. In the fighting that ensued iron railings, bicycle chains and choppers were used.

The next day, a Sunday, a mob of five to seven hundred, shouting 'We'll get the blacks', 'Lynch the blacks', and using knives, bottles, crowbars and dustbins attacked coloureds' houses. Another mob of a hundred youths, armed with knives, sticks and bars, gathered under the arches of Latimer Road station. There were also attacks and fights on the Harrow Road and Kensal Rise.

Similar incidents occurred on the next two days. Only when rain fell on Wednesday did the violent activity subside. But when the sun shone again the next day, racialist shouting and bottle-throwing revived, and with it came petrol-bomb attacks on coloured people's homes in Notting Hill and Paddington. The attackers' intention was to root out the blacks, then assault them.

Violent activity, albeit in a low key, went on for another fortnight. During that period there were reports of assault on coloured people in Harlesden, Hackney, Southall, Stepney, Hornsey and Islington. In Brixton, for days, it was touch and go. Geneva-Somerleyton Roads were sealed off by the police; and repeated attempts by a white mob to break the cordon failed. Besides, unlike Notting Hill, blacks in Brixton were well prepared to defend themselves. It was the same in Wolverhampton's Waterloo Road. 'We were well stocked with bottles, bricks and sundries,' recalls a West Indian leader in Wolverhampton. 'We were waiting for *them*.'

Once the blacks in Notting Hill had overcome their initial alarm, shock and despondency, they tried to help themselves as best as they could. They avoided, as far as possible, leaving their homes; and when they had to, they avoided walking alone after dark. They provided elaborately arranged escorts for those black London Transport employees who had to work late-night or early-morning shifts, and formed vigilante groups which patrolled the area in cars.

This self-defence, coupled with the sentences passed against nine assailants in west London by Judge Salmon in mid September, had a salutary effect. By the end of September, the situation returned almost to normal; but not quite. It could not.

'The Age of Innocence' came to a dramatic end, at least as far as the West Indians were concerned. They were made to realize that they were not 'overseas British' now living in Britain, but were black men and women living in a white society. With this, a new chapter in the racial history of Britain began.

To their dismay and disgust, the West Indians noticed how swiftly the demands of the white mob, chanting 'Deport all niggers', seemed to be reflected by the local Labour MP, George Rogers, who, at the height of white violence against blacks, demanded that 'The government must introduce legislation quickly to end the tremendous influx of coloured people from the Commonwealth.'[7] The sheer presence of black people was to be blamed for the eruption of violence, not white racialism. It was a bitter discovery for the West Indians; and its effect still lingers.

The white authorities and sociologists tend nowadays to belittle the importance and the size of the 1958 race riots by calling them no more than a 'bashing up at football matches'. But many people, white as well as black, feel differently. A recent study of whites in Nottingham by Danny Lawrence revealed that seventy-two per cent of those questioned felt that inter-racial violence could recur.[8] Obviously they still remember the events of 1958. It is the same with blacks. To listen to the violent events that occurred more than a decade ago described in vivid detail by black settlers in Nottingham and Notting Hill, is to become aware, anew, of the deep mark left on their psyche. The memory will rankle for another decade, if not longer, even if no fresh riots break out in the near future.

7. Cited in Paul Foot, *Immigration and Race in British Politics*, p. 169.
8. Danny Lawrence's letter, dated 3 December 1968, to the author.

The Notting Hill riots taught us one bitter lesson:
we were black first and British last.
A West Indian leader in Wolverhampton.

My trip to America (in 1963) made me realize
that we in Britain too needed a radical
approach to achieve racial and social equality.
PAUL STEPHENSON, then a leader of
West Indians in Bristol.

Judged in the light of the recent violence in Northern Ireland the 1958 race riots can only be termed mild. The scale of violence was limited, and so were the areas of rioting. Nobody was killed. However, none of this diminishes, by an iota, the psychological impact that the riots had on the West Indians – in Britain and in the Caribbean. The façade of the West Indian going to 'the country of his flag' came crashing down; the urgent need for self-help and self-organization was realized.

Significantly enough, politically conscious West Indians had realized the need for an organization of their own some time earlier. In 1957, a number of them, concerned with 'unemployment, housing problem and colour bar' had talked to some two thousand West Indians in their homes, pubs and Labour Exchanges, and concluded that 'West Indians want an organization to represent their interests . . . and welcomed efforts to unite [them], and to further British–West Indian unity'.[1]

From this evolved, in March 1958, the *West Indian Gazette*, a monthly publication, under the editorship of Claudia Jones, a Trinidadian by birth. In its inaugural issue the monthly pointed out that 'West Indians in Britain form a community with its own special wants and problems which our own paper alone would allow us to meet'.

In reality, however, the West Indian community in Britain was composed of many sub-communities, each one loyal to its own

1. *West Indian Gazette*, March 1958.

island of origin; and forging a single West Indian identity was not an easy task. Long distances between islands in the Caribbean – stretching across a crescent whose two ends are as far apart as London and Morocco – had fostered individual identities among islanders and inter-island rivalries. The British hegemony over the islands had further strengthened these tendencies by encouraging liaison between each island and the metropolitan country, and discouraging inter-island contacts. For instance, it took ten weeks for a letter to travel directly from Jamaica to Trinidad but only a month if routed via Britain.

But residence in Britain, the common experience of racial discrimination, and associating with people from other Caribbean islands, had begun to undermine the inter-island rivalries. Gradually a West Indian identity was emerging and, sometimes, assuming a formal existence. In Willesden for instance, a West Indian Unity Association was established in 1956. Back home too moves were afoot to create a larger, regional identity: the Federation of the West Indies was in its embryonic stage when race riots in Britain broke out in the summer of 1958. These riots gave further impetus to the idea of fostering and preserving the West Indian identity. They also dispelled the lingering doubts of the 'assimilationist' West Indians (who wished to lose their identity totally) regarding the value of a separate West Indian publication in Britain, such as the *West Indian Gazette*.

The more perceptive among the West Indians in Notting Hill, however, had realized by then that their problems had more to do with colour than with a national identity, present or potential. One such West Indian was Amy Dashwood Garvey (the widow of Marcus Garvey), the founder of the Association for Advancement of Coloured People, who ran a hostel and a club for coloured people in North Kensington. She stressed black self-help.

Another organization in this field was the Coloured People's Progressive Association. It had a three-prong programme: to protect the rights and privileges of its members as citizens; to strive for their social, economic and political advancement; and to work for inter-racial understanding. In the wake of race riots its membership swelled to five hundred, a considerable achievement. The West Indian authorities too had noted with much alarm the events of the summer of 1958. Norman Manley, the Chief Minister of Jamaica, had flown to London with the specific objective of reassuring the West Indian migrants by touring the areas of racial disturbances, and by meeting them informally. Later, in December, when the West Indian Federation was formally inaugurated, it took over the British Caribbean Welfare Service, expanded it, renamed it the Migrant Services Division, and appointed two community development officers to help organize the West Indian settlers in general, and to set up a co-ordinating body for them in the London area.

The murder of Kelso Cochrane, a West Indian carpenter, in Notting Hill on Whit Sunday 1959, gave the matter further urgency. Finally the Migrant Services Division spawned an organization called the Standing Conference of Leaders of Organizations Concerned with West Indians in Britain. Its major aims were: to advise the West Indian High Commissions on problems, opportunities and tensions in the integration of the West Indian peoples; to improve and develop liaison between the West Indian peoples and statutory and voluntary bodies and other interested groups; and to promote a progressive and realistic approach to all matters relating to integration.

The over-elaborate title of the organization and the excessive stress on 'integration' were symptomatic of the ambivalence of *official* West Indian circles. They wanted to foster a distinct identity among West Indian immigrants; and yet they went out of their way to seek affiliation of 'inter-racial' and British bodies, such as the British Caribbean Association, a Parliamentary lobby. To them, as well as to the British authorities, the 1958 race riots notwithstanding, the words 'colour' and 'race' were still taboo. They advised the existing and embryonic local bodies to drop 'Coloured' and 'West Indian' from their titles. The West Indian Unity Association, Willesden, for example, became the International Unity Association. 'Not that it made any difference as far as the composition of the membership was concerned,' recalls its current president, Anthony Green.

Nevertheless, the fact remains that the High Commission of the West Indian Federation brought a dozen West Indian organizations in Greater London together under one umbrella organization.

This was a remarkable achievement because, unlike the Indians and Pakistanis, the West Indians were not then nationals of an independent state, but were, legally speaking, British subjects. Had there been no race riots this would not have happened.

The West Indians in Wolverhampton and the surrounding district formed the West Midlands Caribbean Association in 1959. And a year later the West Indian Standing Conference was inaugurated in Birmingham. In short, West Indians began building and consolidating local and national organizations of their own. This proved to be an irreversible step, and marked the next phase in the racial history of Britain. Much of the West Indian political energy was, from then on, channelled into these organizations, and not into the major British political parties.[2]

In any case, British politics as such did not seem to impinge on the daily life of the West Indians. It was racial prejudice and discrimination that mattered; and these seemed to transcend conventional party loyalties. Before and after the violence of 1958, racialist statements were issued by many local leaders of both the major parties. This made the West Indians even more apathetic to British politics and to the national election campaign in the autumn of 1959.

At this election the Tories were returned to Parliament with a large majority. Although 'officially speaking' coloured immigration and race were 'non-issues' in the election strategy of both major parties, a whispering campaign, based on racialism, was conducted against those Labour candidates who had in the past advocated equal rights for coloured settlers.

After the election the restrictionist lobby, which wanted coloured immigration to be banned or stringently controlled, became active. Its activities, widely reported in the mass media, made the coloured settlers fear that immigration control was imminent. They therefore thought it wise to send for their families, relatives and friends before the gates finally closed.

By encouraging more West Indians to come faster to Britain, black settlers inadvertently provided fuel to the restrictionist

2. Many of the politically conscious West Indians tended to join such fringe British organizations as the Communist Party or the Trotskyite groups, all of which took an uncompromising stand against racialism.

lobby. All that these lobbyists had to do was to quote statistics to show that an 'unarmed invasion' of Britain by black people had begun in earnest: the number of West Indian immigrants had jumped from 16,400 in 1959 to 49,000 in 1960. Let them – so thought many black settlers – for the best way to face the uncertain future was to make the present secure.

Meanwhile rumours of immigration control legislation persisted; and Sir Grantley Adams, the Prime Minister of the West Indian Federation, was obliged to express his fear publicly, in April 1961, that West Indian immigration to the United Kingdom was likely to be stopped before the end of the year, and that some people may even be sent back to the West Indies.

At the Tory annual conference in October the motion demanding control of Commonwealth immigration was passed by a huge majority, an event to which the Jamaican *Daily Gleaner*, a solidly middle-class newspaper, reacted thus:

That this great free centre of the world, the United Kingdom, mother of all modern parliamentary freedoms, should this day fear the entry of coloured people – the core of the problem is colour – and give up the unique basis upon which its own undoubted claims to greatness have grown and flourished. The Britain of the Magna Carta, of habeas corpus, of freedom, has had to bow to fear of race.[3]

Along with the hyperbolic extolling of Britain as the 'great free centre of the world' went the moral rage at her racialism: '*the core of the problem is colour*'. The Prime Minister of the West Indian Federation concurred with this analysis. For, in his cable to the British Prime Minister, he said, 'West Indians are convinced that Britain has begun to take steps which are no different in kind to the basis on which the system of apartheid in South Africa is based.'

If further proof of the racialist basis of the proposed legislation was needed it came with the government's decision to exempt the Irish Republic from its application. With this the last nail was driven into the coffin of the concept of Black British. But the death of one concept often leads to the birth of another.

Just as the 1958 race riots helped to forge a West Indian identity, the 1961 Commonwealth Immigrants Bill made the

3. 13 October 1961.

West Indian and Asian organizations coalesce to oppose it.
For the first time in Birmingham's history 450 West Indians,
Asians and Britons marched under the aegis of the Co-ordinating
Committee Against Racial Discrimination (C C A R D), an
umbrella body of Indian, Pakistani, West Indian and sympathetic
British organizations. At a conference in London, attended by a
hundred delegates, a Committee of Afro-Asian-Caribbean
Organizations (C A A C O) was formed. This Committee immedi-
ately set out to win the support of the coloured Commonwealth
High Commissions and was invariably successful. The Nigerian
High Commission, for instance, deplored 'the racial overtone of
the Bill and the encouragement it ... has in fact given to racialist
and fascist elements in the country'. And the Indian High
Commission also criticized the Bill.

This was a remarkable and highly significant development. For
the first time, coloured immigrants, faced with a threat to their
rights, decided to enter the arena of British politics and apply
direct pressure to safeguard their interests.

C A A C O applauded the Labour Party for its unequivocal
stand against the Bill. It actively co-operated with the lobby –
consisting of the British Caribbean Association, the National
Council for Civil Liberties, the Movement for Colonial Freedom
etc. – committed to the repeal of the Bill. It invited Denis Healey,
as a Labour Party spokesman, to its rally in London, in February,
1962. His pledge that the Labour Party (if returned to power)
would repeal the Act was received with a rapturous applause.
But this euphoria was to prove short-lived.

Within a fortnight of his pledge to the C A A C O rally,
Denis Healey watered down Labour's opposition to the Bill
during the third reading debate in Parliament. With this, the
battle against the Bill was essentially lost. The traditional 'open
door' principle was abandoned in order to come to terms with
the widespread prejudice against coloured people.[4]

The only consolation, perverse though it was, that could be
drawn was that the long, emotional controversy that preceded and

4. Very appropriately, Colin Jordan, the leader of the (Neo-Nazi) National
Socialist Movement, greeted the enforcement of the Act on 1 July 1962
with a rally at Trafalgar Square.

followed the publication of the 1961 Bill, and which filled column after column in serious newspapers, made many black settlers politically conscious and interested in redressing the inequities resulting from racial discrimination.

Now black activists, supported by white sympathizers, turned their attention to promoting legislation against Racial discrimination. The Birmingham-based C C A R D was the first to act. During the summer of 1962 it organized a petition for legislation against racial discrimination and incitement. Later, armed with 10,000 signatures, it lobbied M Ps.

Its lead was followed by the National Council for Civil Liberties which, in conjunction with other bodies, launched a nationwide campaign to collect signatures for a similar petition. But despite the 140,000 signatures, the petition had no effect on the government. The Home Office argued that racial incitement was covered by the Public Meetings Act, 1908, and the Public Order Act, 1916; and that legislation was *not* the best way to tackle racial discrimination.

It seemed to many black settlers that 'other means' might have to be adopted to right the racial wrongs. By then they had, through television and newspapers, become familiar with the instrument of non-violent direct action – namely, sit-ins at lunch counters and bars, 'freedom rides' on inter-state buses, pickets and demonstrations – that negro Americans were using, with some success, to gain racial equality. Due to common bonds of slavery and race, they identified themselves with negro Americans, and began to consider if similar tactics might not be employed in Britain. But when? In what situation?

An opportunity presented itself in, of all places, Bristol, associated in black people's minds with slavery. In April 1963, the Bristol Omnibus Company said to a West Indian applicant, 'Sorry, no coloureds'. This was a signal to the black citizens, many of them settled there for three generations, to take 'radical direct action'. The leadership for such action was provided by Paul Stephenson, a young man born in Bristol of West Indian parentage. He had just returned from a three-month tour of America where he had closely studied the civil rights organizations. As an official of Bristol's West Indian Development Council, he called for the boycott of buses to force the management to rescind their policy of colour bar.[5] This call was followed up by a demonstration against the bus company. The upshot of this agitation was that the issue acquired national importance and caused much embarrassment to the management.

The controversy dragged on for weeks. Finally, however, the management capitulated, oddly enough, on 28 August, the day of the massive civil rights march in Washington D.C. This episode, although minor in scale, was significant, since it broke new ground in the struggle of black people in Britain to achieve racial equality.

There was a growing feeling among coloured people in Britain that their general sympathy for negro Americans should be given formal expression. That summer, under the auspices of CAACO, a few thousand blacks – and their white sympathizers – marched from Notting Hill to the American Embassy in London to express their solidarity with the negro struggle in America for 'freedom and dignity'. It seemed that the pressure of national and international events was making more and more coloured people in Britain politically conscious.

But probably the most important event yet in British politics, for the black settlers, was the victory of Peter Griffiths at Smethwick in the October 1964 Parliamentary elections, when he defeated Patrick Gordon-Walker, an important member of the Labour shadow cabinet. It was in this campaign that there was heard the rhyme:

> If you want a nigger neighbour,
> Vote Liberal or Labour.[6]

Contrary to the national swing of 3.5 per cent against the Tories, Peter Griffiths improved his position by 7.2 per cent over his predecessor.[7]

5. Five years later, black citizens in Willesden carried out a boycott of the shop of a local councillor when he issued a statement in favour of Enoch Powell's speech in April 1968.

6. Peter Griffiths told the Midland correspondent of *The Times*, 'I would not condemn anyone who said that [rhyme]. I regard it as a manifestation of popular feeling.' Cited in Paul Foot, *Immigration and Race in British Politics*, p. 44.

7. It is believed that at least four other Labour candidates lost to the Tories

For the first time in Britain, racialism was *openly* injected into politics at the national level and was seen to pay electoral dividends. The general alienation of black settlers grew as race and immigration were dragged from the fringe of British politics to its centre. A formal recognition of this came when *The Times* published a series of eleven articles on the subject the following January under the ominous heading of 'The Dark Million'.

What were the coloured citizens to do to combat the rising white racialism? This was the question uppermost in the minds of many coloured leaders, who were either involved with the three federal organizations of coloured immigrants – the West Indian Standing Conference (WISC), the Indian Workers' Association–Great Britain (IWA–GB), and the National Federation of Pakistani Associations (NFPA) – or were actively involved in the general politics of race relations. Might not such organizations and individuals be banded together under one banner, on a formal basis? This seemed an admirable idea, but who was to take the initiative, and how? Dr Martin Luther King's presence in London in December 1964 (on his way to Oslo to receive a Nobel Peace Prize) provided the missing catalyst. The end-result was the Campaign Against Racial Discrimination (CARD), an umbrella organization, formally inaugurated at a public meeting, in February 1965 under the chairmanship of Dr David Pitt, a West Indian physician.

At its first conference in July 1965, CARD defined its aims and objectives as 'the elimination of all racial discrimination against coloured people; opposition to all forms of discrimination on the entry of Commonwealth citizens into the U.K.'; and 'co-ordination of the work of organizations already in the field ... for the fight against racial discrimination'. C A R D sought the affiliation of the I W A–G B, N F P A and W I S C. The I W A–G B spurned the offer summarily, as it was already the main force behind the Birmingham-based Co-ordinating

on the issues of race and immigration. For instance, Charles Howell, the Labour candidate for Perry Bar, Birmingham, lost his marginal seat (against the general Labour swing) after the local Tory agent had issued five thousand anti-immigrant leaflets on the eve of the poll. *The Times*, 25 June 1970.

Committee Against Racial Disci imination with similar aims. The
NFPA and WISC, after initial hesitation, joined.

WISC had come a long way since its formative days in 1959.It
had cut its umbilical cord with the High Commission of the West
Indïan Federation (which was itself dissolved in late 1962). It had
replaced the white liaison officer (selected mainly to help foster
'good relations' with the mass media) by a West Indian. It had, by
then, passed through the phase of having 'tea and biscuits' with
British authorities, and was deeply embittered by events since
the 1961 Commonwealth Immigrants Bill. Now it hesitated to join
CARD because it had serious doubts concerning CARD's
potential as a truly militant body. Also, part of its leadership
was receptive to the idea of black militancy and self-help, first
introduced into Britain by Malcom X, an Afro-American radical,
and an electric personality.

After completing an extensive tour of Africa, Malcolm X
stopped in London, in December 1964, on his way back to
America. Among the various West Indians, Africans and Asians
he met was Michael DeFreitas (now Michael Abdul Malik), a
West Indian settled in Notting Hill, who was once a vice-
chairman of the Coloured People's Progressive Association.
Soon afterwards respective groups and study circles led by Roy
Sawh (a West Indian accountant), Jan Carew (a West Indian
writer) and Michael DeFreitas merged to form the Racial
Adjustment Action Society (RAAS). This organization pledged
itself to guarantee 'the human rights of coloured people'; to
protect their 'religious, social and cultural heritage'; to re-
examine 'the whole question of Black Identity'; and to strengthen
'links with Afro-Asian-Caribbean peoples in a common fight for
the freedom and dignity of man'.

The difference between RAAS and CARD went beyond the
rules for membership: CARD was inter-racial while RAAS
was open only to coloured people. CARD was concerned solely
with racial discrimination; RAAS had a broader approach –
'identity as Black men' and 'links with Afro-Asian-Caribbean
peoples'. The two organizations respectively reflected the differences that existed between Martin Luther King and Malcolm X
in America. The philosophy underlying RAAS was that only

black people could help themselves; and it was necessary for them to evolve their own leadership to achieve their ends.

An incident at a Preston rayon mill in May 1965 provided R A A S with just the opportunity to practise its preaching. In order to show their disgust with their union, which had agreed to a fifty per cent increase in work load for a ten shilling rise in weekly wages, the coloured workers, forming a third of the production force, went on an unofficial strike. Among the leading strikers was Abdulla Patel, an Indian university graduate, who worked as a machine-minder. At his suggestion, the strike committee invited the leaders of R A A S to Preston to act as 'advisers'.

The strike lasted eighteen days; and, under national limelight, the venue of negotiations between the strikers and management shifted from Preston to London.[8] The final settlement that emerged could hardly be construed as having given the coloured strikers much 'tangible' benefit. But, in the wider perspective of race relations in Britain, this strike was significant. It exposed a malaise in the trade union movement, namely, that white leadership was unresponsive to and unconcerned with the problems of the coloured members. Furthermore, the blaze of publicity boosted R A A S's morale. Abdulla Patel became a full-time organizer with R A A S and, in association with Roy Sawh, began to lay the foundation for a grass roots movement in the North and the Midlands.

At about this time another plum fell into the lap of the black militants: the White Paper on Commonwealth Immigrants. As against the current yearly intake of 20,000 work voucher holders, the White Paper imposed a ceiling of 8,500, including a thousand for the (white) Maltese. There were further restrictions on the dependants' right of entry. It made the task of the R A A S's organizers and other militants easier. They could argue, convincingly, that the Labour Party was as racialist as the Tory Party, and that there was little to choose between the two as far as coloured citizens were concerned. Hence, instead of following C A R D's line of attempting to generate goodwill in the white

8. Two years later a similar strike took place at a mill in Bradford; but the incident received very little publicity.

community and lobbying M Ps, coloured settlers should concentrate on strengthening 'coloured only' organizations, such as R A A S. The failure of C A R D and the liberal lobby to get the White Paper revoked lent further support and credibility to this argument. The membership of R A A S rose to sixty thousand.[9]

Another factor indirectly contributing to the popularity of the militant viewpoint was the rising incidence of racial violence against the coloured minority following Peter Griffiths's victory. A sample of such incidents, in 1965, included:

January: A Jamaican was shot and killed outside a pub in Islington.

February: A West Indian schoolboy in Notting Hill nearly killed by white teenagers armed with iron bars, axes and bottles.

March: Hate leaflets against coloured people and Jews distributed all over Newcastle-upon-Tyne.

April: A group of black men outside a café in Notting Hill received blasts from a shot-gun fired from a moving car.

May: Incidents of cross burning in London.

June: Crosses burned outside coloured citizens' homes in Leamington Spa, Leicester, Rugby, Coventry, Ilford, Plaistow and Cricklewood.

July: A written warning (allegedly) from the Deputy Wizard of the North London branch of the Ku Klux Klan sent to the Indian secretary of C A R D: 'You will be burnt alive if you do not leave England by August 31st'.[10]

August: A potential race riot in Wolverhampton quelled in time by the use of police dogs and the cordoning off of the street, in the Low Hill area, where 150 whites attacked a black citizen's house with stones, bricks, bottles and sticks.

9. 'The 60,000 strong Racial Adjustment Action Society (R A A S) was founded a year ago for coloured immigrants . . .'' *Nova*, January 1966, p. 21.

10. Robert Shelton, the Grand Wizard of the Ku Klux Klan in America, was reported saying in April (1965), 'We are getting more and more letters of support from Britain. We'll have a subsidiary movement there.' The Home Office said, 'We take the K K K seriously.' *The Times*, 16 August 1965.

A barrage of threatening letters from a Ku Klux Klan branch in London to the C A R D's secretary continued. The last letter, towards the end of August, mentioned 'concerted efforts to attack West Indians, specially those living with white women', and 'the launching of nigger-hunting during September'.

The persistence and specific nature of the K K K threats made the West Indian community and its leaders treat these threats seriously. The attitude of the police, however, seemed indifferent. Not that the police merited much confidence from the black community. Police limitations were underlined by a statement from a senior police officer in Notting Hill expressing heartbreak at 'his helplessness in preventing a white gang from keeping their vow to hound a West Indian family from the district'.[11]

It became clear to the West Indian leadership that the community would have to rely exclusively on self-help. The leaders of W I S C let various authorities, including the Commonwealth High Commissions, know the situation by circularizing the threatening letters. They also set up a special committee to ensure funds and facilities to bail out West Indians should they get embroiled in the threatened racial trouble. Furthermore, plans were made to organize vigilante groups for self-defence in London as well as in Birmingham. At a meeting in Birmingham in mid-August, a resolution was passed calling on all West Indians to mobilize themselves for self-defence against the threats of the K K K since the authorities had shown reluctance to do so. 'We shall fight as citizens, not as strangers,' declared Jeff Crawford, secretary of W I S C. 'Vigilante groups will be set up if trouble starts.'

Unlike 1958, when the West Indians were caught unawares, this time they quickly got ready to face the threat of racial violence, and let it be known publicly. Consequently, racial trouble was staved off.

Two events in the Midlands underlined the fact that at least some members of the black community wished it to be publicly known that blacks were in no mood to let themselves remain perpetual victims of white violence, and that violence was not the monopoly of white racists. A time bomb exploded inside the

11. The *Observer*, 15 August 1965.

Smethwick home of Peter Griffiths on the evening of 26 October. No damage was caused, either to property or human life. However, another bomb which went off the same evening (but was discovered later) damaged a hundred-foot pylon near Stourbridge, eight miles from Smethwick.[12] Both devices were similar in construction, and Superintendent T. W. Shipley of the Smethwick police was reported as saying, 'It is strange that these explosions should happen about the same time'.[13] An unsigned letter by one 'Gregory X', posted on 27 October from Coventry and published on the front page of the *Birmingham Post* of 29 October, said, 'This is to wise you up on the explosions last night. We are sick of being bugged by the whites in this country.'[14]

The point was thus established that any violence against blacks would draw counter-violence against public property and white racialists. Threats and violence against coloured people seemed to have ceased thereafter, at least temporarily, thus proving that retaliatory violence is not always as counter-productive as many liberals, white as well as black, maintain.[15]

The speed and seriousness with which West Indians in London and Birmingham organized themselves, and the emergence in the Midlands of the mysterious 'Gregory X' planting time-bombs, were clear indications that, when threatened with violence, the black settlers were capable of taking care of themselves. Whatever the moral and political issues involved, the British authorities could not have viewed these developments with a benign eye. It seemed obvious that relations between the races were rapidly deteriorating, and that more than 'law and order', or possible breach of the peace, was involved.

12. An explosives expert said, 'There was sufficient explosive to have brought the whole thing down if properly applied.' The *Birmingham Post*, 29 October 1965.

13. ibid.

14. After Asians had been attacked and their cafés damaged as a result of a race riot in Leeds in July 1969, some black militants from Manchester travelled to Leeds to offer support 'to fight off the whites'.

15. In June 1970, Asian leaders in Wolverhampton told the author that only after groups of Asian youths began taking the initiative in assaulting the Skinheads, and other white youths, did the attacks on Asians by the Skinheads subside.

One of the reasons for this deterioration was a lack of national policy with regard to coloured settlers. As a prisoner of its dogma of equality of all British subjects, the Tory government – during whose tenure the bulk of coloured immigration had taken place – had refused to acknowledge that some British Commonwealth citizens were racially different from the others. They maintained that once Commonwealth citizens or overseas British subjects entered Britain they became indistinguishable from the native-born: hence, the question of the relations between the two, or lack of them, simply did not arise. However, the Labour government, installed in the autumn of 1964, showed some realism on the subject. Its 1965 White Paper, while severely curtailing the immigrant inflow, recommended the integration of those already here, thus indirectly recognizing differences between two categories of British citizens.

The one concrete result that stemmed from the White Paper was the creation of the National Committee for Commonwealth Immigrants, an independent body financed by the government The NCCI was charged with the task of 'generally promoting and co-ordinating efforts of liaison' between Commonwealth (that is, coloured) immigrants and the 'host' society. In other words, the government moved, however obliquely, into the field of race relations with its own organization and money. It thus provided a strong counterpoint to the emerging black militancy.

The NCCI began functioning in early 1966. The appointment then of Roy Jenkins to the Home Office proved a strong tonic for it. With a confidence untypical of a fledgling organization it began to seek, and obtain, the co-operation of most black and white leaders in the field of race relations. The net effect was to disrupt the incipient protest movement, and CARD became the first victim of the NCCI's tactics.

Two leading members of CARD – Dr David Pitt and Hamza Alvi, a Pakistani academic – were invited to join the NCCI, and accepted. This led to a rift within CARD, because two of its important constituent bodies, WISC and NFPA, were implacably opposed to the NCCI, which they considered a palliative offered by the government to take the sting out of its restrictive immigration policy. Their argument was powerful in its simplicity: how could C A R D, dedicated to the repeal of the White Paper, let its leaders sit on the Committee which owes its existence to that very document?

WISC had affiliated to C A R D with certain reservations. Events surrounding the 1965 Race Relations Bill had strengthened these doubts. The draft Bill had classified racial discrimination in public places as a criminal offence. However, at the committee stage, racial discrimination was reclassified as a civil mis- demeanour, and complaints were to be handled by a special body, the Race Relations Board, charged with the task of 'conciliating' the discriminator and the victim. C A R D's legal sub-committee and the Society of Labour Lawyers, linked through a common white official, were deeply involved in behind-the-scenes manoeuvring. Rightly or wrongly, WISC as well as NFPA, regarded the C A R D leadership a party to this deplorable climb-down in the Bill's provisions. Along with this disillusion- ment came the realization that the vocal, articulate white members on C A R D's executive committee often managed to have their way on major issues of policy and tactics. On top of that came the decision of Dr Pitt and Hamza Alvi to join a quasi-govern- ment body, the N C C I. That was the last straw. W I S C disaffiliated from C A R D; so did the N F P A. 'C A R D has lost its direction and become dominated by whites,' said Jeff Craw- ford, secretary of W I S C, on the eve of its disaffiliation from C A R D in the spring of 1966. 'We wanted a strong body that would speak out for us, but it [C A R D] has become soft and middle-class, working behind the scenes.'

As if to disprove this image the C A R D leadership organized surveys in Manchester, Leeds and Southall during the summer of 1966. The objective was to discover if racial discrimination in jobs and housing existed; and if so, how much. Volunteers for the projects came mainly from among white university students on vacation. The conclusion of these surveys was unmistakable: massive racial discrimination existed. But C A R D's reports on the subject had very little, if any, impact on the authorities, or even on the liberal Press. After all, they argued, C A R D was a pressure body and, as such, likely to produce biased evidence.

Only the findings of the P E P (Political and Economic

Planning Ltd) survey, released in April 1967, could have any impact on the British Press, politicians and people. The report concluded unequivocally that there was widespread discrimination against coloured citizens in employment, housing and personal services.

To the blacks this was nothing new. They had *known* the facts at first hand all along. But, until then, their complaints had never been taken seriously by most whites who had either dismissed them as allegations made by people with 'chips on their shoulders', or viewed them as' 'difficulties' experienced by *all* newcomers irrespective of colour or race, and which were expected to disappear 'with time'. Now the P E P report proved that *more* discrimination existed than the blacks themselves alleged! With this, the rhetoric of the black 'demagogues' at Speakers' Corner was, overnight, transformed into respectable testimony.

A new life was infused into black militancy, which after its first flourish had begun to subside, partly due to the assassination of Malcolm X, who had first kindled the light here, and partly due to the subsiding of restrictionist demands regarding coloured immigration following the 1965 White Paper and the 1966 general election.

In America too the racial scene was changing rapidly. The influence of Martin Luther King was on the decline. Instead, the demand for Black Power, first heard in Greenwood, Mississippi, in the summer of 1966, was gaining ground. By the spring of 1967, faint echoes of the Black Power slogan could be heard in Britain. Ironically, the P E P report, by confirming black militants' views of British society, acted as a catalyst and brought the Black Power supporters together to form, in June 1967, the Universal Coloured People's Association (U C P A).

The word 'universal' in the organization's title summed up the supporters' ideology. They viewed white racialism in Britain not in isolation but as a part of a world-wide phenomenon, and conceived combating racialism in international, rather than national, terms.

The arrival in London, in July, of Stokely Carmichael, the originator of the Black Power slogan, boosted the morale of black militants in general, and of the U C P A in particular. In his paper to the International Congress of Dialects of Liberation, Stokely Carmichael expounded a thesis which can be summarized thus:

White western [i.e. West Europeans and North American] societies enjoy the fruits of international racism through the exploitation of the Third World, i.e. Afro-Asian-Latin American countries. In recent times these white societies have ruled the rest of the world where they have successfully indoctrinated the people, especially the intellectuals, into accepting their own [basically racist] view of history.

The notion that the west is 'civilized' is a western idea. But, most important, it is the white West that defines what civilization and progress are. Whosoever defines the terms, and makes them stick, is the master. Only when the slave refuses to accept the master's definition can he feel psychologically free, not before.

History shows that western 'civilizations', since the time of ancient Greece, have thrived only on the exploitation of others. Furthermore, the western world has a most barbarous history of violence practised within itself, and on non-western peoples. White societies have often mouthed the ideals of freedom and democracy while committing atrocious violence against non-whites. For example, the white colonies in America were demanding freedom from England on one hand while decimating the (American) Indian population on the other. Where white societies could not decimate the non-white people (as in Asia and Africa), or had reason not to (as with the African slaves in the Western hemisphere), they tried to destroy their sense of dignity, and their indigenous cultures.

But blood is, after all, thicker than water. Present-day Afro-Americans feel emotionally and economically a part of the Third World, even though they are trapped in the bowels of America, the leader of the white west. To counteract the growing imperialistic and racist tendencies of white America manifested in Vietnam and a chain of counter-revolutionary *coups*, engineered with the aid of the Central Intelligence Agency, the Afro-Americans realize the need to attack the white racist, imperialist system from both inside and outside of the American boundaries.

To be most effective the Afro-Americans must co-ordinate their strategy with progressive forces everywhere. That is where organizations such as UCPA come in.

Being a negro by race, a Trinidadian by birth, and an American by nationality, Stokely Carmichael was instantly able to establish a rapport with his Afro-Asian-Caribbean audiences. His speeches and activities in London had an immediate and electrifying impact, especially on the coloured British. The hysterical reaction of the British mass media, his (threatened) expulsion from, and the subsequent ban on his re-entry to, Britain by the government all testified that the powers-that-be were apprehensive of his ideology and, above all, his appeal to the coloured population.

The coining of the term 'Black Power' was a pragmatic act.[16] Stokely Carmichael used it simply as an antithesis to the term 'white power structure' that was then current in the American civil rights vocabulary, and to popularize the idea that 'Negroes should hold offices in negro areas'. But within a year the term had acquired a wider and more profound meaning. In July 1967, Stokely Carmichael defined it as 'the coming together of black people to fight for their liberation – by any means necessary'.[17]

The term liberation – freeing oneself – is applied in socio-psychological and political contexts.

That there is a need for liberation for the Afro-American and Afro-Caribbean becomes clear when one examines the historical background. Having been deprived of the use of their languages and religions, and having imbibed self-contempt, the African slaves in the Caribbean and North America grew up imitating their 'massa', wishing to be Europeans in cultural, and even physical, terms. Abolition of slavery did not free them from this subtle, self-imposed cultural subjugation. They continued to spend millions of hours and dollars on thinning their lips and noses, straightening their hair, and bleaching their skins. It is only when these historico-cultural facts are borne in mind that one can fully appreciate the liberating force of Stokely Carmichael's statements: 'Black is beautiful', 'We're black and beautiful'.

Not that Stokely Carmichael was the first black to say so. Or Elijah Muhammad, the leader of the Nation of Islam in America (popularly known as Black Muslims). No. Fifty years before,

16. The term 'Black Power' was first used in 1959 as the title of a book on independent Ghana by Richard Wright, an Afro-American writer.

17. At the C A R D annual conference in November 1967, Dr David Pitt defined 'Black Power' as 'a right to be respected for what you are – self-respect'.

Marcus Garvey had said, 'The Anglo-Saxons see beauty in themselves to the exclusion of all others. The people of Mongolia, the Chinese, the Japanese ... [do the same.] I shall teach the black man to see beauty to the exclusion of all others.' It is towards this aim that the present-day Black Power advocates and supporters are striving – as far as the cultural plank of Black Power is concerned.

No matter where the African finds himself in the western world, and in what state his racial purity, he is exhorted by the Black Power supporters to discard the stigma attached to kinky hair, flared nose and thick lips which the European, through centuries of domination, has impressed on his psyche. The point about being proud of what one *is*, is so fundamental to normal human existence that it allows no compromise.

What does allow variation is the second plank of the Black Power ideology, namely, the attainment of economic and political power. The forms it takes and the tactics to be employed vary from country to country, and from situation to situation.

As if to underline this difference, in July 1967, George Weekes, a leader of the oil workers in Trinidad, was saying, 'I am certain that if I was to ask anyone at this General Council meeting what is meant by B P, the answer will be "British Petroleum". I say no. Today, in our struggle for Economic Liberation, B P must mean one thing – Black Power ... When we advise the government of Trinidad and Tobago to acquire B P holdings, what we are actually advocating is the transfer of power – White Power – into the hands of Black People, that is to say, Africans and Indians principally in our country.'

What applies to Trinidad in particular applies to the West Indies in general. But certainly not to America taken as a whole. Nevertheless, America is a country of black *islands* scattered in the rural counties of the South and in the urban centres elsewhere. Given this, the achievement of political power by black people at the *local* level is both feasible and desirable. This is already happening.

In Britain there *already* is a concentration of blacks in some factories and services at the local level. Two-thirds of the bus crews in Wolverhampton, for instance, are coloured. The majority of junior doctors in many hospitals are coloured, as are the nurses.[18] Many textile mills in the West Riding are fifty per cent to eighty per cent black. So are paper mills in High Wycombe; and foundries, bakeries, and rubber and plastic works in the Midlands. The black workers, therefore, find themselves as possessors of *industrial* power. This gives them a certain leverage in the overall (industrial and political) power relationship.

Finally, and most significantly, there is the rapidly growing concentration of coloured people in the inner perimeters of cities and towns. Such a situation is pregnant with the promise of Black Power on the American model. The present racial composition of infant and primary schools in these areas is a clear indicator of the future development. In 1968, in fourteen out of thirty-three London boroughs, 'immigrant' children constituted thirteen to thirty-one per cent of the total primary school population.[19] If we bear in mind that coloured settlers are not evenly distributed throughout a borough, but are instead concentrated in smaller areas, it becomes apparent that substantially, or dominantly, coloured enclaves have already formed in the country and that these will get blacker as years go by and today's children grow up. One has simply to stand, for instance, at the intersection of Harvist Road and Chamberlayne Road, London N.W.6, during lunch hour and see children playing in the compound of Harvist Road Infants School to visualize the composition of the area within the next decade: it will be almost exclusively black. And yet the present situation did not develop overnight, nor is it of black settlers' making. It was thrust on them. In the final analysis, it is the cumulative result of thousands of refusals by white Britons, over a generation, to let accommodation, or sell houses, to blacks.

18. This fact is dramatized by the following letter by one C. Anthony Prince of Ealing. 'I took him [my son] to the local hospital casualty department . . . He was X-rayed at 10 p.m. by an Indian radiographer. At 11.30 p.m. a doctor from Pakistan examined him . . . At 12.30 a.m. he was put to bed for the night by a West Indian nurse.' *The Times*, 23 October 1969.

19. *Hansard*, 5 December 1968, cited in *The Report of the Race Relations Board for 1968–69*, p. 73.

6 THE COLOURED ENCLAVES

The ghetto is the geographical expression of
complete social rejection.
CERI PEACH[1]

Before the 1968 Race Relations Act, which outlawed discriminatory advertisements, 'No Coloured' and 'Europeans Only' signs for rooms and flats to let were so common that they hardly evoked comment from coloured people. And yet these signs, by themselves, did not reveal the full extent of racial discrimination in housing. These were merely the tip of an iceberg. Ruth Glass, a sociologist, found this out in her study of West Indians in North Kensington in 1959.

She found that only one-sixth of the 'Accommodation Available' advertisements in the local paper specified 'No Coloured'. But when she followed up the 'neutral' advertisements by telephoning 'on behalf of a West Indian friend', only one out of every six white landlords was prepared to consider the application.[2] In other words, white landlords not attaching the 'No Coloured' restriction to their advertisements were not colour-blind; they were merely practising the English reticence.

A colour bar applied, and still does, as much to the black settlers as it did to the university students from Africa, Asia and the West Indies. Only one out of every twelve landladies on the housing register of London University, for instance, was prepared to accept students of 'all nationalities'.[3]

What about the accommodation agencies? The PEP survey revealed that three out of four accommodation bureaux practised racial discrimination. One agent summed up the situation neatly:

After a few people have bawled you out for sending a coloured chap along to look at a flat, you learn to check up first ... you don't

1. *West Indian Migration to Britain*, p. xvi.
2. Ruth Glass, *Newcomers*, p. 60.
3. *The Times*, 22 October 1969.

have to guess the answer. They just *assume* you won't send them the coloureds.[4]

Yet the P E P investigators found half of their coloured respondents living in rented premises.[5] This was not paradoxical since, almost always, their landlords were coloured as well. Antipathy of whites had made the blacks help one another as much as they could. 'To put it another way,' stated the P E P report, 'awareness of discrimination by West Indians made them order their way of life to avoid it.'[6]

Avoidance of black clients was what – according to the P E P report – two out of three estate agents were found to be practising. The estate agents' stock responses to the black enquirers were: 'No property available'; 'Mortgages will be difficult to get'. If a coloured person approached an estate agent with a particular property, carrying a 'For Sale' sign, in mind, he was frequently told that the house in question was already 'under offer'. As Elizabeth Burney points out in *Housing On Trial*, hypocritical subterfuges were often used in lieu of open discrimination.[7]

Those estate agents who did business with coloured people usually did so under special conditions, which were spelled out by coloured respondents during the P E P enquiry.[8] Some of them had bought houses by paying cash; others had bribed building society officials, through the agent, to obtain mortgages. Others still had been forced to raise short-term loans from banks and/or friends at high interest rates.

Where and what kind of property did coloured immigrants end up buying? Mainly sub-standard or condemned houses in areas of towns and cities that had been, over the decades, steadily

4. Political & Economic Planning Ltd, *Racial Distrimination*, PEP, 1967, p. 73.

5. ibid., p. 75.   6. ibid.   7. ibid. p. 43.

8. One estate agent pointed out in his circular to houseowners in Leyton, that 'we usually obtain a much higher price than the market value from our Commonwealth friends'. *Focus*, March 1966, p. 12. 'In the case of short leaseholds, properties which were virtually unsaleable have sometimes been unloaded at unrealistically high prices on to ill-informed newcomers.' Sheila Patterson, *Immigration and Race Relations in Britain 1960–67*, Oxford University Press, 1969, p. 202.

losing population. The borough of Haringey in London is one example. Between 1931 and 1961, its population declined from 307,500 to 259,200 despite an injection of Cypriot and West Indian immigrants during the 1950s.[9] North Paddington is another example: this parliamentary constituency has been losing voters steadily (about a thousand a year).[10] So has the Central Bradford constituency. A number of central wards in Bradford lost more than twenty per cent of their population between 1951 and 1961. It was only in such areas that houses were available for sale to coloured buyers. As had happened earlier in the job market, black immigrants were offered leavings from the table. And just as certain job categories had, over a period of time, become 'black', a similar development took place in housing.

Once a property was sold to a coloured person, it became part of a 'black' pool of housing. It more or less lost its chance of free circulation. Which white citizen would consider purchasing a property from a coloured vendor in a street that was steadily turning black? Besides that, demand within the expanding coloured community was continually rising, causing unavoidable overcrowding. 'It's better, I think, personally, to live in an over-crowded house than sleep in the railway or the park or something like that,' said a West Indian in Birmingham. 'And if the West Indians didn't let houses to their friends, that would happen, definitely.'[11] Many West Indians tried their best to convert single rooms into homes. Mrs Betty Davison (wife of R. B. Davison), for instance, wrote of one Mrs Rocco, a West Indian in London, living 'in a small room just large enough to hold a bed, dressing table and wardrobe, everything as brightly and gaily painted as possible in the dirty smoke-laden air which thickened the texture of the curtains, obliterating any colour or pattern'.[12]

The West Indian who succeeded in buying a house almost invariably treated his property as a symbol of his material well-being. In contrast with the generally negligent attitude of the previous, native-born, owner who had probably grown up in the

9. The population continues to decline. In 1966, it was 254,200; and the estimate for 1969 was 245,300.
10. *The Times*, 23 October 1969.
11. Richard Hooper edr, *Colour in Britain*, p. 74.
12. R. B. Davison, *Black British*, p. 142.

old, run-down house, the young immigrant was enthusiastic about his newly acquired possession. He painted and wall-papered it; he often added a bath. The result was a general upgrading of the street. 'In some parts of the Midlands, Indian and West Indian households can often be picked out in a drab grey suburban street by the fresh and bright paintwork on the house,' wrote Robert Moore.[13] 'Immigrants have shown themselves ... receptive ... to the idea of improving and modernizing their houses,' stated Elizabeth Burney with regard to the different areas in the south-east, north-west and the Midlands that she surveyed. 'Externally, their attitude shows up in brilliant paintwork and gaudy colour-washes which would endear them to Civic Trust "face-lift" propagandists. Internally (contrary to common beliefs), a higher standard of hygiene may prevail than in "traditional" English homes which have never known a bath, a modern sink, or an inside lavatory.'[14]

Aside from enjoying better amenities in his house, the coloured settler was keen to recover his investment in case he decided to move to another district or town. Quite often he did. Sometimes he even made a handsome profit on the transaction. John Thompson, for instance, bought a house in 1960 in Villiers Street, Wolverhampton, for £1,800. Seven years later he sold it for £2,850 – to a fellow West Indian.[15] Hundreds of similar transactions took place in various areas of coloured settlement. Several estate agents told Elizabeth Burney that 'prices were relatively high for the type of house and locality which was recognizably the "coloured market".'[16]

These instances and statements show that the commonly-held belief among many white residents that arrival of coloured families in a street lowers property values is not always supported by evidence. Nevertheless, the fear of falling property values, and

13. Richard Hooper, edr, *Colour in Britain*, pp. 67–8.
14. Elizabeth Burney *Housing on Trial*, pp. 55–6.
15. Within two years of his purchasing a house in Preston Gardens, Willesden, for £3,300 Peter Woods had an offer of £4,200.
16. Elizabeth Burney, *op. cit.*, p. 44. Professor John Denton's study in Southall revealed 'a property market still buoyant despite steady (and bitterly resisted) expansion of the Sikh settlement there'. *New Society*, 25 April 1968, cited in E. J. B. Rose and Associates, *Colour and Citizenship*, pp. 245–6.

the popular association of colour with low social status, undesirable social behaviour, and a general downgrading of the area accelerated the rate of exodus of the indigenous population from the twilight zones which had begun long before coloured immigration became substantial. On the other side of the colour line there were, as explained earlier in Chapter 3,[17] practical advantages accruing to newcomers from clustering together. The end-result of this two-headed process has been an emergence of coloured enclaves in practically every town and city where coloured immigrants have found jobs. And the development has been rapid. For example, in 1962, only three houses out of fifty-one in Ranelagh Road, Willesden, were coloured; in 1969, the number was thirty-four. The King Edward Road in Chalvey, Slough, became ninety per cent coloured in less than six years. A similar change occurred in Claremont Road, Luton; Lumb Lane, Bradford; Francis Street, Wolverhampton; and Tubbs Road, London N.W.10; to quote, at random, a few of the hundreds of examples throughout the country. In every case, the street is a part of a district which is substantially, or sometimes predominantly, coloured. Most of the sixty-odd boroughs where coloured immigrants have settled have black enclaves. This is the one characteristic that Gravesend shares with Glasgow, and Manchester with Maidenhead. Even Nottingham, a city with a (cleverly cultivated) image of racial 'tolerance' fails, on close examination, to pass the test of a dispersed housing pattern of coloured settlers. The 1966 census showed that eighty per cent of its coloured citizens were living in five central wards which comprise only twenty per cent of the city's area.

Slowly, but definitely, during the early 1960s racial transformation of some of these districts began to reflect itself in the composition of schools. The Grove Lane Infants School, Handsworth, for instance, altered from being all-white in 1957 to eighty per cent coloured in 1965. However, two years earlier, national attention had been drawn to this situation as a result of protest by parents of white children in two Southall schools.

In October 1963, white parents in Southall demanded separate classes for their children because, they claimed, the presence of

17. See pp. 26–7.

coloured pupils was retarding their children's progress. The Minister for Education, Sir Edward Boyle, met the protesting parents. Separate classes for white and coloured children were out of the question, he told them; but he would recommend to the local authority that 'immigrant' children be dispersed throughout the borough.

During a subsequent debate in Parliament Sir Edward Boyle referred to 'the difficulty in places where nearly a whole neighbourhood is taken over by immigrant families [when] the school serving the neighbourhood [would] cease to have a supply of native children'.[18] It was the symptom that worried Sir Edward Boyle, not the root cause – white racialism – which had curtailed coloured immigrants' freedom of choice and had led to the 'take-over' of certain neighbourhoods by them. And his remedy? Disperse 'immigrant' children so that no one school would have more than thirty per cent of immigrants. White children were to be exempt from the dispersal policy because, as Sir Edward Boyle said, 'It is both politically and legally more or less impossible to compel native parents to send their children to school in an immigrant area if there are places for them in other schools.'

Apparently, there were *different* political and legal considerations involved as far as coloured parents were concerned. Or how else could they be compelled to send their children to prescribed schools, a practice which still continues in some towns and cities, and which makes many of them feel that 'coloured people are pushed around like parcels'.[19]

In short, faced with its first test the often-proclaimed official doctrine 'All citizens are equal' failed. As long as coloured immigrants had to fend for themselves in the private sector of employment and housing, the local and national authorities could sit back and justify their inaction with the simple statement: 'Let the

18. Cited in John Power, *Immigrants in School*, Councils and Education Press, 1967, p. 6.

19. Anne Corbett in *New Society* 12 September, 1968. The National Union of Teachers noted this differential treatment when its report, in January 1967, on the subject stated its firm belief that 'any decision made should relate to all children affected and not merely to newcomers'. Cited in John Power, op. cit., p. 33.

newcomer compete in a free market.' But as soon as coloured settlers, albeit inadvertently, impinged on the public service of education, government intervention followed, and a differential policy was instituted.

This happened not because the government wished to help the coloured immigrants but because it wanted to allay the concern of white parents. The seriousness with which the white parents' protest was treated by the highest authority in the country, the Minister of Education, and the speed with which a new policy was formulated *and* executed illustrated this. And the fact that no consultations whatsoever were held with coloured parents further underlined the point.

Since lack of English among children of some immigrants was the publicly expressed cause for concern in Southall, it would have been logical to apply, if necessary, the policy of dispersal to 'non-English speaking' children. Instead, the hastily conceived idea of dispersal was made applicable to *all* 'immigrant children'. Later, in June 1965, this was given an official sanctification in the form of a circular by the Department of Education and Science, entitled 'Education of Immigrants'.[20] This circular, however, did *not* define the basic term 'immigrant child'.

When this omission was pointed out, an 'immigrant child' was then defined as 'a child born overseas, or in the United Kingdom, of immigrant parents who came to the United Kingdom on or after first January ten years previously'.[21] The idea of 'an immigrant born in this country' is patently ludicrous. And it is the height of irony that the Department of *Education* should attempt to make the English language stand on its head.[22]

This juggling with words could only be understood in a political context. Although the Labour administration had committed itself to the integration of 'Commonwealth immigrants', it still felt shy of incorporating such words as 'white', 'coloured' or

20. Circular 7/65.
21. But children born in Eire are excepted. Cited in John Power, *Immigrants in School*, p. 13.
22. 'We seem to spend a great deal of effort to avoid calling them "coloured", but achieve much confusion in our endeavours to define the term "immigrant",' writes G. H. Grattan-Guinness, Deputy Education Officer, Huddersfield. ibid., p. 43.

'black' in its official documents. Its equivocal attitude was well illustrated by the 1965 White Paper on 'Immigration from the Commonwealth'. This document did not specifically mention 'colour' or 'coloured' anywhere; and yet it gave separate figures for 'citizens of Canada, Australia or New Zealand' and 'Commonwealth citizens from other Commonwealth countries and dependent territories'.[23]

'Education of Immigrants' does not make it clear whether the dispersal policy is to be applied to non-English speaking immigrant children or to all immigrant children, irrespective of their proficiency in English. Nevertheless, wherever local authorities follow a dispersal policy they apply it to *all* immigrant children. And 'immigrant children', in practice, means 'coloured children'. This may not be correct technically; but in the common parlance of present-day Britain the words 'immigrant' and 'coloured' have become interchangeable.[24]

'Coloured' means, in the popular mind, anybody who is not white and caucasoid. Hence most Britons make no distinction between West Indians and Asians. This, in fact, is a continuing symptom of the general incuriosity and indifference with which the British, in their days of the Empire, viewed the 'natives'. Until recently, this was equally true even of most of the British teachers and local politicians.

A headmaster in Birmingham, for instance, was surprised and disappointed when the appointment of an Indian teacher did not solve the school's 'colour problem'. It often took years of day-to-day contact with coloured pupils before British teachers realized that there are basic cultural and socio-phychological differences between West Indian and Asian children. Outside school, this realization still remains a prized possession of the 'experts' on race relations. 'Some recent trends suggest that these [West Indian and Asian] groups have distinctive needs which have not always been recognized,' states the editorial preface to the article

23. Cmnd 2739, August 1965, p. 4.
24. Paul Stephenson, the local liaison officer in Coventry, asked a class of twelve-year-olds, 'Who is an immigrant?' and received a reply, 'Someone like you'. He was born in Bristol of West Indian parents. When he pointed out that Prince Philip, the Duke of Edinburgh, is an immigrant, his statement was received with incredulous gasps.

'Education and Race' in the October 1969 issue of *Race Today*, a specialist journal.

Often these differences have been noted, by researchers and others, in terms of indiscipline and unsatisfactory academic performance concerning West Indian pupils. David Beetham is one such researcher. Describing the 'difficulties affecting the educational attainment of the West Indian immigrants' he writes:

Any generalization must be tentative, though the unanimity of opinion on the subject expressed by teachers and Heads is impressive. To begin with there is the problem of language. Though the West Indian has English as his native tongue, it differs considerably from standard English, not only in vocabulary but in structure and syntax as well ... When it comes to work which requires sustained effort the West Indian seems to lack concentration and staying power. Teachers who have experience of both compare the West Indians unfavourably with the Asians in this respect. By nature the West Indian is emotional and exuberant, and this leads to behaviour problems in school. Some attribute these largely to the difference between the educational methods employed in the West Indies and here; used to more Victorian methods of teaching, the immigrant finds it difficult to adapt to the freer discipline of an English school. Others see emotional disturbances as the inevitable reaction to the sudden change from rural surroundings to an urban environment ... Though teachers, therefore, may differ about the precise cause, they nevertheless agree in regarding the West Indian as presenting particular behaviour problems. One teacher ... writes succinctly: 'By nature and upbringing quick, energetic, emotional and noisy, the West Indian disturbs the life of an English school.'[25]

Many teachers attribute West Indian exuberance to the tropical climate in the Caribbean. And yet, Asian children who share with the West Indians all these background elements – Victorian methods of teaching, rural environment, and tropical climate – do not present behavioural and emotional problems in school. On the contrary they tend to be shy and withdrawn, and do not 'misuse' the new freedom of the British school. One is therefore led to conclude that this set of cause-and-effect analysis is superficial. In order to understand correctly the characteristics and personality traits of contemporary Afro-Caribbeans, adults as

25. *Immigrant School Leavers and the Youth Employment Service in Birmingham*, Institute of Race Relations, Special Series, 1968, pp. 11–12.

well as children, one has to study the impact that centuries of slavery has left on them. This has been outlined earlier.[26]

The reference by David Beetham to 'the sudden change from rural surroundings to an urban environment' pertains to the practice common, until very recently, among Afro-Caribbean parents, settled in Britain, of letting their children be raised by elderly female relatives in the Caribbeans and then have them brought over just before they were fifteen. The parents did so partly to comply with the immigration law and partly to ensure that the child acquired British scholastic qualifications, thus improving his chance of getting better jobs than they themselves had. In this they were to be disappointed.

The British employers' resistance to placing black school leavers in jobs other than manual and semi-skilled remained as high as with black adult immigrants. Evidence of this attitude was provided, indirectly, by the 1966 census. It showed that job distribution among coloured immigrants (in Greater London area) was the same as in the 1960 census.[27]

26. See pp. 14–20.
27. E. J. B. Rose and Associates, *Colour and Citizenship*, p. 166.

7 WHITE REJECTION, BLACK WITHDRAWAL

*Even if a coloured doctor walked into a
factory they'd give him a broom.*
RALPH GOODWIN, a West Indian youth in
Islington.

*Nobody believes that thousands of coloured
Britons in Birmingham schools have an equal
chance of life ahead of them.*
The Midlands correspondent of *The Times*.[1]

*On all the [black] youngsters I talked to, the
sudden break with white friends at thirteen or
fourteen had left scars and hardened attitudes.*
COLIN MCGLASHAN[2]

The most depressing aspect of racial discrimination in Britain
has been its blanket application. No matter what the occupation
or earning of a black citizen, he found himself barred from
'respectable' white areas.[3] No matter what the educational
achievement of a coloured school-leaver he was denied the
opportunity of a white-collar job. Keith T., a nineteen-year-old
Trinidadian, educated entirely in Britain, and with three G C E
'O' levels, applied for the following jobs in the summer of 1966 –
'cleaning offices, selling encyclopaedias, canvassing for laundry
orders, doorman at a cinema, bookmaker's assistant, junior
clerk and shop assistant'. He was turned down for each one of
them, whereas the white boy he was with was offered, or kept in
mind for, every one of them.[4]

By the mid-1960s, the proportion of those educated entirely in
Britain among the coloured school leavers was rising. And yet

1. 4 November 1963.   2. The *Observer*, 10 September 1967.
3. 'The few attempts by ambitious Indians and West Indians to obtain
housing in the privately developed estates of lower priced housing . . . have
almost invariably provoked outbursts of intense hostility.' E. J. B. Rose and
Associates, *Colour and Citizenship*, p. 251.
4. The *Observer*, 25 September 1966.

there seemed little evidence that they were catching up with their white counterparts in gaining jobs. This was due to employers' attitudes and policies. A check of the London Youth Employment Offices by a correspondent of the *Observer* showed that white youths in the 'deprived' areas of black settlement such as Islington, Paddington and Notting Hill were almost five times more likely to get skilled jobs than coloured youngsters. Of the 147 firms dealing with the Youth Employment Offices, nearly half had stated 'No Coloured', or were known to be 'unlikely to accept them'. Even Birmingham, generally considered a centre of racialism, fared better than London. There, in 1964–5, the chance of a white youth entering an apprenticeship scheme was three times higher than that for his coloured counterpart.[5] The overall employment pattern in Birmingham, however, is different from that in London.

With its countless offices London has an almost insatiable appetite for office staff. Each year three fifths of the female and one fifth of the male school leavers in the London area find work in offices. This is certainly not the case with coloured youths. Their employment in offices is still rare. It is true that nowadays coloured shop assistants and usherettes at local cinemas are to be seen, but generally only in the areas of coloured settlement. As yet their number is comparatively small.

Outside London the picture is bleak. In the summer of 1968, the vast city centre of Wolverhampton, for instance, did not have a single coloured shop assistant. The explanations given by large stores as well as small shops were 'There just weren't any vacancies' and 'The coloured community, in any case, couldn't speak English well enough.'[6] Leaving aside the Asian community there were then nine thousand West Indians in the city for whom English is their native language. Is it conceivable that not one of them was qualified to be a shop assistant?

In Bradford, of the five hundred coloured youths leaving school in 1968, no more than sixty were expected to get jobs 'with some skill or training'.[7] The number should have been two hundred to

5. *Immigration, Race and Politics*, a Bow Group pamphlet (London 1966), p. 21.

6. The *Observer*, 14 July 1968.   7. *The Times*, 6 December 1968.

bring it to a par with the overall job distribution of the city's school leavers. No wonder then that a West Indian leader complained 'Coloured kids are being educated for labouring jobs; they're becoming the worker ants.'

In short, the skilled and 'face-to-face' jobs that have been more or less out of the reach of adult black immigrants, continue to elude the black youths. Like their parents, the black youths ultimately find jobs; but the time and effort spent by the Youth Employment Officers to achieve even this modest end is quite staggering.

Take London, for instance. During the period 1966–8 there were three jobs for every two school leavers. Given this, there should have been no difficulty in placing youths, black or white, in jobs. But, instead, the Youth Employment Officers described the actual situation in these terms: 'It takes three times as much effort to place a coloured school leaver as the white'; 'Placing a coloured youth is as difficult as placing a physically handicapped white youth'; 'They [coloured youths] are in the same position as women used to be'.

Such statements are the mirror images of the black youth's experiences, whether in Islington, Brixton, Paddington or Handsworth. A typical comment is: 'My white classmates in school – well, they get jobs in two, three days, or weeks. But us, we have .o wait months.' And that too for the modest jobs to which their career teachers or Youth Employment Officers have, insidiously (or tactfully, as they would put it), brought the black youths' sights down to.[8] In early 1968 the author met black youths in North London who had been jobless since they had left school the summer before. More than half of the 143 unemployed youths at the Brixton Youth Employment Office in December 1968 were coloured,[9] although they constituted only one-seventh of the total secondary school population in the area. According to a

8. During an informal conversation a Youth Employment Officer in south London told a West Indian teacher: 'When a coloured kid comes in wanting to join a bank, we try to discourage him . . . He gets to the point where he'd accept *anything* . . . No, we don't tell them directly what the real situation is. That's not our policy. We follow the guidelines as laid out for us.'

9. *The Times*, 6 December 1968.

survey, published in June 1970, the unemployment of young West Indian males in some areas of London is at least four times the national average for all races and age groups.[10]

This situation has to be viewed against a continually changing background – physically, psychologically and economically. Firstly, the old, stock explanations of white employers – 'They don't know English'; 'They speak English with a peculiar accent'; 'They don't have British qualifications'; 'They don't know our way of life' – are becoming outdated as more and more black youths leave British schools, speaking English with local accents, and having had longer and longer periods of schooling in Britain. Unlike their parents black youths make comparisons with their white classmates. 'Why do they [the employers] say "No job" when my white classmate after me gets one?' asked a puzzled and angry West Indian youth from Handsworth.

Secondly, the absolute and relative number of coloured school leavers is rising sharply. Already, in Bradford, they form one-quarter of the total. By 1974, one in six of the school leavers in Inner London and Birmingham will be coloured.[11] Simultaneously, the nature of demand in the British labour market is changing. There is less and less need for blue-collar jobs, and more and more for white-collar.[12] This, in turn, leads to sharper competition between the unskilled white youths and the average black school leaver.

Thirdly, black youths dislike the idea of taking unskilled and manual semi-skilled jobs even more than their parents. They know, from their parents' experience, that 'If you start with a broom you'll end up with a broom'. So they (and their parents) find means of breaking the vicious circle by trying hard and long for suitable jobs, or by staying at school longer and/or going to university or college. All along they are persuaded by school authorities to lower their sights, that is, to take the typecast jobs their parents have.[13] Following her mother's example, Joan

10. *The Times*, 29 June 1970.

11. Michael Banton in *New Society*, 9 November 1967.

12. Between 1911 and 1961, white-collar jobs increased by 171 per cent whereas manual jobs rose by only 2 per cent. Bob Hepple, *op, cit.*, p. 62.

13. 'Our findings [show] . . . that West Indians tend to react to the unfavourable employment situation by taking jobs which are beneath their

Gordon, a seventeen-year-old West Indian girl in Wolverhampton, went to college to train as a nurse. After a year she changed her mind and told her departmental head that she wished to be transferred to Business Studies. He told her that it would be best for her to be a nurse because, 'it is difficult for you people to get jobs in offices'.[14]

Fourthly, working in jobs they dislike engenders dissatisfaction and a general grievance against white society. The author's informal interviews with black youths made him conclude that only one in five considered his job satisfactory.[15] Peter Figueroa's study in north London showed that of those West Indian school leavers who had not got the job of their choice more than half expressed dissatisfaction (compared with one in eleven English boys); and that more West Indians wanted to leave their present job.[16] However, a much smaller proportion of black youths are likely actually to give up their jobs, for they know only too well that they do not have the same choice and latitude in picking up jobs as the whites. This realization only adds to their frustration and bitterness.[17]

Fifthly, most black teenagers do not share either their parents' awe of the whites, or their obsequious dependence on them. The differences go beyond the normal generation gap. For, unlike their parents, born in the Caribbean and brought up on stories of Britain as the land of hope and glory and of 'Queen Victoria the Good' by their ancestors and the education system, the young-

---

abilities and qualifications,' said Dennis Stevenson and Peter Wallis at the end of their survey. *The Times,* 29 June 1970.

14. As a career, nursing is unpopular with English girls. In Birmingham, in 1966, only three per cent of the English girls chose it compared with forty-six per cent of the West Indian girls. David Beetham, *Immigrant School Leavers and the Youth Employment Service in Birmingham,* p. 26.

15. An earlier enquiry by Peter Wright in the Midlands and the North had revealed that seventy-two per cent of the West Indian workers preferred a different job from the one they had. Peter Wright, *The Coloured Worker In British Industry,* Oxford University Press, 1968, p. 151.

16. *Race,* April 1969, p. 506.

17. Fifty per cent of the young West Indian males (aged sixteen to twenty-four) polled in a survey in London (in 1969–70) said that a black man should fight for what he wants; whereas *seventy* per cent of the *unemployed* young West Indians felt the same. *The Times,* 29 June 1970.

sters born and brought up here have no such illusions. Also, growing up in Britain has meant that the vision of the youngsters is not distorted by the physical distance between the West Indies and Britain which, in their parent's case, gave British society a certain glitter. The young West Indians grow up here sharing classrooms with British children, an experience that provides them with a yardstick against which to measure their own progress and behaviour patterns. All this makes them far less likely to accept meekly incquitable treatment by whites. The following example sums up the difference between two generations. 'The foreman told me to brush the floor,' said Joe, a seventeen-year-old West Indian engineering apprentice in London. 'There was a white labourer (whose job it was) doing nothing, so I refused. I got the sack. I told my dad, and he said, "You should have swept." I told my dad, "You're whitewashed, those English people have corrupted your mind".'[18]

No doubt Joe's self-assurance sprang partly from the lack of financial and filial responsibilities that weighed on his father's mind, and partly from the familiarization with white teachers and students that he had gained at school. However, if experience at school familiarizes black children with whites, it also makes them aware of their racial difference through ridicule. Early black arrivals at school suffered most. 'Before I came to this country (thirteen years ago) I had no idea of whites,' recalls Sydney Harris, a nineteen-year-old West Indian in north London. 'I was so young then. But when you go to school here, you realize the difference: you're *made* to realize it. They [the white kids] pick on you and pick on you. First you try to bribe them – sweets, ices, the lot. But then one day you can't stand it any more. You get vicious, real vicious; and you lick them.' Only if one were to ignore such experiences could one concur with the view, widely held in official circles, that the small size of the black minority was conducive to 'integration'.

This view was often linked with another, that racial integration in schools would grow and spread to the rest of society. In spite of its popularity in official and quasi-official circles, this theory was soon to be discredited. Integration at school had few lasting

18. The *Observer*, 10 September 1967.

effects, wrote the Midlands correspondent of *The Times*, in 1963, at the end of a long enquiry; white and black boys were to be seen leaving school separately. Apparently, whatever black-white friendships developed were not continued outside the school gates; or if they were, they were seldom maintained beyond the years of puberty. And almost invariably it was the whites who rejected the blacks. 'From four until fourteen I grew up with white friends,' said Louis, a West Indian youth in London. 'Then they started acting cold. I couldn't join their conversations. I was always left out when they went anywhere. Their mothers looked at me like I was a leper. In the street, with their girl-friends, they'd mutter ''go away'' or put their heads down like they didn't know me. Now I don't see any of them.'[19] In the face of such blatant rejection only spineless black youths would continue seeking white company. To preserve their self-respect black teenagers soon learnt to remain with their 'own kind'.

However disappointing these rebuffs might have been to black adolescents, their parents were not surprised. After all, many of them had undergone similar experiences. During their early years of arrival West Indians had invited their workmates to parties, and christening and wedding ceremonies. Very few, if any, whites had accepted; and fewer still had turned up. In any case, West Indians were seldom, if ever, invited by whites in return. So they got the message, and acted accordingly. Describing such experiences, Wallace Collins, a West Indian carpenter, wrote in his autobiography, *Jamaican Migrant:*

I decided to quit the disenchantment, the uncompassionate yet impolite monstrosity of the white man's society, where I ... tried to convince him that I was a genuine human being as he was ... This metamorphosis took place within me without my knowing it, until I began to intermingle with my own people. ... I felt wanted and desired by my own people ... I belonged.[20]

It so happened that the continual rejection of black schoolmates by whites was accompanied by a steady growth in the number of black students – a situation which released the blacks from

19. The *Observer*, 10 September 1967.
20. Routledge and Kegan Paul, 1965, p. 98.

the pressure to mix with whites during school breaks and on the playground, and simultaneously enabled them to create a self-contained social life. Besides that, larger numbers helped them to counter the fear engendered by the overwhelming presence of whites both inside and outside the school. How real that fear is, is borne out by the statement that a black teenager in Notting Hill made to a friendly white journalist. 'It may sound strange to you,' he said, 'but I feel safer here at night than I do walking down Oxford Street.'[21]

Charles Hines, a young West Indian in Wolverhampton, told the author that whenever he and his friends returned home late at night from a dance-hall in the city centre they devised an elaborate plan to avoid walking alone in the streets. He was uncomfortably aware of the attacks on black men when alone at night, and believed in the axiom current in the community: 'If you're black you've to learn to defend yourself.'

As children grow older, their awareness of and contact with the adult world grows, as does the importance and frequency of their out-of-school activities. At present black children see no visual signs of social integration between races in the adult world: they do not, for example, notice racially mixed groups of adults walking together in the streets, or entering or leaving pubs together. At home their families neither visit white friends' homes nor are they visited by whites. Even West Indian homes with one white parent (usually the mother) seldom have white visitors. The only whites calling at their homes are those who have to do so in the course of their job, that is, meter-readers, postmen, child welfare officers, social workers and policemen.

In his social circle, the black adolescent seldom, if ever, meets West Indians who have either authority or social status. The relatives, friends and neighbours he knows are nearly always factory workers, busmen or nurses. Persons with authority – teachers, youth employment officers, policemen, magistrates, driving-test examiners, Labour Exchange officials – are almost always white. The only institution where he sees black people in authority is the Pentecostal church, but then the congregation there is all black. His social life remains limited to contacts with fellow West

21. The *Observer*, 10 September 1967.

Indians. The only place outside school where he might mix with whites is the youth club, if there is one in his district.[22]

By now, the youth clubs have proved, in this respect, to be the proto-types of factories. That is, they either remain all-white, barring blacks,[23] or become predominantly black; or, if they manage to stay inter-racial, they become places where voluntary racial separatism is practised and accepted. 'It is virtually impossible to find an integrated youth club in the area,' said Bill Harte, a senior white youth leader in Brixton in 1969. 'Sometimes you'll find one which has one quarter West Indian membership, but when you go there, they'll be standing by themselves in a corner.'

However, if the black minority shies away from a full participation in club activities, so do whites when they find themselves in the minority. Describing a visit to a church youth club, the Brixton YMCA's Community Relations Development Project's *Year One* report (published in December 1968) states:

> The membership totals 80, of which two-thirds are coloured. [This evening] . . . by 8.30 p.m. the membership has built up. . . . At 8.46 p.m. there were about 60 members in the club. All, except 12, were coloured. The white members sat outside. The youth leader went outside to them. 'We ain't comin' in yet, 'cos there's too many yobbos in there.'

On their part, the blacks express similar feelings about whites. One of the main reasons given by West Indians for preferring black youth clubs (as revealed by the Brixton Y M C A's survey in 1966) was 'the bad behaviour of English youths'. The other main reason was that '(Black) people speak the same language as me'.

These are also the major reasons why in such inter-racial clubs as the Radford in Nottingham or the St Stephens in Shepherds Bush, voluntary racial separation takes place in club activities.[24] The St Stephens Hall may overflow with black and

22. In 1963, for 10,800 young men in Handsworth, Sandwell and Aston (3,000 of them black) there was no fully-fledged youth club only a part-time one. In contrast, the suburb of Northfield, with 12,000 youths, had eleven youth clubs, open all week. *The Times*, 4 November 1963.

23. For instance, the YMCA youth club in Wolverhampton. *The Observer*, 14 July 1968.

24. There is also the difference in preferences for activities. At the Radford club, for instance, blacks are to be often seen playing cards, dominoes or

white teenagers (almost equal in number), but when dancing begins, whites move up the hall while blacks stay near the entrance The atmosphere seems relaxed and friendly; and yet there is no black-white dancing. The youth leader in charge compares the situation to 'water and oil in the same can: they're in the same hall but they don't cross the colour line'.

This pattern is to be found at discotheque clubs which are often held up as great inter-racial successes. Here, differences of musical taste come to the surface. 'I once acted as a disc jockey at a club, and I could definitely feel the inter-group hostility being channelled through me in the requests for records,' said Bryan Hartley, a white youth leader in London. 'The West Indians would come up to me and say, "Man, can you stop playing this s——?"; and then the whites would refuse to dance when I put on ska or rock-steady.'[25]

The national situation was summed up by the House of Commons Select Committee on Race Relations and Immigration when it reported:

There was an apparently successful multi-racial club in Ealing. Mainly coloured clubs in Wolverhampton and Huddersfield, and all-coloured clubs in Liverpool and Hackney, also appeared to be active. But all such clubs rapidly change in their membership and activity. In particular the success of a multi-racial club, as such, may be short-lived. They tend, all too soon, to become all-coloured or all-white.[26]

In short, youth clubs are already reflecting the values and attitudes of the adult world. Temperamental differences[27] and racial antipathy are proving to be almost insurmountable barriers against creating inter-racial understanding and friendship.

---

snooker, while whites are to be found at ping-pong tables, on the badminton court or in the gymnasium.

25. The *Sunday Telegraph*, 2 February 1969.

26. *The Problems of Coloured School-Leavers*, Vol. I, July 1969, p. 56.

27. 'A different behaviour pattern was found between the West Indian children and the English,' wrote Peter Watson, summarizing the findings of a research team at Birmingham University. 'The West Indians were more depressed, tense, backward; more hostile to adults, more anxious for other children's approval and more likely to show unconcern for adult approval.' Review of *Teaching English to West Indian Children: the Research Stage of the Project*. *New Society*, 25 June 1970.

During the early 1960s it was at least possible to secure the co-operation of different races to launch youth clubs. By the mid-1960s this co-operation was becoming rare. In 1965, for instance, a Methodist minister in Harlesden, concerned with the lack of youth club facilities, sent thirty invitations to young Methodists (half of them white, the other half black) to start a club, but not a single white responded. The result is that the club is now one hundred per cent black. That was three years *before* Enoch Powell, a Tory leader, delivered his first major speech on race and immigration, a speech that was condemned by many liberals for 'worsening race relations'.

Enoch Powell may well be criticized for devoting a whole speech to the subjects of race and immigration, and for using highly charged language. But as far as race relations were concerned, the fact remains that long before his speech, voluntary separatism of races, among youths as well as adults, had become an accepted norm. Nonetheless, many whites and blacks were jolted out of their complacency by Enoch Powell's speech.

In the case of West Indians, however, after their initial anger and apprehension had subsided, the speech accelerated their search for identity. In the Caribbean this process had begun nearly a decade earlier as the hold of British imperialism loosened and as the politics of new African states, particularly the Congo, acquired an international importance. Describing a procession in Port-of-Spain, Trinidad, 'some weeks after the news of (Patrice) Lumumba's death', V. S. Naipaul, a Trinidadian by birth, wrote:

It was an orderly procession made up wholly of negroes. They were singing hymns, [carrying] banners and placards [which] were anti-white, anti-clerical and pro-African in an ill-defined, inclusive way. I had never before seen anything like it in Trinidad ... I thought then that it was a purely local eruption, created by the pressure of local politics. But soon, on the journey I was now getting ready to make, I came to see that such eruptions were widespread, and represented feelings coming to the surface in negro communities throughout the Caribbean.[28]

28. *The Middle Passage*, pp. 84–5.

8

BLACK CONSCIOUSNESS: AN AFRO IDENTITY

It is simplicity itself . . . to link West Indians in Britain with those in the Caribbean and the Americas, and with their African brothers and sisters everywhere.
NEVILLE MAXWELL[1]

My ancestors were Africans taken to the New World to do a job, so obviously I'm not detached. And I cannot see myself or any other black man being detached from his African heritage.
LANCE DUNKLEY, a West Indian leader in Wolverhampton, 1969.

Events in the Congo in 1960–1 caused many people in the Caribbean to identify themselves openly with Africa, whereas the West Indian minority in Britain has needed the stimuli of two immigration laws, four race riots and the emotive speeches of Enoch Powell to consider the issue of their origin. The explanation for this delayed reaction by West Indian settlers lies partly in their status as immigrants, wherein they seem mainly concerned with their personal and economic problems of settlement, with little interest or energy left over to ponder the abstract question of self-identity; and partly in their historico-cultural background.

Although emancipated from bonded slavery the freedmen remained psychologically locked in their past, servile to the values embedded in their psyche. 'The West Indian negro knows nothing of Africa except that it is a term of reproach,' wrote Anthony Trollope in 1860. 'If African immigrants are put to work on the same estate with him, he will not work beside them, or drink with them, or walk with them. '[2] This attitude was coupled with the constant insistence by the post-Emancipation, educated West Indians that they belonged, exclusively, to Western civilization.

1. *The Power of Negro Action*, p. 3.
2. Cited in V. S. Naipaul, *The Middle Passage*, p. 66.

'It is necessary to see ourselves in perspective as far as we can and to recognize that ours is ... a part of that great branch of civilization that is called western civilization,' wrote Dr Hugh Springer in the *Caribbean Quarterly* a century after Anthony Trollope's journal on the West Indies appeared. 'Our culture is rooted in western culture and our values, in the main, are the values of the Christian-Hellenic tradition ... the Greek ideals of virtue and knowledge and the Christian faith.'[3] This statement illustrates, as well as any other, the persistent refusal by many Afro-Caribbeans, especially those of the middle class, to come to grips with their past.

For many West Indians, migration to Britain was a continuation of the same self-denial, a part of the psychological flight undertaken in the belief that residence in Britain would bestow upon them the inheritance of a Christian-Hellenic civilization, and release them, for ever, from the chains of their African heritage. But discriminatory experiences in Britain led many sensitive West Indians to examine their past. 'We had *heard* about slavery in Jamaica but we didn't sort of put it together and put ourselves within,' said Dorothy Pearson, a West Indian nurse living in Slough. 'We didn't think it happened to people we descended from. We thought it was somebody else or some other people we didn't know about. But, coming to this country, you get to realize that we're part of slavery.'

Life in Britain also caused the West Indians to conclude, with much pain and sorrow, that western civilization is the prerogative of white people, and that colour differences count far more than cultural affinity. The result was that most West Indians ceased trying to be accepted in the social niche of white western society and limited themselves to socialization with fellow West Indians, while still nursing a sneaking hope that at least their descendants, born and bred in Britain, would be considered and treated as inheritors of British civilization.[4] In this, too, they

3. Cited in *The Middle Passage*, p. 67.
4. 'No matter how they [the white people] hurt you, you're still not inclined to be really divorced from them,' said Patricia Fullwood, a West Indian housewife in Wolverhampton. 'There's something between us, this love–hate. There shouldn't be, but there is.'

were to be disappointed.[5] 'They [black children] learn English history, but when they want to join English society they're shut out and there's nowhere they can go,' said a West Indian social worker in London in 1967.[6] A year later he heard Enoch Powell stating that a West Indian or Asian does not, by being born in England, become an Englishman.

The cumulative effect on the young West Indians of the general behaviour of the British, the speeches of Enoch Powell, and the continual discussion of race and immigration in the mass media, especially since early 1968, has been to undermine their belief that they are British. The case of Noel Green, born in London in 1958 of West Indian parents, is typical. 'As a young child he wanted to be called an Englishman,' said Anthony Green, his father. 'But now [in 1969] he considers himself a West Indian and a black person.'[7]

To some, this change may seem undesirable, even cruel; but it has its merits, the principal one being that it signifies a halt to the traditional West Indian flight from his past, and his unwillingness to face his problem of identity and origin. As a West Indian nurse in Wolverhampton expressed it:

Each day I'm getting more aware of the fact that I'm black because of the situations that one comes up against. Sometimes you feel, oh, the white man and myself are equal, but there's always something there to tell you that you're not the same, even though you speak the same language, eat the same food, and have the same customs. Therefore you try to find out your background, and the customs of your ancestors.

Part of the credit for this development must go to Enoch Powell. Black militants are openly thankful to him for helping them achieve in a year what might otherwise have taken them a decade. Mainly due to his speeches, the socio-political awareness of West Indians in Britain has increased.

5. The Afro-Caribbeans may well ponder the status of fellow-Africans in America. Although born and bred in America for well over fifteen generations they are still considered pariahs by most white Americans.

6. The *Observer*, 10 September 1967.

7. Reporting the findings of a year-long survey of young West Indians in London, Dennis Stevenson stated, 'When respondents were asked to say spontaneously what nationality they were, more than two out of three said they were West Indian.' *Race Today*, August 1970, p. 279.

In the Caribbean, however, they did not need the stimulus of an Enoch Powell to spur them to examine their past. Political independence since the early 1960s has meant that each island has had to write its own history, and erect a pantheon of national heroes, to help the inhabitants feel a sense of national identity. As a result, previously ignored leaders of slave revolts, and leaders of movements which emphasized self-pride and African heritage, have been resurrected and accorded the status of national heroes. For instance, the late Marcus Garvey, much maligned and ridiculed during his lifetime by the power élite in Jamaica, was declared a national hero by the government of independent Jamaica. His body was flown from London to be re-buried in Kingston, Jamaica, with full state honours.

At universities and colleges much intellectual energy has been channelled into examining those elements of creole life which are African in origin and which had until recently been ignored or altogether denied by the European-orientated élite in the Caribbean. By now, it has been established that popular culture and folklore in the West Indies has much in common with African traditions. The rhythm of creole speech has been noticed to parrellel that of West African speech. The 'nonsense' words in creole language have been recognized as derivatives of African words. Many Caribbean dishes such as *callalou*, *cachop* and *cou-cou*, and the method of preparing soup have been shown to have African origins.

The natural rhythm and grace with which most blacks in the Caribbean and America dance have been related to their ancestors in Africa where dancing is more a form of self- and communal expression than a means of entertainment. Describing the various body movements in '[African] war dances, victory dances, stage dances, remedial dances etc.', Dunduzu Chisiza writes:

We nod our heads, rock our necks, tilt our heads and pause. We shake our shoulders, throw them back and forth, bounce breasts and halt ... We rhythmically shake our hefty rear ends, our tummies duck and peer, our legs quick march, slow march, tap dripple, quiver and tremble while our feet perform feats. 'Dance!'[8]

8. Cited in Neville Maxwell, *The Power of Negro Action*, p. 50.

The West Indians too dance with the same ecstatic abandon as the Africans.

Neville Maxwell points out that African customs and beliefs have been retained, in essence, in the Shango dance in Trinidad, Grenada and Jamaica, as well as in the voodoo and obeah cults throughout the Caribbean. The Trinidadian calypso, too, is African in origin, 'a very important aspect of the "oral", as against the "written" tradition of the African'.[9]

African beliefs and practices, of course, have become amalgamated with conventional Christian practices; and the result is the Pentecostal church.[10] Many of these churches in the Caribbean have their headquarters in America; and thus West Indian Christians maintain contact with their 'soul brothers' in America. In addition to these formal, religious contacts, there is increasing communication between Caribbean intellectuals, writers and politicians and their counterparts in black America and Britain. A three-way dialogue between the black people in the West Indies, America and Britain has developed, and is growing rapidly. What brings blacks in the western world together is their race and common history, their present search for identity and their interest in Africa and Black Power.

Already the term Black Power has proved so popular with the black masses in the Caribbean that many conventional, old-style politicians cannot resist publicly supporting the idea. 'I say Jamaica must restore to her sense of independence and nationhood a basic pride and hope – respect of dignity and self-confidence – which are expressed in that great phrase which ... I salute: "Black Power"!' said Norman Manley, once the Prime Minister of Jamaica, in the autumn of 1968.[11] Some time later Hugh Shearer, the then Prime Minister of Jamaica, made a similar statement, as did Vere Bird of Antigua.[12] This is, however, what is called the 'moderate' version of Black Power, a version that emphasizes only racial pride, but neglects economic analysis. It is considered inadequate by many radical Caribbean intellectuals, industrial workers, the young urban *lumpenproletariat*, and some segments of the armed forces. These radical elements wish

9. *The Power of Negro Action*, p. 50.   10. See Chapter 3, pp. 28–9.
11. *Joffa*, March 1969, p. 47.   12. *Race Today*, December 1969, p. 232.

to engineer a social revolution to free the West Indies from its present subjugation to 'the white *economic* power structure' consisting of corporations based in America, Britain and Canada. They seem to have considerable support.

It was indeed to pacify this force in Trinidadian politics, that was manifesting itself in March 1970 in the form of massive demonstrations, that Eric Williams, the Prime Minister, said,

The fundamental feature of the demonstrations was the insistence on Black dignity, the manifestation of Black consciousness and the demand for Black economic power . . . If this is Black Power, then I am for Black Power.[13]

However, this statement was soon followed by the arrest of prominent Black Power leaders, which led to a rebellion by a considerable segment of the armed forces.[14]

Radical Black Power parties exist in almost all the West Indian islands, bearing such varied names as the Black Panthers and the Young Power (in Trinidad), the Progressive Labour Party (in Bermuda) or the Educational Forum for the People (in St Vincent). They maintain informal contact with Black Power movements in America and Britain. Roosevelt Brown, a PLP leader in Bermuda, was elected a member of the Black Power Conference in Philadelphia in August 1968. As a result the first Caribbean Black Power Conference was held in Bermuda in July 1969. It was attended by two hundred delegates from the Caribbean, America and Africa, an unprecedented event which emphasized identity of colour.

A new feeling of 'Black Brotherhood' seems to be surging across the globe. When, at the 1968 Olympics in Mexico City, black Americans were seen on television giving the Black Power salute, millions of black people in the western world instantly identified with them, and applauded their silent, dignified gesture.[15]

13 The *Observer*, 26 April 1970.
14. The speed with which the American and British governments helped Eric Williams to put down the rebellion by sending small arms by air, and by alerting their war ships in the Caribbean, proved the point that the Black Power radicals had hitherto been making.
15. A white teacher of a predominantly black class in a primary school in London told the author that 'Black children are immensely pleased when

When, in October 1968, Walter Rodney, a Guyanese lecturer and a (radical) Black Power advocate, was banned from returning to the University of the West Indies at Mona, Jamaica, the students rebelled in protest; and troops had to be called in to restore order. To show their disapproval, many Jamaican nationals in London staged a sit-in at their High Commission.

At the time of the Commonwealth Prime Ministers' Conference in London in January 1969, black citizens demonstrated in support of black Rhodesians. Later that year, black settlers in London staged a demonstration against the British government's action in sending troops to Anguilla. When a Nigerian diplomat in Brixton was manacled by the police for a motoring offence, many West Indians in the area protested and 'obstructed' the police, for which some of them were arrested and charged. When Robert Williams, a radical black American leader, was held in a London prison because an American airline refused to carry him to America, some Black Panthers picketed the airline's office in London while the West Indian Standing Conference interceded to act as Robert Williams's spokesman and plead for him at the Home Office. It did not matter that Robert Williams was an American national; all that mattered was that he was a 'black brother' in trouble.

Besides engaging in periodic demonstrative activity, especially against harassment and maltreatment of blacks by the police,[16] many black organizations in Britain, moderate as well as militant, have undertaken projects of self-help and education. The militant Universal Coloured People's Association and the Black Panthers pursue their aim of spreading 'black consciousness' by holding periodic meetings in London and Manchester where Black Poetry is read, Black Music played, and Black Films shown. The moderate West Indian League in London has set up its own youth club; and so has the Willesden West Indian Association. Volunteers from the West Indian Student Centre

---

they see coloured people on television . . . Right away they identify themselves with them no matter what their *nationality* is.'

16. During the summers of 1969 and 1970 at least six demonstrations against police harassment were held in London and Manchester by black militant organizations.

in London go to black districts to coach children in school subjects as well as in Black History. An Afro-Asian Study Circle has been active in Birmingham since 1968, as has been the Afro-Caribbean Circle in Wolverhampton. A Free University for African, Asian and West Indian studies was launched in west London in September 1969 by the British Black Power Party. Plans are also afoot to start Black Studies programmes in Birmingham, Wolverhampton and Nottingham, where a Black Power group is preparing a Black History of the British Empire. Activists at the West Indian Student Centre are drafting an A to Z Guide on the Black Personalities of the World, and plan to have it published by a black publishing house in London, which has already been established.

What impact are these activities having on the West Indian community at large? There is no doubt that more West Indians are joining more organizations and attending more meetings than ever before. In the wake of Enoch Powell's speech in April 1968, old, defunct organizations were revived, and new ones founded. In Manchester alone three black militant organizations were established. To the surprise of many black activists, and others, these organizations have not lost steam. 'We had a speaker from London, and we packed a hall with three hundred West Indians at a week's notice,' said a West Indian leader in Wolverhampton in early 1969. 'A year ago this would have been unthinkable.'

As for the militants, they already have an active national body: the Black People's Alliance. Representatives of more than fifty organizations affiliated to it meet periodically in the Midlands. The number of Black Power militants is estimated, by the (Home Office) Special Branch, at two thousand.[17] For each activist there must be at least a dozen sympathizers.

These numbers apart, it is more meaningful to judge the undramatic, socio-psychological change that the black community has already undergone by examining the proportion of West Indian girls who no longer straighten their hair, the extent to which the West Indians have ceased to consider the word 'black' pejorative; and the attitude they have towards Africa in general,

17. The *Daily Telegraph Magazine*, 23 May 1969.

and African settlers in Britain, in particular. In all these areas, signs of change are unmistakable. In Leeds, for instance, nearly a third of the West Indian girls have 'gone natural' in their hair style. When asked to tick off the appropriate term to describe their race – coloured, black, negro – two-thirds of the young West Indian males in a survey conducted by the author in London (in 1968) chose 'black'. Two years earlier such a result would have been totally unexpected. (With their fathers, such a response would still be unlikely). With the young West Indians the disc 'Say It Loud/I Am Black And Proud', released in 1968, still remains the most popular ever.

But, most significantly, change has come in the attitude of the young as well as old West Indians towards West African settlers in Britain. Until recently, locked in their historic conditioning, the West Indians and West Africans eyed one another warily from a distance. The West Indians thought Africans 'savage' and 'uncivilized'; whereas most Africans considered West Indians as 'descendents of slaves'. That is changed. Today, Africans are warmly welcomed in West Indian circles as 'brothers'. Together they blame the white man for warping their minds and for creating the gulf that existed between them for so long.

The young West Indians are even more interested in Africa and Africans. 'We must find out about Africa because that's from where our ancestors came' and 'All black people belong to Africa' are commonly expressed sentiments among them. The scene of Tarzan knocking down six Africans with one swipe no longer amuses them. It offends. 'Films and television about Africa always show the bad things about black races, never the achievements,' says Barry, a West Indian youth in London.[18]

Nor are the images and descriptions of Africans swinging from trees, and eating one another, accepted as true because, as many West Indians argue, all the books have been written by whites.[19] 'But even if these stories are true,' says Kate McNish in Wolver-

18. The *Observer*, 10 September 1967.
19. 'As long as Europeans are . . . to write and speak . . . on African affairs, this distortion, wilful or innocent, of our history, culture, standards and values will continue,' writes Neville Maxwell, a West Indian leader. *The Power of Negro Action*, p. 15.

hampton, 'it was the way people lived there. It was their *way of life*.' Most West Indians are no longer shameful or apologetic of their African ancestry. Consequently when they see West Africans with their tribal marks or in native dress they no longer sneer but, instead, respect this as a manifestation of a way of life that is different from the white man's. The presence of West Africans in Britain, retaining their native customs, is, to them, living proof that they (the West Indians) have not always been black duplicates of a white culture.

Although black, and negroid by race, the West African can be distinguished from the West Indian by his accent, dress, hair style and mannerism. At the less obvious, psychological level too his attitudes and behaviour towards whites are different from those of the West Indian, because of the variations in their historical experiences with respect to the whites. Unlike the West Indian, the West African did not undergo a traumatic uprooting nor did he suffer the indignity of slavery. Hence he has not developed the feeling of 'intimate enmity' towards the British that the West Indian has.[20] He does not suffer from the anxiety and neurosis about his colour, something that is part of the West Indian sub-conscious. He does not wish to be white, nor is he a product of a 'white-biased' society. Indeed, in his culture white is the colour of death. He does not suffer from self-contempt nor does he wish to run from his past. Quite the contrary. The West African is rooted in his past and in his own socio-cultural tradition.

In the case of West Africans, migration to Britain does not disrupt their social continuity, or undermine their loyalty to their tribe, religion or language. They remain Yorubas, Ibos, Hausas, or Fantis, especially when these tribal origins are recognized and accepted by the West African community in Britain, and also because their close friendships and immediate social life tend to be centred around members of the same tribe. Many African women retain their original dress. As a rule the West Africans maintain a much greater interest in their country of origin and

20. A study by F. H. M. Raveau in France showed that whereas seventy-five per cent of the French West Indians nursed memories of racial persecution only fifteen per cent of the French Africans did so. Renck and J. Knight, edrs, *Caste and Race*, Churchill Socy, 1966, p. 267.

do not seek to submerge themselves into British society. Like the Asians in Britain, they never fully give up the idea of ultimately returning to their home countries.

Furthermore, the African retains a strong sense of the family with its well-defined structure of rights and obligations. As a father he takes keen interest in the future of his children who, in return, offer him respect. He encourages them to be studious and ambitious; and he expects them to look after him in his old age.

In his dealings with white people the West African is likely to be more natural and self-assured than the West Indian. He is also more likely to take his Rachman-type landlord to the Rent Tribunal, and more inclined to enter private business. He believes in himself and is very much a man on his own.

The main reason why cultural and social differences between the West Africans and West Indians have not attracted popular, or even academic, interest is the imbalance between the size of the two communities. Compared with the West Indians, the number of West Africans in Britain is small. Furthermore, this small community is not concentrated in a particular area of the British conurbations, but is scattered throughout the areas of coloured settlement. Hence no single district with a special flavour of West African life has emerged. If it had, it would most likely have been a cross between Afro-Caribbean and Asian settlements. For, although biologically the same as the Afro-Caribbeans, the West Africans are, in their psychological make-up, nearer to the Asians. Both, West Africans and Asians, come from settled societies with their distinctive histories, traditions cultures and folklores, and therefore possess a certain inner calmness and self-assurance. The West Africans were ruled by the British, but the rulers did not interfere with their tribal system and social structure. Hence, their sense of cultural being was not impaired.

A similar situation prevailed in India under the British raj. And, as we shall presently see, Indians have maintained their cultural identity as strongly as have the West Africans.

PART II: ASIANS

1

THE COOLIES OF THE
EMPIRE – AND BRITAIN

The [European] manufacturers and traders who
were the harbingers of imperialism in the hills
and plains of Asia and the forests of Africa
went there with certain definite economic
objects: they wanted to sell cotton or calico,
to obtain tin or iron or rubber or tea or coffee.
But to do this under the complicated economic
system of westen civilization, it was necessary
that the whole economic system of the Asiatic
and African should be adjusted to and
assimilated with that of Europe.

LEONARD WOOLF[1]

Unlike the modern West Indies, which are the creation of Europe
(that is, Britain, Spain, France and Holland), present-day Asia
and Africa do not owe their existence to European colonization.
The people of the West Indies in the New World are now where
they are because they were transported from Africa and Asia,
involuntarily or voluntarily, as part of the colonial policies of
European powers. This is not the case with those non-European
parts of the Old World which fell under the imperial rule of
Europe. Basically, these lands in Asia and Africa have continued
to be populated by the indigenous people with histories that stretch
back to the dawn of civilization.

When Britain conquered parts of Asia and Africa, she
concerned herself mainly with the economic and political administration of these colonies. Throughout her imperial and pre-
imperial history, Britain's overriding concern remained economic
– first, trade and then, with rapid industrialization at home,
adequate supplies of raw materials for British factories, and
guaranteed colonial markets for her manufactured goods. In
order to achieve this economic end, Britain in India, for instance,
established an administrative machinery charged with the tasks

1. *Imperialism and Civilisation*, Hogarth Press, 1928, pp. 37–8.

of tax collection and the maintenance of law and order, and buttressed it later with an educational system designed to produce clerks, *babus*, to staff her bureaucracy at a low cost. Britain left the social structure and culture of the Indian masses well alone. In any case, it seemed a Himalayan task to mould Indian society with its distinct history, religions, languages, literature and folklore into a European image. Moreover, there was no profit to be made from it.

On the other hand, the value of India as an economic asset came into sharper focus as a result of the abolition of slavery. On Emancipation, in 1834, the freed African slaves left the estates, unwilling to work for their old masters under any circumstances. This led to an almost total collapse of the economic system of the plantation colonies. One of the colonies so affected was Mauritius, a small island in the Indian Ocean which the British had obtained from France in 1815.

When faced with an acute labour shortage, the Mauritian planters considered tapping the vast Indian sub-continent for labour. They contacted the East India Company and secured its permission to engage agents in India to recruit labour. They offered their Indian agents lucrative commissions of £3 to £6 per recruit.

Given this monetary incentive, the agents worked hard to produce 'volunteers'. To their gullible audience of landless labourers in the bazaars of Madras and Calcutta, they painted glamorous pictures of life 'across the waters'. They guaranteed free passage to a 'land of milk and honey' – and back, if the actual situation turned out to be less rosy. And, above all, they promised free land, an irresistible proposition to the land-starved people. With these baits, many young labourers – mostly Hindus of lower castes and Muslims – were lured into the planters' net.

Little did the illiterate labourer realize that, by his thumb impression on a contract, he was committing himself to 'semi-slavery'; because the contract bound the labourer to a planter for five years under a small, fixed wage, with a further five years' labour under the same or any other planter on the island, before allowing him free passage home *if* he chose to return home. That was the origin of 'indenturing' labour from India, a practice that continued until 1916, when it was outlawed by the Indian authorities.

The first batch of indentured Indian labour arrived in Mauritius in 1834 to work on sugar plantations. The scheme worked unbelievably well for the planters. Its success led the planters in British Guiana to initiate a similar scheme four years later. Subsequently, it was extended to Trinidad and Jamaica.

From then on, whenever and wherever the plans of British capital were frustrated by the unavailability, or lack of co-operation, of indigenous labour in the colonies, Indian labour was invariably imported. This happened in Ceylon, Malaya and Burma for the development of coffee, sugar, tea and rubber plantations, and tin mining; and also in South Africa, in 1859, for mining and the development of cotton fields. Later it occurred in East Africa for the construction of railways. The Indians became the coolies of the Empire, for ever serving the interests of the British capitalist, who found them hardworking, docile and reliable.

During the early phase of the indentured system the morale of Indian labourers was, however, low. They were overworked, underpaid and badly housed. They suffered sexual deprivation and jealousy due to lack of women. Internecine violence and suicide rates ran high. In time came resignation and acceptance. They also succeeded in tempering the harshness of an alien environment by grouping together on a linguistic and religious basis, thus partially recreating the socio-cultural milieu they had left behind. The later practice of being grouped in culturally homogenous work gangs gave them a sense of security and comradeship.

At the end of their contracts, some of them, spendthrift and enterprising, bought small plots of land with their own savings. With these, they established roots in the new country. They brought their families. Thus a small community of 'free' Indians emerged. It grew. It attracted 'voluntary' immigrants from India – traders, skilled craftsmen, even professionals – to service the agriculturist settlers. In short, the milieu of the Indian village and Indian society was recreated in the Caribbean, Mauritius, the Fiji islands and south-east Asia. Unlike the West African slaves there was no rupture of continuity, no annihilation of the past. The Indians carried their past with them and recreated the present in its image as, indeed, did the English settlers in North America, and the Iberians in South America. There was, however, one crucial difference. Indians were not the conquerors or imperial colonizers in whom the ultimate political and economic power rested, but were themselves colonial subjects, mere labourers and petty farmers.

From this brief history of Indian settlements abroad emerge two elements which are relevant to the issues of immigration and race in contemporary Britain. Firstly, Indian settlements overseas are a direct result of the actions taken by British entrepreneurs to further their economic interests. Secondly, like the British and the Chinese – that is, people with a strong culture of their own – the Indians are adept at recreating substantially the environment they have left; and they do not totally discard their culture, whatever the direct or indirect pressures.

The voluntary immigrants, who followed the indentured Indian labourers into various British colonies, were mostly from Gujarat and the Punjab, the two areas in the Indian sub-continent with a tradition of migration.

In modern times, the business enterprise of the Ismailis (a Muslim sect) and the merchant castes among Gujarati Hindus has often stimulated travel and migration to other parts of India and abroad. There is also a fifteen-centuries-old tradition of overseas trade from the ports of Gujarat – which is a coastal state facing the Indian Ocean – with East Africa, Persia and the Arabian Peninsula. Hence, foreign trade and travel among Gujarati businessmen is not new. Also, unlike peasants, merchants do not feel attached to the soil and are willing, for business reasons, to migrate to distant places. Nowadays they are to be found in all parts of the Commonwealth and the rest of the world.

The fertile plain of the Punjab has been, through the centuries, a scene of major battles between the invading foreigners (from the ancient Aryan tribes to the Moghuls) and the indigenous people, and is thus a 'melting pot' of varied human stocks. As such, it produces people who are generally dynamic, thrusting and energetic. Of the three major religious groups – Hindus, Muslims and Sikhs – in the Punjab, the Hindus were inhibited from migrating abroad out of caste considerations. The higher caste Hindus, aware that caste taboos could not be maintained in an alien land, or even on board a ship, would not normally contemplate migration. But the casteless Sikhs and Muslims were far less restricted in movement as well as in their choice of occupation.

As people with a martial history, Sikhs joined the police and the British army in large numbers. In this capacity they were often sent to other British colonies such as Singapore, Malaya and Hong Kong.[2] Thus their knowledge of the world outside India grew. With that, they became more adventurous. Increasingly, Sikh (and Muslim) craftsmen and artisans joined the voluntary outflow into those parts of the Empire where Indian labourers had already settled – in south-east Asia, the Caribbean and East Africa.

In one instance – that of the Fiji islands – Sikh agriculturists, *jats*, became the pioneering Indian migrants. They developed sugar-cane fields in the islands during the 1880s. From there, they grew familiar with New Zealand and Australia. In the early 1900s, a shipload of Sikh immigrants disembarked in Australia, but the next ship was refused disembarkation by the authorities.[3] Undeterred by this rebuff, the Sikh migrants crossed the Pacific and disembarked at Vancouver in British Columbia. There, they mainly engaged in lumbering and, in time, set up a chain of saw-mills. By 1910 – when the Canadian Immigration Act came into operation and barred free entry – more than five thousand Sikhs had settled in British Columbia, enough to create the substantial Sikh community which now exists there.

After the First World War there was a steady, but numerically insignificant, trickle of Sikh immigrants into Britain, since it was the only country in the Empire retaining an 'open door' policy. They were mainly craftsmen; but only those who were fluent in English managed to find jobs in factories. The large majority had to explore areas of self-employment, and often became

2. For instance, Sikh soldiers were used by the British to suppress the Boxer Rebellion in China in 1900.

3. The Australian immigration law came into force in 1901.

pedlars. They sold hosiery, woollens and knitwear from door to door in the working-class areas of London, the Midlands and Glasgow.

Of course, there were, at any given time, hundreds of Indian students and doctors in Britain. But comparatively few took up permanent residence. Instead, they returned to India to capitalize on their British qualifications in law, medicine or engineering. The case of R. B. Jillani was exceptional. He secured a degree in civil engineering, in London, in 1935. Then, with the help of his professor, he found an appropriate job. He stayed, and was called up when the Second World War broke out, as were most Indian doctors and graduate-students. Thus the number of Indians *resident* in Britain increased. But, even then, their total was small.

It is estimated that in 1949 there were no more than eight thousand Indian and Pakistani settlers in Britain, including one thousand doctors. Broadly, the Indian and Pakistani communities could then be divided into Lascars (seamen), mostly from (the then) East Pakistan; doctors and students; and pedlars, mostly Sikhs.

Post-war labour shortages created a favourable climate for the Sikh pedlars. The handicap of language no longer seemed to matter. Being able-bodied was enough – especially to the managers of Midlands foundries. The Sikhs vastly preferred indoor, steady work with an assured pay packet at the end of each week to precarious outdoor peddling. This wage-earning community was later to prove to be the nucleus around which Indian immigration to Britain grew.

The post-war boom in Britain happened to coincide with two major, inter-related upheavals in the Indian subcontinent: the partition of British India into Pakistan and India on the eve of Independence in 1947; and the conflict between these two states regarding Kashmir. As a result of the partition of the pre-Independence Punjab, nearly four million Muslims from the Indian side crossed into the Pakistani Punjab, while a slightly larger number of Sikhs and Hindus moved in the opposite direction. The pressure on land, already high in the less fertile Indian Punjab, increased even further. Some of the displaced Sikhs had relatives and friends in England, who through their letters and generous remittances to India, showed that they were doing rather well. The bewildering situation of partition and displacement induced the youngest male members of a few hundred families to migrate to Britain, where they were readily absorbed in unskilled factory jobs.[4]

For generations, it has been customary for young Sikhs leaving the farms to join the Army[5] or to migrate to other parts of India. Sikhs are therefore to be found in all the major cities of India – except in the south – engaged in semi-skilled and skilled jobs. For instance, in Calcutta, a city one thousand miles to the east of the Punjab, Sikhs drive most of the city's taxis.

The pressure to migrate is the highest in the most thickly populated districts of the Punjab, namely, Jullundur and Hoshiarpur. These adjoining districts contain $2\frac{1}{2}$ million people, as many as Jamaica and Guyana put together. (The population density of Jullundur is 914 per square mile; that of Britain, 535.) It was from these districts that migration to Fiji and Canada had earlier taken place.

The conflict between India and Pakistan over Kashmir also led to a considerable uprooting of populations across boundaries. One of the affected areas was Mirpur, where the terrain is rocky and the agricultural output low, and where, over many past generations, young men seeking jobs have often been forced to travel to other parts of the subcontinent – or even overseas, to secure work as seamen and deckhands with British and other shipping lines. The disturbed conditions in Mirpur during 1947–50 gave further impetus to the traditional exodus. Almost concurrently, word was spreading among Pakistani seamen that jobs were easy to get in Britain, and that they could more than double their earnings by taking up jobs on the land. Consequently more and more Pakistani seamen began to desert ships in Britain to take up factory jobs.

As with the West Indians, initial contacts in Britain were crucial for Indians and Pakistanis. For instance, J. S. Nehra,

4. Even at the best of times, the labour of the youngest male member is not needed at the family farm.

5. Although only two per cent of the total Indian population, in 1920, Sikhs formed twenty per cent of the Indian Army.

came to England to join his brother who, after serving in the Royal Air Force during the last war, had settled in Nottingham. Gurbachan Singh Gill came to London, during the early 1950s, because his father-in-law's family had been living there since 1936.

In some cases, adventurous Sikhs travelled to the Far East first, and then managed to gain contacts for eventual travel to Britain. Umerao Singh Basi, born near Jullundur, is a case in point. He longed to 'go abroad' as soon as he had matriculated. He joined a relative in the Philippines, worked, saved, secured addresses of distant relatives resident in London, and joined them. For a living he took up peddling.

Overall, however, the rate of migration from India and Pakistan was very low. In 1955, for example, there were only 7,350 Indian and Pakistani immigrants, about a quarter of the number from the West Indies, even though the combined population of the principal areas of migration – the Punjab, Gujarat, Mirpur and Sylhet (in Bangla Desh) – was fourteen times that of the West Indies.[6] The recession of 1958 had a dampening effect on immigration. The number of Indian and Pakistani immigrants dropped to 3,800 in 1959. The following year it returned to the 1955 level. The reasons for this low rate of migration to Britain were partly historico-psychological and partly administrative.

Although the British ruled India for two hundred years, social contact between the Indians and the British was insignificant. The vast majority of Indians had, at most, distant, occasional glances at the white District Collectors or Superintendents of Police,[7] men who conducted their personal and social life in an exclusive circle of their own. Such a situation was in direct contrast to the African slaves' experience in the Caribbean. There, the white planter and his assistants, living in a mansion surrounded by slaves, and cut off from other whites, could not completely shield their everyday life from the view of the house-

6. In 1961, the population of the Punjab was 20.3 million; that of Gujarat, 20.6 million; Sylhet, 0.7 million; and Mirpur, approximately 1 million.

7. This applied not only to the Indian masses but also to the élite. 'They [the British] look upon us as beings of inferior order,' wrote L. L. P. Garu, an Indian professor and intellectual, in 1866 'Does not this sort of conduct . . . tend to demoralize us and to estrange us?' *The Social Status of the Hindus*, p. 35.

slaves and field hands. Also, the white masters' frequent submission to their weakness for free sexual gratification with slave women, and the subsequent creation of a substantial mulatto population, subverted their (moral) efforts to impose and maintain a racial apartheid.[8] Whereas, in India, by successfully maintaining their aloofness, the British were able to engender in the Indian mind an awe of the white man and his country of origin.

The feeling of awe among the Indians went hand in hand with the view of England as an alien land where people had strange customs, dress, religion and dietary habits. This (factually correct) view was so widely prevalent that no efforts could have conditioned the minds of the Indians, whether at the popular or élitist level, to believe that Britain was their mother country. And, indeed, no such exercise was seriously attempted by the British.

Hence, unlike the West Indians, Pakistanis and Indians never visualized their migration in socio-cultural terms. For them, the economic consideration was the sole motive for migration. However, the idea that Britain offered better economic opportunities occurred only to that tiny fraction of the Indian sub-continent's population whose relatives, or close friends, had earlier made the long journey. Often, those in the Indian sub-continent, contemplating a similar journey, thought concretely in terms of joining relatives or friends already in Britain rather than of going to Britain *per se*, a proposition which, in its abstract form, they found much too intimidating.

Furthermore, there were the administrative controls rigorously applied by the Indian government. In 1954, the central government deprived the Indian state governments of their right to issue passports. It then introduced stringent educational and financial requirements for successful passport applications.[9]

A similar situation prevailed in Pakistan. Many Pakistanis

8. It is estimated that nearly one fifth of Jamaicans and Barbadians have some white blood in them. In the West Indian vocabulary, they are called 'coloured' whereas people of pure African stock are called 'black'.

9. In spite of good academic qualifications and financial references, it took the author six months (in 1957) to secure a passport in India.

could come to England only through a circuitous route: they would first obtain a passport for travel in the Persian Gulf region, or for pilgrimage to Mecca. They would undertake the journey and then, at the Pakistani embassies abroad, have the passport endorsed for travel to England.

With such stringent control *at source*, Indian and Pakistani migration to Britain was kept to an absolute minimum – until 1960. In that year the Supreme Court of India ruled it unconstitutional for the Indian government to refuse passports to its nationals, that is, to deny them the fundamental freedom to travel. The only device by which the central government could then discourage its nationals from migrating was to deny them foreign exchange, which it did, and still does.[10] However, such a restriction was meaningless to those who already had relatives and friends in Britain.

In its importance, the Indian Supreme Court judgement in 1960[11] must be compared with the Walter-McCarran Act of 1952 in America. Soon after this verdict, rumours of impending restrictions on Commonwealth immigrants began to circulate. Both these factors led to an abrupt rise in Indian and Pakistani arrivals in Britain. Their numbers swelled from 7,500 in 1960 to 48,000 in 1961. And an almost equal number arrived during the first half of 1962.

In 1962 Commonwealth Immigrants Act had another far-reaching effect on Asian immigrants. As with the West Indians, it compelled them to discard their original plan of a few years' stay in England before returning home with their savings. It even forced some 'mature' students, such as G. S. Bhandari, in London for a course in advertising, to stay permanently. Moreover, it led Indians and Pakistanis already here to advise male kinsmen to join them, and thereby gain a toehold, before the doors finally closed. The result was an excessive imbalance of sexes. According to the 1961 census, the male–female ratio among Pakistanis in Bradford was 40:1, and among Indians 3:1.[12]

10. Each traveller is entitled to carry only £3 as 'travelling allowance'.
11. Indirectly, it led to a relaxation of rules regarding passport issue in Pakistan.
12. Cited in Eric Butterworth, *A Muslim Community in Britain*, Church Information Office, 1967, p. 14.

Those who could not get in before 1 July, 1962, queued for work vouchers under the new system. But this did not mean that they left for Britain the moment they received work vouchers. Indeed, of the work vouchers issued to Indians and Pakistanis during the first year of the 1962 Act's operation, only twenty-two per cent were actually utilized.[13] Why? Because Britain was undergoing an economic recession in 1962–3. In other words, once the political hysteria of 'beat the ban' subsided, the old economic law of demand and supply became operative: economic recession proved a more effective deterrent than the Administrative and legislative controls of the 1962 Act.

Indian and Pakistani immigration previous to the 1962 Act can, in retrospect, be divided into two phases: before 1960, and after. During the earlier phase, its size was small, being less than a third of the West Indian immigration. It consisted principally of people with a significant knowledge of the English language and/or Britain, namely, seamen, ex-Army personnel, university graduates, clerks, teachers, doctors and other professionals; and it was controlled at source by the Indian and Pakistani governments. During the latter phase, immigration increased, equalling that from the West Indies; and the profile of the average immigrant changed. More often than not, the Asian immigrant was now an agriculturist, generally unfamiliar with the language and culture of Britain. But, throughout, one factor remained constant: the importance of the contact or sponsor in Britain. During the 'beat-the-ban' rush of 1961–2, the houses of early settlers virtually became reception centres.

13. Cited in Paul Foot, *Immigration and Race in British Politics*, p. 188.

2 MONEY IS ALL: THE RISE OF ASIAN ENTERPRISE

Why am I here? For money ... I miss the freedom of my village in the Punjab. Sometimes I think that England is like a sweet prison.
GURDAS RAM, an Indian worker in Slough.

Our food is a constant reminder to us that we're Indians or Pakistanis ... Our language? Well, language is the food of mind.
MUHAMMAD FARUQI, a Pakistani settler in Bradford.

The English are not the only nation of shopkeepers. We are too. And we're proving it daily – in England.
ABDUL LATEEF, a Pakistani businessman in Birmingham.

The factors that kept the West Indian immigrants together – discrimination by whites, a sense of racial and temperamental alienation from the host society, lack of funds and the need for the companionship of fellow countrymen – applied equally to the Asians. Indeed, in their case, alienation from British society was further accentuated by cultural differences and unfamiliarity with English. The newcomers had to rely heavily on the assistance and guidance of the early English-speaking settlers. The latter hardly ever failed to oblige.

The early settler helped the latecomer not out of any monetary or altruistic considerations but out of a sense of mutual obligation towards kinsmen and fellow-villagers that is characteristic of a rural, agrarian society everywhere, be it in India or Pakistan, Cyprus or Sicily. In such a society much value is attached to blood relationships and friendships; and readiness to help friends and relatives even at the cost of personal convenience and expense is the touchstone of inter-personal relationship. Therefore, the early settler was often generous in rendering moral and material help to his relatives or fellow-villagers in *pardes*, an alien land. He would let an unemployed relative or friend stay with him free of charge until he found work. He would charge lower rents from tenants related to him than from others. If he knew English well he would freely help those who did not.

The language barrier of the Asians had individual and collective consequences. For instance, lack of English excluded the average Asian immigrant from employment on public transport. He therefore sought, and found, work in factories where gang work, or a menial task, was offered; that is, where demands on his English were minimal. Two such industries were heavy engineering (foundries, steel mills) and textiles, located mostly in the Midlands and the North. Demand for unskilled and semi-skilled labour in these industries was high. Consequently Asians had little difficulty getting jobs. In Bradford, a woollen textile centre for instance, there were 250 Pakistanis in 1953. Eight years later there were 3,500; but they were *all* employed.[1]

The cumulative effect of all these factors has been to keep most of the Asian immigrants out of the Greater London area. Whereas, in 1966, nearly three-fifths of all West Indian immigrants in Britain were living in Greater London, the corresponding proportion of Indian and Pakistani immigrants was only half as much.[2] Comparatively fewer Asians than West Indians are at present employed on trains and buses in London and elsewhere.

Economic considerations also led many Asians to settle in the provinces. Living is, after all, cheaper in, say, Tipton, Staffordshire, than in Tooting, London: rents are lower; travel costs less, and so do cinema tickets; and temptations to spend are fewer.[3] All these were important considerations for the Asian immigrant. His *raison d'être* for being in Britain was economic, much more so than in the case of the West Indian. Summing up a general feeling in the Asian community, Gurnam Singh, an Indian settler

1. Jobs on the Bradford local buses, however, remain the exclusive domain of 'educated' Pakistanis and Indians. A study in Coventry, reported in the *Morning Star* (5 January 1967), showed that half of the Indian bus conductors were university graduates.

2. Breakdown of 1966 census published as Appendix X in the *Report of the Race Relations Board for 1969–70*, p. 58.

3. A (single) Pakistani worker in Bradford can live on £5 a week.

in Wolverhampton, said, 'Money is our mother; money is our father; money is all'. That is why many Asians seek jobs offering overtime. An 84-hour week is not uncommon with Pakistani workers in the West Riding. 'To let go an overtime hour is like dropping a tenbob note in the street,' said Akram Ali, a Pakistani machine winder in Keighley.

Economic pressures on the average Asian immigrant are immense. He most probably mortgaged his meagre assets to raise a loan for travel to England. So the loan must be repaid. At the same time his immediate family, and his parents, living in an Indian/Pakistani/Bangla Deshi/ village, have to be supported. Additionally, the demands of other members of the joint family have to be met.[4] After these obligations are discharged, money is to be saved either to buy a house and to pay for the fares of his wife and children to join him or, alternatively, to finance his travel and a long holiday at home, The complex web of social and filial obligations drives the Asian immigrant to work as long and hard, and as submissively, as he can.[5]

Saving fifty per cent of his income is quite common among Pakistani and Bangla Deshi workers; the comparative figure for the average Briton is five per cent.[6] Taeeb Ali, a Bangla Deshi millworker in Bradford, for instance, saves £14 a week. He remits £10 a week home, a sum on which he not only supports his family but *also* pays for the university education of his two brothers.[7] Taeeb Ali is typical of the Bangla Deshi immigrants in Britain, nearly seven-eighths of whom are, even today, living here without their families. Previous to the 1962 Act this was true of Indian

4. In the social milieu of present-day rural Punjab or Bangla Desh, a male expatriate's social status is measured by the size of his weekly remittances.

5. 'The majority of managers in the interview surveys found Asian workers very amenable to discipline,' writes Peter Wright. One personnel manager commented: 'With Asiatics it [supervision] is easy enough. If you say, "Run around the car park", they will run around the car park all day.' Another said, 'I think the Pakistanis are all regarded as excellent workers. They will do as they are told until the cows come home.' *The Coloured Worker in British Industry*, pp. 118, 132.

6. In 1963, the estimated remittances to Pakistan from Britain amounted to nearly £26 million. E. J. B. Rose and Associates, *Colour and Citizenship*, p. 443.

7. The *Observer*, 14 June 1969.

and Pakistani immigrants as a whole. That is, before 1962, Asian immigrants were predominantly male and single.

However, being unaccustomed to the western way of life, most of them did not visit dance-halls or clubs. They did not seem interested in dating white women. Therefore such limitations as a colour bar at a dance-hall or club did not disturb them. At the time of the national controversy over a colour bar operating at a dance-hall in Wolverhampton, in 1958, Rashmi Desai noted that the Indian immigrants to whom he talked 'did not admit any great feeling of corporate indignation ... they considered the privilege of dancing to be of doubtful value. Some welcomed the affair as a deterrent to those immigrants who would otherwise want to go dancing ... There was no collective militancy among the Indians. ... As individuals also most of them were indifferent.'[8]

For the Muslims among Asian immigrants there was (and still is) a religious taboo against drinking – so pubs were generally out of bounds. Whatever drinking a Muslim eventually succumbed to took place in his bed-sitting room in an all-male company. For his entertainment the Asian immigrant went to an Indian or Pakistani film, or listened to Indian music in Asian cafés. His sexual gratification came from the odd white prostitute who dropped in to service a houseful of Pakistani or Indian men. That cost little. Life became literally 'bed to work, work to bed'. And he did not mind.

Outside the economic field, the average Asian had no aspiration or expectation. He had come to Britain knowing full well that white people were culturally alien, quite apart from his own. And he had neither the inclination nor the intention to participate in 'their' life. It was therefore not surprising for the PEP survey team to find that 'a coloured community in a West Riding town' – in fact, Pakistanis in Keighley – complained the least about racial discrimination. This was so because the Pakistanis had only minimally exposed themselves to situations where they might be discriminated against. 'By avoiding notice the Pakistanis hope to avoid trouble,' explained a Pakistani leader in Nottingham.

8. Rashmi Desai, *Indian Immigrants in Britain*, Oxford University Press, 1963, p. 127.

By creating a self-contained life of their own and by being genuinely indifferent to British social life, many Asians saved themselves from the indignities and rebuffs inflicted on the West Indians.[9] Their expectations from British life, outside employment, were less; their attempts to socialize with white people almost non-existent. Consequently racial tension in cities such as Bradford, where Asians form the bulk of the coloured settlers, is much less than in, say, Brixton where the West Indians are the predominant group.[10]

Most of the bitterness expressed in the Asian community has come from English-speaking and educationally qualified persons. And that, too, mainly in the sphere of employment. They almost invariably found following up job advertisements in newspapers or professional journals a wasteful experience. Either no interview calls came or, when they did, British employers often treated their university degrees and professional experience as worthless. A typical experience was that of an Indian teacher in London who made nearly three hundred applications but did not obtain a single interview.[11] Consequently, many qualified, experienced teachers became bus conductors.[12] A holder of M.A. and LL.B. degrees from the Punjab became a moulder in a Southall rubber factory; a police officer from Delhi, a machine operator.[13]

Nor did the subsequent system of B vouchers, issued to people

9. Referring to 'poor and illiterate' African workers who neither speak nor write French, F. H. M. Raveau states, 'They have regrouped themselves in Paris and France and have achieved a cultural *homoeostasis* which shelters them from the psychocultural trauma of displacement.' *Caste and Race*, p. 267.

10. 'Those who have the most clear-cut and distinct culture of their own are the least likely to become involved in friction; they do not wish to enter or to become integrated in the British system,' writes James Wickenden. 'They are not hurt by rejection from a society they have no wish to enter; the chances of social misunderstanding are thus less.' *Colour in Britain*, pp. 18–19.

11. The *Morning Star*, 8 September 1967.

12. Fifteen of the Indian bus conductors in Coventry in 1966 were qualified teachers. The *Morning Star*, 5 January 1967.

13. A survey by the Campaign Against Racial Discrimination in Southall, in 1966, revealed that there were nearly one thousand Indian and Pakistani

with special skills (that is, teachers, doctors, engineers and scientists) improve the situation. Before leaving his country a qualified Indian/Pakistani teacher or scientist felt, with some justification, that possession of a work voucher would ensure him an equivalent job. But this was not to be. Most British employers treated the work voucher as another meaningless piece of paper.[14] Of the 3,500 Indian and Pakistani teachers who were issued B work vouchers between 1965 and 1967 only a few hundred managed to find teaching jobs.[15]

This situation prevailed not only amongst those with Indian or Pakistani degrees, but also those with a British education. The case of Zulfikar Ghose, a poet and writer, is illustrative. He was born in Pakistan but finished his schooling in London. Later he obtained a degree in English and Philosophy at Keele University. In his autobiography, *Confessions of a Native-Alien*, he states:

I wrote to some daily papers ... two put me on their availability lists ... To this day, I have heard nothing from them ... I wrote off to some advertising agencies. Some interviewed me and felt that my background of journalism and poetry was an excellent one for being a copywriter ... I have heard nothing more ... I wrote to several head-masters who advertised for teachers. Not one replied.[16]

Employment was one area in which Asian immigrants were totally dependent on British society. They could not all become grocers and restaurateurs.[17] Ambition and enthusiasm were not enough. Capital was needed. And capital, during the early period of settlement, was better used for buying a house than starting a

---

university graduates, eighty-four per cent of whom were engaged in manual, semi-skilled jobs.

14. In spite of an acute shortage of doctors, many Asian doctors have had to apply forty to fifty times before securing a job.

15. Referring to the July 1962 – October 1965 period, John Power, a British educationist, doubts 'whether even ten per cent of them [those Commonwealth teachers with B vouchers] have found employment in English schools'. *Immigrants in School*, p. 25.

16. Routledge and Kegan Paul, 1965, p. 158.

17. A survey of Indians in Coventry, in 1965, showed that only four per cent were self-employed. In comparison seventy per cent were in unskilled and semi-skilled jobs, and eighteen per cent in skilled factory jobs. Dewitt John, *Indian Workers' Associations in Britain*, Oxford University Press, p.29.

business, particularly when, like the West Indians, the Asians too realized that the only way they could solve their housing problem was by purchase.[18]

In some cases, business-minded Asians soon realized that buying a house could also prove a worthwhile capital investment, and acted accordingly. For instance, ten Indians in Handsworth formed a mortgage club. Each member paid £10 a week into the pool. Thus in ten weeks they accumulated £1,000. With this sum, they bought outright – in the name of one member – a short lease property, where there was very little competition from white Brummies. They then rented out the house. Shortly, with the rent money, and their own savings, they bought another house in the same street in the name of the next member on the list. And so on. Until, in less than eighteen months, each of them had a house of his own plus income from rent.

The elements of self-help and enterprise apparent in that project were soon to be applied to other areas, particularly in meeting needs arising out of linguistic and religious differences, and the special sartorial and culinary habits of the Asians. The earliest examples of this were the Indian grocers' shops.

The gradual expansion of the Asian community and the corresponding increase in the demand for Indian spices, pickles, vegetables and *chapatti* flour led some enterprising Asian immigrants, with previous business experience, to become traders. Often this enterprising immigrant began by importing groceries in bulk from India or Pakistan and engaging his recently arrived family in packaging goods in small quantities. To build a clientele, he delivered groceries by van to Asian households. At first, while he held his factory job, he limited deliveries to weekends; but as his clientele grew, and with it his business confidence, he gave up his job and became a full-time retailer.

When he saved sufficient capital he bought a shop and stocked British as well as Indian items. He added Indian sweets, snacks

18. 'Though there are major linguistic, ethnic, religious and social differences between them [the West Indians] and the Pakistanis and Indians,' writes Ceri Peach, 'from the point of view of the host society, they were all in the same economic and social position, occupied largely the same type of locality and their distributions were explicable only when they were considered together.' *West Indian Migration to Britain*, p. xvii.

and vegetables, and West Indian items – yams, tinned okra, brown rice, green bananas, etc. – to his stock. His apparent success aroused envy. Other ambitious Asians, anxious to relieve themselves of the drudgery of factory work, followed his example. More Indian groceries opened.

At present, indeed, there is an over-abundance of Asian grocers. An Asian community of fifteen thousand in and around Southall, for instance, is now served by over thirty grocers and butchers. In Bradford, the number of Pakistani grocers and butchers rose from two, in 1959, to fifty-one in 1967.[19] A whole network of retailers and wholesalers dealing in Indian groceries and vegetables has grown up.

Asian enterprise also went into clothing. Aware that Indian and Pakistani women like to buy cloth and sew their own dresses, Asians opened draperies. Trained Indian and Pakistani tailors started tailoring – at home or in business premises. Others opened goldsmiths' shops, since Asian women prefer golden ornaments individually made. And so it continued.

The result was that, by 1965, in Bradford there were 105 'immigrant-owned' commercial and business premises. These included grocers, butchers, cafés, restaurants, travel agencies, photographic dealers, booksellers, car-hire firms, draperies, sweet shops, electrical goods stores, estate agencies, banks, dry cleaners, coal merchants, furniture dealers, tailors, car driving schools and barber shops 'complete with showers'.[20]

Obviously such dynamism and business acumen could not, for ever, remain circumscribed within the 'immigrant' market. It had to break out; and it did. Nowadays Asians in Nottingham, for example, buy taxis as soon as they have saved enough from working overtime on the Corporation buses. Others put their money into off-licence shops. Asian publicans are to be found in the Midlands and the North.

But, more significantly, Asians entered the garment and mattress manufacturing industry in London's East End and

19. E. J. B. Rose and Associates, *Colour and Citizenship*, p. 443. During this period the number of Pakistani cafés in Bradford rose from three to sixteen.

20 Eric Butterworth, *A Muslim Community in Britain*, p. 18.

elsewhere. In Birmingham they have created a clothing industry where none existed before. Each week a score of Asian entrepreneurs turn out thousands of anoraks and quilted car-coats at highly competitive prices. Some of them cut the cloth in one place, then distribute it to 'outworkers' – that is, Asian housewives – thus slashing overhead costs while, at the same time, tapping the unused skills of Asian women in their own homes. Others employ their family and near-relatives to keep the costs down. It is a hard life for all, but financially rewarding and psychologically satisfying.

Kareemi Fashions Ltd. is a case in point. Its owner, Adbul Kareem, a trained gentlemen's tailor, worked with the Indian Army and the Pakistani Railways, cutting uniforms. He came to Birmingham in 1960, and won a City & Guilds diploma in ladies' tailoring. However, he failed to secure a suitable job. So he worked in a post office, saving as much as he could. In 1966 he brought his family over from Pakistan. Two years later, goaded by the idea that he must have something of his own to pass on to his children, he set up a clothing firm. 'At first it was hard going,' he recalls. 'I went from store to store to get the buyers to look at my samples.' Now, with long-term supply orders from a few large stores in Birmingham, he does not have to worry overmuch, except that he considers it unbusinesslike to be tied to one line – anoraks.

This was precisely the view of Gurbachan Singh Gill, in 1957, when, with the aid of his family, he began to manufacture shirts (with such brand names as 'Soho' and 'Superlene') in the East End of London. Since then, in spite of the lack of credit facilities from his British bank, he has expanded and diversified his company, which now makes 'everything that fits the human body'. His present clientele is eighty per cent British.

Such a preponderance of white customers holds true in another context: Indian, Pakistani and Bangla Deshi restaurants. There are now nearly two thousand such restaurants in Britain. A large majority of these are owned and staffed by Bangla Deshis. Pioneers in this field were those (the then) East Pakistani seamen who worked as cooks on British ships plying between Britain and Pakistan/India. When they settled in Britain they first established cafés in dock areas and then graduated to running restaurants in better districts.

Running a restaurant is, by its very nature, a small business, and not highly profitable. And yet it is attractive to many Asians because it offers a congenial atmosphere, comradeship, plenty of food, and a slower pace of work than is expected in factories.

Travel was another business which attracted ambitious Asians, aware of the fact that British travel agencies were unpopular with most Asians due to the language barrier. Initially, money was to be made out of transporting Indians and Pakistanis to Britain. Successive immigration control regulations, however, curtailed this traffic. But then, with settlement and comparative prosperity, Asian immigrants developed a pattern of periodic visits home for holidays. Asian travel agencies stepped in to arrange charter flights. Besides that, these agencies go to great lengths to find routes and airlines that offer the cheapest flights to India, Bangla Desh and Pakistan, sometimes at rates as low as half the scheduled fares. As such, even English-speaking Asians find it in their economic interest to approach Asian, not British, travel agencies.

The settlement of thousands of Asians brought another avenue of business within the enterprising Asian's range – estate agencies. Starting in the late 1950s, and especially in the early 1960s, there was a fairly rapid build-up of Asian families and, consequently, of Asian house-owners. During the period of 1959–63, the number of Asian house-owners in Southall, for instance, quadrupled.[21] By the mid-1960s, there were enough houses under coloured ownership and a sufficiently large turn-over of property *within* the coloured community to make it feasible for some Asians to establish estate agencies. They did. And they prospered. As new entrants to business they tried hard to please their clients. They showed none of the superciliousness with which many well-established white estate agents treated their coloured enquirers. On their part, most coloured clients placed their trust and confidence in Asian agents to a degree they could never do in the case of white agents. Thus Asian estate agencies thrived and multiplied. Six years ago there was only one Asian estate agency

21. E. J. B. Rose and Associates, *Colour and Citizenship*, p. 455.

in Southall; now there are at least seven. And all are doing well.

From there on, it seemed logical to establish mortgage companies, followed by private loan companies and finance brokers. The arrival in Britain, since 1965, of many Asian entrepreneurs from East Africa, as well as their capital, has given a further fillip to the financial and business activity of the Asian community. In some cases they have acquired financial control of British firms which continue to be managed and staffed by white Britons.

Simultaneously Indian, Pakistani and Bangla Deshi banks in Britain have been expanding and opening branches throughout the country. The Habib Bank of Pakistan, for instance, now has a dozen branches.[22] These banks have proved very popular with non-English-speaking Asian settlers who generally feel intimidated by the atmosphere of a British bank, and find it cumbersome to fill in forms, and answer questions, in English. At Asian banks, on the other hand, they find the atmosphere congenial. Urdu- or Bengali-speaking staff are always co-operative and willing to help, aware that remittances to India or Pakistan or Bangla Besh are beneficial to their respective country's economy and balance of payments position.

In short, a complex infra-structure of Asian business establishments, estate agencies, mortgage companies, banks and financial brokerage firms has grown. In some areas it is almost independent of the larger economic structure; in others, not so.

All this led to another, rather unexpected, development: the establishment of an Asian Press in Britain. The major stumbling block to the successful launching of an Indian-language journal in Britain hitherto had been the lack of a distribution channel, since British distributors had refused to co-operate. Mahmood Hashmi, an experienced Pakistani journalist and broadcaster, settled in Birmingham, and then working as a teacher, visualized the potential of Asian shops as sales outlets for an Urdu journal he wished to publish. That was in 1960. By then, the need for such a publication had been felt by thousands of Asian settlers.

Because of the language barrier many Asians felt cut off from

22. In Bradford, for instance, there are *six* Pakistani banks.

the primary sources of information and entertainment: English-language radio, television and papers. Even the English-speaking Asians missed detailed news about their home countries. Subscribing to an Indian/Pakistani newspaper by air was costly, and listening to short-wave broadcasts by All India Radio or Air Pak inconvenient. An Indian-language journal published in Britain was the only solution.

By conveying this point and by appealing to their communal sense, Mahmood Hashmi was able to secure the co-operation of most Asian grocers and butchers regarding distributing his Urdu weekly newsmagazine *Mashriq* (*The East*). His beginning, in 1961, was modest: a weekly publication of twelve pages at 2/6. Now the size has tripled, but the price has been halved.

As in other fields, Mahmood Hashmi's successful lead has been followed by others. At present there are at least nine Indian-language weeklies – four in Urdu, two in Punjabi, one each in Gujarati, Bengali and Hindi; and one monthly in Urdu, *Afaaq*, from Nottingham. In addition there is one English-language weekly, *India Weekly*. The combined circulation of the Indian-language weeklies is over 70,000, a third of which is accounted for by the pioneering *Mashriq*.

For thousands of Indians and Pakistanis these weeklies are the only windows to the outside world. Aware of this, the editor of *Mashriq* crams his news magazine with news of the sub-continent, reports from its correspondents in Britain; important British and international news; correspondence columns; reviews and comments on Asian films; and special columns for women and on questions pertaining to the immigration laws. Its popularity and usefulness can be judged by the statement of a local Community Relations Officer in the West Riding: 'My only way to get through to the local Asian community is to write to *Mashriq*.'

The healthy state of these publications is due to the advertisers, predominantly Asian, who buy a third to a half of the total space, an indication of the strength of the internal economy of the Asian community. A very substantial share of the advertisement revenue comes from Asian film distributors and exhibitors – another Asian industry which has emerged to meet a keenly felt need of the community.

The pioneer in this field was a non-profit organization, the India League, which was the spearhead of the Indian independence lobby. After 1947 it redefined its major aim as creating better understanding between the Indian and British peoples. One of the means employed to achieve this objective was to show Indian films, suitably sub-titled in English, to predominantly English audiences in London.

However, as the size of the Indian community in Britain grew, some enterprising Indians discerned a business potential in catering for Indian audiences alone. The result was that, by the mid-1950s, Indian films were being sporadically shown, for profit, over the weekends in hired cinema halls. A legal difficulty arose: films could not be shown publicly on Sunday mornings, the only time cinema halls were available for rent at reasonable rates. To overcome this hurdle cinema clubs were organized. By the late 1950s practically every town with a substantial Asian community had weekend Indian films.

Gradually, as films, in general, have declined in popularity with British audiences and an increasing number of cinema halls have fallen into disuse, Asian entrepreneurs have been able to buy them outright. At least fifteen cinemas in London, the Midlands and the West Riding are now owned by Asians. Here, throughout the week, Indian and Pakistani films are shown.

All told, every weekend some two hundred cinemas from Maidenhead to Middlesbrough and from Glasgow to Gravesend show Indian films to an estimated audience of 100,000. It is a £1½ million-a-year business, two fifths of which goes to the cinema owners; and a third to the film distributors who, over the years, have built up a library of twelve hundred films; the rest is profit. In the beginning it was possible to import an Indian film for £150; nowadays the price can be as high as £10,000, an indisputable index of the popularity of Indian films.

Similarly the BBC's programmes in Hindustani on radio and television are immensely popular. It is estimated that nearly eighty per cent of Asian immigrants listen to or watch these programmes each Sunday in spite of the fact that they are broadcast early in the morning.

The idea of having programmes for immigrants mainly 'to

make them feel at home' was first aired at a CARD meeting in the early 1965. Soon afterwards the BBC called a meeting of prominent West Indian and Asian spokesmen. The (English-speaking) West Indians were not keen on a separate programme but the Asians were. The result was the BBC's Immigrant pro-gramme, with the twin-headed objective of education and enter-tainment. The first programme was broadcast in October 1965.

Initially the stress was on education and instruction. These programmes were generally well received. The course of English lessons by direct method teaching was popular, especially with the Asian housewives. A sale of more than thirty thousand booklets, to be used in conjunction with this programme, indicated its popularity. Nowadays the stress is on producing a magazine-type programme consisting of interviews, discussions and entertain-ment.

Besides these specific aids, the general process of acculturation has been at work, particularly among Asian men who must, in any case, daily leave home to work. Thus their familiarity with the English language and culture grows. An overwhelming majority among them now understands English. A survey of Asian immigrants in Keighley in 1968 revealed that only one in seven had 'no knowledge' at all of English.[23] However, four out of five Pakistani and Bangla Deshi women did not know English. The reason is obvious. Such a housewife is not compelled by economic necessity or tradition to participate in the (English-speaking) outside world. Her place is in the home. Outside it, as long as she can manage shopping and the laundromat, she can survive. After all, human beings adjust themselves only to the degree which their immediate environment demands. That was why very few, if any, British *mem-sahibs* in India, for instance, managed to wade through the Hindustani/English primer.

The acculturation and socialization processes are, of course, more pronounced in the case of Asian children who attend British schools. Many are bilingual, and enrich the English language – undetected and unacknowledged though it may be at

23. Out of the 187 Pakistanis interviewed during a survey in Bradford only thirty could speak no English at all, that is, one out of every six. E. J. B. Rose and Associates, *Colour and Citizenship*, p. 321.

present – with their idiom, imagery and original turns of phrase. No one knows for sure whether *their* children will be bilingual or unilingual. But whatever may happen to their mother-tongue, it seems their religious identity will remain unaltered, as has been the case with the descendants of Jewish immigrants in Britain.

Under the pressure of mass education, designed to serve an industrial society based on mass production, the minority languages such as Welsh and Gaelic tend to fall into disuse.[24] But this does not apply to minority religions since these are not, in any way, involved in the complex mechanisms of production in an industrial society. Jews, scattered throughout the world, speak different languages, but are nevertheless Jews. The Indians in the Caribbean are another case in point. Even when they have lost touch with their original languages, most of them remain, by religion, Hindus, Muslims, and Sikhs, and have names that identify them as such.

24. Only 80,000 people in Scotland speak Gaelic. *Race Today*, September 1969 p. 154. Of the 2½ million people in Wales, only half a million speak Welsh.

NO FACES LIKE SIKH FACES

I constantly tell my sons that there are no faces like Sikh faces in the entire world. They must never forget that.
GURNAM SINGH, a Sikh settler in Wolverhampton.

No religious identity is as sharp and dramatic as a male Sikh's. This is as true in the western world as it is in Africa or the Philippines, or even India, where the nine million Sikhs form only a tiny minority among her 550 million people.

Sikhism is a comparatively young religion. Its founder, Guru Nanak, was born in 1469 (near Lahore, Pakistan). However, it was the tenth, and the last, Guru, Gobind Singh, who two centuries later gave Sikhs the distinct look they now have. He prescribed the five symbols of Sikhism – *kess*, long hair; *kanga*, comb; *kachha*, long underpants; *kara*, steel bangle; and *kirpan*, dagger; and moulded the Sikh sect into a militant brotherhood, the *Khalsa Panth* (the Pure Brotherhood). He called his followers *singhs* (lions).

The physical and sartorial prescriptions were, in fact, designed to make the (*Khalsa*) Sikhs distinctive from the surrounding Hindus and Muslims, a people apart, and give them a lasting identity. Both purposes were well served. Long hair and beards gave the Sikhs an instant unity, and also put to rest the nagging fear of the founders that Sikh converts would gradually be reclaimed by their original religion, Hinduism, noteworthy for its inclusive tendencies. These prescriptions, therefore, became the cornerstone of Sikhism, and to question them was tantamount to questioning its very foundations.

Wearing a dagger at all times, however, proved too cumbersome for the ordinary Sikh and fell into disuse. But the Sikh's right to wear it has never been questioned or disallowed in the Indian sub-continent. Of course, Sikhs migrating to Britain do not arrive wearing daggers. They do not even keep one at home, which, by custom and tradition, they should. This is just one example of how Sikhs have adapted to the British environment. On the other hand, the steel bangle, which is easy to wear, has been almost invariably retained by the Sikhs in Britain.

The Sikhs' main dilemma in Britain proved to be the beard and turban. They noted, dejectedly, that time after time they were turned down for jobs for which other Indians and Pakistanis were freely hired. The almost universal objection of British employers, in both private industry and public services, seemed to them unjust and depressing. In spite of his war service, and years spent as a Japanese prisoner-of-war, the bearded Gurbachan Singh Gill was jobless for three months when he first came to London in 1950. By chance, he approached a personnel officer who, as an ex-Indian Army Officer, had a certain regard for bearded Sikhs, and secured a job. He was lucky. Thousands of other Sikhs were not. They were faced with a bitter choice: to cut their hair or return home.

When faced with this situation, Trilok Singh Dhami, a newcomer to Wolverhampton, booked a passage home. But relatives and friends prevailed upon him to reconsider. He went through an agonizing reappraisal of his religious identity. Reluctantly, he cut his hair. 'Afterwards I felt less than a man,' he now recalls. 'I didn't want to go out in the street: I didn't want to be seen by people. It was like I had got a scarred face overnight.' As with Trilok Singh so with thousands of other Sikhs. Caught in the conflict between religious identity and economic interest, they submitted to the latter, but only at the cost of suffering a sense of spiritual degradation.

Cutting their hair, however, did not signify diminution in the Sikhs' devotion to their religion. Quite the contrary. Having compromised with the outward form, they felt impelled to reiterate their attachment to Sikhism in other, more significant ways. They attended, more often than before, religious services on Sundays, held in homes or rented halls, and contributed generously towards *gurdwara* funds. As a result of regular and generous contributions from Sikhs, various *gurdwara* committees in the country were able to buy properties and establish proper *gurdwaras*. As early as 1957 the Sikh community in Birmingham, for instance, bought an old church in Smethwick and converted it into a *gurdwara*, thus, inadvertently, contrasting their religious ardour with British Christianity.[1] Now there are at least forty *gurdwaras* in Britain.

In an alien land, a *gurdwara* becomes more than a place of worship: it becomes simultaneously a social welfare centre, a hub of communal activity. It also acquires a socio-psychological significance, becomes an important link with the past. It helps to maintain religio-cultural continuity. The familiarity of the carpeted floor, the decor, the gaudy pictures of the Gurus, the smell of incense, the hymns and the loud reading of the *Ad Granth* (the Sikh holy book) reassures the worshipper that though his environment has changed radically the essence of being a Sikh has not. The long, leisurely service on Sunday mornings provides a relief from the rigid demands of an industrial society. And the presence of fellow-Sikhs all congregated in one place, on the same carpet, generates anew a feeling of 'belonging'.

The function of a *gurdwara* does not cease after the Sunday service. It remains open to Sikhs at all times of the day and night. A hungry Sikh can walk in and cook a meal for himself in the refrectory, if one is not already prepared. A homeless Sikh can sleep there during the night and stay during the day. The *gurdwara* committee in Southall owns a house where homeless Sikhs are transferred after a fortnight at the *gurdwara*. The generosity of the *gurdwara* has to be experienced to be fully appreciated.

Like other immigrant groups in Britain the Sikhs have maintained an interest in politics at home. For a long time their specific point of interest was the agitation for a Punjabi-speaking state (with a Sikh majority) in India, which had been brewing since 1956 and which reached a climax in 1966. The leader of this movement was Sant Fateh Singh, a revered religious leader of Sikhs, who visited Britain in the spring of 1966.

The Sikhs from all over the country turned up in their thousands at Heathrow airport to give Sant Fateh Singh a tumultuous

1. Suggestions have been made, seriously, that old, unpopular churches, instead of being closed, be handed over to Asian immigrants for the pursuit of their religions.

reception. He became, during his short visit, the undisputed spokesman of the Sikh community in Britain. He led deputations to British authorities at local and national level to have the ban on beards and turbans on Sikh employees in public transport removed. He reminded British politicians of the services that Sikhs had rendered to the British in India and abroad: 83,000 Sikhs 'in beards and turbans' had died for Britain in the Second World War. More pertinently, he argued that if Sikhs in beards and turbans could operate a tank they could certainly drive a bus or ring a bell without endangering the safety of passengers or causing an offence. The Sikh leaders in Manchester had been repeating these points, and more, to the local councillors since 1959, but without any success. Now Sant Fateh Singh was able to convince the local Transport Committee that religious edicts were involved. As a result, Sikh employees on the buses were granted a special dispensation, provided the colour of their turbans matched that of their uniform. The Sikh's sense of righteousness was further strengthened when, in November 1966, their demand for a Punjab-speaking state was conceded by the Indian government. It seemed to Sikhs here as well as in India that the history of Sikhism – self-preservation against heavy odds – was being re-enacted in modern times.

However, by January 1967, the tricentenary of Guru Gobind Singh,[2] Manchester's lead had been followed by only a few local councils. This realization came to the Sikh community through a dramatic event in Wolverhampton.

In August 1967, Tarsem Singh Sandhu, a bus conductor, returned to work (after a long illness) wearing a turban and a beard. He was told to remove them if he wished to continue working. He refused. Thereupon he was summarily suspended. The incident highlighted, once again, the illiberal policy of many local authorities on this issue.

As a result, thousands of clean-shaven Sikhs, who had learnt to live with their shorn hair with a certain resignation, were jolted into re-thinking the whole issue. It did not matter whether given the freedom to wear beards and turbans they would all

2. This occasion led to the formation of the Central Committee of Gurdwaras (Great Britain).

return to them, but to regain that freedom, in principle, became to them a very important issue. And to show their solidarity with a fellow-Sikh, who had been victimized for following his religious edicts, they gathered from all over the country in Wolverhampton, in February 1968, to march silently, with dignity, in a mile-long procession from the *gurdwara* to the Town Hall. But the local council was unmoved.

The Shromani Akali Dal (SAD) – a national body interested exclusively in the religious affairs of Sikhs – formed in the wake of the February 1968 march, kept up pressure on the Wolverhampton council.[3] But nothing happened. The local councillors, aware that the issue had been transformed into a battle of will and nerves, remained obdurate. Finally, in sheer desperation, Sohan Singh Jolly, the SAD's president, warned the council that if its decision was not reversed by 13 April 1969 (which was the start of the Sikh New Year), he would immolate himself. The councillors were unmoved, and let it be known publicly.

By late March, this controversy had aroused deep interest among the Sikhs here and in India. On 6 April, thousands of Sikhs, wearing black arm-bands, marched towards the British High Commission in New Delhi.[4] The event was widely reported in the British press, although the underlying point was not stressed. The message was clear: if Sohan Singh Jolly were to burn himself in Wolverhampton the repercussions would not remain limited to Britain but would involve India as well, very likely jeopardizing the lives and property of British nationals resident there.[5]

However, the British High Commission in Delhi and the government in London seemed to have grasped the grave implica-

3. The SAD now claims a membership of nearly thirty thousand out of an estimated Sikh population in Britain of three hundred thousand.

4. In Wolverhampton, a whole chain of Sikhs pledged to burn themselves – one every fifteen days – until the ban was lifted. *The Guardian*, 8 April 1969. Outside Wolverhampton, fourteen Sikhs pledged to follow the example of Mr Jolly.

5. During his subsequent visit to Britain, Jathedar Santokh Singh, one of the leaders of the Sikh demonstration in Delhi, told his audience at various meetings, 'The death of Jolly could have had serious repercussions on British interests in India . . . it would have definitely put the lives of British nationals in danger.' *Race Today*, October 1969, p. 188.

tions of the case. On 8 April, Ernest Fernyhough, a junior minister of the government, was despatched to Wolverhampton to meet the local Transport Committee.

On 9 April, after a two-and-a-half hour meeting, the Transport Committee decided to lift the ban. Announcing the decision Alderman Ronald Gough, the Chairman of the Committee, maintained that their decision 'in the first place' had been 'right and proper'. He conceded the national and international implications of the case when he added:

> We feel we have been pressured; but we had to take into account the wider implications ... Mr Fernyhough put to us what might happen if he [Mr Jolly] did take his life.[6]

Alderman Gough also mentioned 'the anxiety by and on behalf of the High Commissioner for India' as one of the factors taken into consideration.

Whatever the reasons and explanations, the Sikhs finally won their point. 'This is not a victory for myself,' said Mr Jolly, 'but a victory for the whole Sikh community.'

The national controversy on Sikh busmen has unfortunately overshadowed the more widespread, and continuing, injustice against Sikhs in industry. There, the ban on employing bearded and turbaned Sikhs has been almost total. Latterly, when Sikhs already in employment suddenly appeared wearing turbans, most employers made their disapproval known in strong terms; only a few turned a blind eye.

But even the 'liberal' employers have generally failed to *recruit* Sikhs wearing beards and turbans. In Wolverhampton, for instance, nearly half of all bearded Sikhs in employment in industry are said to be found in one factory. Why? Because the personnel manager of this firm, by virtue of his association with Sikhs in the Indian Army, is sympathetic towards them. He is even known to confront clean-shaven Sikh applicants with the question: 'If you can't be true to your own religion, how can you be loyal to my firm?' But then he is considered, by the Sikh community and others, to be an exceptional case.

If Sikhs are, for various reasons, assertive regarding their

6. *The Times*, 10 April 1969.

religion, Hindus are exceptionally unobtrusive. In spite of their substantial population in Britain they have established only a handful of temples – and one Hindu centre in London, which is more a community centre than an exclusive place of worship.

It is somehow in the nature of Hinduism and its followers to be amorphous and vague rather than crystallized and dramatic. For instance, unlike Sikhs, Christians, Jews or Muslims, Hindus do not have a single book which to them is the repository of absolute truth. Instead, there is voluminous religious literature and scripture.

Then there are the social implications of Hinduism, such as the caste system, which are an integral part of life in (Hindu) India. The twin principles of specialization and division of labour which originally led to the evolution of the caste system and which, incidentally, underlie modern industry, seem, on the face of it, quite sound and rational. It was the hereditary nature of the caste system which made it unjust and undemocratic. However, the rapid urbanization of modern India is undermining the hold of this traditional system: an urban environment is ill-suited to the maintenance of caste taboos.

Hindu Indians migrating to an urbanized, western country such as Britain, are aware of the practical difficulties of maintaining caste differences and taboos among themselves, and with respect to the British. They are thus psychologically prepared to compromise their caste standing in Britain. In this they are further helped when they discover that the British tend to distinguish between people solely on the visual marks of colour and race.

This does not imply that caste differences among Hindus in Britain disappear altogether. They do not. Between the Brahmins, the highest caste, and the Untouchables, the lowest caste, a distinction remains. And yet there are no practical or *public* manifestations of this difference, simply because those who differentiate hold no levers of power – economic, legal or moral. It remains a matter of 'internal' relationship, meaningful only to the sub-community. At most, such considerations may be emphasized during election campaigns for the prestigious positions in the local Indian Workers' Association or the Indian Association. Nothing more.

About the only Hindu taboo that manifests itself in a wider context is the abstinence from beef. Many Hindu employees, for instance, avoid beef at works canteens. Hindu (as well as Sikh) children are instructed by their parents to avoid beef at school lunches.

Among Indian immigrants, almost all Gujaratis are Hindus, as are a small proportion of the Punjabis. Although these groups speak different languages they share first names because of the common religion. As in the western world, first names in the Indian subcontinent show religious influence. Hindu names are often Sanskrit in origin, the language in which Hindu scripture is written: Shiv, Kanti, Ashwin, Pushpa, Chitra, Ashok, Om Prakash, Praful, etc. Accordingly, Muslim names are Arabic in origin since the Koran is written in that language: Haroon, Zeenat, Kareem, Abdul, Farrukh, Mansur, Rasheed, Razak and so on. Sikh names are identical for both boys and girls – Gurjeet, Amolak, Man Mohan, Charan, Sukhdev, Gurdayal, etc. – because these are chosen at random from the holy book, *Ad Granth*. The distinction is made later in life when the suffix Singh is added for men and Kaur for women.

Whatever else may be the influence of the British environment on the Indian, Pakistani and Bangla Deshi immigrants and their children, their names will not be radically altered. In the case of children going to predominantly white schools some adaptation may ensue – Jagjit may become Jock or Sundri become Sandra, for ease of speech – but the essence will remain. This is likely to happen in the whole socio-cultural make-up of the Asian community.

Since surnames among Hindus indicate caste or sub-caste, the founder of Sikhism (a Hindu by birth), rebelling against the Hindu caste system, advised his followers to drop them. He himself was simply called Guru Nanak, and his followers, Sikhs (that is pupils). The equality of all Sikhs is periodically reiterated through *langar*, a communal meal shared by fellow-Sikhs all sitting at the same (floor) level. Earlier, the propagators of Islam, a religion which made a substantial impact on the Hindu population of India, too, had stressed its castelessness and the equality of all Muslims before Allah.

4   EQUAL BEFORE ALLAH

> *A Bulgarian Moslem is likely to conduct his*
> *family affairs (e.g. marriage, death, inheritance,*
> *etc.) much more like an Indonesian Moslem,*
> *rather than like a Christian Orthodox or a*
> *Communist living next door.*
> FARRUKH HASHMI[1]

Though physically less obtrusive than Sikhism, Islam lays down stricter and more thorough-going edicts for its followers. One edict requires the Muslim to offer prayers, facing Mecca, five times a day. This is possible in a rural, agrarian society, but not in an urban, industrial environment. The 9 a.m.–5 p.m. syndrome and shift work, whether in Pakistan or Britain, forces a paring of the ritual. The final burden, therefore, falls on the afternoon prayer on Friday, which corresponds with the Christian Sunday.

It was the absence of a large meeting-place for Friday prayer that led the Pakistani Muslims in Birmingham, for instance, to form the Pakistani Welfare Association (PWA) in 1957. Funds were collected, and soon the PWA bought a house to be used for Friday prayer as well as other religious and social functions.

Historically, Muslims were the first non-Judaeo-Christian community in Britain to establish a place of worship of their own. The Shah Jehan mosque in Woking, financed by the Muslim ruler of Bhopal, then an Indian princely state, was built in 1900. Arab seamen in South Shields built their own mosque during the inter-war period. During the war, in order to meet the religious needs of Muslim seamen and servicemen, a mosque was opened in London's East End.

However, the vast majority of the eighty mosques that now exist in Britain have been established during the past decade and,

1. *The Pakistani Family in Britain*, Community Relations Commission, 1969, p. 7.

almost always, by local Pakistani settlers. The Pakistani community in a town would organize a mosque committee to raise funds, buy property, and appoint an *iman* (religious leader) to lead prayers on Fridays and religious days, perform marriage and burial ceremonies, and impart religious instruction to the children.

Mosques are first and foremost places of worship, but in the present British context, they tend to become part of the Pakistani community's social welfare system. Of course much depends on the vigour and devotion of the *iman*. Haji Taslim Ali, the resident *imam* of the east London mosque, provides a welfare service to the Muslim community of seven thousand, ninety-five per cent of whom are Pakistanis. He and his wife teach Muslim children (thirty to forty at a time) Arabic and the Koran, collect and distribute old clothes within the community, and look after children if their mothers are hospitalized and cannot make satisfactory alternative arrangements. Besides that, as an interpreter, he is on call for interpretation at coroner's inquests, in courts and with the police.

Plans are constantly being made to upgrade present mosques, to buy better properties, and to build traditional mosques with a dome and four minarets. One such mosque in Birmingham, when finished, will accommodate 2,500 worshippers at a time. Another mosque to be built in London will be even larger. Part of the contribution for these projects has come from the London embassies of various Muslim countries. Besides that, Urdu weeklies such as *Mashriq* and *Asia* provide channels through which appeals are addressed to the national body of Pakistani Muslims, estimated now to be in the region of a quarter million (half as many as the Jews in Britain).

These ambitious, multi-nation, co-operative projects continually remind Muslims in Britain that Islam is a unifying force which often transcends nationality and race.[2] The response of Muslims in Britain to the burning, in July 1969, of the El Aqsa

2. The first conference of the Union of Muslim Organizations of the U.K. and Ireland was held in London in July 1970. The main functions of this confederate body are to safeguard the interests of Muslims and to submit their demands to the government.

mosque in the Israeli-occupied sector of Jerusalem was a dramatic evidence of this fact, as well as of the hold that religious leaders and institutions have over Muslims. Protest marches and meetings were organized in London and some major provincial towns. Thousands of Muslims participated. In Bradford, for instance, responding to a call from *imams* and leaders of Markazi Kameet Tabligh-ul-Islam, eight thousand Muslims, principally Pakistanis, gathered for a protest march and meeting. Commenting on the event, Stuart Bentley wrote in *Race Today* of 'the persistence of religious institutions transposed to a new and alien society and their efficacy in mobilizing support', and compared it with the 'considerably less support' given by Muslims to local anti-Powell demonstrations.[3]

Many mosque committees work in conjunction with the local Islamic Cultural Centre of the Muslim Education Board to ensure that the religious identity of Muslim children is not blurred as a result of growing up in Christian Britain. They often object to the local education authority regarding the Christian instruction given to Muslim children in schools. Once their protest has been registered, they co-operate with the authorities by providing volunteers to instruct Muslim children in Islam. As a result, more and more Muslim children are receiving Islamic instruction in school. In any case, the circumcision of male children leaves an ineradicable religious identity mark. This edict is invariably followed by Muslim parents.

Another edict that a devout Muslim should follow is fasting during the month of Ramadhan. In a country such as Pakistan, where religious fervour runs high, the entire social milieu is changed during Ramadhan. Life is rearranged to fit the pattern of fasting between sunrise and sunset. In rural Pakistan, in particular, eating between sunrise and sunset during Ramadhan almost amounts to committing a sin. This socio-religious custom is transferred intact to Britain. Indeed, in the new Christian environment, this practice signifies something more: it reiterates religious identity and keeps alive a communal feeling.

Middle-class, westernized Pakistanis, employed in white-collar jobs in a city, may disregard the edict and go unnoticed and

3. October 1969, p. vii.

uncommented by the Pakistani community. But for the bulk of Pakistani settlers, living in the coloured quarters of Birmingham, Bradford or London, deviation can create a scandal. Unnoticed by others, Pakistani enclaves in Britain undergo an internal transformation during Ramadhan: the sale of dates (used traditionally for breaking a fast) and yoghurt (considered alleviative for an empty stomach) rises; and the takings of Pakistani cafés decline. The only Britons who notice the change are those employing large contingents of Pakistanis. In those cases, where Pakistanis staff entire sections of factories, work-breaks are often adjusted to fit the fasting pattern.

Thus, through prayers on Fridays and fasting during Ramadhan, Muslims in Britain preserve and reiterate their religious identity. In addition, there are religious taboos on food and drink, constant reminders of their Islamic allegiance. Alcohol is forbidden, although, in the socio-cultural climate of Britain, where drinking beer is as much a part of life as drinking tea, some compromise is inevitable. Even so, drinking in pubs, likely to be noticed by fellow-Muslims, remains minimal. Anyhow, why go to a pub when there are, in the areas of Asian settlement, cafés and 'social clubs' where the tea is strong and sweet, and juke boxes spin out the latest Indian and Pakistani film songs, thus recreating an atmosphere reminiscent of Mirpur, Lahore or Campbellpur?

Abstinence from pig's meat is observed as strictly by Muslims as it is by Jews. Knowing this, many Pakistani immigrants, during their early years of settlement, would go to a Jewish butcher. Also, *kosher* meat sold there is nearest to the Muslim *halal* (legitimate) meat: in both cases, a bird or animal is killed by cutting its jugular vein and letting the blood drain; the only difference is in the prayer that is said during the ritual.[4] Now, of course, there are many Pakistani butchers selling *halal* meat.

Like Jews, Muslims do not consider Jesus the son of God but only one of the prophets in the line of Abraham, Isaac, Jacob,

4. It is worth noting that although this religious practice by Jews nowadays goes unnoticed and uncommented, the slaughter of sheep by this method at a Lichfield slaughterhouse by Muslim butchers brought protests of 'cruelty' from rural district councillors. *The Times*, January 1970.

Moses and David. Muhammad, the founder of Islam in the seventh century, himself made no claims to be the son of God – only the last of the prophets. Nevertheless, Islam shares with Judaism and Christianity a common ground: the monotheistic doctrine. The Koran may be read as the last of the volumes beginning with the Old Testament. Aware of this fact, many British clergy, in the areas of Pakistani settlement, have tried to woo Muslims into the fold of Christianity by distributing literature in Urdu. But their attempts have proved singularly unsuccessful.

Theological sophistries aside, Pakistani Muslims know only too well, from direct observation and experience, that the gospel of Christian brotherhood and love is seldom practised by most white Britons towards West Indians, who are fellow-Christians. They also know of the general lack of interest of white Christians in their own religion. Consequently they remain contemptuously indifferent to the proselytizing overtures of the British clergy.

In any case, religion does not exist as a separate entity but is a part of the general culture of a society. And as far as British and Indo-Pakistani cultures in their 'native' form are concerned, they stand apart. The languages, culinary and sartorial habits, social customs and the very loci of thinking of the two peoples are different. Along with these socio-cultural differences there exists a general feeling, on both sides, of self-sufficiency. Cultural pride, tradition and socio-psychological confidence have enabled the Indo-Pakistani immigrants to preserve their languages, cuisine and dress; to recreate their religious institutions; and to establish in Britain thousands of business enterprises which cater for the special needs of their community (as well as the general needs of others).

One of the remarkable features of self-made Asian entrepreneurs has been that they have often pursued their business objectives while simultaneously maintaining interest in the well-being of their community. Indeed, in some instances, such as Muhammad Faruqi in Bradford, success in business has been accompanied by growing interest in the communal problems. It was a Pakistani businessman in Birmingham who founded the first Pakistani social organization in 1956. Balbir Singh Sandhu, a prosperous Indian grocer in Wolverhampton, was the first president of the local Sikh *gurdwara* committee. An Indian estate agent in Southall has been well known for his social work in the Indian community. The increasing demands of his expanding and diversified business have not deterred Gurbachan Singh Gill from active participation in the affairs of Southall's Sikh community. It seems that the economic prosperity of the Asian entrepreneur and the confidence with which he conducts himself in the white world inspire admiration from the community which has, by virtue of circumstances, relied heavily on its English-speaking members for guidance and leadership.

COMMUNAL LEADERSHIP

*I spend most of my time in Handsworth filling
in all kinds of forms, writing letters, advising
my fellow-countrymen on their problems. It's
tedious work; but that's the only way to win
my countrymen's respect, and keep it.*

An Indian leader in Birmingham.

Very early in the history of Indo-Pakistani immigration, a
person conversant with English became a valuable asset to his
group. During every step of their settlement non-English-
speaking immigrants called on him for help. It began with the
Labour Exchange, and National Insurance and National Health
Service forms, and continued with postal savings account, bank,
income tax form and electoral registration papers. In between
were letters to and from the High Commission in London
concerning foreign exchange and passports, and from local
authorities regarding, say, rates and overcrowding. The result was
that the English-speaking kinsman or fellow-villager felt over-
taxed.

The case of Manmohan Singh Basra in Wolverhampton is
illustrative. He arrived there in 1953 from Singapore (where he
had settled after leaving the Indian Army in 1950). Soon after his
arrival he found himself filling in forms and scribing letters for
fellow-Indians to the extent that he hardly had a moment to
relax. As a result, he and other socially active Indians decided to
establish a formal organization dedicated primarily to providing
voluntary service to the community. Supported by a membership
of 150, they founded the Indian Workers' Association, South
Staffordshire, in 1956. The reason for assigning this name to their
organization was historical.

Three Indian workers – Udham Singh, an active member
of his electrical workers' union and a delegate to the local Trades
Council; Ujjagar Singh; and Akbar Ali Khan – had formed the
first Indian Workers' Association in Coventry in 1938. They had

chosen this name to distinguish their organization from the middle-class Indian League (formed in 1929 and concerned exclusively with Indian independence) and the Birmingham Indian Association, consisting of students and doctors. In time, the I W A in Coventry became dormant, and was largely forgotten. But Udham Singh survived as an Indian martyr, for in 1940 he assassinated, in London, Sir Michael O'Dwyer, who, as the Lieutenant-Governor of the Punjab, had approved of the action of Brigadier-General R. E. H. Dyer[1] in massacring hundreds of Indians in Amritsar. Udham Singh was subsequently hanged, and it was to honour his memory that the Indian settlers in Coventry named their newly formed organization, in 1953, the Indian Workers' Association. During the subsequent years their lead was followed by the Indian communities elsewhere in the country.

By 1957, there were enough local I W As in Britain to draw the attention of Prime Minister Nehru who, during a visit to London, advised the I W A leaders to form a central body. He also advised the Indian High Commission officials to help bring this about. The 1958 race riots – when a group of Sikhs was attacked by white hooligans in Notting Hill – provided further impetus to centralization.[2]

At its first conference in September 1958, the Indian Workers' Association of Great Britain adopted a constitution and spelled out its aims and objects, which were to organize Indians:

to safeguard their conditions of life and work;

to promote co-operation and unity with the trade-union and labour movement in Great Britain;

to fight against all forms of discrimination based on race, colour, creed or sex;

to co-operate with other organizations, national and international, striving for friendship, peace and freedom; and

to undertake social welfare and cultural activities, to further above aims and objects.

1. Brigadier-General R. E. H. Dyer died a natural death in 1927.
2. The 1958 race riot in Nottingham led to the formation of the first Indian organization there, the Indian Association.

Right from the beginning the leadership of the local I W A consisted of two major groups: the moderate entrepreneurs and the political radicals. The moderates stressed social welfare work whereas the radicals advocated trade-union and political activities. The aims of the national organization, as it emerged in September 1958, were broad-based enough to contain both groups.

The leftist element continued to exhort the I W A members to participate in trade union activities, and even to initiate unions where they did not already exist. In this they were quite successful. Many local I W As can justly claim that their members, in spite of victimization and threats from employers, managed to originate unions. Also, without exception, I W A members supported whatever militant action was taken by established unions in factories and public transport, because they believed that the economic lot of Indian workers was intimately interconnected with that of British workers.

Due to their diligent interest in trade unionism some Indian workers became shop stewards and even union officials. Local I W As gained enough standing and acceptance to be invited by employers, particularly in the Midlands, to help resolve problems, social as well as industrial, arising out of the employment of Indian workers.

Also the I W As showed admirable vigour and initiative in combating racial discrimination and opposing racialist immigration policies. The Birmingham I W A, for instance, was the first in Britain to foster, in 1960, an anti-discrimination umbrella body of various coloured immigrant and British organizations – the Co-ordinating Committee Against Racial Distrimination; and the first to lead a demonstration of black and white citizens against the 1961 Immigration Bill.

The I W A - G B (with a national membership of twenty thousand) actively participated in the formation of the Committee of Afro-Asian-Caribbean Organization which lobbied against the 1961 immigration legislation. Later, in 1963, it supported the struggle of black Americans for civil rights.

Simultaneously I W As maintained active interest in local politics. When, in April 1963, Peter Griffiths, then the leader of Smethwick Conservative councillors, suggested to the (Conservative) Home Secretary that all immigrants who had been unemployed for six months be deported,[3] the Birmingham CCARD wrote to the Joint Chairman of the Conservative Party that 'The Conservatives in Smethwick are not only damaging the Conservative Party, but far more seriously are pursuing a policy which will ultimately result in a second Notting Hill'.[4] To that the Joint Chairman replied that local Conservative Associations were autonomous bodies. Thereupon the Smethwick IWA decided to campaign actively for Labour candidates at the local elections in May 1963. This had an important bearing on Labour's political fortunes, a fact acknowledged, indirectly, by Peter Griffiths who, after the elections, wrote in the local paper:

There were the voters in their turbans and saris, and the babel of many tongues as the Indian Workers' Association gave instructions to non-English-speaking voters ... It is fair to assume that more than a quarter of Labour's voters could not speak English.[5]

During the 1964 general election the Smethwick IWA, once again, worked hard for the Labour candidate, Patrick Gordon-Walker; but he lost. So did the IWA in Southall actively canvass for the Labour candidate. He won, although by a reduced majority of 1,800 votes, a clear indication that but for the IWA's support (of nearly 2,500 votes) he would have been defeated.[6]

The IWA, Southall, began in 1957 with a membership of 120. Now its membership is nearly 12,500. Its £16,000-plus assets include the freehold property that accommodates its office and reading room, and part-payment on a cinema hall (with a seating capacity of 1,850) which shows Hindi and Punjabi films throughout the week.

It was probably the first Indian or Pakistani organization in Britain to elect its officials by ballot vote. That was in 1963. Since then three elections have been hotly contested, an index of the community's interest. The IWA election in April 1968 aroused more passion and controversy in the Indian community than did the local council election that followed a fortnight later.

3. Paul Foot, *Immigration and Race in British Politics*, p. 43.
4. ibid., p. 73.   5. ibid., p. 46.   6. ibid., p. 181.

Each week some 300 to 350 Indians use the Southall I W A's reading room, where air-mail editions of Indian newspapers in Hindi, Punjabi, Urdu and English are made available. A full-time welfare officer gives guidance to Indians and Pakistanis (who can join as associate members) in how to obtain house mortgages, or apply for council housing; supplies information on all aspects of immigration and (British) nationality; provides help in finding accommodation and jobs for those members who have failed to do so on their own; and, of course, fills in all kinds of forms as well as drafts letters to various authorities.

There is also a part-time female welfare officer. She looks after the special interests of children and widows. She conducts a weekly class to teach English to Indian women at times that suit them and in an atmosphere they find congenial.

The Southall I W A also sponsors cultural evenings of Indian dance, song and music. Sometimes, it finds itself playing a specific trade-union role – especially in instances of industrial injury to its members. It engages in political lobbying at the local and national levels. Indeed, it comes nearest to the ideal of active community organization which blends social welfare work and cultural activity with political lobbying.

Almost concurrent with the formation of I W As was the emergence of local Pakistani organizations, and for similar reasons: language difficulties and cultural identity. But it was not until 1963 that a successful attempt was made to form a national body. Twenty-three local organizations joined together to form the National Federation of Pakistani Associations in Great Britain (N F P A).[7]

At the local level Pakistani organizations have been concerned, almost exclusively, with social welfare services, providing Pakistanis with an interpreter service, advising them on police and legal matters (such as how and where to lodge a complaint with the police, which solicitor to contact, etc.), or guiding the male immigrant who wishes to bring his family to Britain – a complex

7. Before the establishment of Bangla Desh, in December 1971, more than thirty-five local Pakistani organizations were affiliated to the N F P A. Its annual conference in March 1970 (in Birmingham) was attended by three hundred delegates. Of its six (elected) top officials, three were from the Eastern wing and three from the Western wing.

exercise involving the Pakistani High Commission and the Home Office in London, and the British High Commission in Pakistan. The leadership at the local level comes mainly from among the Pakistani restaurateurs, estate agents or teachers, who are considered by the community to be well equipped to deal with the Town Hall, the Chamber of Commerce, the building societies or the police. Their political views are often moderate.

At the national level, however, the radical element, mainly from the Eastern wing, managed to remain in the forefront since the N F P A's inception in 1963. The worsening racial situation in Britain strengthened the hands of this group. Nevertheless, the N F P A, when asked to affiliate to C A R D, did so. But as mentioned earlier,[8] this affiliation did not last long.

The N F P A consistently and diligently tried to redress Pakistani settlers' problems and grievances, and did not shirk even from criticizing the Pakistan High Commission, if and when necessary. At first its leaders protested, orally and through letters, against the bureaucratic sloth shown by the Commission's staff in their dealings with Pakistani nationals. But when this tactic proved ineffectual, N F P A leaders organized, in early 1968, a protest march and demonstration against the High Commission in London. The event received much publicity, embarrased High Commission officials, and jolted its staff out of their complacency.

But by far the most disturbing and demoralizing experience for Pakistani and Indian settlers was the 1968 Immigration Bill designed primarily to bar Kenyan Asians (with British passports), from entering Britain.[9] One of the prominent and vocal critics of this Bill was the I W A - G B. It brought coachloads of its members from the Midlands and North to London to join a demonstration against the Bill on 25 February. But it was all in vain. The Bill was passed; and the Act became effective on 1 March as originally planned.

8. pp. 57–8.
9. This Bill arrested the trend among Indian and Pakistani settlers towards acquiring British nationality. 'Many of them who had taken up British papers wanted to change back to their original nationality,' said J. S. Nehra, an Indian leader in Nottingham in November 1968. 'But it's not easy to do so.'

It seemed clear to many Indian and Pakistani leaders that racialism in Britain was on the rise, and that a broad front of coloured people's organizations was needed to combat it. As in the past, the I W A - G B took the initiative. Its general secretary, Jagmohan Joshi, sounded out various coloured leaders and found the response encouraging. It was decided to hold a national convention shortly of various coloured representatives. Then came the news, on 4 April, of Martin Luther King's assassination in America. Interest in the project mounted.

In spite of that, the I W A - G B stuck to its original plan of inviting to the convention only those black organizations which had, in the past, taken an uncompromising stand against racialism. Prominent among twenty such organizations were the West Indian Standing Conferences in Birmingham and London, and the N F P A. The convention was scheduled for 29 April in Leamington Spa.

In the interim came Enoch Powell's speech on 20 April. The dramatic, and at times hysterical, support he received from many whites further fuelled the interest of black organizations in the forthcoming convention. On 29 April, fifty representatives of various Afro-Asian-Caribbean organizations arrived in Leamington Spa. At the end of six hours' deliberation they announced the formation of the Black People's Alliance, 'a militant front *for* Black Consciousness and *against* racialism'. Summing up the general feeling among conferees, Jagmohan Joshi, the convenor, said:

Powell's speech and its aftermath . . . is just one step in a continuous campaign which was started at the end of the 1950s by the political parties to whip up racial antagonism to make political gains . . . There has been no distinction between Conservative and Labour parties.

Accordingly, the B P A pledged 'to fight racialism from *all* quarters: Labour government, Tories, employers, unions, police, Press, etc.; to expose the Labour government and its racialist policies over immigration, and phoney protection accorded through marginal laws like the present Race Relations Bill, etc.; and to seek allies from the majority community while exposing false allies such as the "do-gooders" who have been using black organizations to further their own vested interests and political ambitions'. In short, the B P A, although remaining a broad front of coloured organizations, did *not* reject the hand of those whites 'genuinely' interested in combating racialism.

From an historical viewpoint, the emergence of the B P A confirmed a certain pattern in racial politics: 'white' action leading to 'black' reaction, generally of withdrawal and self-help. The 1958 race riots led to the establishment of the West Indian Standing Conferences in London and Birmingham, and the Indian Workers' Association – Great Britain. The 1961 Immigration Bill created a temporary alliance of West Indian and Asian organizations. Now the 1968 Immigration Act and Enoch Powell's speech led to the formation of a permanent front of Afro-Asian-Caribbean organizations: the Black People's Alliance.

From the original twenty, the number of black organizations affiliated to the B P A has grown to more than fifty. Each organization maintains its independent existence and functions at the local level. The general stress is on the quiet, undramatic work of education, organization and recruitment. However, when offered an appropriate occasion, the B P A decided to show its strength in the streets.

During the Commonwealth Prime Ministers' Conference in January 1969, the B P A led a march of five thousand black – and two thousand white – supporters to Downing Street demanding that the 1962 and 1968 Immigration Acts be repealed and that a strong Race Relations Act with 'the backing of strong punitive sanctions' be passed. It was the first time ever that coloured organizations had, on their own initiative, staged a march in London to voice their views, a lead that was to be followed later by a Birmingham-based Indian organization.

Its two thousand members marched in Birmingham to protest against the virtual ban on the entry and settlement of fiancés from the Commonwealth imposed by the government in late January. This is an issue which vitally concerns thousands of Asian settlers with nubile daughters who cannot find suitable matches in Britain. 'This restriction has caused more resentment among Indians and Pakistanis against the government than all the acts and racialist speeches put together,' said an official of the

Southall I W A. 'More and more of them are joining our organization and pushing us to do "something".' A Pakistani leader in Bradford, well-known for his moderate views, termed the restriction as 'the first stage of the repatriation of the blacks'.

Pressure of events, inter-organizational rivalries and the persistent insensitivity of many British leaders and institutions, at local as well as national levels, have gradually led many moderate and 'non-political' Asian organizations and leaders to take stands that are anything but 'non-political'.

The Nottingham Indian Welfare Association is an example. It calls itself 'non-political', and stresses its co-operation with the Indian High Commission and the government-sponsored N C C I (now the Community Relations Commission). And yet, reacting to the national climate of racialism and competition from a rival, militant I W A, it pointed out in its 1968 annual report, 'Immigrants are greatly apprehensive about the next general election, which can cause some very ugly incidents if immigrants are to be made scapegoats for political aims by an individual or a party.'[10] Controversy over Sikh turbans in Wolverhampton buses caused it to demand the repeal of this restrictive regulation in Nottingham. The cavalier attitude of trade unions towards coloured members led it to press employers to consider granting three months' leave without pay every third year to coloured employees to enable them to visit their distant home countries.

Meanwhile the socio-cultural life of the community is not neglected. This organization, like many others in the country, provides cultural evenings of Indian music, dance and drama on days of religious and national importance, thus keeping alive cultural and national identities.

Many Pakistani organizations present *mushayaras* – poetry evenings – in Urdu, thus preserving a long-established tradition ingrained among Urdu-speaking people. To encourage continued use of Urdu in writing, *Mashriq* runs a column for young readers to help them find pen-friends. As for the formal teaching of Indian languages, this role is steadily being taken over by religious

10. As it happened the Tory candidate for Nottingham South injected the issue of coloured immigration into his election campaign in June 1970. He defeated the sitting Labour M P.

institutions. Mosques and Islamic Cultural Centres often teach Arabic and Urdu, languages that share a common script. Sikh *gurdwaras* have formed classes to teach the Punjabi script because the Sikh holy book is written in that script.

But even if children do not learn to read and write their native language, they grow up speaking it at home and with other Indian and Pakistani children. Although parents wish their children to have a British education they do not necessarily want them to forget their mother-tongue or disown their cultural heritage. The general attitude of Asian adults was summed up by Mihir Gupta, chairman of the Indian Association (U K), when he asked the white man 'to leave us alone to our culture, our music and our language'.[11]

The vast majority of Indians and Pakistanis in Britain do not wish or intend to give up completely their socio-cultural identity. By preserving their cultural identity, Asian settlers are, sub-consciously, practising the philosophy of Black Power.[12] For, once the sensationalist, nihilistic wrapper of the 'Burn, baby, burn' slogan (with which the term Black Power is associated by many white Britons) is discarded, the Black Power concept is seen to have two basic elements: racial and cultural pride and integrity; and racial or ethnic self-help.

Intellectual analysis and interpretation apart, the Black Power slogan also symbolizes an attitude of mind. In that context, many Asian settlers show a remarkable (albeit unrecognized) rapport with it. For instance, 'Black is beautiful' does not sound different from 'We have beauty of our own, they [the whites] have their own; in *quality* we're equal, but we're different from one another'. The latter statement, expressing a commonly held view among Asians, comes from an Indian housewife in Wembley.

However, though the views expressed above are identical, the sources from which they spring are not. By asserting that 'Black

11. *The Times*, 2 December 1968.
12. The authors of the 'Black Man In Search of Power' series of articles in *The Times* seem to have grasped this point, for they write: 'The idea of coloured identity and separation fostered by Black Power in America exists already among many Indians and Pakistanis in Britain who . . . look inwards toward their own social and religious communities and outwards toward their homelands.' *The Times*, 16 March 1968.

is beautiful' the African in the western world is trying to regain his self-dignity, lost through centuries of slavery and cultural imperialism; whereas the Indian or Pakistani settler, having been generally spared the experience of cultural imperialism, is stating something that is an accepted norm in his polyglot nation-state.

Indian and Pakistani societies can best be described as pluralistic, where many linguistic, religious and racial groups co-exist peacefully. (It is as if western and eastern Europe existed as two nation-states.) Indians and Pakistanis, therefore, grow up accepting, and respecting, the religious, linguistic, dietary and sartorial differences of their fellow-nationals. Adherence to the 'different *and* equal' concept, whether applied within their own communities or with respect to the British, is maintained when they migrate to Britain. Gujarati-Indians, for instance, continue to eat Gujarati food (with its main emphasis on vegetables and lentils), wear saris, Gujarati style, and socialize mainly among fellow-Gujaratis. So do Punjabis and Bangla Deshis. None of this disturbs or agitates the Indian or Pakistani settlers. They do not aspire to a stifling uniformity in culture or language either here or in their home countries. And yet there *is* unity in diversity among them, just as there is an underlying common set of values, generally labelled the 'western values' that unifies such diverse cultures as the French, American, Dutch, British and German. Indians, Pakistanis and Bangla Deshis, for example, share common attitudes towards birth and death, marriage and family, parents and teachers, money and education. Underlying the different super-structures there is a common foundation, vaguely called 'eastern values'.

6   CULTURE OF THE INDIAN SUB-CONTINENT

Instead of calling it Western and Eastern
way of life, let's call it an industrial and an
agrarian way of life. We're not really much
different that way from the people in
Southern Italy or Sicily or Cyprus.
An Indian teacher in London.

Those who ask us to change our way of life
overnight should first answer the question,
'Do English people living in our countries
ever adopt our way of life?'
HAIDER KHAN, a Pakistani leader in Bradford.

In order to understand properly the social norms, values and attitudes prevalent in the Indian, Pakistani and Bangla Deshi communities in Britain one must first examine their economic and historico-religious background. The economy of the Indian sub-continent is basically agrarian; and three-quarters of the population live in villages. Agrarian life revolves around seasons which determine times for sowing seeds and harvesting crops. It is no accident that Holi, the Hindu festival of colours, and Divali, the festival of lights, coincide with harvest times. It is also easy to see why the cow came to be revered: she gave milk, considered a nutritious food and used as a base for many dishes and sweets; and she bred bullocks, used for agricultural production and carting.

Hinduism, an ancient religion, which grew out of Indian soil, remains deeply embedded in the Indian people. So much so that periodic breakaway religious sects have not been able to sustain a different outlook and social practices for long. Sikhism is a case in point. Though considered casteless, its followers have succumbed to social distinctions based on occupations which are considered hereditary: *ramgharias*, craftsmen; and *jats*, peasants.

Islam was, however, introduced into India through foreign Muslim invaders whose commanders, during the eleventh century became rulers of northern India. Gradually, through force and persuasion, Muslim rulers won converts from within the indigenous population. On conversion Hindus changed their names and adopted the new religious practices but did not, could not, alter their dress, habits, language or method of cooking. Consequently religious taboos on food, drink and tobacco (forbidden to Sikhs) became crucial marks of distinction. Indeed animosity between Hindus/Sikhs and Muslims became epitomized in their attitude towards the cow: Muslims were considered 'cow-killers'; Hindus, 'cow-worshippers'. Even today this emotive point of religious difference can, and does, lead to violence and rioting in the Indian sub-continent.

Within religious and caste delineations, life is communal and is institutionalized through the joint-family system. (It is worth noting that the joint-family system, a miniature form of tribal life, is not peculiar to the Indian sub-continent but is the hallmark of many agrarian societies throughout the world.) A joint family includes married brothers and their families as well as unmarried brothers and sisters, all living under the tutelage of the eldest male member – usually the father or grandfather. Belongings are shared between the families and, if the family house is large enough, all members live within it, while maintaining separate hearths. All orphans, widows and aged members of the joint family are cared for. The head of the family has authority over all others, even those who are married and are themselves fathers.

Thus the feeling of belonging to a group larger than one's immediate family is ingrained in people from rural India or Pakistan or Bangla Deshi. Individualism, as fostered by western culture is almost unknown. Children are not allocated separate rooms in which to live and sleep, and do not, therefore, grow up thinking in highly individualistic terms. Moreover, the nature of work – labouring on the family farm – produces a group, rather than individual, identity. On maturity the male child does not detach himself from the family and start on his own, but remains part of the joint family, loyal and respectful.

In the family, the role and functions of father and mother are well defined. Father is the boss, the provider and disciplinarian, and makes the important decisions. Mother cooks, sews, maintains the house and brings up the children.

The proverbial submissiveness of the Indian women, however, is deceptive. Under the coat of plasticity and self-effacement there lies granite. She has ways of subtle pressurizing and arm-twisting, and generally gets her way in areas she considers exclusively her own. She is the central arch of the Asian family. Michael Kraus's description of southern Italian immigrants in America – '[They] had tight knit families, father-orientated but mother-centred'[1] – applies equally to Asian immigrants in contemporary Britain.

Viewed against this socio-economic backdrop, it becomes clear why marriage is conceived as an alliance of families rather than a union of mates attracted to each other through 'romantic' love. Careful and extensive enquiries regarding the family tree, and the social and material standing of the prospective bride and groom by family elders precede the 'arrangement of marriage'. (Abdul Kazi, a Pakistani teacher in London, compares the arranged marriage system with 'two countries wishing to sign an important treaty'.) This marriage custom is transferred almost intact when people from the Indian sub-continent emigrate. If no suitable match can be found within this community in its new country of settlement, then marriage alliances are arranged in the towns or villages of the Indian sub-continent. Such a practice persists among, say, Sikh settlers in Canada who have lived there for more than three generations. A study of Sikhs in Vancouver by A. Mayer revealed that eighty per cent of post-war marriages had been arranged in India. These included many Sikhs born in Canada.[2]

Although the pattern of arranged marriage is to be found among all major religious groups – Hindus, Muslims and Sikhs – the religious significance of marriage varies. In Hindu and Sikh scriptures marriage is regarded as a spiritual union and therefore considered indissoluble. The Hindu law, reformed in 1955 by the Indian Parliament, allows divorce; but the country's divorce rate

1. Michael Kraus, *Immigration, The American Mosaic*, p. 69.
2. Cited in E. J. B. Rose and Associates, *Colour and Citizenship*, p. 459.

particularly among its rural populace, is negligible. The Koran, on the other hand, regards marriage as a civil contract. Therefore divorce among Muslims, easy to obtain, is much more frequent.

The practice of polygamy among Muslims, which often fascinates the western male and horrifies the western female, stems from the following Koranic verse: 'then you may marry other women who seem good to you: two, three or four of them. But if you feel that you cannot maintain equality among them, marry only one. '3

However, Pakistan abolished polygamy in 1961. A government decree stipulated that a second marriage could be contracted if, *and only if*, the first wife consented in writing. Legalistic considerations apart, there is, for the average Pakistani peasant, the economic problem of supporting two wives. According to a Pakistani leader in London, no more than one in six hundred Muslim settlers in Britain have two wives.

But whatever be the differences due to religious allegiance, rural society in the Indian sub-continent is marked by a high degree of marital fidelity. Extra-marital sexual liaisons in a village, where all the inhabitants know one another, can be difficult, even dangerous, to initiate and maintain. Besides there is the notion of 'honour' that the wronged husband is expected to uphold if he is not to lose face. This mode of thinking persists among Asian settlers in Britain. Avtar Singh Ojagger, a resident of Britain for sixteen years, says, 'If I knew my wife had been unfaithful to me, I'd give her a hiding. I wouldn't be able to sleep at night until I had straightened her out.'4

Attitudes towards sex and sexual matters tend to be prudish. The subject is seldom discussed openly, or even mentioned. Physical demonstrations of love or affection in public, even between man and wife, are rare.

Husband and wife do not jointly participate in socializing within the village community. They do not visit the village tea-shop together, or play cards together under the peepul tree, or jointly participate in the nocturnal confabulations around a

3. In the Arabia of Prophet Muhammad's day, when polygamy was common among all tribes, such a condition was considered restrictive!
4. *New Society*, 22 February 1968.

communal *hookah* in the village square. This pattern continues in Britain. Indian, Pakistani and Bangla Deshi women are rarely to be seen eating in Asian cafés and restaurants, much less sipping tomato juice in pubs.

Places of worship, however, are the exception. Hindu temples and Sikh *gurdwaras* are visited by both men and women. But, on entering, men and women congregate separately. This is the practice in India; and it continues, undisturbed, in Britain. Among Muslims the question of a mixed congregation simply does not arise; prayers and religious meetings are conducted for men and women in separate rooms or halls. This pattern is followed invariably in the Muslim world.

In general, continuation of old traditions in an alien environment is reassuring to Indian, Pakistani and Bangla Deshi immigrants, for it reiterates their distinct religio-cultural identity and creates psychological security. Referring to 'the great mass of immigrants from China and India' in south-east Asia, Guy Hunter states that 'deeply held in their traditional views and beliefs [they] found an emotional shelter and security in a strange land by holding to their own roots'.[5]

Religious practices aside, there are social attitudes that are commonly shared by Asian men and women. For example, education is highly regarded. Since higher education was, and still is, closely associated with ability to read, write and speak English, Asians fluent in English are much respected, as are all those who have white-collar jobs, a legacy of the bureaucratic British raj.

Coupled with respect for education goes deference for the teacher, the guru, much fortified by traditional Hindu philosophical ordering of 'entities'. This philosophical concept begins with the 'One Supreme Being' at the top, and comes down through primary, secondary and tertiary gods and goddesses to certain human beings who, in a given context, are to be revered: parents in relation to children; husbands to wives; teachers to pupils; and priests and ascetics to all the rest. This historico-religious conditioning, more than anything else, explains why Indian children in

5. *South-East Asia; Race, Culture and Nation*, Oxford University Press, 1966, p. 57.

Britain generally show respect for their parents and teachers in spite of the contrary tendency often shown by British children.

However, traditional values and attitudes, long preserved in the rural environment of the Indian sub-continent are being undermined by the communications explosion and by growing contacts between the village and the town, to which many villagers, under economic pressure, migrate. But as long as the movement of the villagers is to the cities or towns within the same linguistic state, cultural shock is minimal. It is when, say, a Sikh peasant or craftsman travels to distant Calcutta or Bombay that bewilderment sets in. To offset it, he seeks out fellow-Sikhs, Punjabi restaurants and Sikh *gurdwaras*. (It is as if a kilted Scot from the Highlands moved to Athens: no doubt, he would seek the company of fellow-Scots [in kilts], and look for a pub and a Presbyterian church).

A more pronounced bewilderment strikes the rural Indian or Pakistani immigrant when he arrives at Heathrow airport. At the end of a twenty-four-hour flight he finds himself in a country with two centuries of urbanization, industrialization and secularization.[6] Furthermore, the nature of English society is vastly different from his own. English society values privacy, tidiness, primness, order and quiet; whereas the rural Asian has grown up in a society where working, sleeping and eating in the open are quite normal. English society values restraint in speech and behaviour, reserve and formality; whereas the Asian is used to informality, frankness and loud speech often accompanied by gesticulation. English houses in urban areas are enclosed and compact; houses in the rural areas of the Indian sub-continent are open and haphazardly built where windows are not curtained nor doors tightly fitted to minimize draught, and where the residents are not in the habit of closing the door every time they enter or leave a room. Early immigrants from the Indian sub-continent demonstrated these differences dramatically as, unaware of

6. Though remaining nominally Christian, modern western society has, by and large, lost interest in religion; whereas the Muslim or Sikh immigrant comes from a rural environment where religion is part of the general milieu. Even if the western country to which the Sikh or Muslim migrates were religious, that is Christian, it would still provide a secular environment for him.

English values and practices, they continued to live and act as if they were still in their villages. Unknown to them, the English were offended and scandalized.

However, with continued residence in Britain and guidance from their community leaders, came a realization of English values and taboos. Conscious and subconscious efforts were made by Asian settlers to moderate blatant differences. Some Sikhs, for instance, shaved their beards not merely to improve their chance of employment but also to minimize their exotic appearance in a new environment. With time also came familiarization with English.

Change in employment, from agricultural to industry, induced a more profound change of attitude. Industrial employment made rural Asians time-conscious, altered their rhythm of life from the seasonal cycle of work and leisure to the weekly cycle of work and relaxation. Simultaneously it robbed them of the sense of freedom they had in a village society. 'Life here is like a machine,' complained Ajit Singh in Slough, reflecting a widespread feeling in the community. Effects of subservience to the work cycle and obsession with economic betterment manifested in other spheres of life. If, for example, Guru Nanak's or Lord Krishna's birthday fell on a week-day, it was celebrated on the preceeding or following Sunday.

In time religious fervour and intense interest in day-to-day events in Indo-Pakistani politics subsided. Revulsion against beef or pork became less. A weekly or fortnightly visit to the *gurdwara* or mosque, and a perusal of an Urdu or Punjabi journal, published in Britain, were considered quite adequate. In contrast, increasingly more time and energy were spent in coping with the problems of buying a house and arranging to bring the rest of the family to Britain.

Once his family arrived, the Asian's life became home-centred. Visits to the pub became less frequent as his leisure time was spent in upgrading his house and his savings used for buying furniture, household gadgets, car and television. A larger number of families from the Indian sub-continent in towns made an active social life possible. With a car at the door, visiting friends and relatives in or out of town over the weekend or during holidays became feasible. While the material life of Asians became almost indistinguishable from their English neighbours', their social life remained solidly grounded within the self-contained Indian, Pakistani or Bangla Deshi community. Their deeply religious wives recreated, at least partially, a religious aura at home. Small altars of Hindu gods and goddesses were built; and portraits of Sikh *gurus* decorated the walls.

And yet Asian women have not proved themselves totally immune to environmental influence. Pakistani women have, more or less, discarded the veil; while Indian women have tightened their *salvars* (baggy trousers), making them more elegant, or have limited the use of saris to warm, dry days and formal occasions. When their sons have bought tight trousers or pointed shoes, or grown long sideburns, they have not protested or disapproved over-much. 'Our children must move with times,' says Avtar Singh Ojagger from Southall; and his wife agrees.

But a firm line is drawn in the case of teenage daughters. They must dress modestly, must not, like 'the cheap English girls', exhibit their anatomy. They must, under all circumstances, remain chaste before marriage. They must be told – as they often are, by Gurmeet Singh, an Indian settler in Wolverhampton – that 'in our society it's the man who shows his body, not the woman; and that is what makes us different from the whites'.

An overwhelming majority of Asian settlers consider English society morally decadent. A survey conducted by the author (for *New Society*), in 1968, revealed that all Asian respondents thought British marriages unstable; and all but one thought British marriages adulterous and white women 'over-sexed'. 'Every time you pick up a [British] paper you see divorce cases,' said Dilawar Singh Nijjar, an eighteen-year-old engineering apprentice in Southall. 'White men and women go off with one another even when married,' said Amrit Kaur Sondhi, a Sikh housewife who works in a canteen kitchen at Heathrow airport.[7] Gulwant Singh, a Sikh settler in Wolverhampton, read aloud a headline from *Des Perdes*, a Punjabi weekly published in Britain, 'Last year 1,100 English girls aged sixteen or under became unwed mothers', and chuckled. Such stories in the Indian language

7. *New Society*, 22 February 1968.

Press in Britain confirm what Asian settlers themselves see in parks, pubs and streets, and on television.

Apprehensive of the morally corrupting climate, many Pakistani males dread to bring their wives and daughters to Britain. If they do, they try to minimize their chance of sexual adventure by restricting them to chores at home, by themselves doing the family shopping, and by locking their homes when, say, they have to work night shifts. Undoubtedly their sense of insecurity is genuine.

Many Pakistani and Indian husbands disapprove of the idea of their wives attending evening classes in English, not only because that would interfere with their housework, but also because of their unexpressed fear that if their wives became familiar with English and mixed with the British, they would end up behaving like the white women. They consider home as the last citadel of security where they can withdraw from a generally unfriendly, alien and competitive environment and assert their manhood without challenge or question. No wonder then that they wish to preserve the *status quo*, and prevent their home environment from being transformed into another area of doubt, challenge and competition.

A faithful and obedient spouse and a stable, loyal family provide the Asian with evidence that his culture is morally superior to the white man's. Furthermore, these elements, buttressed by clear, unambiguous delineation of duties and obligations, provide him with an environment where his counsel to his children is most likely to be taken seriously. He frequently tells his young son that 'Without education you're nothing', and his adolescent daughter that 'Your destiny lies with your future husband: you must become a good cook and seamstress and learn to keep a house'. It has been the parents' experience that the more interest they show in their children the better response they get from them.

However loving, albeit restrictive, the atmosphere at home, Asian children, educated in the generally liberal, 'think-for-yourself' atmosphere of British schools find themselves at the centre of a cultural conflict. When very young, they feel confused and culturally ambiguous. But as they grow up they often resolve the problem by adopting some aspects of western culture and behaviour while retaining many of the traditional values and attitudes.

The main difference between the two generations of Asians is this. The adults, reared and educated in the Indian sub-continent, were not strongly exposed to British values, Christian thought and the history of western civilization; whereas their children are. Consequently whatever compromises the adults made in response to the new environment did not detract from the core of their culture. With their children, however, compromises tend to be achieved by their shedding parts of their hereditary cultural core.

7

ASIAN CHILDREN: CULTURAL SYNTHESIS?

You can talk to an English boy without him thinking anything of it, but if you talk to an Indian boy he thinks you're fast.
SUKHDEV KAUR, an Indian girl in Southall.

I feel I'm different from the Indians because I've been in England for so long; and yet I'm quite different from the British people because I've not been here long enough.
GYAN CHAND, aged 25, a resident of London since 1955.

Some of the rules and practices prevalent in the schools, which are taken for granted by British parents, have proved causes for concern among many Asian parents. School uniforms for girls is one example. As early as 1955, Jaswant Singh, an Indian settler in Gravesend, objected to his daughter having to wear a skirt, thus 'showing her legs'. He based his protest on cultural grounds; and it was accepted. His daughter was allowed to wear a blue *salvar* in school.

Since then similar objections have been raised by some Indian and many Pakistani parents. The latter have quoted the Koran to back their opposition to skirts for their daughters. The appropriate Koranic verse 'enjoins the believing women ... to draw their veils over their bosom and not to reveal their finery except to their husbands, fathers, husband's fathers, sons, stepsons, women-servants, brothers, brothers' sons ... and children who have no carnal knowledge of women'. Some education authorities (such as Leicester) have waived the school uniform regulation for Muslim girls; while in other cases, Muslim parents have accepted a compromise by which their daughters wear uniforms only within school premises, but not outside.[1] Objections have also

1. When, however, neither party gives in, children's education suffers. This happened at a Walsall school when, in October 1969, the Headmaster banned *salvars* in school. Thereupon five Muslim parents kept away their

been raised, and exemptions won, regarding gym slips and swimming lessons for Asian girls.

Once past adolescence, most Asian girls wear traditional dress at home. They often do the same if and when they go to college. When, for instance, Mehtab Aslam, a Pakistani girl in Cricklewood, joined a technical college her mother insisted that she wear a *salvar* because 'she said that I was a grown-up girl, and that I was going to a co-educational college'.

School assembly and scripture classes are other examples of conflict between the values at home and school for the Asian child. Muslim parents, generally more particular about their faith than Sikhs or Hindus, have been prominent in raising the issue, and they have often succeeded in getting their children exempted from assembly and/or scripture class.

Muslim parents who fail to act in time realize later the confusion that Christian instruction creates in their child's mind regarding his own religious identity. Faiz-ul-Niyazi, a Pakistani in Southall, became aware of the effect Christian instruction had on his daughter when, once hearing a religious service on the radio, she crossed herself instantly. He began to 'instruct' her differently; but that only confused the child who thought that either her teacher or her father was telling lies.

One would expect school authorities to arrange instruction in Islam or Sikhism wherever there is a large number of Muslim or Sikh children. This has not yet happened. At most, the authorities have agreed to allow volunteer instructors if the Muslim or Sikh community would provide them. Some local Muslim organizations have done so.

Among Sikh and Hindu parents the issue has not caused much concern because of the pervasive feeling that the long-term effect of Christian instruction on the child is minimal, and that children treat religious instruction as one of the 'subjects' to be studied at home. The counter-argument advanced by many – including some Indian teachers – is that it would be better if the Sikh or Hindu child regarded Sikhism or Hinduism as one of the

---

daughters from school rather than let them wear skirts. This situation continued for months. *The Times*, 7 January 1970.

'subjects' and learnt about his own religion rather than Christianity.

The authors' interviews with many Indian school leavers revealed that they treated assemblies as school 'routine', and held liberal views on religion: 'All religions are the same – love thy neighbour, don't kill, that sort of thing; only they say it differently'; 'Religion is in one's heart'; 'There's only one God, whichever way you worship Him, through Christ or the Ten Gurus'.[2] All this sounds admirably liberal and is much appreciated by school authorities until you ask the authorities if English children would mind attending Sikh or Muslim assembly, or study their scripture.

In the case of Hindus, liberalism is blended with feelings of inclusiveness and self-confidence. They can accommodate the Pope as 'a holy man' or consider Jesus as 'one of the gods' in the massive Hindu pantheon without, in any way, impairing the essence of Hinduism. They also have a quiet confidence regarding their religious survival. If eight centuries of Muslim rule did not obliterate Hinduism, they argue, a generation of exposure to Christianity is hardly going to make much difference. 'I'm born a Hindu, and I'll die as a Hindu.' says eighteen-year-old Rajesh Sharma from Southall, succinctly expressing a widely prevalent feeling.

Moreover, if a Hindu mother worships before the altar of gods at home, fasts regularly on days of full moon, conducts *puja* (prayer) at home, and reads aloud the Hindu epic stories of Rama and Krishna, she keeps alive the spirit of Hinduism in her children. There are also religious day celebrations when Hindus congregate in rented halls and conduct services, periodic reminders of being Hindu in a Christian environment.

Religious identification is generally much stronger among Muslims. The Muslim child is made aware of his religious faith when he notices that during Ramadhan the pattern of eating at home is altered radically. Then there is always a copy of the Koran at home. If the child was born in Pakistan and can read Urdu, he has no difficulty reading it. If not, he is helped by his parents or the local mosque or the Islamic Cultural Centre. In the

2. *New Society*, 1 June 1967.

case of Mehtab Aslam, for example, her mother wrote down the words of the *nimaz*, the Muslim prayer, in Roman script. Mehtab memorized it and began to pray as often as she could. Then she read the Koran in English which she described as 'more logical and rational ... not like the Bible which just seems to be full of miracles without any explanations'.

Thirteen-year-old Anwar Hussain in Bradford, who knows parts of the Koran by heart, often argues with his Christian classmates that if Jesus was the Son of God, then Mary must have been God's wife. Some of his Muslim friends spend as much as ten hours a week at the mosque learning the Koran and praying. A general Islamic air pervades the Pakistani community in Bradford just as a Judean air did within the Jewish community in the East End of London until its recent migration to suburbia.

As for the Sikhs, the simmering controversy regarding bearded Sikhs on buses has kept the issue of their religious identity alive. The obstinacy of various local authorities has goaded many Sikh parents to prescribe long hair and turbans for their male children. For instance, at the time of controversy on this issue in Manchester, 135 clean-shaven Sikhs underwent baptism at the Sikh *gurdwara*, thus returning to long hair and beards.[3] Following Sohan Singh Jolly's successful battle with the Wolverhampton local council, at one mass baptism ceremony alone 200 Sikhs, many of them young, resolved to wear long hair. In general, the proportion of clean-shaven adult males in the Sikh community – which reached a peak during the mid 1960s – has been declining steadily. And a similar trend is to be noticed among young Sikhs.

The question of long hair often crops up in another context: with regard to Indian and Pakistani girls who attend British schools. Aesthetic and cultural values, rather than religious edicts, are involved.[4] In the Asian community, long hair is considered a sign of female beauty; and often cotton or silken braids are used to give hair extra length. Asian girls at school, on the other hand, see most British girls with short hair, and feel tempted to follow suit. But they cannot do so until and unless their mothers consent. And it is hard to persuade them. Female hair may be trimmed

3. E. J. B. Rose and Associates, *Colour and Citizenship*, p. 465.
4. Except in the case of Sikh girls.

but to have it shortened, like a man's, at the hairdresser's – the very idea is alien to most Asian men and women. Asian parents also refuse to allow their adolescent daughters to wear make-up. Girls have to be in their late teens before they are permitted to do so and that too only minimally.

Since the Asian girl's life is predominantly home-bound, parental control is tighter than in the case of boys who, like English male teenagers, are not expected to be home-bound to the same extent. Many Asian boys can, and do, go to English cafés, for instance, and eat what they like. On the other hand a visit to an English (or even an Asian) café by Asian girls, alone or in a group, would create a scandal and win them the label of 'morally loose'. However, the hold of religious taboos on food and drink remains so strong that even those boys who eat pork or beef outside the home often do not admit it to their parents. Muhammad Akram, for example, has eaten pork and bacon, and found it 'too greasy'; but his parents do not know. 'They'd be appalled if they knew,' he says. 'They don't even buy margarine because someone told them that it had pig's fat in it.'[5]

In short, despite the corrupting influence of the Christian environment, most Asian children grow up following basically the dietary taboos of their inherited religions. The proportion of habitual beef-eaters among Hindu or Sikh youths does not seem higher than is the case with their male parents. The percentage of clean-shaven Sikh youths is by no means larger than among adult Sikhs. And mosques are drawing as many Muslim youths as adults.

As for the children's linguistic identity, it is seldom in doubt at home where Punjabi, Urdu or Gujarati thrive as spoken languages. However, both children and parents aspire to become fluent in English as they, very rightly, consider it a prerequisite for economic progress. The child's knowledge of English means that, unlike his parents, he does not feel excluded from the British world of information and entertainment. At any given time he has a choice of Hindi as well as English films. He often goes to both and is enriched by the varied experiences. If, for instance, an Indian film is historical, it infuses in him national pride. If it is

5. *New Society*, 1 June 1967.

religious it fills in gaps that exist in his knowledge of Indian religions. On the other hand, if the film is set in modern India or Pakistan or Bangla Desh it informs him, however obliquely, of the social ethos prevalent in his country of origin. Even if he realizes, after some time, that the story-line of most of these 'social' films is identical – namely, the conflict between romantic love and arranged marriage – the theme is going to be relevant to him as he reaches marriageable age.

Another attraction of these films is their music and songs. Even the most anglicized Asian will openly confess his weakness for Indian film songs, especially the poetic and imaginative lyrics. These lyrics, often sung to western tunes and background music, are seen by many as complementary to the Beatle songs with Indian music in the background. Obviously in this area a cultural synthesis is taking place, both here and in India; and young Asians growing up in Britain are the first to detect, and appreciate this development.

Admiration for Indian music and songs, however, does not prevent young Asians from listening to and appreciating conventional or 'pop' western music. Almost invariably juke boxes in Asian cafés provide a combination of popular Indian/Pakistani film songs and a few of the current Top Twenties in Britain.

Besides going to the cinema or cafés, Asian teenagers watch television, read comics or novels, and visit friends or clubs. Social visits among boys of the same age-group are common. When large numbers of Asian children live in a particular district or go to the same school, there is a tendency for different linguistic groups – Punjabi, Gujarati, Bengali – to socialize among themselves. In this they are following the parental pattern.

Social contacts between Asian and English boys are minimal. In spite of his ten years' residence in Wolverhampton and a sociable disposition, Subash Chandra Ohri, an Indian student, for instance had made one English friend. He estimated that only one out of twenty Asian students could claim an out-of-school friendship with an English boy.[6] Here again the young world is very much a replica of the old.[7]

6. The *Observer*, 14 July 1968.
7. Neither his active involvement in the local Indian community's affairs,

Asian children, following their parents' advice to be studious, show little interest in 'frill' activities at school, such as joining clubs. David Beetham's study of schools in Handsworth, in 1966, showed that only one out of eight Asians joined school clubs and societies; the proportion of English students was three times higher.[8] Uniformed organizations – namely Brownies, Scouts, Girl-Guides, etc. – are the exception, because Asian parents consider these to be a 'legitimate' part of school activities. Indeed, Asians join these enthusiastically. In Southall, for instance, there is a waiting list of Asian students wanting to enrol in the schools' Air Training Corps.

Studiousness of Asian pupils is also reflected in their disinclination to join out-of-school clubs. A study of schools in Handsworth showed that whereas one out of two English students joined out-of-school clubs, only one in seven Asians did so.[9] In the latter case, more often than not, such a club is likely to be a sports club: hockey, cricket or football. Club members practise daily or weekly, and play matches against other Asian clubs (bearing such names as Punjab Tigers, Pak Players, Indian Giants) or local English teams.[10]

There are also Indian youth clubs in the country; but the number is small because the youth club, with its indoor-games and weekly dances, a by-product of the urban western environment, is not popular with most Asian parents. They fail to grasp the meaning or usefulness of such an institution; and even if they let their sons join, they never let their daughters. They wish to keep teenage daughters away from the sexually tempting company of boys, a decision they view within the general context of the restraining function of parents. However, without the goodwill and

---

which brings him in contact with many English people, nor his thirteen years' residence in Slough, has won G. S. Kumra the friendship of an English family.

8. *Immigrant School Leavers and the Youth Employment Service in Birmingham.* p. 15.

9. ibid., p. 15.

10. There are now so many Asian teams in the country that each summer national tournaments in cricket, hockey and football are held, and trophies awarded.

respect of their children such restrictions would not be as effective as they often are.

Various factors, historical and contemporary, internal and external, have combined to create and sustain a harmonious, loyal and stable family system among Asian settlers in Britain: traditional cohesiveness of the family with its clear demarcation of the roles of the father, mother and children; a substantial concurrence between the social attitudes of parents and children; hard-working fathers, anxious to provide for their families; social pressures by the 'in' community on its members to conform to traditional values; and the general cultural and racial alienation from British society.

The cohesiveness of the Indian, Pakistani or Bangla Deshi family is, as explained earlier, rooted in the rural, agrarian base in the Indian sub-continent. This is invariably weakened when families migrate to towns and cities. However, the fact that Asian immigrants to Britain are exposed to the influence of competitive and divisive forces of the urban centres in an alien and unfriendly environment simultaneously generates counter-forces of self-protection and communal help, factors that tend to keep the migrant families, individually as well as collectively, cemented together. The cohesive element will remain strong as long as there is overt identification – such as skin colour – of the settlers, and antipathy towards them from the British.

Although at ease with the English language, children of Asian settlers feel culturally alien, since the influence of traditional values epitomized in their parents, remains strong. To a considerable degree they share their parents' social values. Attitudes towards nakedness and sex is one example. Recalling her school days when she had to change for swimming or showers, Mehtab Aslam says, 'I was surprised at the English girls who simply used to stand there and change. They didn't seem to be embarrassed whereas I used to try and hide everything, and felt conscious of myself.' The explanation of this difference of attitudes lies in the variation between the home environment of the Asian and English children. Mehtab, for instance, had never seen her mother or father sun-bathing in the back garden. Nor had she seen ever her mother expose her breasts, or even legs, at home. She had therefore grown up subconsciously feeling that nakedness was undesirable, even immoral.

Attitudes towards the child-parent relationship is another example. Most Asian teenagers and parents feel that British adolescents have too much freedom; that the idea of an independent existence at seventeen or eighteen, away from parents, is too awesome to be considered seriously; and that marriage need not signal a break with parents and/or the setting up of an independent household. On the eve of his marriage twenty-year-old Jessa Singh, in Glasgow, summed up the feelings of most young Asians when he said, 'My parents, they grew me up. They did all the planning [for my marriage]. So I can't chuck them. I like us all – mother, father, sisters, brothers – to stay together.'

The Asian child's traditional respect for his parents is further enhanced in the present circumstances by his awareness of the unflagging energy with which the mother devotes herself to the upkeep of the house and the care of children, and of the father's hard work for the family's economic welfare. The child often tries to reciprocate by being submissive, so as not to add to the already considerable burdens and worries of his parents. Ahmad Abbas, a Pakistani youth in Birmingham, for instance, says of his father:

He has to deal with hot iron and all that in his factory. So when he comes home, he's always tired and bored. And I always get the idea he's been working hard to feed us, his children. I feel really sorry for him.

On the other side, G. S. Kumra, an Indian settler in Slough, says of his children:

I give them all that they want at home. There's no deprivation, economic or social. In return I know, for example, where my son is when he's away from home. He's twenty-two; but he always tells me.

Although Asian teenagers, particularly girls, aspire to have less restricted existences than they now have, they certainly do not want (what they consider) the 'excessive freedom' that their British counterparts seem to have and enjoy. When given a choice between freedom and security they often opt for security. They do so partly because they lack the courage to face the risks and responsibilities that go with an independent existence, and partly because of the confidence and trust they place in their parents' wisdom and judgement.

Quite a few independent minded Asian teenagers toy with the idea of breaking from their parents, but only a small proportion actually do so. And still fewer manage to sustain the break. Munawar Sultana, a nineteen year-old Pakistani girl in Bradford, sums up the situation thus:

> I say, 'Oh, my parents this and that,' and I could live without them. But I always come back to them, no matter how much I rebel against them. I come back to what they've taught me ... No matter what I say now about my parents and their way of life, I'll find myself teaching my children exactly what they've taught me.

Such sentiments are not limited to girls: they are shared by most Asian boys as well. A sample of Asian boys was asked by the author 'If you fell in love with a girl but your parents did not approve of the marriage, what would you do?' Eighty-two per cent replied that they would yield to their parents' decision. 'I can't put a girl before my parents,' said Harnam Singh, a Sikh youth from Southall. 'I mean, they brought me up. Their blood runs into my veins, and the girl has only my feelings towards her. I know that my parents have a feeling for me which is greater than my own feeling for *myself*.' It is not that Harnam Singh is a recent arrival in Britain and thus holds strongly to traditional values. Quite the contrary. He arrived thirteen years ago, when he was six. His schooling has been completely British; and he speaks English with a local accent. What is more, unknown to his parents, he has dated English girls, although not in Southall. There, white animosity is much too strong, as is the grapevine in the Indian community.

The young Mehtab Aslam illustrated the strength and pervasiveness of the communal grapevine in Cricklewood – an area that does not have a large, or concentrated Indo-Pakistani community – with the following example: 'If a Pakistani sees me walking with a boy to the bus stop in the morning (on my way to college), the word goes around that I'm passionately in love with this boy. My mother knows it by the time I return from my college. She gets upset; and I've to promise to behave "decently" in future to avoid scandal in the community.' Social pressure against deviation from traditional behaviour is of course stronger in areas where there are concentrations of Indians and Pakistanis. British education may implant seeds of individualism and liberalism in the Asian child's mind, but in the climate of his home and neighbourhood these seeds cannot sprout and grow.

If an Asian youth wishes fully to adopt western values he has no alternative but to sever his connections with the family and totally disown his religious and cultural heritage. But then how does British society treat him? Does it reward him with social acceptance and equality of opportunity, or does it treat him as it does the West Indian youth? If the latter, which is often the case, then the rebellious youth is lost to both worlds, voluntarily cut off from one and unaccepted by the other. In that case, he must *eventually* return to his original flock.

To be fair, Asian parents are not clinging completely to the traditional ways of rural India or Pakistan. They cannot, even if they wish to. They are changing. One of the areas of change is in the role of women. They are slowly taking on a wage-earning role. Two factors have brought about this shift. One is the need to overcome the boredom that many Asian women experience on being removed from the gregarious atmosphere of the joint family in their native villages and on being confined, instead, to the four walls of their British homes with their nuclear families. The other is the constant pressure to increase family income to meet rising demands and aspirations. Consequently a sizeable minority of Asian women in such places as Southall and Slough have begun to work in factories. Of course, before husbands allow this, they make sure that their wives will be working in a 'hen-house' in a factory, such as packing departments; that there will be other Asian women at the work place; that there will be private or company transport to and from the factory; and that they will not have to wear skirts. However qualified and guarded, there is, nevertheless, a change. And the young Asian cannot fail to notice it since it is taking place in his home.

He must notice too that his community's marriage custom is changing. No longer are the matches arranged 'blindly', as was the case in his parent's days, without any consultation with the boy or the girl. Instead, a liberal version of the arranged marriage has evolved and become popular. This works as follows. When a boy or girl reaches marriageable age, parents start looking for a suitable match through a network of relatives and friends. When they are satisfied with the boy's background, education and financial standing, and the girls' character, family background and ability to manage a home, the stage is set for the next step: exchange of photographs. *If* there is mutual interest shown by the boy and the girl, then a meeting, under parental guidance is arranged. The boy and the girl meet, talk to each other, perhaps go to the cinema together. If they feel they like each other, the marriage is on. If not, another round of enquiries, pictures and meetings ensues. In this way the *final* decision rests with the boy and the girl, and not with the parents as used to be the case.

In some instances, a young man who feels sufficiently enamoured of a girl is known to have approached his parents to initiate enquiries which have led to marriage. Thus a move spurred by romance culminates in a traditionally 'arranged' marriage. As social liberalization proceeds, this pattern of romance-leading-to-arranged-marriage will prevail in the Asian community.

It seems that the practice of dating and love-marriages will not become popular within the Asian community for a long time to come, except perhaps with the middle-class families.[11] Some of their children will date and marry on an individual basis, mostly with their parents' consent. Thus young Asians will follow the western *value* of individualism without getting entangled with western *people*.

At present the incidence of inter-marriage between the Asians and the British is very low; and disapproval of such marriages among Asians, particularly in the working class, remains high. A survey by the author, in 1968, showed that seventy per cent of the Asian respondents disapproved of Anglo-Asian marriages.[12]

11. The size of the Asian middle class has been bolstered by the operation of B work vouchers under the 1962 Commonwealth Immigrants Act and the arrival of thousands of Asian businessmen and professionals from East Africa.

12. *New Society,* 22 February 1968.

However, their disapproval was based on cultural, *not* racial, grounds. 'A white girl will find it difficult to adjust to our way of life,' said Savitri Bhandari, a Hindu housewife. 'How sad it will be for me not to be able to talk to my own daughter-in-law unless she learned Punjabi or Hindi. Will she?'[13] Kripal Kaur, a Sikh housewife in Southall, made a similar point:

We're a hospitable people. If a friend drops in at midnight we'll feed him. If a relative arrives we'll ask him to stay the night. How will an English girl put up with all that? How will she restrain herself from going to pubs, keep away from dancing with other men? It'll be hard on her.

What Kripal Kaur has probably learned from her observation of British society, her daughter, Manjeet Kaur has realized through personal experiences in British schools. As the only Indian girl in a girls' infants school she was a figure of 'much friendly curiosity'. She picked up English quickly, got on well with her classmates, and had only English girl-friends. 'Up to thirteen I was totally English,' she now recalls. 'At fifteen, I began to realize I was different. Because then English girls were going out with boys, something I could not do. I found I had less and less to talk about with my English girl-friends: all they talked about was boy-friends, hair styles and pop singers. I couldn't cut my hair; and English pop singers bore me to tears. So, at seventeen, I realized that I was an Indian. I went to India for a holiday. I loved it.' Here, in a nut-shell, is a case history that illustrates the psychological transformation that the Indian or Pakistani child growing up in Britain often undergoes. As a child matures he becomes increasingly aware of the gap that exists between his parental culture and the British counterpart.

And yet this is only a part of the story. There is still the racial dimension to the Anglo-Asian relationship, Indeed, to most British, Asians are merely 'coloured', a racial tag. As the only Indian student in a girl's school Manjeet Kaur may not have been a recipient of racial abuse or ridicule, but the experiences of many other Asian pupils in British schools have been unpleasant.

13. ibid.

8

ASIAN YOUTH:
RACIAL CONFLICT

If any English girls start quarrelling with me
and calling me bad names like 'you wog'
or 'blackie' or 'nigger', then I tell them,
' You're white pigs' . . . I don't care.
GURENDRA KAUR, a Sikh girl in Birmingham.

Once I was walking down a street. And
there was this car standing with four or five
Englishmen in it. They started shouting
'Oh blackie! Blackie!' I was afraid,
you know. I ran. They laughed at me.
That's why I now hate everyone of them,
these English people.
A Pakistani boy in Bradford.

Present evidence suggests that colour consciousness arises in an
Asian child through one or more of the following ways: parent's
or close friends' experience; personal experience; and observation of social reactions. When, for instance, an Asian child finds
that, in spite of a university degree, his father is working as a
moulder in a factory or as a bus-conductor, he cannot help
becoming aware of colour prejudice, particularly when his Urdu-
or Punjabi-speaking parents generally refer to the British as *gore*
or *chite log* (white people) and to Indians, Pakistanis or Bangla
Deshis as *kale log* (black people).[1]

However, the commonest source of discovery is a personal, or a
close friend's, encounter with English students at school. On the
very first day Deepak Singh went to a senior school in Southall an
English boy called him over at break time, shouted 'You black
wog!' and punched him. Deepak Singh was shaken. He told his
father; but the latter refused to take any action, and said, 'You
must learn to take care of yourself.' He did. He hit the white

1. An Indian boy told the author that his father (a businessman in Delhi)
had made two hundred applications for an office job during his first four
weeks in England in 1958, and had secured one interview.

boy back the next day. This was the tactic more and more Asian boys were to adopt later, and to find effective. But initial experiences have left indelible marks and are still recalled in detail.

Jasbir Singh Khatra, for example, still remembers the hoots of 'Not another one!' that greeted him when he entered his class in a Southall senior school for the first time. (In those days, there were very few Asian or West Indian students in that school). He sat next to an English student; and the latter walked away. 'That's how it started,' recalls Jasbir Singh. 'They started to keep to themselves, and we to ourselves.'[2]

Ridicule of Asian children on a racial basis is not limited to senior schools, as is commonly thought by many white Britons. It occurs at junior school level as well. On his first day in a predominantly white junior school in Burley, Leeds, the young Abdul Malik was so badgered with taunts of 'black' and 'dirty' that he refused to go to school the next day. His mother, herself a teacher, had to tell him that English children are not white, but have 'pig's skin'. Fortified with this knowledge, Abdul Malik returned to school.

In Preetam Sahgal's case, colour consciousness came subtly, through his registering the reaction of white students to a television programme. He said,

> Everything is all right in my boarding grammar school [in East Anglia]. I'm the only Indian boy there. Every Saturday afternoon we watch sports on television, and then one of the Pop shows. There's an Indian boy in the dancing crowd. When the camera pans on him, a cry of disgust goes up from the English boys in the hall. That's when I realize what they *really* think of me. It could be me on television.[3]

It seems that colour prejudice exists in boarding grammar schools to the same degree as it does in secondary modern schools; the only difference lies in its expression. Whereas white middle-class

2. Dispersal of Asian, and West Indian, children over a wide area has further strengthened separatist tendencies. Groups of Asian children arriving, by bus, from districts as far as six miles away from the school feel more, not less, isolated from their English classmates.

3. *New Society*, 1 June 1967.

pupils are generally subtle and muted, working-class children are often crude and open.[4]

If, however, by chance or design, school proves to be a haven of colour blindness or racial tolerance, there is still the outside world which is not so well-ordered and structured. There is always the chance that an Asian adolescent walking down the street would hear the 'Black bastard!' shout from a passing car or motor-cycle. If and when he does, he is not likely to forget it for a long time.

More importantly, there are the stories of assaults on Asian people and property by whites that continually circulate in the community. Mr. A's windows were smashed again by white youths. The other day Mr. B's grocery was broken into.[5] Mrs. C's handbag was snatched by a white youth while she was walking down the street. Mrs. D had her sari plastered with eggs thrown from a passing car as she stood at a street corner. Abdul gave up his job as a bus conductor after having been assaulted by white passengers twice in a week during late-night shifts. The other day Mr. Singh was assaulted and robbed of his wallet and watch as he was returning home from work late at night.[6] And so on.

Violence against Asians reached a climax and became national news during the spring of 1970. From early April to the end of May, the national Press reported numerous instances of violence (one of them fatal) on Asians by Skinheads in London's East End,[7]

4. 'Boys from the local public school [in Tettenhall a middle-class suburb of Wolverhampton] thought coloured people's "manner" and "bearing" rather degrading,' wrote John Heilpern. The *Observer*, 14 July 1968.

5. Describing an Asian-owned shop near her residence, Doris Lessing wrote, 'The shop was broken into once, twice, again, again, again ... The windows were now barred over glass, and boarded up behind the glass, which was shattered, and stayed so; there was no sense in putting new panes in'. *New Statesman*, 26 December 1969.

6. Just under a quarter of all members of the Pakistani Students' Federation in London had been attacked in 1969. The areas included Notting Hill Gate, the Chelsea–Fulham district, Shepherds Bush and King's Cross. *The Times*, 16 April 1970.

7. Ghulam Taslim, son of the *imam* at the East London mosque, had documented thirty-eight attacks on Pakistanis that had occurred in the past few months. *The Times*, 7 April 1970.

Southall, Redhill, Aylesbury, Wolverhampton, Coventry, Birmingham, West Bromwich, and Luton.[8] Under the circumstances, Asian youths could hardly remain unaware of racial differences.

In some areas of Asian settlement, British and Asian youth gangs have been engaging in periodic brawls and fights since the mid-1960s. Karnail Singh, a nineteen-year-old Indian youth in Gravesend, showed the author scars on his face from wounds received in one such fight in 1966. Describing the situation in Southall in early 1968, a white youth said, 'You get done by an Indian group if you're walking on your own, and vice versa. If an Indian is walking on his own he gets done by one of our groups. It's a bit dicey at the moment round here.' On the other side, Harnam Singh said, 'They kick our heads in, and we knife one of them'.

This then was the situation before the controversy over the 1968 Immigration Bill further aggravated it.[9] It was apparant that this legislation was aimed primarily at barring entry into Britain of British Asians from East Africa. As such, Asian settlers' confidence in the white man's word, never too high, plummeted to a new low. Many Indians and Pakistanis, who had earlier taken up British nationality in Britain, re-applied for their original nationality.

Soon afterwards came Enoch Powell's speech in Birmingham. Old fears and suspicions of Asians were revived once again as they felt their economic security, gained over a decade of hard work, suddenly threatened. White antagonism, never far from the surface in Southall or Balsall Heath, manifested itself openly. 'That's when the English boys started openly hating black youths like me,' said Jasbir Singh Khatra. 'There were open arguments – in the classroom. They said that we lived in what they called "unhygenic conditions".' Such arguments flared right across the country. In Bradford, for example, Ramesh Patel, an Indian

8. In a major confrontation between three hundred Skinheads and two hundred Asians in Luton, twenty-five people were injured.

9. 'Every time I appeared on television or issued a Press statement I received many threatening and abusive telephone calls and letters,' said Dhani Ram Prem, an Indian leader in Birmingham. 'This had never happened before.'

student challenged his white class-mates with a bet of £5 to come to his house and decide whether it was cleaner than theirs. No white boy accepted the bet. 'I feel now I'm being looked at as a coloured person *all the time*,' said a Kenyan Asian youth in Handsworth.

Following Enoch Powell's speech, a gang of white youths armed with iron bars appeared outside a Southall school. They beat up a few Asian boys at random before the police arrived. This incident may now be regarded as one among many, but it triggered off a profound transformation among many young Asians.

For instance, it considerably altered the attitudes and outlook of Ranjit Randhawa. He never used to read newspapers before; now he is an avid reader of the *Guardian*. He used to admire Gandhi and Martin Luther King; now he takes interest in Black Power. He asserts 'I'm black, and I'm beautiful,' a statement particularly relevant to him, jet black as he is. He is now ashamed to realize that he once agreed with his mathematics teachers statement that 'If black people had an option they'd all choose to be born white'. He derides his father, a local community leader, for his belief in 'the white liberal version of integration'. He says, 'Before Enoch Powell's speech I was accepting English life, going on slowly, moving with the wheels. But it [the speech] made me stop and take a completely different look at myself and my people.' As a result he has become keenly interested in Indian music and culture, and in events in India. Even his attitude towards the system of arranged marriage has changed. 'I used to think it's a whole lot of rubbish; but now I see that it's got many advantages.'

Ranjit Randhawa's case is an important one as he is representative of a generation of British born Asian children growing up in Britain. He speaks Punjabi but cannot read or write it. He had his hair cut. He even dropped the suffix Singh as he was critical of the beliefs and practices of Sikhism, his parental religion. But Powell's speech, and the national and local events thereafter, reversed the trend. Enoch Powell gave a further impetus to Asians to preserve their culture when he declared in a speech, in November 1968, that the West Indian or Asian, by being born in England does not become an Englishman. In a way, his speeches can be seen as both a cause and a symptom of the trend towards de-anglicization among many Asian settlers and their families.

Most Asian adults make a clear distinction between economic and educational opportunity, and anglicization. As stated earlier, they have little or no intention of giving up their *basic* religo-cultural identity. But they are determined to make steady progress in the economic field. As such they put much faith and hope in their children's education. They often go out of their way to provide the children with a home environment that is conducive to study. They would much rather spend money on their children's education than buy household gadgets or new furniture. Muhammad Faruqi, a Pakistani restaurateur in Bradford, for example, spends £8 a week on the private tuition of his already brilliant son. 'Every penny that I earn is for the education of my children,' says Hameed Baksh, a Pakistani bus driver in London. In this he is reflecting a traditional norm; because in the Indian sub-continent, it is not uncommon for a father to mortgage his property to raise a loan to pay for his son's university education. No wonder then that many Asian children in Britain, actively encouraged by their parents, stay at school beyond the age of fifteen.

David Beetham's study of Handsworth schools showed that among fourth-year students eighty-one per cent of the coloured students wanted to stay at school beyond the statutory age limit; the corresponding figure for English pupils was thirty-six per cent. Furthermore, ten per cent of the coloured pupils, compared with one per cent of the English, proposed to go on to 'full-time further education'.[10]

Asian pupils' enthusiasm for education is being increasingly recognized by the British. 'On the whole Indian and Pakistani children work hard, sometimes too hard, and are deeply motivated by the wish for academic success,' wrote Valerie Knox in *The Times*.[11] 'In many cases Asian children arrived in Slough with little or no English,' said Charles Smyth, the Slough Chief Education Officer, 'but once the handicap was overcome they often forged ahead and became pacesetters at around the age of thirteen or fourteen. Another factor was the young immigrant's dedication

10. *Immigrant School Leavers*, pp. 14–15.   11. 22 March 1968.

to school work, aided by the Asian parents who set great store on education.'[12]

Most Asians do not consider scholastic achievement as an end in itself but hope that their better academic performance will lead to better jobs. And better jobs, in the main, do not necessarily imply becoming doctors, accountants, computer scientists or university lecturers. Their aims remain basically realistic, as is shown by David Beetham's study. He found that seventy-five per cent of Asian school leavers wished to become motor mechanics, engineers, electricians and radio/TV repairers. (On the other hand only twenty-one per cent of English school leavers wished to enter these trades.)[13] But their actual achievement fell woefully short. Only twenty-five per cent managed to enter 'recognized skilled crafts'.[14]

The reason for this wide gap between the aspirations and achievements of Asian school leavers is to be found, principally, in the attitudes and beliefs of Youth Employment Officers and personnel managers. It seems that many Youth Employment Officers continue to employ the tactic of subtly persuading Asian youths to lower their aims to even more 'realistic' levels while most personnel managers continue to associate young Asians with the traits and disadvantages they associate with adult immigrants, that is, that they cannot speak English fluently and that they are not used to machinery and are therefore slow in their movements and accident prone. Hence personnel managers seem almost as reluctant to let young Asians into skilled jobs as they were with their parents.

Similarly office jobs continue to elude young Asians almost to the same degree as they did with their parents. Once again managerial attitudes and beliefs are involved. Julia Gaitskell's study of employment opportunities in office jobs in Croydon, in

12. The *Slough Observer*, 11 July 1969. In a survey conducted by the author (for *New Society*) in 1968, Asian respondents frequently complained about school time-tables for their 'excessive stress on play and games'; lack of a pass and fail system at the end of the academic year (as is the case in schools in the Indian sub-continent); British teachers' leniency regarding homework; and the general lack of formal discipline and punishment at school of the kind that they had experienced.

13. *Immigrant School Leavers*, p. 17.   14. ibid. p. 32.

1966–7, amply bears this out. She concludes that 'the belief that coloured workers are not suitably qualified for white-collar work is widely held and self-reinforcing'. The following examples from her study illustrate the managerial attitudes and beliefs:

The manager of one company explained why he had rejected an applicant for a secretarial post – 'Asian ... a charming woman, forty-ish, capable, been here a long time. Her English was good although not her first language. But we both felt [he and the personnel officer] that if she got excited her English would fall down.' Later in the interview he expressed the opinion 'they [coloured people] do get wildly excited'. An even more interesting comment from another company was: 'He [Lieutenant-Colonel of Engineers, a graduate of Rangoon University] had sapper experience in the post-war Indian Army. Hard to judge whether he was any good ... it was not the British Army, after all.'[15]

All kinds of excuses are invented to deny well-qualified Asians (as well as West Indians) jobs in offices. There is an implication in one of the above-mentioned cases that, had the Indian applicant had British Army experience, his chance of employment would have improved. But present evidence does not support this view. For, in the same study, Julia Gaitskell states that, 'Private employment exchanges reported that, *even with British qualifications*, it was extremely difficult to place coloured applicants in office jobs'.[16]

Nor has the enforcement of the 1968 Race Relations Act made much difference. In the summer of 1969, Roger Jowell and Patricia Prescott-Clarke, respectively a director and research officer at the Social and Community Planning Research Centre, conducted a study to discover racial discrimination in white-collar jobs. They sent out 256 applications for 128 jobs (in sales and marketing, accountancy and office management, electrical engineering, and secretarial) in the East Midlands, West Midlands Greater London and Slough/Reading area – that is, two applications per vacancy. The two letters, matched in terms of personal and professional details, were sent from different parts of the same town; but one was written and signed as if it came from a

15. Cited in E. J. B. Rose and Associates, *Colour and Citizenship*, p. 321.
16. ibid., p. 321. (Author's italics).

British-born white and the other from an Australian/Cypriot/ West Indian/Asian. All applicants stated that they had received their higher or further education in Britain. The result was that whereas the British and Australian applicants were successful (that is, were invited for interviews or sent application forms) in seventy-eight per cent of the cases; the Asians were successful in a mere thirty-five per cent.[17]

These studies and case histories show that the reluctance of most British employers to consider coloured applicants for jobs other than unskilled or semi-skilled is strong. Rational considerations of academic qualifications, trade skills. and experience tend to be overshadowed by unfavourable attitudes and beliefs, and mental reservations. These managerial attitudes and beliefs are, it seems, deeply rooted, which is understandable. After all, contacts between the British and coloured 'natives' stretch far back in the past, a past during which Britain became the most powerful imperial nation ruling vast stretches of Asia and Africa, the coloured continents of the Old World.

17. *Race*, April 1970, pp. 397–413.

PART III: WHITE BRITONS

1　THE 'OPEN DOOR' CLOSES

*The central principle on which our status
rests is largely dependent on the 'open door'
to all Commonwealth citizens. If we believe
in the importance of our great Commonwealth
we should do nothing in the slightest degree
to undermine that principle.*
ARTHUR BOTTOMLEY, (Labour) Shadow
Commonwealth Relations Secretary,
5 December 1958.

*We all know perfectly well that the core
of the problem is coloured immigration. We
must ask ourselves to what extent we want
Great Britain to become a multi-racial
community.*
SIR MARTIN LINDSAY, a Tory M P,
5 December 1958.[1]

*The Labour Party is opposed to the restriction
of immigration as every Commonwealth
citizen has the right as a British subject to
enter this country at will. This has been the
right of subjects of the Crown for many
centuries and the Labour Party has always
maintained it should be unconditional.*
Secretary to the Parliamentary Labour Party
in a letter to Sir Cyril Osborne, 2 June 1961.[2]

*The Government are firmly convinced that an
effective control is indispensable. That we
accept and have always accepted ...*
SIR FRANK SOSKICE, (Labour) Home
Secretary, 17 November 1964.

The presence of coloured immgirants in Britain today can only
be explained in terms of the Commonwealth. And the Common-

1. Cited in Paul Foot, *Immigration and Race in British Politics*, p. 130.
2. ibid., p. 170.

wealth evolved out of the Empire. The history of the Empire, in turn, is tied up with Britain's efforts to emerge as the supreme sea-power, 'the ruler of the waves'. However, the initial impulse was simply to explore the high seas, to follow the example of Christopher Columbus by sailing west. John Cabot did precisely that in 1497. He discovered Newfoundland.[3]

Barbados was another island that fell into English hands as a result of explorations in the New World. That happened in 1605. Two years later the first permanent English settlement in America took place. It was named Jamestown, after King James I. The following year Lord Chief Justice Ellesmore spelt out the legal position of the colonizers when he declared that 'King James I is one King over all his subjects in whatsoever of his dominions they were born'. Thus arose the concept of overseas British subjects.

By 1608, a sea-route to India had been found and the East India Company established to trade with the eastern hemisphere. As India was already well populated the question of British settlement there did not arise even when Britain had, during the eighteenth century, acquired political hegemony over large parts of the sub-continent. After the Indian Mutiny in 1857, the British Parliament removed the intermediary East India Company, and placed India under direct rule. Thus millions of Indians became British subjects.

British authorities, however, showed a contrasting attitude towards the colonies settled by the people of British stock, and the subject-territories inhabited by the 'natives'. For instance, whereas, in 1867, Queen Victoria made Canada a self-governing colony (that is, a dominion), a decade later she formally acquired the title of Empress of India. The remaining territories colonized by British people – Australia and New Zealand – were granted dominion status in 1907.

The First World War unified the Empire as never before. But the attempt made at the Imperial War Conference in 1917 to organize a central organ of government in London to guide the unified Empire, after the war, failed. Instead, for the first time,

3. But it was not until 1583 that formal claims to Newfoundland were made by England.

the idea of a British Commonwealth of Nations, a family of independent dominions, was aired before a generally receptive gathering of politicians. However, it was not until 1931 that the Statute of Westminster formally established the British Commonwealth of Nations.

On the eve of the Second World War, the British Empire was divided into the Commonwealth; India; and the colonies and protectorates. For all practical purposes, the British Commonwealth was 'The White Man's Club'.

After the war, India would have become the first coloured dominion had not her nationalist leaders insisted on complete independence. But having won independence in 1947, Indian leaders decided to remain within the Commonwealth provided it did not conflict with their plans to inaugurate, at a later date, the Republic of India.

The Labour Party, then in power, was anxious to retain India in the Commonwealth. This necessitated a fundamental change in British law and custom. The result was the British Nationality Act, 1948, which was supported by both major parties.[4] This Act divided British citizenship (until then assumed to be a common possession of the British monarch's subjects) into two categories: citizenship of 'the United Kingdom and Colonies'; and citizenship of independent Commonwealth countries, which then meant the white dominions, India and Pakistan. In other words, citizens of a Commonwealth country possessed, as an additional attribute, the *common status* of being British subjects. Thus arose the concept of the New Commonwealth, which, for instance, allowed Indian nationals to retain their status as British subjects even when India became a republic and the Queen lost her right to appoint a Governor-General to India.

Although the *constitutional* relationship between Britain and India and Pakistan altered, there seemed little change in British *attitudes* toward the coloured colonies, past or present. For instance, no effort was made by the British government to tap the manpower resources of India or Pakistan to solve her labour shortage problem.

Britain was then suffering from an acute scarcity of labour. In

4. Paul Foot, *Immigration and Race in British Politics*, p. 45.

June 1946, James Callaghan, then a young MP, called for 'an addition to our population which only immigration can provide'. The fuel crisis in 1947, stemming directly from a labour shortage in the mines, dramatically highlighted the problem. A special Polish Resettlement Act was passed to enable Polish ex-servicemen to settle in Britain. 120,000 Poles did so.[5] The following year, the government sponsored the European Voluntary Workers Scheme. 90,000 European workers, mostly from European Displaced Persons Camps, were imported under this scheme.[6] Meanwhile, instead of helping the West Indians, who had come to Britain under the wartime Overseas Volunteers Scheme, to stay, the government encouraged them to return home, and finally wound up the scheme in 1947.

When, in June 1948, nearly five hundred West Indians boarded the *Empire Windrush*, 'the news of the passenger list began to worry both Whitehall and the House of Commons'.[7] Their arrival in England became a subject of debate in the Commons. 'Merely to read the House of Commons debate of June 1948,' writes Professor Gordon Lewis, 'is to be made to appreciate how British political leadership, including Labour, managed to see it [the arrival of the *Empire Windrush*] not as a free movement of voluntary labour but as a sort of slave transportation engineered by evil agencies somewhere in the Caribbean.'[8]

The old fears and prejudices associated with dark skin were revived and expressed not only in Parliament but in the popular Press as well. Apprehension on this subject was never fully dispelled. Meanwhile, the labour shortage persisted, grew worse even, thus providing an economic magnet for West Indian migrants.

By the early 1950s, as European post-war reconstruction got under way, the European sources of labour dried up. In contrast, the 1952 McCarran-Walter Act began to divert West Indian mi-

5. In contrast, the West Indian ex-servicemen were given no official or unofficial encouragement to settle in Britain. Nor was any attention paid to the ex-serviceman in India and Pakistan.

6. As a result the number of aliens in Britain rose from 159,000 (excluding the 80,000 European refugees) before the war to 429,000 in 1951.

7. Christopher Serpell, *The Listener*, 20 March 1969.

8. *Race Today*, July 1969, p. 79.

grants from America to Britain. Consequently, apprehension in Britain at the rising 'black tide' grew. And with it, voices of alarm.

One of the politicians to raise the alarm was Sir Cyril Osborne, a Tory M.P. Even before the McCarran Act became law he had begun to demand control of coloured immigration. The five-fold increase in West Indian immigration – from 2,000 in 1953 to 10,500 in 1954 – strengthened his case. He received support from the Central Council of the Conservative and Unionist Associations – the policy-making organ of the, then ruling, Tory Party. In 1955, the Central Council demanded that the laws pertaining to aliens be applied to the Commonwealth immigrants.[9]

Demands for coloured immigration control also came from the Labour-controlled Birmingham Council and certain Labour M.P.s representing constituencies in London.

But the government did not yield to these pressures, for reasons that can broadly be divided into external and internal. The leaders of both major parties considered the Commonwealth as 'one of Britain's principal sources of diplomatic influence'. This source was impressive not only in its magnitude – it covered nearly a quarter of the world population spread out from Australasia to northern America through Asia and Africa – but also, more importantly, in its unique exemplary nature. As the head of the Commonwealth, described as 'multi-racial society',[10] Great Britain was seen as a first-rate *moral* leader, setting an example to the rest of the world.

The 1950s were notable for high idealism in regard to the New Commonwealth, blended with a self-congratulatory mood. To have transformed Britain's hitherto imperial role into moral leadership of her ex-colonies – freely bestowed upon her by the latter – pleased and excited British leaders. Never before in the history of empires, they often proclaimed, had there been such a development. They felt that for the New Commonwealth to be meaningful there had to be at least one *common* element, and that

9. Paul Foot, *Immigration and Race in British Politics.*, p. 130.
10. 'The Commonwealth is a multi-racial society and it is in this that its unique opportunity of serving the world and the greatest single peril to its survival both consist,' wrote the authors of *Wind Of Change – The Challenge Of The Commonwealth*, a Conservative Political Centre publication (London 1960), p. 29.

was to be the opportunity for *all* Commonwealth citizens freely to enter or leave the mother country. To limit that right was to undermine the very foundation upon which this institution was built, and to cast a shadow on the quality of moral leadership expected of the mother country.[11]

Internally, coloured immigration was a local issue, limited only to some parts of London and the Midlands. It had not yet impinged on the national mind.

However, the 1958 race riots altered the internal situation considerably. The British public at large became aware of the coloured immigrants' presence. Once that happened, the task of the proponents of immigration control became easier. It was the presence of coloured people that had created a 'colour problem', they argued. So the solution to the problem lay in banning, or severely restricting, coloured immigration.

George Rogers, the Labour M.P. from North Kensington, where the riots occurred, demanded quick legislation to end 'the tremendous influx' of coloured immigrants. Lord Home (later Sir Alec Douglas-Home), then a junior minister for Commonwealth Relations, said in a speech in Vancouver that 'curbs will have to be put on the unrestricted flow of immigrants to Britain from the West Indies'.[12] In this he was supported by the delegates to the Tory Party conference later that year, who by a substantial majority passed a motion demanding control of Commonwealth immigration. The Tory conference was well in tune with the popular mood on this issue because a public opinion poll had earlier shown that seventy-five per cent of those questioned wanted coloured immigration to be controlled.

It was the first time that the general public was polled on this subject. And the results revealed a conflict between the external and internal interests of the country: between the ideal of free entry into Britain of all British subjects, irrespective of colour or

11. 'Is [this] domestic difficulty here [due to the recent increase in the West Indian immigration] an adequate reason for abandoning the whole concept of the Commonwealth,' asked Lady Holly Huggins, an eminent Tory leader, in 1959. 'If we are not prepared to pay that price we shall imperil our whole colonial policy and our whole Commonwealth ideal.' Cited in Paul Foot, *Immigration and Race in British Politics*, p. 155.

12. Cited in Paul Foot, op. cit., p. 131.

race, and the unfavourable reaction of most white Britons to coloured citizens in their midst. This conflict ran straight through Whitehall. There, it was symbolized by the opposing stands taken by the Commonwealth Relations Office and the Colonial Office on the one hand, and the Home Office on the other.[13]

Besides this matter of principle, the government was faced with a genuine administrative problem. Most of the coloured immigrants then were from the colonies in the Caribbean and, as such, were citizens of 'the United Kingdom and Colonies'. To subdivide further this category would probably have necessitated new legislation, a step which could certainly have exposed the government to charges of racialism by critics in Britain and by the coloured Commonwealth countries.

The timing was awkward too; because, in 1958, the West Indian colonies were being federated, and the Federation was to be groomed rapidly for independence. It was hoped that once the Federation was on its feet, it could be persuaded, like India and Pakistan, to control emigration at the source.

All these factors combined to make the government stand firm on the principle of free movement when Sir Cyril Osborne's motion calling for immigration control was discussed in Parliament in December 1958. The motion was defeated, but the debate revealed, more clearly than ever before, the reasoning of many of those demanding immigration control. Sir Martin Lindsay, a Tory M.P., warned that 'A question which affects the future of our own race and breed is not one we should merely leave to chance'.[14] Frank Tomney, a Labour MP, said, 'The coloured races will exceed the white races in a few years by no less than five to one. This will be a formidable problem for the diminishing members of the white races throughout the world'.[15]

Contrary to its outward posture the government was not totally unresponsive to popular feeling. Just a week before the Commons debate on immigration a well-briefed staff member of the *Economist*, wrote:

They [i.e. officials] think that the liberal line – uncontrolled

13. E. J. B. Rose and Associates, *Colour and Citizenship*, pp. 211–12.
14. Cited in Paul Foot, op. cit., p. 130.
15. ibid., p. 190.

immigration – can be held for a few more years, but not indefinitely
... this school in Whitehall and beyond feels that when the tide
of colour rises to a ceiling yet unspecified ... British voters will
demand that some check is imposed.[16]

But when a General Election was announced a year later, the
Tory Party was eminently successful during its election campaign
in generating a euphoric feeling among the voters: 'You never
had it so good.' It was therefore in the interests of Tory candidates, individually and collectively, not to bring up the unpleasant
and controversial issue of coloured immigration in their election
speeches and thus tarnish the 'happy, affluent' image. Because it
supported the 'open door' policy the Labour hierarchy was only
too willing to oblige by keeping quiet on this subject.[17]

Once the election was over, however, the issue was revived.
Undeterred by the statement of R. A. (now Lord) Butler, the then
Home Secretary, in July 1960, 'It is very unlikely that this country
will turn away from her traditional policy of free entry,' Sir Cyril
Osborne kept up the pressure to control Commonwealth immigration. In this he was now actively supported by a group of
newly-elected working and lower-middle class Tory MPs from
the Midlands. Aware of the value of grass-root support, these
lobbyists tried to direct mass opinion in such a way as to produce
the maximum pressure at the right places. The establishment of
the Birmingham Immigration Control Association in October
proved an additional help to them as it encouraged its members
and sympathizers to secure signatures for a mass petition and
deluge MPs with letters.

Soon afterwards, the Home Secretary directed an inter-
departmental committee to re-examine the mechanics of immigration control. [18] This committee favoured control based on the
availability of jobs in Britain. The details were leaked to the Press

16. Cited in E. J. B. Rose and Associates, op. cit., pp. 214–15.

17. Nevertheless, a lot went on behind the scenes, which James Griffiths,
the deputy leader of the Parliamentary Labour Party, felt obliged to point
out later. 'The most depressing aspect of the election result is the whispering
campaign based on racialism against Labour candidates who stood for
equality, and self-determination, for the colonial people.' *West Indian
Gazette*, November, 1969.

18. E. J. B. Rose and Associates, *Colour and Citizenship*, p. 218.

in January 1961, 'possibly by ministers anxious to test the temperature of the voter'.[19]

On 9 February 1961, the *Birmingham Evening Mail* reported that the Home Secretary had told senior ministers that Commonwealth immigration would be controlled. The government duly denied the report and, once again, opposed Sir Cyril Osborne's bill to control Commonwealth immigration. Three months later (in May) the government let each MP know through a circular that there would be no immigration control legislation 'for at least a year'.[20] Nevertheless, by July, the *Observer* was confidently forecasting an outline of future legislation: a labour permit would be the prerequisite for settlement in Britain.

A Gallup poll taken in June showed sixty-seven per cent in favour of restrictions, six per cent for a total ban, and twenty-one per cent for continued free entry. The figures had hardly changed since the 1958 race riots. But there was one important difference. Now the Tory government, and the Tory Party, were more than willing to fall in line with public mood, and did so with speed.

On 11 October, the Tory Party conference passed a motion in favour of immigration control. On 31 October came the government decision, in the text of the Queen's speech, 'to control the immigration to the United Kingdom of British subjects from other parts of the Commonwealth'. The appropriate Bill was published the *next day*. The second reading of the Bill began on 17 November; and the Committee stage and the third reading of the Bill commenced after the Christmas recess. On 27 February the Bill was passed by 277 to 170 votes. The Act became operative on 1 July 1962.

This Act restricted entry to those Commonwealth citizens who had current work vouchers issued by the Ministry of Labour (now the Department of Employment and Productivity). Very shrewdly, the Tory government did not include the actual scheme of control in the Act. Thus the scheme could be changed through the administrative decisions of the Ministry without reference to Parliament.

19. ibid., p. 218.
20. Paul Foot, *Immigration and Race in British Politics*, p. 135.

In 1962 the Ministry of Labour designed a graded system of work vouchers: category A, for those Commonwealth citizens who had specific jobs to come to; category B, for those who possessed special skills or qualifications; and category C, for unskilled persons without definite prospects of employment. Right from the beginning, the government had indicated that they might, from time to time, impose limits in the C category. But, in practice, this category was abolished altogether in August 1964. A year later limits were to be imposed on the number of A and B work vouchers – and that too by a Labour government.

Throughout the late 1950s and the early 1960s, when the issue of immigration control was raised and publicly debated, the Labour Party consistently opposed restrictions. Popular sentiment and opinion polls notwithstanding, the party stuck firmly to its position. But in the end the party bowed before popular opinion. It took much longer than the Tory Party to yield to the voters' pressure; but when it did, it did so completely.

There was a variety of reasons for the delayed change in the Labour Party's position on Commonwealth immigration. The party had come into existence in 1900 to fight for the under-dog. As such, it identified itself, emotionally at least, with the exploited millions in the colonies. It was favourably disposed to the idea of self-rule by India. It was also committed to the socialist doctrine of the 'Brotherhood of Man'.

More specifically, the New Commonwealth was the creation of the post-war Labour government. Therefore the Labour Party, even when in Opposition, remained deeply attached to the concept of a multi-racial Commonwealth. When the demand for immigration control first arose in 1955, it was the Commonwealth Sub-Committee of the party's National Executive which stated publicly that it had no doubt that 'the [immigration] problem is based on colour'. Following the 1958 race riots, the Labour Party stated that 'any form of British legislation limiting Commonwealh immigration into this country would be disastrous to our status in the Commonwealth and to the confidence of Commonwealth people'.

Until then appeals to the 'Commonwealth ideal', like the 'Brotherhood of Man', had the advantage of, what Paul Foot calls 'electoral irrelevance'.[21] But as the ideal began to be associated, by more and more Britons, with increasing numbers of black faces in streets, pubs and factories, it lost its electoral irrelevancy.

Indeed, it became an electoral liability, as shown by the results of the 1959 general election[22] and, later, in April 1961, the by-election in a Birmingham constituency, when the Birmingham Immigration Control Association's candidate secured twice as many votes as the Labour candidate.

And yet the national leaders of the Labour Party remained firm on their commitment to the 'open-door' policy. To them – and especially to Hugh Gaitskell, the party's leader in Parliament – upholding a moral principle was more important than short-term electoral popularity. The Labour Party declined a second reading of the Commonwealth Immigrants Bill in November 1961 because the Bill introduced control, and because 'it was widely held to introduce colour bar into our legislation'. The latter was a valid claim, and was confirmed when the Tory Home Secretary stated, during the Parliamentary debate, that controls would not apply to the Irish Republic because of 'practical difficulties'.

But the question still remained: how long could a mass organization, such as the Labour Party, continue to disregard popular opinion on a subject that mattered to British voters in direct, personal terms? The conflict between a moral ideal and a practical reality became dramatized in the person of Patrick Gordon-Walker, the Shadow Foreign Secterary, who represented Smethwick. Along with Hugh Gaitskell, Patrick Gordon-Walker made a passionate speech against the Bill in Parliament in November. During the Christmas recess, however, he was made aware of the strong disapproval of his stand by many of his white constituents. Consequently he had to refrain from attacking the Bill during the final debate in February 1962, not from any lack of sincerity, but perhaps because of the need to be wholly representative of his constituency. He did not vote for or against the Bill: he either abstained or was paired.[23]

The final summing up of the Labour stand was left to Denis

21. op. cit, p. 191.   22. See footnote 17, p. 192.
23. Paul Foot, *Immigration and Race in British Politics*, p. 174

Healey, the Party's spokesman on colonial affairs. He qualified Labour's opposition to the Bill thus:

> If the information collected by a serious survey of the whole problem revealed that immigration control was necessary, we should regard it as essential to consult the other Commonwealth governments ... to see how this could be achieved with the minimum of damage to their interests and to their confidence of our loyalty and good will.

Despite repeated questioning he refused to state whether or not the Labour Party, if elected to power, would repeal the Act. Thus the Labour Party started to register, and to yield to, popular feelings on this issue.

After the change of leadership, following Hugh Gaitskell's death in January 1963, the Labour Party began to smell victory at the polls, and became more responsive to the voters' feelings. A straw poll of Labour MPs taken in July 1963 revealed that opinion had moved considerably in favour of control.[24] Some MPs even suggested giving unqualified support to the 1962 Act when it came up for renewal in November. But a complete renunciation of its previous policy, reiterated until recently with moral fervour, would have meant a politically embarrassing admission of poor judgement, which the Tories would probably have exploited to the hilt. So, in the end, a compromise was hammered out.

Harold Wilson, the new leader, spelled it out in Parliament. 'We do not contest the need for control of immigration into this country,' he said, and then went on to suggest that certain 'loopholes' in the Act must be eliminated. He offered a bargain to the Home Secretary: if the government would initiate consultations with the Commonwealth governments to get control from their end, his party would not vote against the renewal of the Act. This offer was disparagingly turned down. The Labour Party therefore had no choice but to vote against the Act. This was madness, or so thought many Labour supporters up and down the country.

Letters began arriving at the Labour Party headquarters in London warning that Labour would probably lose the General Election (expected at any time) on the issue of coloured immi-

24. Paul Foot, *Immigration and Race in British Politics*, p. 175.

gration. Most of the letters pointed out that 'it was easy to sit back in London and be idealistic about the matter, but that living with the problem was a more serious business'.[25] The point was not lost on the drafters of the Labour Party manifesto for the October 1964 election. They stated:

Labour accepts that the number of immigrants entering the United Kingdom must be limited. Until a satisfactory agreement covering this can be negotiated with the Commonwealth, a Labour government will retain immigration control.

During his whistle-stop tour, Harold Wilson himself had a taste of the popular mood. Almost everywhere he spoke in England, the question of coloured immigration was raised. In some cases the Labour candidates took an offensive stand against their rivals. Nearly fourteen per cent of the Labour candidates (compared with eight per cent of the Tories) mentioned immigration in their election speeches, stressing that their party would continue immigration control.[26] As if this were not enough, some Labour candidates blamed the Tories for 'the whole wave of immigration'. 'Labour has not been in power for thirteen years to control the flow of immigrants, and before that Southall had not been in difficulties,' said the Labour candidate in Southall.[27] 'Large-scale immigration has occured only under the Tory government,' said a leaflet issued by the agent of Dr David Kerr, Labour candidate for Wandsworth Central.

Just before election day, the Smethwick Labour Party issued a leaflet on Patrick Gordon-Walker's behalf: 'Immigrants only arrived in Smethwick in large numbers during the past ten years – while the Tory government was in power.' None of this cut much ice with the Smethwick electors. Patrick Gordon-Walker's votes went down from 20,670 to 14,916. He lost. And his defeat was greeted with chants like 'Where are your niggers now, Walker?' and 'Take your niggers away.' Patrick Gordon-Walker was made to pay the price for his anti-immigration-control speech in Parliament three years earlier which had, it seemed, earned him the label of 'Nigger Lover'.

25. ibid., p. 178.   26. ibid., p. 181.
27. The *Middlesex County Times*, 5 October 1964.

This epithet remained with him even when he contested, in January 1965, a very safe Labour constituency in Leyton, specifically vacated for his benefit. He lost again. This time his defeat reduced the Labour government's majority to three. Almost simultaneously a private poll indicated that ninety-five per cent of the voters favoured stringent control of coloured immigration. The Labour government was visibly shaken. It seemed to have realized that simply being for immigration control was not enough: controls had to be tightened. Furthermore, the government had to be *seen* to be getting tough on the issue.

The Tory Opposition was competing with the government in its enthusiasm for further controls. In February 1965, Sir Alec Douglas-Home, the then Leader of the Opposition, demanded a reduction in the number of Commonwealth immigrants allowed entry, and the inclusion of dependants in the limit set on overall numbers. The following month Sir Cyril Osborne introduced a motion in Parliament that only those Commonwealth citizens whose parents or grandparents were born here should be allowed to enter until local authorities had solved their problems.[28] 162 Tories voted for this motion, including Sir Alec Douglas-Home, Edward Heath, Enoch Powell and Anthony Barber.

Not to be outdone, first the Home Secretary, and then the Prime Minister, stated that 'evasions' were almost fatally eroding the Act. 'Since the Act is not working as intended,' said Harold Wilson in March 1965, 'a fresh examination of the whole problem is necessary.' In a speech at a Labour Party rally, Richard Crossman, the Minister for Housing, criticized the Tories for instituting 'completely ineffective controls'.[29]

To prove that *Tory* controls were indeed ineffective the government produced figures of 'evasions' among Commonwealth immigrants. During 1963 and 1964, it was claimed, some 10,255 citizens from the New Commonwealth had 'evaded' immigration controls.

Close study of a plethora of statistics produced by the govern-

28. Three years later, this principle was incorporated by the Labour Government in its Commonwealth Immigrants Act *without* the qualification of local authorities 'solving their problems'.
29. Cited in Paul Foot, op. cit., p. 183.

ment revealed that the figure of 10,255 was arrived at by subtracting the 'total deliberately admitted for settlement' from the 'net overall gain'. Corresponding subtraction for the countries of the Old Commonwealth (Canada, Australia and New Zealand) showed a difference of 15,538. But a footnote to the table of 'Evasion Figures' stated: 'It is doubtful whether most of these have the intention of permanent settlement'. By offering a favourable, yet subjective, judgement on one set of figures, the government showed that it was (racially) biased. 'The so-called "evidence" has been presented selectively to create public alarm about evasion by coloured immigrants alone,' wrote Sheila Patterson.[30] But this might well have been the government's intention.

The exercise of referring to the 'evasions' and associating these with coloured immigrants seemed to serve a dual political purpose. It demonstrated that the Labour government was ever vigilant, and had indeed detected 'evasions' that had taken place during the Tory administration. This meant one-up for Labour. Also, constant repetition of the 'facts' of evasion,[31] was expected to demoralize the liberal lobby, and likely to moderate its criticism of the restrictive measures that the government planned to announce within the next few months.

This is precisely what the White Paper, presented to Parliament in August 1965, did. It increased the immigration officer's discretionary powers, authorizing him, among other things, to make police registration a condition for entry if he doubted the entrant's genuineness. It gave the Home Secretary power to deport a Commonwealth citizen. As for the numbers, the White Paper placed a limit on work vouchers at 8,500 a year, a reduction of about 11,500 from the current yearly intake. Furthermore, the permissible age for the entry of dependent children was lowered from eighteen to sixteen.

Among those who approved of the White Paper were Sir Cyril Osborne and Peter Griffiths, the victor of Smethwick. Their stand was vindicated. More significantly, a Gallup poll showed that

30. *Immigration and Race Relations in Britain, 1960–67*, p. 34.
31. 'By constant repetition, the government's estimates of "evasions" have acquired the status of fact,' wrote Sheila Patterson, op. cit., p. 34.

while eighty-eight per cent of the population supported the White Paper, only five per cent opposed it.[32] Government action was well in step with the general feeling in the country. Provincial papers, tuned to popular opinion at the local level, called the White Paper 'sensible', 'realistic' and 'reasonable'.[33]

In contrast, the national Press, particularly the 'quality' papers, condemned the document, pointing out the immorality of slashing Commonwealth immigration while Irish and European immigration continued unabated.[34] This then was the measure of the chasm that lay between the British mass and the liberal, intellectual minority. Although small in size, the liberal lobby was quite vocal. In criticism of the White Paper, the National Council for Civil Liberties came out with a publication, *Prejudice or Principle*; the Campaign Against Racial Discrimination produced *A Spur To Racialism;* and the Young Fabians, *Strangers Within.* Plans were made to raise the issue at the impending TUC conference; but these failed. The TUC leadership adroitly managed to avoid a debate on the subject.

Liberal hopes were then pinned on the emergency motion at the forthcoming Labour Party conference asking the government to withdraw the White Paper. These hopes were never realized. The motion was lost. The only major block of votes for the motion came from the Transport and General Workers' Union; but that was not enough to win an overall majority. Commenting on this the *Economist* wrote:

The representatives of the British working man faithfully reflected his aversion to any spirit of universal brotherhood which touched him too closely.[35]

As expected, Harold Wilson staunchly defended the White Paper. He went on to repudiate 'the libel that government policy is based either on colour or racial prejudice'. But then had not the Tory leaders too resented and repudiated the label of racialism thrown at them by critics at the time of the 1961 Commonwealth Immigrants Bill? What, then, was the *fact*? 'The Bill's real

32. ibid., p. 410.   33. ibid., p. 45.
34. Thirty thousand Irishmen migrated to Britain in 1965.
35. 12 October 1965.

purpose was to restrict the influx of coloured immigrants,' wrote William Deedes, the then Minister without Portfolio, seven years later. 'We were reluctant to say as much openly.'[36]

This time the Tory leaders were in no doubt concerning the *real* purpose of the 1965 White Paper. They fully supported it. At the Tory conference later that year they harped on the fact that the Labour government had been so quickly, and so thoroughly, converted to their viewpoint. Satisfied with this achievement, they refrained from making further demands for controls. It seems the 'Dutch Auction on Restrictionism' was over – for the time being at least.

From a historical viewpoint, the period 1961–5 saw the collapse of *laissez-faire* policies regarding coloured immigration and the settlement of coloured immigrants. A *laissez-faire* policy is very comfortable to follow: it means doing nothing. And this is exactly what the Tory government did regarding coloured immigration until popular anxiety forced its hand in 1961.

Simultaneously, however, another problem had grown. It concerned coloured settlers. They were being denied equal opportunity in jobs and housing, and equal access to public places. The *laissez-faire* policy in this case meant refusal by the authorities to admit that such problems existed. But as the traditional 'open-door' policy regarding Commonwealth citizens became vulnerable, slightly more attention was paid to the problem of their settlement. For instance, from 1961 onwards, Fenner (now Lord) Brockway's Bill against racial discrimination – submitted to Parliament almost every year since 1951 – began receiving bipartisan support.

36. *Race Without Rancour*, a Conservative Political Centre publication, 1968, p. 10.

2 COLOURED IMMIGRATION AND RACE RELATIONS: A COMPOSITE POLICY

Nobody thinks prejudice can be cured by legislation ... But legislation can check open and offensive manifestations of prejudice.
TOM DRIBERG, a Labour MP, 6 October 1967.

This [1968 Commonwealth Immigrants] Bill ... must be considered at the same time, and in accordance with, the [1968] Race Relations Bill ... which is to be introduced by the government during the next six weeks.
JAMES CALLAGHAN, (Labour) Home Secretary, 22 February 1968.

For this [1968 Race Relations] Act to work, you need goodwill from both sides. That's just not there.
A Pakistani garage mechanic.[1]

Fenner Brockway's views and attitudes on race and immigration were in total contrast to Sir Cyril Osborne's. Whereas Sir Cyril Osborne, from the early 1950s, devoted himself to the question of coloured immigration, Fenner Brockway concentrated on redressing the problem of racial discrimination in Britain. He first introduced a Private Member's Bill on the subject in 1951. Nothing came of it. He made the next attempt in 1953, but was again unsuccessful.

By then, however, the Commonwealth Sub-Committee of the Labour Party's National Executive showed enough interest to invite an opinion from Kenneth Little, an early researcher in the field of race relations. In his memorandum Kenneth Little concluded that there was 'a good case both in principle and in fact for enactment ... of ... legislation ... as a means of stirring the national conscience and of creating a new standard of public

1. *Daily Mirror*, 24 April 1968.

behaviour in relation to coloured people'.[2] But the Labour Party took no further action.

As for the Tories the problem was non-existent. In 1954, Sir Winston Churchill (as Prime Minister) refused to instruct ministers to prevent the operation of a colour bar because 'the laws of this country are well known, and . . . there is no need for new instructions'.[3] A similar sentiment was echoed two years later by Gwilym Lloyd-George, the then Home Secretary, when he said, 'I have no information that there is any particular problem as far as these people [the Commonwealth immigrants] are concerned'.[4] That this view was shared by most legislators became apparent when, in 1957, Fenner Brockway's Bill on racial discrimination was talked out in Parliament because less than forty members were present.

Even the 1958 race riots did not shake off the complacency of the Tories. The Tory government viewed the race riots in terms of law and order and a breach of the peace. British law was quite unambiguous regarding that; and the stiff sentences imposed on the rioters amply illustrated this, it argued. However, the Labour Party was sufficiently disturbed by the event to demand that the government outlaw 'the public practice of discrimination'. The Tory response to that was aptly summarized by Lord Chesham: '[an] Act . . . would run the risk of recognizing the existence of discrimination in a way which might draw attention to it, and would tend rather to foster it than do away with it'.[5]

The Tory government's wish to leave the *status quo* undisturbed was much too strong. And despite the riots, it persisted. The government resisted demands for immigration control as firmly as it did the demands for law against racial discrimination. But as practical considerations and popular opinion began to undermine the doctrine of 'open door', realism began to creep into the assessment of the coloured settlers' position in British society.

In fact, following the 1962 Commonwealth Immigrants Act,

2. Cited in Bob Hepple, *Race, Jobs and the Law in Britain*, p. 129.
3. ibid., p. 130.
4. Cited in E. J. B. Rose and Associates, *Colour and Citizenship*, p. 200.
5. Bob Hepple, op. cit., p. 130.

a composite doctrine gradually began to emerge: control the number of coloured immigrants coming in, and assure equal rights to those already here. The Labour Party showed signs of following this pattern of thinking. It combined its shift towards immigration control with a stronger commitment to law against racial discrimination and incitement.

When elected to power in 1964, the Labour administration formally announced its decision to introduce a Race Relations Bill. But before the Bill was published, in April 1965, enough hints had been dropped regarding impending (further) restrictions on Commonwealth immigration to cancel, in advance, much of the enthusiastic support that this Bill would otherwise have received from the liberal lobby. Many liberals now considered the presentation of this Bill more as an example of political tightrope-walking rather than proof of the Labour government's positive commitment to racial equality.

The Race Relations Bill's declared intention was 'to prohibit discrimination on racial grounds in places of public resort ...; to penalize incitement to racial hatred; and to amend Section 5 of the Public Order Act, 1936'. The absence of vital areas of housing and employment from the Bill was criticized by liberal opinion both inside and outside Parliament. Answering this criticism, the Home Secretary maintained that the Bill was concerned 'basically ... with public order'.[6]

The only consolation to the liberals was that the practice of racial discrimination was classified as a criminal offence. But this was precisely where the Tory Opposition found the Bill objectionable, and declined it a second reading (in May 1965). The Opposition spokesman declared that they would tolerate the measure if the Home Secretary drastically cut Commonwealth immigration,[7] and withheld the Bill until conciliatory procedures regarding racial discrimination had been thrashed out. This offer was rejected; and the Bill was given a second reading by 258 votes to 249.

But then, quite inexplicably, Sir Frank Soskice, the Home

6. Bob Hepple, op. cit., p. 133.
7. The Tory Party thus officially linked further controls on Commonwealth immigration with legislation against racial discrimination.

Secretary, retracted his position to accommodate the Tory viewpoint before the Committee stage of the Bill began. He substituted criminal sanctions against the discriminator with conciliation between the discriminator and the discriminated to be undertaken by a special body, the Race Relations Board. His gambit paid off. He secured the co-operation of the Tories on the Committee. By early August, the government established its restrictionist bona fides on immigration by publishing the White Paper, thus winning further Tory approval. Consequently, when the Race Relations Bill was finally passed into law in September, it had the stamp of a bipartisan measure.

Taken together the 1965 White Paper and the 1965 Race Relations Act signalled the convergence of the two major political parties on the issues of immigration control and racial justice. An advance, albeit minor, on the front of racial justice for the coloured minority was agreed to by the Tories in exchange for a retreat by the Labourites on the front of immigration control. The Tories tempered their opposition (expressed as late as 1964) to a law against racial discrimination; the Labourites committed themselves firmly to 'realistic controls, flexibly administered', as their 1966 election manifesto stated.

By March 1966, when the General Election took place, Labour had established its restrictionist bona fides with the voters. As a result, many traditional Labour voters in areas of coloured settlement, such as Smethwick, who in 1964[8] had abstained from voting in protest against Labour's softness on coloured immigration, returned to the fold, thus enabling Labour candidates to regain their seats or improve their majorities, and making Peter Griffiths redundant. The Labour victor over Peter Griffiths became so effusive over the result that he declared jubilantly, 'We've buried the race issue!' But his was not to be the last laugh, as subsequent events were to show.

The Tories wanted to tighten controls even further. Their manifesto proposed that new entrants be allowed in only on a

8. 'In 1964, the experts say, the race issue probably cost Labour another three seats besides Smethwick, which they could have won without it,' wrote Nora Beloff, the political columnist of the *Observer*. 15 March 1970.

probationary basis for two years, and that they be required to register the number of dependants they wished to bring over. More significantly, the idea of government financial assistance to those immigrants who wished to return home, first mooted by Sir Alec Douglas-Home in February 1965, was enshrined in the document. However, these proposals were not flaunted with much enthusiasm during the election campaign because of the realization among Tory leaders that, since October 1964, the British voters had been subjected to a continual barrage of argument and counter-argument on this issue; and that it was time to let passions cool.

After the elections the country did have a comparatively calm period in this field. It seemed that the leaders of the two main parties had reached a tacit understanding to keep race and immigration out of party politics.[9] In any case, they were generally agreed on a common prescription of minimum coloured immigration and maximum 'integrative' effort.

An example of the tacit understanding and 'gentlemanly behaviour' between the two parties was provided by Duncan Sandys, a former Tory cabinet minister. In October 1966, he privately warned Roy Jenkins, the then Home Secretary, of the danger of a 'flood' of Asian immigrants from Kenya. He was asked to refrain from publicizing his fears. He did so. It was thus that a comparative calm was maintained on this highly sensitive issue. 'For the moment ... there is a feeling of stabilization,' wrote Enoch Powell in early 1967, 'and the subject has disappeared below the surface of public consciousness.'[10]

This feeling, however, could be maintained only as long as *all* prominent politicians refrained from injecting the subject into party politics; and the British public remained assured that coloured immigration was at its lowest possible level, and declining. Any indication of a contrary trend was, and is, likely

9. 'Political leaders have expressed a wish to keep it [the issue of race and immigration] out of party politics,' wrote William Deedes, a Tory MP and a former minister. *Race Without Rancour*, p. 21.

10. Enoch Powell then went on to prophesy that 'There will be subsequent phases, when the problem will resume its place in public concern and in a more intractable form, when it can no longer be dealt with simply by turning the inlet tap down or off.' The *Daily Telegraph*, 16 February 1967.

to revive public unease. Signs that this might happen began to appear in early 1967. And on the very issue on which Duncan Sandys had been asked to keep quiet: Asians from Kenya.

The central question about the Asians in Kenya was this: could those with British passports enter Britain freely? That is, were they exempt from the 1962 Commonwealth Immigrants Act, or not? This question was raised *publicly* as early as February 1967, and was answered quite unambiguously by, among others, Donald MacColl, a former Deputy Passport Officer in Kenya: Yes, they were exempt.[11]

This was in contrast to the government's silence on the issue. The *Guardian* quoted one Asian, who had entered Britain, as saying that, 'British officials had made no attempt to apprise us of our rights, unless they were asked point blank whether a particular person was free to come here. The position had been deliberately obscured.'[12]

Confusion and obscurity continued for some time until the Court of Appeal ruled that the 1962 Act did not apply to residents of former British colonies with passports issued by the British government.[13] That was when the fear of yet another 'black tide' gripped those Tory leaders who had made it a point to safeguard Britain's racial interests. Enoch Powell was one of them.

In a speech at Deal on 18 October 1967, Enoch Powell said, 'Hundreds of thousands of people in Kenya, who never dreamt they belonged to this country, started to belong to it like you and me ... It is monstrous that a loophole in legislation should be able to add another quarter of a million to that score [of Commonwealth immigrants].'

There was no loophole in the 1962 Act. It applied to the nationals of independent Commonwealth countries and overseas British subjects whose passports were issued by the Colonial governments, such as in Hong Kong. But the passports to Asian and European settlers in Kenya were issued by the British government through its agent in Kenya – the British High Commission.

11. The *Guardian*, 4 February 1967.   12. ibid.
13. Cited in *Immigration And Race*, Conservative Political Centre, London, 1968, p. 5.

This had happened because of pledges given to *both* these groups of settlers by the Tory government at the time of Kenyan independence in 1963:[14] they could, if they wished, retain British citizenship after independence and receive British passports. The main reason for offering this pledge was to save them from becoming stateless.

In any case, the number of Asians in Kenya entitled to British citizenship and passports in 1967 was nowhere near the quarter-million that Enoch Powell stated. At the time of independence there were 185,000 Asian, and 53,000 European, settlers in Kenya. Of these Asians, 60,000 automatically became Kenyan citizens, as they and their fathers were born in Kenya. Another 10,000 were nationals of India and Pakistan. The remaining 115,000 were offered the choice of Kenyan citizenship if they applied within two years after independence. Some 20,000 did so (compared with 975 Europeans). It meant that 95,000 Asians either had, or were entitled to have, British passports.

In spite of their British passports and the Home Office's silence on the subject, they were placed into a distinct category 'Exempt U.K. Citizens' and counted, when they entered Britain. 6,149 such citizens came to Britain in 1965; and 8,846 in 1966.

In 1967, the Kenya government, in pursuance of its Kenyanization policy, passed a law according to which non-citizens could work and live in Kenya only on a temporary basis. This led to a rise in the migration rate of Asians with British passports. By September 1967, 8,443 had entered Britain. And it was at this stage that Enoch Powell blew his policemen's whistle.

Not that the government needed this warning. They were well

14. Duncan Sandys was the Commonwealth and Colonial Secretary when this happened. Iain Macleod, once Colonial Secretary in a Tory government, said in an open letter to Duncan Sandys: 'We did it. We meant to do it. And in any event we had no other choice.' (The *Spectator*, 23 February 1968.) Further confirmation came from Hugh Fraser who served at the Colonial Office from 1960–2, and from Lord Landsdowne, a former Colonial Junior Minister, who said, 'I understood, as Mr Iain Macleod understood, what we were doing. I understood we were making a solemn undertaking to these people.' However, Duncan Sandys maintained that no specific undertaking was given either to Parliament or in the legislation. Cited in E. J. B. Rose and Associates, *Colour and Citizenship*, pp. 611–12.

aware of the 'danger', but were in a moral cleft-stick, as the *Sun*, commenting on Enoch Powell's speech at Deal, pointed out: 'No feasible way of legally differentiating between them [European settlers in Kenya] and Asiatics who are granted passports by the High Commission in Nairobi has been devised'.[15]

The situation paralleled that in 1961. Then, too, the Tory government had to design a Bill which would serve the purpose of controlling coloured immigration without being labelled 'racialist'. But at least then the Tory government had stated publicly that Commonwealth immigration would not be controlled for a year. The Labour government did nothing of the sort. It kept quiet.

As it was, repeated statements by right-wing Tories were beginning to draw public attention. What they needed to capture public imagination was a dramatic news-story. It came. In January 1968 there were front-page reports in the Press of clandestine arrivals of Pakistanis. Public anxiety on coloured immigration, never fully dormant, was revived; and the drama of 1961-2 was re-enacted. Just as the small-pox cases in December 1961, attributed to the arrival of a Pakistani girl-immigrant, had led to hysteria, the clandestine arrivals, and subsequent arrests, of Pakistanis had a similar effect now. In that climate the issue of Kenya Asians was soon blown up into a major crisis.

By early February, Enoch Powell was speaking of 'the cloud no bigger than a man's hand, of communalism and communal agitation in Britain'. Sir Cyril Osborne predicted ominously that 'If we go on like this, there will be more blacks than whites in seventy years' time'. Duncan Sandys formally asked the government 'to subject those Asians in East Africa who acquired U K passports on Independence to the same restrictions as other Commonwealth immigrants', and followed this up with a motion in Parliament (on 13 February) containing a provision for tighter restrictions for Commonwealth immigrants.

Outside Parliament panic seemed to seize the mass media. The

15. 19 October 1967. The *Sun* went on to say, 'Mr Edward Heath and his colleagues are alarmed at the possible charge that they would like to discriminate on purely racial grounds in favour of Europeans as against Asiatics.'

Daily Mirror, on 15 February, ran a leader article on the front page headlined: 'ON IMMIGRATION – A free-for-all? Or government control? Or an Alf Garnett election?' It went on to warn that 'The country now faces the prospect of an *uncontrolled* flood of Asian immigrants from Kenya.'[16]

This size of this potential 'flood' was 66,000 people,[17] because, of the 95,000 Asians theoretically entitled to settle in Britain, 29,000 had already done so. Even if all the 66,000 had come in 1968, they would not have made up the net loss of 84,000 that Britain had suffered due to excess of emigration over immigration in the preceding year.

But in the emotional climate of mid-February 1968, the number of those who could come to Britain 'tomorrow' was inflated from day to day: from the original quarter-million to a million, and then to two million![18] 'Fearing betrayal, the Asians are coming faster,' wrote the *Sunday Times* in an editorial on 18 February. 'Fearing a deluge, the British, led by politicians who exaggerate its proportions, are running daily more scared.'

Two days later the bipartisan policy on coloured immigration formally collapsed. The Tory shadow cabinet demanded a tightening of existing controls, return of illegal immigrants, registration of dependants by applicants for work vouchers, and financial help for those wishing to return home. It was the first time since the 1966 general election that the Tory shadow cabinet issued a public statement on this issue. On Kenya Asians, it proposed that the entry of British passport-holders be phased.

The government legislation that followed two days later went much further. The Bill restricted the right of entry *only* to those British passport-holders who had substantial connections with the U K by virtue of birth, or their fathers' or grandfathers'

16. 'Immigration lends itself to maritime metaphor,' wrote Brian Wenham in the *New Republic* of 16 March 1968. 'The damage done to whitey's psyche by this puffed-up prose must be considerable.'

17. Or the population of one British town, such as Chesterfield, Derbyshire.

18. Curiously enough, the alarmists, among them the Lord Chancellor, Lord Gardiner, forgot to add the three million Irish from the Republic of Ireland to this score.

birth, in the U K. Thus a 'non-racial' device was employed to make a 'racial' distinction between the Asian and British settlers in East Africa.[19] As for the rest, they were to be allowed in at the rate of 1,500 special vouchers a year.[20] For the Commonwealth immigrants already here, there were further restrictions on the ages of dependent children and parents wishing to join them.

There was a strong protest against the Bill, especially its 'grandfather' clause, from the liberal quarters. But, on the whole, Labour backbenchers evinced little interest or concern. At the Parliamentary Labour Party meeting on 22 February, there was a greater outcry against the location of a new airport than against this Bill.[21] This provided a dramatic contrast to the 1961–2 period. The 1961 Commonwealth Immigrants Bill had aroused strong passions. The public controversy on the Bill had continued for months. The Parliamentary debate had dragged on for weeks, whereas the 1968 Commonwealth Immigrants Bill was presented, debated, and passed through both houses of Parliament in a week. The Act became law immediately – on 1 March 1968.

From both legal and moral viewpoints, the 1968 Act was far more objectionable than the 1962 Act. The latter curtailed the rights of Commonwealth citizens; but then the British Commonwealth was not a national or supra-national entity. The 1968 Act curtailed rights implicit in a document issued by the British government. It denied, in the words of the International Commission of Jurists, 'the right of every person to enter the country of which he is a citizen, which has been recognized in the universal declaration of human rights and all the other human rights conventions that have been adopted by the international community since the war'.[22] Furthermore, as the Commission

19. '[The Home Secretary] Mr. Callaghan's pitiful sophistries, such as the claim that the distinctions made by his new Act are "geographical and not racial", cannot disguise what every honest person knows – that this is the first incontestably racialist law to be placed on the statute books,' stated the *New Statesman* editorial on 1 March 1968.
20. In May 1971 this quota was raised to 3,000 vouchers a year.
21. The *Guardian*, 23 February 1968.
22. The *Guardian*, 12 June 1968.

pointed out, 'The fact that these citizens are non-white inevitably gives the legislation a racial character'.[23]

The overriding factor in both cases, however, was the same: to keep the inflow of coloured immigration to an absolute minimum. If it became necessary even to devalue British passports to achieve this objective, so be it. That seemed to be the general feeling among British legislators. Only 62 (out of a total of 630 MPs) voted against the 1968 Bill; and only 31 against the third reading.[24] This, among other things, made the *New Statesman* declare, 'The government, shadow cabinet and a large majority in the House of Commons endorse ... [the] attitudes that people are coloured or white before they are human beings and British citizens, that official impartiality between races is a pipedream'.[25]

The Bill was introduced and passed in such haste that no opinion polls could be taken.[26] However, polls taken after the Bill's passage showed overwhelming support for restrictions on coloured immigration: eighty-one per cent among Labour voters, seventy-eight per cent among Tory supporters, and seventy-three per cent among Liveral voters.[27] Overall, thirty-nine per cent were for a *total* ban on coloured immigration. There were no doubt 'millions of Alf Garnetts in the country' – as David Ennals, the Junior Minister at the Home Office, put it – whose minds were closed on this issue. They seemed unable, or unwilling, to register the fact that work vouchers for coloured Commonwealth immigrants had been cut drastically from 28,678 in 1963 to 4,721 in 1967. If the current total figures for coloured immigrants (in 1967) remained more or less at the 1964 level (of 53,000), it was because there had been an increase in the number of

23. According to a report released by the European Commission of Human Rights, the British government itself admitted that the 'intention and effect' of the 1968 Commonwealth Immigrants Act is one of racial discrimination. The *Observer*, 22 November 1970.

24. Cited in David McKie and Chris Cook, *Election '70*, Panther Books, 1970, pp. 100–101.

25. 1 March 1968.

26. However, Richard Boston wrote, 'The government claims [that] a large majority of the population – perhaps 75 per cent – was in favour of the Act.' *New Society*, 28 March 1968.

27. But in Parliament, the Liberal Party unanimously opposed the Bill.

dependants of immigrants, already here, arriving. An immediate drastic cut in absolute numbers was impossible without a legislative bar on the families. Such legislation, besides being inhuman *per se*, would contravene the European Human Rights Declaration, to which the United Kingdom is a signatory.

As it was, the Labour administration had some moral qualms in introducing the 1968 Immigrants Bill. Anticipating an outcry from the liberals, James Callaghan, the Home Secretary, had pleaded, while moving the Bill's second reading, that the Bill must be considered in conjunction with the (liberal) Race Relations Bill to be introduced in Parliament soon, and that both these Bills were, in his view, parts of 'a fair and balanced policy on this matter of race relations'.

From a rational viewpoint, immigration – from whatever quarter – should be an issue in itself. It should be considered as a part of population control and its rate tied to the economic state of the country. Social justice for racial minorities should be an issue in itself. But since the presence of coloured people in the country is related mainly to the immigration of the past generation, the two issues have become hopelessly entangled. And this interleaving has been given official recognition, the latest example being the establishment, in November 1968, of the Select Committee on Race Relations and Immigration in the Commons.

A generation of coloured immigration (1948–68) also gradually translated the previously latent contradiction in British society between regard for 'human dignity' and a general contempt for poor, dark humanity into an open conflict between the moral principle of equality for all British subjects and the very real social fact of racial antagonism towards black settlers in their midst.

When, in 1958, racial antagomism against black settlers manifested itself dramatically, the Tory government, for all its public disclaimers, registered the intensity of public feelings which led it, in 1961, to compromise the hitherto sacrosanct principle of freedom of movement for all British subjects born in or out of the United Kingdom. This measure had a calming effect; but it did not last long. As racial antagonism began to rise again, the Labour government instituted further restrictions on the (predominantly coloured) Commonwealth immigrants in the form of the 1965 White Paper. Simultaneously it passed the 1965 Race Relations Act to assure the coloured minority equal access to places of public resort.

The calm that followed proved, once again, short-lived. To defuse a potentially violent situation in early 1968,[28] the government now deprived a class of *British* passport-holders of their rights. Following the already familiar pattern the government tried to resolve the conflict between a moral principle and the popular pressure by giving in to the latter at the cost of the former. But in spite of the government's haste to carry through the appropriate legislation in a week, the British voters were not reassured, as the opinion polls clearly indicated. Fed by alarm and rumour the public mood had grown irrational.

Under the circumstances, what chance was there that the majority of the public would view the impending Race Relations Bill, meant to assure equal opportunity to coloured citizens in employment and housing, as a part of 'a fair and balanced policy on race relations'? Very little.

After all, only three years earlier the Labour government itself had not regarded racial discrimination in housing and employment serious enough to include it in its 1965 Race Relations Act, thus placing the onus on those, who disagreed with its viewpoint, to produce hard evidence, and also to convince the public at large. It was in that spirit of challenge that (backed by a grant from a private trust) the National Committee for Commonwealth Immigrants and the Race Relations Board jointly commissioned Political and Economic Planning Ltd to undertake a survey on racial discrimination in Britain.

The survey was conducted during late 1966 and early 1967 in six different areas of coloured settlement.[29] It included interviews with nearly a thousand immigrants (West Indians, Asians and Cypriots); five hundred potential discriminators (that is, employers, trade-union officials, employment bureaus, accommodation agencies, estate agents, local housing authorities, car insurance

28. 'If nothing is done [about coloured immigration], there will be race riots,' warned a Tory M P from the Midlands in mid-February 1968.
29. These were: Brent, Islington, Keighley, Sheffield, Slough and West Bromwich.

firms, etc.); and four hundred tests of 'situations' in employment, housing and personal services. The report was published in April 1967.

Its conclusions can be summarized thus. Firstly, coloured settlers consistently under-reported racial discrimination. Only thirty-six per cent of coloured respondents claimed personal experience of discrimination in jobs whereas a ninety-per-cent discriminating-factor against coloured applicants was revealed in a series of 'situation tests'. A similar under-reporting occured in the case of private housing. Secondly, the thesis that the problems faced by coloured newcomers were due to their immigrant status was disproved. Only six per cent of the Cypriots, who have been arriving in Britain during the same period as the West Indians and Asians, experienced discrimination in jobs whereas forty-three per cent of the West Indians, by far the most anglicized group, did so. Similarly, only eleven per cent of the Cypriots, compared with nearly sixty-six per cent of the West Indians and Asians, encountered discrimination in private housing. Thirdly, discrimination was higher among the educationally qualified coloured settlers than among the unqualified. Of those who did not speak English, only twenty-five per cent claimed personal experience of discrimination in employment whereas seventy per cent of the English-speaking coloured people with *British* qualifications did so. This, indeed, was the most disturbing discovery made by the report, for it was an ominous pointer towards the pattern of the future.

The PEP report received wide publicity and seemed to have established the point that racial discrimination was widely prevalent. An opinion poll taken soon afterwards showed that nearly sixty-six per cent of the respondents thought there was 'a great deal' or 'quite a lot' of discrimination against coloured people; another thirty per cent thought 'not very much'; and only one per cent thought 'not at all'.[30]

The proponents of a law against racial discrimination in housing, employment and personal services felt they had won their case, and that government action would follow as a matter of course. But they were mistaken. 'It would be absurd for the

30. The *Sunday Times*, 7 May 1967.

government to take a snap decision on extending the legislation to cover discrimination in housing, insurance and so on until it had looked at other ways of dealing with the problem,' said David Ennals, the Junior Minister at the Home Office.[31]

There seemed little urgency in government circles even when the Race Relations Board had stated in its report in April 1967 that, 'No effort should be too great to prevent the development of American patterns of *de facto* segregation in this country. Similarities in housing patterns and employment already exist in fact.'[32]

The comparison with America was pertinent and timely. What could happen in Britain if matters were allowed to drift, out of neglect and complacency, became frighteningly clear to the government when racial violence flared up first in Newark, New Jersey, and then in Detroit, in July, resulting in the loss of hundreds of millions of dollars' worth of property and the deaths of many people. As chance would have it, coloured audiences in London were, at that time, being stimulated to greater political awareness by the speeches of Stokely Carmichael, a young, militant black American leader. These events seemed to jog the British government out of its lethargy.

On 23 July, when rioting was at its peak in Detroit, David Ennals was saying, 'The forces of law should be against disccrimination ... I shall be surprised if there is not an important announcement soon in the field of race relations.'[33] The announcement came within twenty-four hours. Speaking in Parliament, Roy Jenkins, the Home Secretary, committed the government *in principle* to legislation against racial discrimination in housing and employment.

From then on, liberal lobbyists never seemed to tire of scaring their white audiences by pointing out the American example. Anthony Lester, a white official of CARD, for instance, warned the Labour conference in October: 'Unless the victims of discrimination are given an effective remedy the coloured population in this country will have no alternative but to take its remedy

31. The *Guardian*, 22 May 1967.
32. *The Report of the Race Relations Board for 1966–67*, p. 16.
33. The *Guardian*, 24 July 1967.

in the way it has been taken in some cities of America.'[34] This tactic proved effective.[35] For the conference *unanimously* endorsed a resolution calling for extending (the present) legislation against racial discrimination to include housing and employment.

However, outside the Labour Party there was still much opposition to such legislation. It came not only from the Tories and the Confederation of British Industries, but also from the TUC. The Labour government itself seemed oversensitive about the prospect of engendering fears of 'persecution' among the white voters. Its spokesmen constantly reiterated that this legislation would be 'exhortative' and 'declaratory'. There was also much delay in actually producing the appropriate Bill.

Finally, in April 1968, *nine months* after the government's commitment to it in principle, the Bill was published. It covered housing accommodation, business premises and land. In employment it covered hiring, training, promotion and dismissal. It also included the provision of goods, facilities and services in banking credit, education, entertainment and travel. It outlawed discriminatory advertising such as 'No Coloured' and 'Europeans Only' signs.

The proponents of the Bill argued that the law had an important role to play in combating racial discrimination. A law is the embodiment of public policy and gives a prop to those who do not want to discriminate but are unable to withstand social pressures to do so: for example those white landlords who do not wish to upset their present tenants and/or neighbours by taking in coloured tenants; and white shop-managers who refuse to employ coloured shop-assistants for fear of offending white customers. As for the discriminated minority, a law provides it with a means of redressing its grievances, thus relieving social tensions which, if allowed to build up, could explode violently. A law would thus help bring about change gradually and peacefully in Britain, and would help preserve the liberal image of British democracy.

34. *The Times*. 7 October 1967.
35. 'Fear of the American situation happening here' was the most frequent reason (for the 1968 Race Relations Bill) given by coloured respondents in a poll by the *Daily Mirror*. 24 April 1968.

The Bill's supporters also argued that the 1968 Race Relations Act was not designed to make prejudiced thinking illegal, but only discriminatory behaviour and action which is, by liberal, humanistic standards, undesirable.

The opponents of the Bill criticized it for the following reasons: it put the blame on the wrong party, the indigenous population; it entailed unprecedented interference by Whitehall in the everyday life of citizens; it severely circumscribed individuals' freedom of action; it would, by virtue of these points, worsen the situation by causing further resentment against blacks; it created a privileged minority; it was unworkable; and, most importantly, it could not change the attitudes from which discriminatory action and behaviour stemmed.

The first argument was centred around the concept of national culture. Duncan Sandys, a Tory leader, enunciated it thus: 'If the newcomers wish to be treated without distinction, they must make a greater effort to conform to British standards and the British way of life.'[36] Cypriot immigrants, of course, had made little effort to anglicize themselves, and yet they met with minimal discrimination; whereas West Indians, culturally nearest to the British, had met maximum discrimination. This meant that race, not culture, was the overriding factor. And the racial stock of a person cannot be made to 'conform' to an extraneous standard. Anyway, the 'cultural case' argument did not prove sufficiently weighty to be accorded the central position by the Bill's opponents. Nor did the argument that the Bill created a privileged minority – although both Enoch Powell and the *Daily Telegraph* advanced it. The latter predicted, 'Those who feel obliged to give actual privilege to coloured clients or employees may be inclined to find lawful ways of avoiding contact with them.'[37] This was a curious statement to make. Whites possess all the advantages that numbers and long settlement confer. Coloured immigrants, on the other hand, are numerically small, economically depressed, and psychologically insecure. Under the circumstances it was hard, for many intelligent people, to visualize the coloured minority being elevated to a privileged position.

The other major argument concerned the practicability of law.

36. The *Guardian*, 9 April 1968.   37. 10 April 1968.

A body of Tory lawyers, for instance, called the Bill 'unworkable legal nonsense likely to bring the law into contempt.' But this was really begging the question. If it was agreed that racial discrimination existed and was considered a social ill, then it was a challenge to legislators to design a law that would 'work'. However, this criticism had a practical merit in so far as it provided a politically convenient escape hatch for those who held a morally ambivalent attitude towards the Bill. Among those who took this easy way out was the Tory shadow cabinet. It reaffirmed its 'condemnation of racial discrimination' and accepted 'the need for steps designed to improve the situation', but declined to give the Bill a second reading because 'on balance [it] will not in its practical application contribute to the achievement of racial harmony'.

This, in turn, led to the central core of the opposition's standpoint – that the Bill entailed excessive Whitehall interference in the everyday actions of citizens and circumscribed their freedom. These were the arguments that caught popular imagination. 'Talking to white people over garden gates you get the impression that non-discrimination in housing concerned them seriously,' wrote Roy Perrott in the *Observer*.[38] Enoch Powell pointed out this aspect of the Bill when he objected to the idea of 'a citizen [being] subjected to inquisition as to his reasons and motives for behaving in one lawful manner rather than another.' However it was left to Ronald Bell, a Tory M P, to sum up this viewpoint:

The Bill deeply encroaches upon the proper sphere of the freedom of the individual and, by exacerbating ill-feeling between people of different races in this country, will lead to permanent hostility and endemic violence.[39]

This was a valid point; but it raised a moral dilemma. If freedom of choice for one person led to the diminution of the freedom of another individual (for reasons beyond the latter's control), how was one to resolve the conflict, especially when the latter belonged to a group which, being numerically small and economically weak, was unable to counter-act? However intellectually stimulating this line of argument (and counter-

38. 14 April 1968.   39. *The Times*, 11 April 1968.

argument) might be, its practical value and importance during the public debate on the Bill was negligible.

What actually happened was that reiteration of Ronald Bell's viewpoint by many others, backed by vocal demonstrations, had a profound effect on the government: it refused to yield to pressure from many white liberals and coloured leaders to strengthen the enforcement clauses of the Bill.[40]

As discussion on the Bill proceeded, first on the Commons floor and then in Committee, the enthusiasm of its supporters, never too high, waned. So much so that when the final vote was taken on 9 July, no more than 182 out of nearly 360 Labour and Liberal M.P.s could muster enough courage to vote for it. Even the liberal newspapers, which had no white constituents to face, considerably moderated their support for the Bill. *The Times*, a consistent standard-bearer of liberalism on race, for instance, stated editorially:

> The fear of the white community that there will be too much interference by authority into their ordinary way of life is much more acute in these new areas of legal concern. So ... the Concilia-tion Committees [of the Race Relations Board] would provide an assurance of realism as well as of a moral conscience. It is true that the coloured population needs to be reassured as well, but with the public opinion in its present mood the first essential is to prove that the law will be applied in a practical fashion.[41]

So 'realism' blended with 'a moral conscience' was the formula *The Times* recommended to the Race Relations Board. But the advice was rather superficial. For, since its inception, in 1966, to enforce the 1965 Race Relations Act (concerning access to places of public resort) the Board had always followed the principles of 'persuasion and conciliation'. Indeed, its administrative organs were called the 'conciliation committees'; and they still are.

The Board now enforces the second Race Relations Act, which became law in November 1968, in the following way. On

40. When, for instance, a delegation of the West Indian Standing Con-ference met David Ennals, the Junior Minister at the Home Office, suggesting that penalties against discriminators be stiffened, the latter reportedly refused to accept the suggestion because 'the government was under "heavy fire" from the other side.'

41. 9 August 1968.

receiving a complaint the Board instructs one of its regional conciliation committees to investigate, hear evidence, discuss, and
form an opinion; and – if discrimination[42] is proved – to conciliate
the parties within four weeks; that is, to secure from the proved
discriminator an undertaking of future compliance with the law.
If the discriminator refuses, the Board has the authority to take
the respondent to a county court. If found guilty, the respondent
may be made to pay damages to the victim for 'loss of opportunity' due to discrimination. *In theory*, therefore, there is the
threat of court action but, in practice, it has been used so rarely
that it can be considered as almost non-existent. For instance, of
the 697 cases investigated by the Board during its first year under
the 1968 Act, court action was taken only once, and that too
unsuccessfully.[43]

Of the complaints investigated from 1 April 1969 to 31 March
1970, fifty-two per cent pertained to employment; nine per cent
to housing; ten per cent to public places; sixteen per cent to discriminatory advertisements; and the rest concerned general
facilities and services such as car insurance, credit facilities, etc.[44]

In the field of discriminatory advertisements, the Board upheld
ninety-four per cent of the complaints investigated. This is not
surprising because it is the one area which, by virtue of its explicit
nature, lends itself to straightforward judgement. It is also easy
to conclude whether the Act has succeeded in its intent in this
case. It has. There is little evidence to contest the Board's claim
that 'the "No coloured" [advertisements] . . . have now virtually
disappeared'.[45] In other areas, especially housing and employment, however, the situation remains bleak.

42. 'For the purpose of this Act a person discriminates against another
if on the ground of colour, race or ethnic or national origins he treats that
other . . . less favourably than he treats or would treat other persons . . .'
Race Relations Act 1968, p. 1.

43. By 31 March, 1972, the Board had investigated 2,967 cases but had
taken court action only seven times. Of the five court cases, *finally* settled
by then, the Board had lost two.

44. Corresponding figures for 1971–2 were: employment, 55 per cent;
housing, 14 per cent; public places, and general facilities and services, 25 per
cent and discriminatory advertisements, 6 per cent.

45. *The Times*, 26 November 1969.

The 1968 Act had been in force for nearly a year when the following report appeared in *The Times*. When the London University Lodging Bureau informed, by letter, 2,835 of the landladies on its register that in future 'the only landladies on the university's books would be those [who were] prepared to take students of all nationalities', and enclosed a slip to be returned, indicating agreement, only 265 (nine per cent of the total) agreed.[46]

There is no reason to believe that before the enforcement of the 1968 Act the proportion of discriminating landladies was even higher than the present ninety one per cent. In other words the Act had not led to any decline in racial discrimination. And yet of the thirty-six complaints regarding renting private housing investigated by the Board, only eleven per cent were upheld as discriminatory! This means that the Board had considerable difficulty in 'proving' discrimination.

Similarly, in employment, of the 513 complaints investigated, only seven per cent were upheld as discriminatory.[47] The possible reasons (considered simply or jointly) for this result can be: (a) discrimination in British industry and services is, *in fact*, minimal; (b) the Board is finding it difficult to prove discrimination; (c) the victims of discrimination were not lodging complaints in all possible cases; or (d) coloured settlers continue to apply principally to those firms which they know already have coloured employees.

It seems unlikely that substantial discrimination in employment disappeared between the publication of the PEP report in April 1967 and the Race Relations Board's report in November 1969. Indeed, it did not, as the following inquiry indicated.

Nearly six months after the 1968 Act became law, and two months after the Employment Agents' Federation had discussed racial equality in employment and its general secretary had

46. *The Times*, 22 October 1969. Nine months later, the situation had hardly changed. By then, only ten per cent of the landladies had agreed to the non-discrimination condition. The *Daily Telegraph*, 6 July 1970.

47. By January 1972, this figure had gone up to ten per cent! Of the 1,241 investigations completed, the Board had found discrimination in only 124 cases.

assured Alexander Mitchell of the *Sunday Times* that it was 'absolutely untrue' that any of its members practised racial discrimination, Alexander Mitchell, posing as the head of an accounting firm, telephoned the offices of ten employment agencies for either temporary or permanent staff. Of these, nine firms agreed to send him only white staff.[48] Under the 1968 Act, both the insistence on a white employee and the agency's compliance are illegal actions. A larger survey by Mitchell revealed that all-white employment was practised by embassies, airline offices, merchant bankers, major heavy industries and Parliament.[49] So one has to reject the view that racial discrimination in British industry and services is minimal.

Next, the question of 'proving discrimination'. Either it is difficult *per se* to prove discrimination in employment or the Board has set very high standards for accepting evidence; or both. It seems that the Board is following a very cautious policy in pronouncing discrimination.[50] This analysis comes from Bob Harrison, a West Midlands conciliation officer from September 1968 to March 1970. Arguing from the point of view that it is very difficult to prove discrimination, he urged the Board to be 'more easily convinced of discrimination' than is the case at present.[51]

Then there is the ambivalent attitude of the victim of discrimination towards lodging a complaint, a subject on which the Board itself said,

> The victim may not even know that he has suffered discrimination. Moreover, those who are aware of the humiliation of being discriminated against prefer to forget it and get on with life, taking care in future to avoid situations where they are likely to encounter so degrading a rebuff.[52]

48. 4 May 1969.   49. ibid.
50. Under the present law the complainant is at the mercy of the Board. He cannot appeal against its judgement, and cannot go to a county court on his own.
51. The *Birmingham Post*, 4 March 1970.
52. *The Report of the Race Relations Board for 1968–9*, p. 22.

And, in employment, this is done by,

... continuing to 'play safe' by confining themselves to areas in which there is little risk of discrimination, or to areas in which large numbers of immigrants are already employed.[53]

Consequently there are 'very few complaints against firms who do not employ coloured immigrants or who only employ them in certain jobs'; [54] and the overall percentage of the complaints upheld by the Board remains small. This has a two-fold effect: it makes most white people and politicians feel, 'After all, we're not prejudiced'; while it makes most coloured citizens feel that it is 'no use' complaining.[55] 'As immigrants are unlikely to be aware of the character of the complaints and the reasons for their rejection, confidence may be further diminished and the tendency to play safe reinforced,' says the Board's report.[56]

Anyway, the mass of coloured citizens never placed much hope or confidence in the Race Relations Act in the first place. A survey of coloured people by the *Daily Mirror* showed the following results:

A third had either not heard of the Race Relations Bill or, if they had, were not interested one way or another.

Only a quarter felt it could be enforced in housing; another third had reservations; and the rest [two-fifths] felt it couldn't be enforced at all.

More than half felt that the Bill would somewhat ease the problem of discrimination in jobs, whereas a third felt it wouldn't help at all.

Eighty-five per cent felt that whites would find loop-holes in the law.[57]

Against this backcloth, the Board's performance of upholding

53. ibid., p. 13.   54. ibid., p. 12.

55. 'The view expressed by the committee last year that there is a danger that coloured workers may measure the effectiveness of the Act only by the number of cases where opinions are formed that discrimination occurred, is still relevant, and, despite close contacts with coloured workers, this view is, we believe, widely accepted by immigrant organizations and individuals,' said the West Midlands conciliation committee. *The Report of the Race Relations Board for 1969–70*, p. 38.

56. *The Report of the Race Relations Board for 1968–9*, p. 13.

57. 24 April 1968.

only seven to eleven per cent of the complaints in jobs and housing can only reinforce coloured citizens' initial mistrust of, or lack of confidence in, the Act and its effectiveness.

The law, as it stands now, does not offer much opportunity to the Board to break this vicious circle. At most the Board can initiate complaints on its own, a power it has, until now, used sparingly.[58] Political events and atmosphere seem actively to dictate its stance. This is particularly borne out in the report of its West Midlands conciliation committee:

Certain events in the West Midlands area have made the atmosphere in race relations more difficult. The Committee has tried to avoid becoming involved in the controversy, but must record its view that the climate of opinion among certain sections of the community seems less favourable to its work than it was a year ago.[59]

Meanwhile the Board continues to act almost solely on individual complaints received by it. The problem of finding proof of discrimination in jobs remains acute because of the difficulty of isolating racial prejudice from other considerations in employment or promotion decisions. But even if a complaint is upheld it means only individual satisfaction. This leaves the general *pattern* of discrimination undisturbed. Consider, for instance, a foundry or a rubber-moulding firm which has all-coloured labour in its factory but all-white staff in its offices. Such a pattern of discrimination can be unearthed by the Board if it has the powers to subpoena the firm's documents and personnel. Under the present law the Board does not have such powers. So, in future, even if the Board improved on the percentage of complaints upheld, the large pattern of discrimination could still remain *basically* unaltered.

The solution therefore lies in amending the present law to give the Board subpoena powers; to allow the individual plaintiff to go to court directly if he so wished; and to empower courts to have the 'proved' discriminator put things right by offering the job or house withheld by him earlier. But in the present climate, for

58. Of the 982 complaints investigated by the Board during April 1969 – March 1970, only 29 (three per cent) were initiated by the Board. During the subsequent two years only 8 per cent of the cases were so initiated.
59. *The Report of the Race Relations Board for 1968–9*, p. 34.

any major political party to advocate or support such measures would amount to committing political suicide. The Race law is therefore likely to remain unchanged for a long time to come; and the indications are that the Board will continue to tread softly.

However, as Duncan Sandys and Tom Driberg have both pointed out, there is a limit to what can be achieved through legislation. The field of race relations is so wide and varied in its social, economic, political and psychological ramifications that no single law, organization, or approach can fully cover it. Various approaches and organizations at different levels can co-exist and complement one another. For instance, the enactment of the 1968 Race Relations Act did not make redundant the local voluntary organizations established earlier to foster harmonious race relations. These local bodies had always been considered by the liberal lobbyists as complementary to their efforts for a law against racial discrimination. Indeed, voluntary local organizations, such as (inter-racial) liaison committees, had begun springing up at just about the same time that Fenner Brockway began his efforts in Parliament to have racial discrimination outlawed – in the mid 1950s.

3

INTER-RACIAL HARMONY
AND INTEGRATION

It (the local voluntary liaison committee)
is a smoke-screen: fashion parades, food
plates, steel bands. It's just a show. The
liaison officer gets a steel band on stage
and they think we've got integration.
A Pakistani member of the local liaison
committee, Nottingham.

I would accept a coloured man as a friend
inside the works but not outside.
A white worker, Pentland Alloys Ltd.[1]

You meet each other outside the squadron,
you wouldn't believe that ten minutes earlier
you had been in the Training Corps talking
to each other as friends. Outside, your
attitude is quite different.
A white student in Southall, member of the Air
Training Corps, in a television documentary.

In the early days of coloured immigration the initiative to form
inter-racial liaison committees often came from the local Council
of Social Service. This happened, for instance, in Nottingham in
1954. There the CSS's initiative was supported by the local
Council of Churches. The result was the Nottingham Consultative Committee for the Welfare of Coloured People, soon to be
renamed the Nottingham Commonwealth Citizens Consultative
Committee.

Although the name was changed, the Committee's main function remained the same: social welfare work for immigrants, for
whom the CSS, in its building, set up a private counselling and
employment advisory service. Whatever 'liaison' took place was
between social and religious welfare organizations, and not
between black and white communities. Indeed, 'black' and

1. Peter Wright, *The Coloured Worker in British Industry*, p. 185. In this
book, all firms have been given fictitious names.

'white' categories did not even exist, because, as Robert A. Burt, a social researcher, points out, 'The dominant response of the formal social organizations dealing with the West Indian immigrant population has been the refusal to view the social problems within racial categorizations.'[2]

Even the 1958 riots did not significantly alter this attitude, prevalent among social workers and the few interested civic leaders. Generally speaking, local councillors seemed reluctant either to help form local liaison committees, or to support, morally or financially, multi-racial organizations already in existence. They felt that forming such committees was an admission that race relations in their boroughs were bad. So they thought it best to claim 'No problem here' or, at most, say 'We're watching the situation carefully.'

Only in the case of Willesden was the International Friendship Council sufficiently disturbed by race riots to conduct a survey of white people's attitudes. But the recommendation of its report – that a major educational programme be launched in the borough in conjunction with schools and trade unions – was never followed up.

Nevertheless, in general, the issues of racial and communal relations slowly began to engage the attention of those involved with local liaison committees. Also, more such committees were formed in the country. But the majority of these proved short-lived. They collapsed because of the 'tea-and-bun' approach, whereby at the opening party, attended by a few local dignitaries and some West Indians and 'Singhs' (chosen from the electoral rolls), there were a few speeches, followed by applause and a few cups of tea; and everyone went home.[3]

The Tory government, following its *laissez-faire* policy, took no notice of, or interest in, these local committees. Even the Commonwealth Immigrants Advisory Committee, appointed by the government after the 1962 Immigrants Act, took two years to appoint a full-time secretary and to instruct her to help bring about 'integration' of Commonwealth immigrants (on an annual budget of £6,000).

2. Cited in E. J. B. Rose and Associates, *Colour and Citizenship*, p. 383.
3. Paul Foot, *Immigration and Race in British Politics*, p. 224.

There were then, in April 1964, thirteen local committees, but only four, supported partly by local councils, were operational; the rest were paper organizations. The active committees were engaged in (a) collecting information regarding Commonwealth immigrants – how many there were, from where they came, and their pattern of settlement; (b) informing the newcomers on such subjects as house purchase, rent control, electoral registration, social welfare services (that is, generally acting as a 'coloured citizens advice bureau'); and (c) fostering better 'immigrant-host' relationships through multi-racial parties and the like, which, as mentioned earlier, were generally unsuccessful.

And yet the 1965 White Paper on immigration from the Commonwealth singled out, for instance, the 'International Friendship Councils', and the 'Commonwealth Citizens Consultative Committees', for creating 'a climate of mutual tolerance in which the stupidity of racial prejudice cannot survive'.[4] This was all the more ironic because, in spite of the existence of a local liaison committee, Nottingham had experienced a racial flare-up in 1958.

But at least the national government noticed the existence of local liaison committees and recognized a 'need for a wider sharing of experience' in this field. It committed itself to setting up a National Committee for Commonwealth Immigrants 'to build up a comprehensive body of doctrine which can be flexibly applied to a variety of local situations'.[5] It also outlined three 'conditions' for the 'success' of present or future local liaison committees. These had to be joint projects of the immigrants and the 'host community', had to have the full backing of local authorities, and had to be non-sectarian and non-political.[6]

The NCCI interpreted the last condition so rigidly that it disqualified (from official recognition and financial support) those local inter-racial committees which could possibly be termed 'campaigning' committees simply because they did not preclude the use of protest action to combat racial discrimination. In other words, the old school of 'social-welfare-for-the-newcomers' was once again in the saddle, backed now by government money and prestige. The only difference was that the local

4. Cmnd 2739, pp. 15–16.   5. ibid., p. 17.   6. ibid., p. 16.

Councils for Social Service lost the initiative: now the NCCI became the sole prime-mover.

The NCCI adopted existing social-welfare-type inter-racial organizations, and formed others. It evolved a formula for establishing new committees, which was to invite social workers, churchmen, local councillors, trade unionists, and coloured immigrant leaders, and set up an inter-racial committee, to be categorized generally as a voluntary liaison committee (now called a community relations council).[7] The NCCI also encouraged Town Halls to appoint full-time liaison officers by underwriting their salaries. In this it was not always successful because the enthusiasm of the NCCI, or the national government, was not generally shared by local authorities. Yet the attitude of the Town Hall was, and remains, the most important element in the success or failure of the local VLC/CRC.

In spite of the continued efforts by the hierarchy of the NCCI – now the Community Relations Commission[8] – to isolate social welfare of coloured citizens from 'politics', this subject remains, in the final analysis, political. After all, the welfare of coloured citizens depends on the *political* decisions of city fathers. It is for political reasons that, with a few notable exceptions, local councils have been unenthusiastic about liaison committees and community relations councils.

Local authorities show their step-motherly attitude towards the CRCs in various ways. For example, they try to stress their dissociation from the CRCs by allocating them office accommodation away from the Town Hall, or by letting them stay in the office of the local Council of Social Service. They starve them of monetary and secretarial help. The liaison officer for Brent, the borough with the highest proportion of coloured immigrants in Britain, does not even have a secretary, only secretarial help from the Town Clerk's department.[9] Another in a Buckingham-

7. There are at present eighty community relations councils in the country.

8. The NCCI went out of existence when the second Race Relations Act led to the establishment of the Community Relations Commission in November 1968. As a statutory body, therefore, the CRC is even more 'non-political' than its predecessor.

9. The Brent CRC receives a grant of £1,360 a year from the local authority. The breakdown is: towards the liaison officer's salary, £400;

shire town, with a fifteen per cent coloured population, has to depend on a voluntary part-time secretary.

The position of the liaison officer himself is hardly enviable. At worst, he is treated as no more than a paid secretary to the CRC executive committee; at best, as a 'Minister for Bantu Affairs', specializing in handling coloured citizens with grievances against the Town Hall.

As for the CRC itself, whether it functions as a mere talking forum or as an active advisor to the Town Hall depends on three factors ranked according to their importance: the attitude of the councillors; the diplomacy and aggressiveness with which the liaison officer conducts his job; and the calibre and influence of its committee members, especially those representing coloured citizens.

Many coloured immigrant organizations affiliate themselves to the local CRC solely because their leaders realize that they have no other channel through which to express their community's problems and grievances with regard to housing, education, relations with the police, and employment. But then a close association with the CRC exposes the coloured leaders to a trap which is that many shrewd councillors on the CRC committees attend to the personal grievances of the coloured leaders and their friends while continuing to neglect the *general* problems of the coloured community. 'There is a tradition among power-wielders in Britain to try to detach the leaders of a protesting minority from their ranks through acts of patronage,' says a well-read and perceptive Pakistani leader in Slough. 'The local white leaders have the power to place a coloured man in a job, to make sure that his children get accepted in school right away, even make a discreet phone call to his building society or bank ... They try to separate me from my people by telling me that I'm different. And I know it. But not all of us are so self-aware.' In other cases, many councillors consider appointing a coloured liaison officer as *the* answer to the local 'colour problem'. In practice, this often ends up as a symbolic act, leaving the core of the problem untouched.

The main problem lies in the fact that the local liaison

accommodation, £250; secretarial help, £210; and cash (for essential expenses, activities, etc.), £500. *Race Today*, February 1970, p. 58.

committees are non-elective bodies and have to be 'non-political'. Literal subservience to the latter condition sometimes leads to ludicrous situations. For example, in its annual report in June 1968, the Wolverhampton liaison committee made no reference at all to the 'River of blood' speech by Enoch Powell, one of the local M Ps, or even to its own executive committee's decision to draw the Attorney-General's attention to that speech as material 'likely to lead to racial hatred'.

Repeated suggestions by popular coloured leaders that the credentials of immigrant organizations affiliated to local C R Cs be checked, and that at least coloured representation on the C R C committees be based on direct or indirect elections, have always been turned down by those in authority. Why? 'Because,' explained a Pakistani leader in Nottingham, 'such elections will throw up vocal coloured leaders, the kind with whom the local authorities do not wish to deal.' The local authorities' apprehension is well justified, as was shown in the case of Birmingham.

There, bowing to popular pressure from the coloured community, the local liaison committee set up a subsidiary body – the Advisory Committee for Commonwealth Immigrants. Its chairman was to be elected by the various coloured organizations affiliated to the liaison committee. As a result, a vocal spokesman of the coloured community, Mihir Gupta, was elected the chairman. But this was seemingly not to the liking of the liaison committee. And so the liaison committee withdrew its support and services from the Advisory Council 'as at present constituted'.[10]

Because local C R Cs are not under any popular pressure from coloured citizens, they do not feel obliged to show positive results in spite of the fact that, over the years, they have become quite business-like. Most C R Cs now operate through sub-committees – on housing, education, employment and 'integration'. Regrettably, however, more often than not, this professionalism has proved a decoy for inaction.

The example of the Nottingham C R C illustrates this. It is not only the oldest body of its kind in the country, but is considered 'one of the more active and committed of the local committees'.[11]

10. *Newsletter*, November/December 1968, p. 451.
11. E. J. B. Rose and Associates, *Colour and Citizenship*, p. 388.

And yet Elizabeth Burney found, in mid-1966, that only 'about twenty' coloured families had been housed on the council estates.[12] The education sub-committee of a CRC in another Midlands town failed to secure the appointment of a leader for the city's 1,500 coloured youths. In the autumn of 1968, the employment sub-committee of the Nottingham CRC was 'thinking' of formulating a questionnaire to discover the pattern of job distribution of coloured citizens, oblivious of the fact that the imminent enforcement of the 1968 Race Relations Act would make it foolhardy for a firm to provide incriminating evidence against itself.

Finally there is the local CRC's function to promote 'peaceful integration'. In practice, this means organizing inter-racial dances, international exhibitions of food and dress, and the like. At these occasions, the mere presence of the mayor or a local MP is to be construed as a token of the white community's goodwill. Commenting on such social gatherings, the authors of *Colour and Citizenship* state: 'They could become a matter of non-representative English meeting non-representative immigrants, a dilemma familiar to many middle-class voluntary workers in the field.'[13]

That deliberate efforts have to be made by a quasi-official body to help the 'mixing' of races, and that these efforts attract only 'non-representative' members of different races, in a country that does not have segregated schools, factories or public services, proves one thing – that contacts between people of different racial stock which occur in the structured world of work and education do not lead to social contacts. It is a sad situation, but it does exist, as a close examination of factories and educational institutions which, throughout the country remain 'integrated', clearly shows.

As regards 'integration', there is a common tendency among the British to think of it in a general, undefined way. One often hears statements such as 'Are the immigrants integrating?'; 'If Sikhs want to integrate they must discard their beards and turbans'; 'It takes two to integrate, and one side hasn't even

12. Elizabeth Burney, *Housing on Trial*, p. 200.
13. E. J. B. Rose and Associates, op. cit., p. 385.

begun'; 'They don't want to integrate' (said across both sides of
the colour line). This is misleading and imprecise. To be precise
we should always specify the kind of integration we have in
mind – economic, educational, social, political. And each kind
should be discussed separately.

Since the size of coloured immigration was related to the manpower needs of Britain, the economic integration of coloured
immigrants occurred almost immediately. Coloured workers are
now an integral part of the British economy. 'Building, engineering and heavy foundry works to a high degree depend on
immigrant workers,' wrote Roy Perrott and David Haworth,
industrial correspondents of the *Observer*.[14] 'So do many menial,
but essential jobs that whites do not care for. The cotton industry's
revived fortunes would not be possible without the ready supply
of Asians in the North ... Foundries, which demand heavy work
in hot conditions, would be lost without coloured workers.'
To this list must be added glass works, paper mills, rubber works,
bakeries, hospitals, post offices, and public transport. If coloured
workers were withdrawn, hundreds of factories, hospitals and
public transport systems would close down or be rendered in-
operative.

But then the economy would grind to a halt within a few
months if blacks withdrew their labour in Rhodesia or South
Africa. In other words, economic integration of races can exist
side by side with educational, social and political apartheid as,
indeed, it does in South Africa. One is therefore led to examine
the social implications of the employment of coloured labour
in the British economy, and to ask whether (a) the coloured
worker has been accepted socially by his white co-workers and
(b) whether personal relationships have resulted through formal
contact at work.

The introduction of coloured workers into British industry was
of course gradual, and was pioneered by English-speaking West
Indians. This development appears, superficially at least, conducive to their social acceptance. It is also in tune with the
current theory that the smaller the number of coloured settlers

14. 28 April 1968.

the better their chances of acceptance. But available evidence does not support this thesis.

In his study of coloured workers in the Midlands and the North, Peter Wright describes the case of Grange Graphite Company (a fictitious name) where only eight per cent of the employees are coloured. And yet, 'they [the white workers] don't like them,' said the firm's personnel manager. 'It's like the USA and Red China: they don't like them, but they try to pretend they aren't there.'[15]

One is inclined to speculate that, when the proportion of coloured workers becomes preponderant in a factory, the remaining whites will accept the situation with a certain resignation. But this is not always the case. Consider, for instance, the Muirhead Foundry (a fictitious name) with three-quarters of its workforce coloured. Yet, 'the white employees in general were still strongly opposed to the employment of coloured labour'.[16]

Peter Wright's interviews with white workers revealed that although only twelve per cent were not prepared to accept coloured immigrants as workers, sixty per cent would, 'other things being equal', prefer to work where only white people were employed. His overall conclusion is that the acceptance of coloured workers by the whites (in firms already with coloured employees) is 'largely of a negative nature'.[17]

It seems fair therefore to sum up the prevalent attitude among white workers towards blacks as: a negative acceptance blended with avoidance. Negative acceptance is the dominant element when the overriding demand of production imposes a certain discipline and elicits co-operation. But once this pressure is off – as, say, during tea- and meal-breaks – the element of avoidance projects itself fully and leads to voluntary racial separation. 'You never see English and coloureds sitting together in the company's bus,' says a personnel manager. 'You don't see them walking down the yard together either. The situation hasn't changed at all since 1956, and it shows no sign of changing.'[18]

15. Peter Wright, *The Coloured Worker in British Industry*, p. 168.
16. ibid., p. 167.
17. ibid., pp. 169–70.
18. ibid, p. 180.

The theory that contacts between whites and blacks at work would lead to friendships that would be maintained, even fortified, beyond the factory gates now stands discredited. And this has happened because of white workers' attitudes, not blacks'.[19]

Interviews with white workers on this subject led Peter Wright to conclude that the majority did not wish to associate socially with coloured people. 'Even those white workers who were willing to accept coloured immigrants as friends at work were, in the main, unwilling to do so outside,' he stated. Some of the statements by white workers were:

I shouldn't really pal with them.
Once my day's work's done, I don't want anything to do with them.
If I had money, I would go to Australia or New Zealand where they're not permitted.[20]

It may be argued that one is dealing here with adults whose opinions and attitudes, for better or worse, are well set, and are not likely to change. After all, until a generation ago, half of the British population had not even seen a coloured person, much less dealt with him as a bus conductor, nurse or factory workmate. We must, therefore, place our hope in the next generation. Let us keep our schools 'integrated'; let children of different races mix freely in school, know one another, become friends; and racial antipathy and separation will disappear. This seems a fair and logical proposition.

Also, education happens to be the responsibility, in the main, of public authorities, and is therefore quite different from, say, industry, which is chiefly in private hands. It becomes, therefore, essential to examine governmental policies, or lack of them, at local and national levels.

Until the protest by white parents in Southall, in October 1963, brought the subject into public focus and forced the hands of the local authority and the national government, there was no public policy to speak of. Whatever may have been the motives of the protesting parents, their action at least made the authorities realize that the 'integration-through-schools' concept would not

19. As stated above (p. 80), black workers' efforts to socialize with whites were quietly rebuffed.

20. Peter Wright, *The Coloured Worker in British Industry*, pp. 184–5.

automatically be translated into reality, and that they would have to design and implement specific policies to achieve the desired end.

The events in Southall also highlighted the fact that 'predominantly immigrant schools' were emerging there, and elsewhere, not only because of the increase in the number of coloured children but also because of the tendency among 'some parents ... to take native-born children away from schools when the proportion of immigrant pupils exceeds a certain level which suggests to them that the school is becoming an immigrant school'.[21] Here one notices white adults' attitudes intruding into the world of children, and white parental decisions paralleling those of white workers who cease to seek employment with firms which, they feel, are 'going coloured'.

However, the functions of factories and schools are quite different. Besides teaching the child how to read and write and to express himself, an important function of primary and secondary education is to socialize the child, to ease his way into the adult society. For children of immigrants, school is, in addition, an important tool of acculturation.[22]

Evidence received by the Commonwealth Immigrants Advisory Council in 1963 suggested that 'if a school has more than a certain percentage of immigrant children among its pupils the whole character and ethos of the school is altered'. In that case, the Council felt, 'Immigrant pupils ... will not get as good an introduction to British life as they will in a normal school'.[23] In other words, a substantial presence of coloured children in a particular school would minimize their contacts with English pupils, thus simultaneously retarding the acculturation process and weakening the foundation on which a racially integrated society was expected to be built. Hence the Council recommended that the catchment areas of schools be so planned as to keep schools (racially) mixed, and if that failed or proved unfeasible,

21. *Second Report of the Commonwealth Immigrants Advisory Council*, Cmnd 2266, February 1964, para. 26.

22. Acculturation is a process whereby groups of individuals with different cultures come into first-hand contact, with subsequent changes in the original cultural patterns of either or both groups.

23. Cmnd. 2266, para. 26.

dispersal of children should be carried out rather than let *de facto* segregation set in.

The Council's recommendations were apparently well-intentioned and 'non-political'. But, with white parents protesting vocally, the issue acquired a political slant. The national government became more concerned with reassuring white parents than with ensuring a 'good introduction to British life' for coloured children. When the Department of Education and Science, for example, recommended the policy of dispersal of 'immigrant children' to the local education authorities in June 1965, the only italicized paragraph in the circular read: 'It will be helpful if the parents of non-immigrant children can see that practical measures have been taken to deal with the problems in the schools . . .'[24] And yet the 'integration of immigrant children' was not totally forgotten by the national government. Its White Paper on Commonwealth immigration, published two months later, stated that '[it can be] more readily achieved if the proportion of immigrant children in a school is not allowed to rise too high'.[25]

As always, the word integration was not qualified. If it meant the absence of segregation, then the question of proportions did not arise. As long as there was *one* white child in a school which had, otherwise, become all-black, that school still remained, technically speaking, 'integrated'. If it meant social integration, then such a statement had, by 1965, a ring of irrelevancy. By then enough evidence had become available to prove that the concept of 'social-integration-through-schools' was fallacious, as was the idea that smaller numbers of coloured students in schools lead to social integration.

In 1962, a study group of the London Council of Social Service carried out a broad survey of Brixton, Willesden, Hackney, Notting Hill and Paddington, concentrating on the position and problems of younger or second-generation immigrants. Its report, *Immigrants In London*, published in late 1963, stated:

Most study group members . . . noted with disquiet that these good [race] relations often did not extend beyond the structural

24. Cited in E. J. B. Rose and Associates, *Colour and Citizenship*, p. 268.
25. Cmnd 2739, p. 11.

world of the school or beyond the early years of puberty and school leaving. When children left school they seemed to slough off the school pattern completely and to accept the values and norms of the place of work, the youth club and the neighbourhood.[26]

About the same time, the Midlands correspondent of *The Times* wrote, 'So many people believed that mingling black and white children would solve the "colour problem". A lengthy enquiry in Birmingham has shown that this is not accepted by many experts.'[27]

The most favourably placed people to observe and judge the situation in schools are those directly in touch with pupils, namely teachers. So their observations must be taken seriously. 'There appears to be very little real integration of races,' said a headmaster in Birmingham. 'Toleration, acceptance, some respect for each other's ability, team partnership and an occasional friendship but little more.'[28] This precise statement is probably the most accurate assessment of the situation.

In his article 'Neighbourhood School', a schoolteacher (from London) wrote:

Boys of one race tend to sit together in the classroom, to play together, to go around together. This has no harmful effects unless the heat is on. Occasionally there is a bust-up in the street after school – 100 boys may be involved, tension is at snapping point, noses are broken: it always so happens that whatever started the fight, it always finishes as black versus white, two clearly divided factions.[29]

If these occasional punch-ups do not occur *within* school premises it is because of the general understanding among pupils that school is not the place for them. Just as demands of production in a factory elicit tolerance and co-operation among whites and blacks, so the disciplinary aura of school helps to keep racial antipathy at a low level. Outside the school gates, however, we see this antipathy translated into racial separation.

The study group of the London Council of Social Service ascribed the phenomenon of racial separatism primarily to

26. London Council of Social Service, p. 40.
27. *The Times*, 4 November 1963.
28. ibid.
29. *New Society*, 23 June 1966.

parental influence.[30] But even if there were no directives by parents, children would find no model of social integration among adults to emulate. 'Children learn the great things of life by the examples set by adults around them, and relationship to people of other races is no exception,' says the Wolverhampton Association of Schoolmasters. 'It would be presumptuous for a small body of teachers to pretend that they could overcome fears and prejudices *built up over generations*.'[31]

Here, then, is the main reason behind the resistance of most white Britons, whether in factories or schools, towards socialization with blacks: 'fears and prejudices built up over generations'. In other words, the British, in general, are meeting coloured people, in their midst, not with an open mind but with preconceived notions. This prejudice seems to have emanated from historical contacts with people of coloured races, which almost always led to a relationship of dominance-subservience, and which continue to bedevil relations between whites and the coloured races.

30. *Immigrants in London*, p. 40.
31. National Association of Schoolmasters, *Education And The Immigrants*, April 1969, p. 43.

4

WHITE POWER,
WHITE POWELL

*To trust people means for an MP not to be
afraid to voice their anxieties, their instincts
and their aspirations.*

ENOCH POWELL

*Not in living memory have groups of workers
across the country gone on strike in favour
of a Tory politician, as they did for Enoch
Powell ... a Tory whose views on every
aspect of politics apart from race and
immigration they barely understand, and
would reject even if they did.*
The *Economist*, 26 April 1968.

No one expressed the thoughts and feelings of the majority of white Britons on the subjects of race relations and coloured immigration as well and as lucidly as Enoch Powell did in his speech in Birmingham on 20 April 1968.

After stating that 'the supreme function of statesmanship is to provide against preventable evils', Enoch Powell illustrated the evil, indirectly, by quoting a middle-aged constituent: 'In this country in fifteen or twenty years' time the black man will have the whip hand over the white man.' By then, 'on present trends', there will be in this country 'three-and-a-half million Commonwealth immigrants and their descendants ... the official figure given to Parliament by the spokesman of the Registrar General's office'.

Having posed the 'danger', he suggested remedies to reduce it. Stop, or virtually stop, further inflow, a process he likened to 'watching a nation busily engaged in heaping up its own funeral pyre'. But that was not enough because, even then, 'the prospective size of this element in the population would still leave the basic character of the national danger unaffected'. He therefore urged the implementation of 'the second element of the Conservative Party's policy: the encouragement of re-emigration'. A determined pursuance of such a policy could then 'appreciably alter the prospects for the future'.

Although he agreed with 'the third element of the Conservative Party's policy' that 'there should be no discrimination or difference made between them [all who are in this country as citizens] by public authority', he emphasized that it did not mean that 'the immigrant and his descendants should be elevated into a privileged or special class or that the citizen should be denied his right to discriminate in the management of his own affairs between one fellow-citizen and another . . .'

He pointed out, 'The discrimination and the deprivation, the sense of alarm and resentment, lies not with the immigrant population but with those among whom they have come and are still coming.' He illustrated this with the case of an old-age pensioner, now the only white left in a once respectable street (in Wolverhampton), now filled with negroes. Her story is that, 'She is becoming afraid to go out. Windows are broken. She finds excreta pushed through her letter box. When she goes to the shops, she is followed by children, charming, wide-grinning piccaninnies. They cannot speak English, but one word they know. "Racialist", they chant.'

Under the circumstances, to enact the 1968 Race Relations Bill (then before Parliament) was to 'risk throwing a match on to gun powder'. 'As I look ahead,' concluded Enoch Powell, 'I am filled with foreboding. Like the Roman, I seem to see "the River Tiber foaming with much blood".'

The next day his speech was termed by Edward Heath, 'racialist in tone and liable to exacerbate racial tensions'. A liberal-minded Tory leader called the speech 'the most disgraceful public utterance since the days of Sir Oswald Mosley'. Its moral distastefulness was underlined by Dai Francis, a miners' leader, who pointed out ominously, that 'If you substitute the word immigrant for Jew, and read the speeches of Hitler and Goebbels there was no difference between them and Mr Powell'.[1] But according to

1. Colin Jordan stated, 'What Enoch Powell said in his speech constitutes what I said in a pamphlet – for which I got 18 months [imprisonment] under the [1965] Race Relations Act' [for incitement to racial hatred].

Enoch Powell, moral right or wrong does not enter the picture here: for an M P, trusting 'people' means voicing their aspirations, instincts and anxieties. This he had done very well in his Birmingham speech. His use of highly-charged phrases and images – 'foaming with much blood', 'match on to gun powder', 'heaping up its own funeral pyre', 'whip hand over the white man', 'excreta pushed through her letter box' – was probably intended to capture popular imagination. And it did.

110,000 letters poured into his office, unprecedented in the history of Parliament.[2] All but 2,030 supported him. One national poll showed that eighty-two per cent considered Enoch Powell right in making his speech. Another revealed that seventy-four per cent agreed with him 'in general'. His support came from all sections of the community, stated the pollsters: from all parts of the country; from those who live near or work with coloured people, and those who do not. Captain Henry Kerby, a Tory M P, claimed, 'At last the nation has found a leader brave enough to break the all-party conspiracy of silence which for too long had shrouded this sinister and festering issue.' If this was so, the silence was broken with a vengeance.

Thousands of workers stopped work and staged demonstrations in support of Enoch Powell up and down the country – in London, Birmingham, Coventry, West Bromwich, Southampton, Southall, Nottingham, Gateshead, Norwich, Preston and Tilbury amongst other places.[3] They marched either to their Town Halls or to local newspaper offices. In London, 1,500 dockers marched on Parliament on 23 April (a Tuesday), the day the Race Relations Bill was to be debated.[4] They submitted a petition asking that the government 'seriously consider their continuous threat

2. A letter from thirty-nine immigration officers at Heathrow airport 'heartily endorsed' his comments on the immigrant situation. 'Were you [Enoch Powell] to pay a weekend visit here to witness the Asian influx,' it said, 'your fears for the future of this country would doubtless be increased.'

3. According to Roy Perrott and David Haworth of the *Observer*, 'The token strikes were spontaneous and usually started by people who were not normally politically active'. 28 April 1968.

4. All but twenty-one of the three thousand West India Dock workers decided on a protest march, each foregoing £5 to £8 for a day's work.

to our living standard by this blind policy of unlimited immigration being imposed on us'.[5] The following Friday (26 April), 4,400 dockers struck again. They marched on Parliament, and were joined by the Smithfield meat-porters.[6]

Of course, there were trade-unionists who expressed opposition to Enoch Powell's speech. Shop stewards at the Ford factory in Dagenham, for instance, pointed out that 'historically, attacks on racial or religious minorities are attempts to divert attention from major problems in an era'. The National Union of Railwaymen and the Association of Scientific, Technical and Managerial Staff (ASTMS) condemned Powell's speech. But in no case were these resolutions or Press statements translated into demonstrations by ordinary workers against Powell.

The anti-Powell march in Wolverhampton was a pathetic affair. Eighty people, mostly students and intellectuals, participated. Not a single trade union or political party banner, or leader, was to be seen. The anti-Powell demonstration in London too was mostly a students/intellectual effort. The clashes that took place outside Parliament were between dockers and students, not between pro- and anti-Powell workers.

Furthermore, almost every condemnation of Enoch Powell from leaders brought a backlash from the rank and file. When an ASTMS official in Birmingham, for instance, issued an anti-Powell statement to the Press, he was immediately upbraided, on the telephone, by union members, who asked him to 'mind the Union business, instead of looking after those nig-nogs'. Edward Heath's action in removing Enoch Powell from the shadow cabinet, as a result of his speech, was disapproved by sixty-one per cent of those questioned by pollsters.

For the first time, it seemed, the rank and file were sufficiently incensed by the moralizing tone of their leaders that they spoke up in contradiction. They expressed themselves freely. Whites discussed coloured people and immigration in buses, pubs and works canteens openly, without regard to the feelings of the

5. Unlimited immigration from the Commonwealth had ceased six years before, in 1962.

6. By 25 April, the total cost of the work stoppages was estimated at over a quarter of a million pounds. *Daily Express*, 26 April 1968.

coloured people present. Voices were no longer lowered. Coloured workers were often taunted by white work-mates with 'When are you going back home?' In some places white hostility did not stop at words.

In Sheffield, for example, the windows of practically all Indian and Pakistani restaurants were broken. In Wolverhampton, within a fortnight of Enoch Powell's speech, there were at least a dozen instances of assaults on West Indians and Asians, and their property.

Previously there had been expressions of mass anxiety on coloured immigration, accompanied sometimes by violent outbursts against coloured people; but those expressing such feeling lacked a nationally known and respected leader around whom they could rally. Now, almost overnight, Enoch Powell became their spokesman and leader on this subject.

By speaking the (hitherto) 'unspeakable', Enoch Powell emerged as a man of courage. His dismissal from the Shadow Cabinet won him the status of a martyr. 'Free Speech' was prominent among the placards used by his supporters. The events and statements following Enoch Powell's speech were prominently and meticulously reported in the British Press. This in turn had a liberating effect, and made many white Britons speak and behave without their customary inhibitions. And this had an immediate political effect because of the adroit timing of his speech by Enoch Powell.

Public apprehension, which had risen to a high point over the Kenya Asian issue, had hardly subsided when the government – in order to retrieve the moral ground it had lost as a result of passing the 1968 Immigrants Act – leaked an outline of the proposed legislation on race relations to the Press. Thus the issue of race – and therefore of coloured immigration – remained very much in the forefront during the interval between the Immigrants Act in March and the 1968 Race Relations Bill published in early April.

The all-inclusive nature of the Race Relations Bill enabled its opponents, such as Enoch Powell, to engender a fear in the public mind. 'We won't be able to say a "boo" to a nigger without being reported,' said a London docker marching for

Enoch Powell.[7] Consequently popular opposition to the Bill increased. A Gallup poll taken after Enoch Powell's speech showed that forty-six per cent of those interviewed disapproved of the Bill while only thirty per cent approved, an all-time low. A poll taken a year earlier (by the Opinion Research Centre) had shown thirty-one per cent against such a Bill, and fifty-eight per cent for.

By delivering his speech three days before the Parliamentary debate on the 1968 Race Relations Bill, Enoch Powell succeeded in weakening the liberal lobby and frustrating its efforts to get the Bill's enforcement clauses strengthened. He managed to throw the Labour government on the defensive. Even Edward Heath, who had strongly disapproved of Enoch Powell's speech, was driven to blame the Labour administration for creating 'all sorts of fears' by attempting to change the law on race relations.

The result was that public attention became diverted from constructive measures for improving race relations to the old premise of coloured immigration control. On that front it seemed almost impossible fully to reassure the British public. In spite of the 1968 Immigrants Act, seventy-five per cent of those polled in an opinion survey, in mid-April, felt that immigration controls were not stringent enough.[8] And, like an experienced military strategist, Enoch Powell kept up the pressure through well-timed[9] and well-directed speeches, and gained ground.

A few weeks after the Race Relations Bill was passed by the Commons in July, he stated publicly that he had not forgotten the issues of race and immigration. Throughout the summer he drew public and Press attention; and rumours were rife that Powellite forces would challenge Edward Heath's leadership at the forthcoming Tory Party conference. The threat seemed real enough for Edward Heath to devote an entire speech to immigration on 20 September, at York (which has a negligible coloured population). He demanded that 'the number of im-

7. The *Observer*, 28 April 1968.
8. After Enoch Powell's speech, this percentage rose to eighty-three.
9. He delivered his second major speech on this subject ten days before the 1968 Race Relations Act became effective; and his third a few days before the Race Relations Board's first, ever, case against a building firm was to have been considered by the Leeds County Court.

migrants entering Britain, both under the voucher system and as dependants, must be severely curtailed'. He re-stated the Tory position as regards ending 'the immediate, unconditional right to stay in Britain' for Commonwealth immigrants, and added that a check must be kept on the whereabouts of all such immigrants during the four years before they are allowed to become permanent residents. On re-emigration, he said, 'It remains an important part of our policy that those Commonwealth immigrants who wish to return to their countries of origin will be eligible to receive assisted passage from public funds.'

Edward Heath's intent seemed to be to bridge the gap between the Powellite position and the official Tory policy. He had good reason to placate the Powellite forces. An opinion poll then taken showed Powell running almost neck-and-neck in popularity with Edward Heath as 'the leader of Opposition'; thirty-five per cent were for Powell as against forty per cent for Heath.

At the Tory conference in October, however, in the most frequently applauded five-minute speech, Enoch Powell devoted himself exclusively to airing his anxiety about the future of England which, he prophesied, would be changed 'beyond recognition' due to the settlement of coloured immigrants and their 'offspring', rather than lambasting Edward Heath's leadership of the Party.

The following month he delivered another major speech, calling for 'a programme of large-scale voluntary but organized, financed and subsidised repatriation and re-emigration' of coloured immigrants. This was to be undertaken 'preferably under a special Ministry for Repatriation or other authority charged with concentrating on this task'.

Two months later, in January 1969, Edward Heath demanded (in a speech in Walsall) that the government should take powers, by the following August, to enable it, if it so wished, to stop all immigration. He also proposed that the government should have the power to restrict the entry of dependants (of immigrants already here). Only three months earlier, Edward Heath had said, 'It is not Conservative policy to stop all immigration into Britain'. Now he called it a matter of urgency. Among those who applauded his speech was Enoch Powell, who shared the platform with him.

Enoch Powell had good reason to applaud since Edward Heath's speech was, in the words of Anthony Shrimsley, the political editor of the *Sunday Mirror*, 'a remarkable concession to the strength held by forces of Powellism in the Conservative Party and the country'.[10]

James Callaghan called Edward Heath's speech 'slick and shifty'. Three days later he proceeded to bar male Commonwealth citizens from entering Britain to marry their fiancées and settle here 'unless there are compassionate circumstances'. The previous year only 1,676 such males had entered Britain; but even that number seemed excessive to the government. Denying them entry in the future was an administrative decision and did not need legislative action.

However, a few months later the government did not shirk from passing a law which, in its practical application, considerably reduced the freedom of dependants to join the Commonwealth immigrants already here. To have its way with a minimum of fuss and publicity, the goverment juggled the legislative procedures. After the 'liberal' Immigration Appeals Bill (which entitled an immigrant, from the Commonwealth or elsewhere, to appeal to a judicial authority if dissatisfied with the government's decision) had passed the Commons and reached the Committee stage in the Lords in May 1969, the government introduced an amendment requiring dependants of Commonwealth immigrants to obtain entry certificates (equivalent to visas) before coming to Britain.[11] Lord Stonham, the government spokesman, told the Lords (on 8 May) that the amendment was introduced at the last moment in order to reduce to the minimum the risk of a rush by the dependants to enter Britain. Within a week the Bill was passed.

Whatever the arguments about the morality of legislative manoeuvring regarding entry certificates, this law resulted in a severe reduction in the inflow of dependants which was, of course, the *unexpressed* objective of the government. For instance,

10. 26 January 1969.
11. Only a week earlier the Home Secretary had told the Commons that entry certificates would not be made compulsory for Commonwealth immigrants.

the number of dependants from (the then) East Pakistan went down from 225 per month during February – April 1969 to 32 a month during June-July 1969. Thus, without openly saying so, the Labour government substantially conceded one of the important (official) Tory demands on immigration control.

By then, however, Enoch Powell had moved beyond the mechanics of immigration control: his mind was now fixed firmly on repatriation. In June, he produced an estimate of the cost of the repatriation scheme: 'To give each family £2,000 for passage and resettlement would cost £260 million assuming that 600,000 to 700,000 coloured immigrants are involved. Raise this to £300 million to include all the costs of administration.'

The government responded by slapping yet another restriction, this time on the issue of A work vouchers for Commonwealth citizens: in future, employers in Britain would be required to *prove* that no suitable local labour was available before the Department of Employment and Productivity issued them an A work voucher for a Commonwealth citizen. (This was not the case previously.) Clearly the Labour government had tightened the screw on the entry of coloured immigrants, as far as it considered possible, through both administrative and legislative actions.

However, the Tory manifesto for the June 1970 general election proposed still tighter control on Commonwealth immigrants along the lines proposed by Edward Heath in his York speech in September 1968.[12] And indeed, when returned to power, the Tories passed the Immigration Act, 1971, incorporating these principles. This is a comprehensive law and replaces the Aliens Restrictions Act of 1914, the Commonwealth Immigrants Acts of 1962 and 1968, and the Immigration Appeals Act of 1969. The new Act covers the immigrants entry, residence, deportation, repatriation and the acquisition of citizenship.

This law restricts 'the right of abode in the United Kingdom' to 'patrials,' that is – to put it simply – those who are either born here, or Commonwealth citizens whose parent(s) were born here. The 'patrial concept stems directly from the clause in the 1968 Commonwealth Immigrants Act, which allowed

12. See pp. 246–7.

right of entry to those British passport holders who had substantial connection with Britain by virtue of birth, or their fathers'
or grandfathers' birth, in this country. It was this clause which
earned the label of 'racialist for that Bill. The same happened
with the latest Bill; and rightly so. 'Taken with other clauses,
this (patrial) clause defines the Bill as a whole as racially discriminatory,' wrote the *Sunday Times*.[13]

If the government's intention was simply to reduce the number
of immigrants into Britain it was not necessary to introduce
a new Bill. The already existing legislative and administrative
powers were adequate and had enabled successive governments
to reduce the number of work vouchers from 28,678 in 1963 to
3,052 in 1970. The new law may well reverse the trend, for it
confers the right of unrestricted entry and settlement on more
than two million Britons who have emigrated to Australia,
New Zealand and Canada since 1945, *and* their children, not to
mention those who migrated before 1945. But it seems that as
the nationals of the Old Commonwealth countries are white,
no 'problem' of bad race relations is envisaged. Which seems
to prove that racial considerations were involved, notwithstanding
constant denials by Reginald Maudling, the then Home Secretary.
After all, had not James Callaghan, his predecessor, also reacted
similarly with regard to the 1968 Act?

According to the new law, a non-patrial – that is, a Commonwealth citizen without a parental relationship with Britain, or an
alien – will have to obtain a work permit to get in. However, a
work permit will be issued only for a specific job and a specific
time. On arrival the non-patrial may have to register at a police
station. He will have no right to settle in Britain until controls on
him are lifted – normally after four years.

The sections pertaining to the non-patrials are full of such
unspecified powers as 'if the Home Secretary deems it conductive
to the public good', 'any person appearing to an immigration
officer', 'if he is . . . of good character and has a sufficient knowledge of English', and so on. In general, wherever there was a
choice between the provisions for aliens and the Commonwealth
immigrants laws, the harsher was chosen.

13. 28 February 1971.

In particular, this Act empowers 'a constable or immigration officer' to 'arrest without warrant anyone who has, or whom he, with reasonable cause, suspects to have, committed or attempted to commit an offence under this section (24)' – that is, to enter Britain illegally, to stay beyond the allowed period or to fail to observe any restriction imposed on him. This means, theoretically speaking, that every black citizen, no matter how long he has been a resident in Britain, is liable to be arrested without warrant, a situation that can hardly help to improve race relations. And yet Reginald Maudling claimed that the 'main task' was 'to secure improved community relations' and that 'immigration policy should therefore be designed to meet the needs of community relations policy'.[14]

This is hardly the case. The first priority of the Tory government was, and remains, to counter 'the fears of *our* people' (as Edward Heath once put it) regarding 'inadequate control' over coloured immigration. And it is the same 'fears' that dominate the thinking of Enoch Powell as well.

The only difference is that, unlike other political leaders, Enoch Powell's sights are fixed on the future – a future of ' "a large alien wedge" in our towns and cities'. This he is determined to avoid not only for the sake of white Britons but, as he often claims, also for the welfare of coloured immigrants and their descendants. For he argues, 'If those who are concerned, think that this fact [of the development of a "large alien wedge"] is being deliberately ignored and overlooked, the danger will be that there will be a tendency for people to be treated differently.'[15]

This statement implies that when the size of the coloured community in Britain was small there was no tendency for (coloured) people 'to be treated differently'. Where is one to find the evidence to support this view? In those cities where small numbers of coloured people first settled half a century ago. It so happens that studies have been made in two such cities – Liverpool and Cardiff.

14. The *Financial Times*, 25 February 1971.
15. The *Guardian*, 1 June 1969, reporting the BBC's *Panorama* programme.

A Working Party of the Liverpool Youth Organizations Committee conducted an inquiry into the position of the second and third generations of coloured youth. The findings of the Working Party, published in October 1968, were summarized by the authors of *Colour and Citizenship* thus:

[The coloured youths] meet discrimination in employment, and when they move outside the coloured quarter they feel insecure ... 'The long-standing myth in Liverpool of non-discrimination between people of different racial characteristics' ... is a cloak for indifference and lack of understanding. ... [There is] evidence of hostility to colour in white downtown areas [of Liverpool].[16]

Earlier, in December 1966, Lord Simey had stated in the House of Lords:

I come ... from Liverpool where our coloured citizens are nearly all locally-born. They have been educated in our schools, they speak the common language of Liverpool, but because of their colour they are given unskilled jobs. They are the first to become unemployed in a slump; they have the worst accommodation, the worst social services, and the worst neighbourhood to live in.[17]

A more detailed and scientific study of Bute Town, Cardiff's dock area, was conducted by Leonard Bloom in 1966–7. He compared and contrasted three generations of coloured settlers and some post-war coloured immigrants with a sample of Italian and Greek immigrants of first and second generation. He found that Italians and Greeks who first settled in Bute Town have now dispersed throughout Cardiff where they easily find employment: they have been, more or less, (socially) accepted. But not so the coloured settlers. His general conclusion, as summarized by the authors of *Colour and Citizenship*, is, 'We see a second and third generation [of coloured settlers] which lives in a quasi-ghetto, is denied the opportunities available to white English-speaking immigrants, is less ambitious, and achieves less than they [the white immigrants] do'.[18]

The author's survey of Bute Town, Cardiff, for *New Society* in 1967 revealed the following:

A generation ago, northern Bute Town was all Greek and Cypriot;

16. p. 490.   17. Cited in Wilfred Wood and John Downing, *Vicious Circle*, p. 24.   18. pp. 488–9.

80 per cent of central Bute Town was coloured. Now, practically no Greeks and Cypriots live there: they have all left for the suburbs through self-help and economic prosperity. During the same period only a third of the coloured population has been able to move out, primarily with the help of the city council. Over the past two generations, a coloured community of 4,000–5,000 has produced only four professional people: two teachers, one architect and one civil engineer who, ironically enough, is now working in America.[19]

And to imagine that coloured people first settled in Liverpool and Cardiff after the 1914–18 war!

One must therefore conclude that the unequal treatment accorded by the British to white (that is, Irish and European) immigrants and black (that is, West Indian and Asian) immigrants after the Second World War, was, in fact, a duplication of the pattern established long before. The only difference was in the scale of the problem. It seemed larger, and engaged national attention, because the number of coloured settlers after the 1939–45 War was higher than that after the 1914–18 War. This was so because of the difference between the economic circumstances of Britain after the two wars. The end of the First World War saw a rise in unemployment in Britain; whereas the contrary happened after the Second World War.

Historically, the economic needs of Britain have regulated the flow of immigrants from, say, Ireland. Industrial Britain has been drawing the poor, unemployed men from mainly agrarian Ireland since the nineteenth century. The Irish workers played a crucial role in the construction of canals, railways, roads and houses, as well as providing manpower for the mining industry in Britain; and still do so in the construction industry.[20] And yet, Enoch Powell, well read in economic theory and history, maintained in his speech in November 1968 that 'supplying labour or skills . . . has nothing to do with immigration.'

19. 21 September.
20. The tragedy of Ireland is that she sells her cattle but gives her people away,' said an Irishman in London. According to the 1966 census, in Greater London alone there were 287,610 Irish-born people, nearly 3½ per cent of the total population. Jeremy Bugler in *New Society*, 14 March 1968.

> *After the [Second World] War there was*
> *firstly a shortage of workers . . . [Secondly]*
> *they felt that because they had fought for*
> *freedom, they deserved a job, and could*
> *pick and choose, so they didn't like*
> *settling down. We tried employing continentals*
> *and refugees, but it didn't work out . . .*
> *in 1950 [we] employed Indian workers.*
> Labour Manager, Edge Tools Ltd.[1]

> *We do find they [coloured tenants] are happier*
> *in the older properties which are very often*
> *in the districts where many of them live.*
> An official of a Housing Department and
> member of a Housing Committee.[2]

> *Certainly by 1981, the map of British towns*
> *will add black belts and white rings to established*
> *features such as green belts.*
> CERI PEACH[3]

Post-war Britain was afflicted with an acute labour shortage. Demand for labour was high due to a massive backlog of postponed projects and post-war reconstruction; and war casualties had reduced the total size of the labour force. Furthermore, there was heavy emigration from Britain during the post-war years. Even the arrival of thousands of immigrants from Europe, Ireland and the Commonwealth failed to balance this loss of manpower. For instance, emigration exceeded immigration by sixty-four thousand in 1953. With the exception of 1952, there were more unfilled vacancies than unemployed workers during the years 1946–56.[4]

1. Peter Wright, *The Coloured Worker in British Industry*, p. 42. In this book, all firms have been give fictitious names.
2. PEP, *Racial Discrimination*, p. 72.
3. *West Indian Migration to Britain*, p. 100.
4. In June 1956, for example, the excess of unfilled vacancies over unemployed people was 174,000.

Some industries and services were worse hit by the labour shortage than others. 'In 1954,' recalls a works manager of a Midland foundry, 'you couldn't get an armless, legless man, never mind an able-bodied one.'[5] Many employers paid regular visits to Ireland, and even Italy, to recruit labour. But these visits were not always fruitful. The above-mentioned Midland foundry, for example, hired thirty-six men in Ireland; but only eight took up their jobs, and only one stayed for any length of time.

West Indian workers, appearing in the British labour market in the early 1950s, on the other hand, offered certain advantages to employers. They were already here; they were English-speaking; and they were anxious to work. But that did not mean employers engaged them as a matter of course. They hired them begrudgingly, only as a last resort. 'We had no alternative really', 'We couldn't get enough non-coloured labour', 'Shortage of white labour'; these were the statements frequently made by employers in the Midlands and North.[6] Seventy per cent of the firms surveyed by Peter Wright attributed the employment of coloured workers to labour shortage.[7] One personnel manager summed up his company's policy thus:

Coloured workers are not employed unless they are urgently needed for specific jobs ... unless absolutely essential ... We get a lot of coloured people coming for jobs and we have to turn them away. If a coloured man comes for a job, they [my staff] tell him there is no vacancy, but if a white man came along within a few minutes they would take him on.[8]

This means that establishments without an 'urgent need' of labour did not, and *still* do not, consider employing coloured labour. And that covers a large proportion of companies. When Peter Wright sent out questionnaires (during 1961–4) to 150 firms known to employ coloured workers, only one third

5. Peter Wright, *The Coloured Worker in British Industry*, p. 42.
6. ibid.
7. ibid., p. 44.
8. ibid., p. 62. This practice still exists, to a large extent, not only in private industry but also in public services. The fact that no coloured bus crews are to be seen in many parts of the country is due to the reason, given by bus companies and local authorities, that enough white labour is available. E. J. B. Rose and Associates, *Colour and Citizenship*, pp. 309–10.

completed the questionnaires. Of these, twenty-nine per cent reported that they had no coloured workers at all. 'No doubt the figures would have been higher had random sampling been used,' he concluded.[9] In 1966-7, using a sample of forty firms, the PEP surveyors directed a set of applicants – an Englishman, a Hungarian, and a West Indian – with identical qualifications to apply for the same job. The English applicant was offered a job or kept in mind in thirty cases; the Hungarian in seventeen cases; and the West Indian in three. That is, twenty-seven out of thirty firms discriminated against the coloured applicant.

Those few establishments which were driven to consider coloured applicants due to the unpopular nature of their work (such as foundries and rubber moulding), or low wages (such as bakeries and textiles), or shift work (such as paper manufacture, glass works, bakeries and public transport) were generally apprehensive of the reactions of their white labour. Hence they considered it necessary to consult their workers. When they did not, strikes often ensued. For instance, the operating staff on the West Bromwich buses went on strike in 1955 when an Indian was recruited as a trainee bus conductor. Twelve years later, in the same town, workers at a light engineering firm struck when a West Indian woman was hired as a trainee press-operator. Other typical examples were:

Over 100 lorry drivers came out on an unofficial strike in East London because they objected to the recruitment of a coloured person.[10]

Forty-nine workers at a North London factory refused to work with three new coloured workers.[11]

Workers at a Banbury firm voted for a 'colour bar' after a Pakistani had been hired.[12]

Employees of a cartage firm refused to work with a (British born) coloured fitter.[13]

If, as was often the case, white workers' representatives opposed the idea of coloured recruitment, managements reassured

9. Peter Wright, op. cit., p. 58.
10. The *Guardian*, 28 February 1964.
11. The *Guardian*, 7 January 1965.
12. *The Times*, 14 June 1962.
13. The *Guardian*, 21 September 1962.

them that only those jobs for which white labour was not available would be given to coloured applicants. Since local labour was most difficult to get for dirty, tedious, dead-end, low-status, unskilled jobs, employers placed coloured applicants in these positions irrespective of their skills and experience. In short, coloured labour was taken in to fill the vacuum at bottom.

Peter Wright's analysis of thirty-eight firms in the Midlands and North showed that fifty-eight per cent of the coloured workers were employed in unskilled jobs compared with ten per cent of the British.[14] 'Generally speaking, the coloured worker tended to obtain the jobs white workers valued least,' he wrote.[15] This meant a considerable job downgrading for coloured immigrants. This also meant that employers were able to serve their economic interest while still retaining their own, and their white workers', prejudice against coloured people by keeping them 'in their place'.

The other restriction that managements, in (unofficial, un-recorded) consultation with the unions, imposed on the employ-ment of coloured workers was that of quotas. Shirley Joshi's study of eleven firms in Birmingham with coloured labour revealed that six of these had fixed quotas for coloured workers at ten per cent.[16]

In some cases managements were unable to maintain quotas at the agreed levels because of a perennial dearth of white labour, and also because they found it cheaper and less troublesome to engage coloured labour. They let their economic interest become the sole guiding factor. Hence, the emergence of firms with more coloured labour than white.[17] But taking British industry as a whole, such firms constitute a tiny minority. The vast majority of the firms continue to limit the number of coloured employees

14. *The Coloured Worker in British Industry*, p. 81.

15. ibid., pp. 46–7.

16. 'Unofficial quotas ranging from 5–10 per cent are applied in many firms in the South and Midlands,' writes Sheila Patterson in *Colour in Britain*, p. 78.

17. 'The Confederation of British Industry is uncomfortably aware that . . . there is a degree of sweated labour in the Midlands and the North, where most of the factories that employ more coloureds than whites are to be found,' wrote Roy Perrott and David Haworth. The *Observer*, 28 April 1968.

because, as a personnel officer in the North explained, 'If over half the employees were coloured, the firm would get a name for being a coloured works and we wouldn't get white workers. . . . We are turning coloured workers away at the rate of fifteen to twenty per day. We could employ another three hundred coloured workers without difficulty if we wanted to.'[18] The personnel manager of a firm in West London also admitted that, 'Twice we have reduced or stopped taking coloured people on, temporarily, in order to maintain a balance, say, of twenty per cent to thirty per cent coloured.'[19]

More typical still is the firm which manages to keep coloured workers at the lowest job level by barring them direct recruitment to skilled jobs, and by refusing to promote senior coloured employees to better jobs (in terms of pay and work conditions), or to supervisory posts. Management has almost invariably refused to treat coloured applicants' experience and skills on a par with the British. Also, evidence suggests that the higher the skill required for a job, the greater the resistance among white workers to the employment of coloured people.[20] White skilled workers have, in many cases, taken militant action to force managements to fall in line with their feelings. For instance, sixty-four workers in a machine shop of a Keighley factory went on strike when two Pakistanis were engaged as machine operators. As a result, the management backed down. It agreed not to employ coloured workers for skilled jobs.[21] In another case, when a coloured employee was promoted from crane driver to machine operator at a steelworks, eighty white machine operators threatened to strike. The coloured man was relegated to his old job.[22] It was therefore not surprising that many firms placed a limit above which a coloured employee was not to be allowed. 'The highest job done by any coloured worker (with us) is fork-lift truck operator,' stated the personnel manager of the Grange Graphite Co.[23]

Prejudice by white employers and workers against coloured people manifests itself most strongly when it comes to supervisory

18. Peter Wright, op cit., pp. 63–4.   19. *The Times*, 27 January 1965.
20. Peter Wright, op. cit., p. 83.   21. *Telegraph & Argus*, 27 July 1961.
22. The *Sunday Times*, 23 February 1964.
23. Peter Wright, op. cit., p. 74.

positions. The idea of *recruiting* coloured candidates as super-visors has seldom been seriously considered by management. But as the proportion and seniority of coloured workers in certain firms has risen, the question of *promoting* a few to super-visory posts has been considered. 'Now with thirty-two per cent of the work force coloured,' said the personnel manager of an asbestos firm in the North-West, 'we could well promote one or two of the senior ones, but we are not sure of the reaction [of white workers].'24 In another case (a heavy engineering company in the Midlands) management had 'made it a policy never to employ a coloured man in a position such as part of a team in hot rolling, where in the course of events he would rise to a position where he would have to give orders to a white man.'25

Even a temporary situation of subordination to a coloured supervisor seems unbearable to most white workers. When, for example, a senior coloured employee stood in as a foreman at a Lancashire firm white workers refused to take orders from him. One of the white workers told a reporter, 'We have no objection to working alongside them. But we do object to taking orders from them.'26 Instances such as this corroborate the finding of Clifford S. Hill. His survey of the attitudes of whites in North London showed that eighty-three per cent of those interviewed objected to working under a black person.27 No wonder then that 'instances of upgrading [of coloured employees] to super-visory positions with some authority over white workers have been almost non-existent'.28

Although there are, at present, coloured supervisors in British industry, they are to be found only 'at the manual worker level', and exercise 'authority only over other coloured workers'.29 This has become possible because some departments or sections in certain firms have become almost all-coloured. Take the case of 'Bradfield Foundry' in the Midlands. The first coloured worker

24. The *Guardian*, 18 August 1966.
25. Peter Wright, *The Coloured Worker in British Industry*, pp. 75–6.
26. *Lancashire Evening Telegraph*, 25 and 26 June 1965.
27. *How Colour Prejudiced is Britain?* Panther Books, 1967, p. 137.
28. E. J. B. Rose and Associates, *Colour and Citizenship*, p. 301.
29. W. W. Daniel, *Racial Discrimination in England*, Penguin Books, 1969, p. 108.

was hired there in 1953. By 1962, however, some seventy-five
per cent of the total labour force consisted of 'foreign workers'.[30]
Under the circumstances it should not be surprising to find a few
coloured supervisors at this foundry. However, this practice is by
no means widespread. Night shifts at many textile mills in the
West Riding are all-coloured, and yet the supervisory staff
remains almost all-white.

Reluctance to promote coloured employees to supervisory
positions remains quite strong even among the managing authorities of the public services – such as transport and hospitals –
which, as Enoch Powell agrees, should not discriminate. Through
its National Health Service, the government has emerged as an
important employer of coloured settlers. Of the quarter-of-a-
million nurses and midwives working in British hospitals, at least
a third are from the coloured Commonwealth. And yet no more
than five per cent of the senior nursing staff are coloured.[31]
A similar pattern is discernible among doctors in the N H S
hospitals. Nearly half of the junior doctors were born outside the
U K and Eire (that is, in coloured countries), but only one-sixth
of the Senior Registrars.[32]

Public transport authorities have shown resistance towards
promoting coloured drivers to the position of inspectors. In
1967, the West Indian Standing Conference pointed out that in
the preceding year not one of the twenty-one West Indian bus
conductors who had applied for promotion had succeeded.
Some of them had a record of ten years' unflawed service. Repeated applications by an Indian bus driver in Wolverhampton
with an exemplary fourteen years' record, local accent and a
university degree, were quietly ignored by management. But the
[white] union secretary told him frankly, 'White employees will
not take orders from you'.[33] No doubt the secretary was voicing
the general feeling among white busmen.[34]

30. Peter Wright, op. cit., p. 79. This percentage would be still higher if one
were to exclude the administrative staff from the 'total labour force'.
31. Oscar Gish in *Newsletter*, November/December 1968, p. 455.
32. E. J. B. Rose and Associates, op. cit., p. 307.
33. The *Observer*, 14 July 1968.
34. The first [reported] coloured bus inspector in the country, an Indian
in Oxford, was first threatened and then beaten up outside his home in

At the grass-roots level trade union leadership has generally tended to reflect the racial prejudice of the rank and file. This is in direct conflict with the purported policy of the Trades Union Congress which, in 1955, condemned 'all manifestations of racial discrimination or colour prejudice whether by governments, employers or workers'. But to pass lofty resolutions at the annual conference is one thing, to put them into practice in everyday situations quite another.[35]

Indeed, trade unions at factory level have often worked in league with management to restrict equal opportunity for coloured settlers – in recruitment, types of jobs available, promotion, and redundancy. One of the earliest public exposures of union collusion with management occurred in Birmingham in 1954. The local Transport and General Workers Union had banned the employment of coloured people as bus crews, in spite of the fact that the transport authority was nine hundred workers short.[36] Since then there have been many cases of the local unions' discrimination against coloured workers. Some of the *reported* instances are:

A chapel of a union branch voted by thirty-eight votes to twenty-four to oppose the recruitment of coloured people.[37]

Led by a trade union secretary, forty dustcar drivers threatened to strike on public holidays if a coloured employee was promoted to the position of a dustcar driver.[38]

A personnel manager in West London was reported saying: 'Officially there is no colour bar in unions. But you get pressure from the shop-floor ... They do a bargain, the same with wages. They say, "Get the proportion of coloured down to ten per cent".'[39]

Eight coloured workers who had been trained by management

February 1968. He resigned. In another, less dramatic instance, over forty railway passenger guards in Birmingham protested to the British Railways against the promotion of two coloured employees to become relief passenger guards. The *Birmingham Post*, 27 March 1961.

35. In any case, the T U C represents only two fifths of the total labour force in Britain.

36. *News Chronicle*, 1 March 1954.   37. *Daily Herald*, 11 April 1961.

38. *Daily Herald*, 10 October 1963.   39. *The Times*, 27 January 1965.

at a synthetic fibre factory in Burnley, Lancashire, to operate crimping machines were unable to take up their positions because the white crimpers denied them union membership (and it was a closed shop).[40]

This is but a minute sample of the cases reported in the Press which in turn is a small sample of the numerous informal, oral agreements made between union officials and company managers. These reported instances, however, give an indication of the general attitudes of union members and officials.

It is therefore not surprising to find that very few, if any, local union officials take the trouble to enrol coloured workers. This, in spite of the evidence that coloured workers are as willing to join unions as whites. Indeed, in many factories where coloured workers have found themselves in the majority they have introduced unions where none existed before. West Indian workers, for instance, established a union at a confectionery firm in High Wycombe. West Indian and Indian workers founded a union at a foundry in Wolverhampton.

As mentioned earlier,[41] Indian workers, guided by the local Indian Workers' Associations, have been particularly active in this field. For example, they established a T G W U branch in a rubber factory in Southall; and in December 1965, they declared an unofficial strike in protest against the management's policy of victimizing trade unionists. Later the strike received 'industrial support' from the regional office of the T G W U, but not 'full official support'. The union's regional secretary refused to blacklist the firms which continued to deal with the rubber factory because, he argued, 'It will put a lot of people out of work in a few days'. The strike failed.

Another instance where white racialism won over trade unionism occurred in Tipton in April 1967. 350 Asian foundry workers, members of the TGWU, struck because twenty-one workers, all coloured, were made redundant. The principle of 'Last in, first out' was not applied because the manager was concerned with 'protecting my countrymen'. A proposal for work-sharing was rejected because 'that would antagonize white workers', of whom there were 150. The white workers did not

40. The *Sunday Times*, 15 September 1968.   41. See p. 141.

strike.[42] In contrast to the above cases, 'there has never been any suggestion that at times when industrial action has been taken by unions immigrant members have been anything other than wholehearted in their support'.[43]

As coloured workers realize, more and more, that they are not receiving the expected help from unions, and that union officials are not responsive to their special needs (such as long, unpaid holidays every three years, etc.) they are driven to the conclusion that unions are beneficial only to white workers.

'In practice,' say the authors of *Colour and Citizenship*, 'they [unions] have often acted in ways which have alienated the coloured worker. ... They have failed, with a few notable exceptions, to organize and involve coloured workers ... have failed to educate their members to face the challenge presented by the presence of the coloured worker in British industry.'[44]

The lack of interest by the trade unionists in racial equality for coloured citizens became apparent when major unions at the local and national levels failed to respond to the repeated appeals by CARD's leaders to affiliate to CARD. With the exception of the TGWU, all major unions, more or less, boycotted the Anglo-American conference in February 1967, on 'Racial Equality in Employment', sponsored by the National Committee for Commonwealth Immigrants, a quasi-official body. Only eighteen trade unionists attended the conference.

The employers and employers' associations showed a similar lack of interest in this conference. The NCCI had to send out six hundred invitations to fill fifty seats allotted to industry. At the conference, a spokesman of the Confederation of British Industry stated that 'Our experience is that up to now no serious problems have arisen'. The Director of the Engineering Employers' Federation made a similar statement.[45]

It seemed that far too many employers and managers felt virtuous in having a few black faces among their work-forces. They were, and still are, unconcerned about the distance that lies between what a black employee *can* do and what he is actually

42. The *Observer*, 30 April 1967.
43. E. J. B. Rose and Associates, *Colour and Citizenship*, p. 313.
44. ibid., p. 317   45. The *Observer*, 26 February 1967.

doing. They are unaware of the frustration felt by many competent black workers denied promotion out of (unstated, but known) racial considerations, and of the rising expectations of black school leavers. However, as in the case of unions, there have been a few exceptions. The Junior Chamber of Commerce in Keighley is one.

Concerned with future prospects for coloured school leavers, educated completely in Britain, the JCC conducted, in 1966, a survey of local employers. They found the results depressing. They could not find a single white-collar job for coloured school leavers. And they summed up the employers' attitudes as ranging from 'wooden indifference to frank hypocrisy'. Some of the recorded responses from employers were: 'A large textile firm, "Not prepared to employ any Pakistani men or women"; a large firm ancillary to the textile industry, "It is not the policy of our company to employ immigrants"; a printing firm, "We are not anticipating employment of coloured personnel ... Unions would not take kindly to their introduction"; and, a large bank, "We can not foresee any possibility of employing these people." '

Undoubtedly the same employers, if questioned in *public*, would have begun their answers with, 'Let me make one thing clear: we are absolutely against racial discrimination ...' It is rare to come across the frankness with which the secretary of the Woolcombers' Association in Bradford expressed himself to a reporter of the *Guardian*: 'He [a coloured person] has to be twice as good as an Englishman for the same job'.[46] This is the true attitude of most white employers and trade unionists. And it is this attitude which has, within a generation, led to the creation of 'industrial ghettoes' for coloured settlers.

Even in those cities and towns where the spectre of a one-quarter coloured population by 1985 haunts the Powellites, coloured workers are still concentrated in comparatively few, generally unpopular factories and services. Even where coloured workers form a substantial minority (of say thirty to thirty-five per cent) of the total labour force they are to be found in the least

46. 18 August 1966. On the other side of the colour line, a West Indian bus conductor in London was quoted saying, 'You've got to drive twice as well as a white man to get the job.' The *Sunday Times*, 6 June 1965.

popular jobs, departments or shifts. Resistance to hiring or promoting coloured people to skilled jobs or supervisory posts remains strong, as does the resistance to giving them white-collar jobs.

This can be read as a summary of the housing conditions of coloured settlers if one were to replace 'few, generally unpopular factories and services' with 'the decaying inner rings of the city' 'the least popular jobs or departments' with 'old, slum properties', and 'skilled jobs or supervisory posts' with 'houses in the suburbs'.

As far as the general attitude of whites towards blacks goes, the statement 'A coloured person has to be twice as good as an Englishman for the same job' runs parallel to 'In both the public and private sectors [in housing] a coloured applicant has to be superlatively respectable in order to receive the same treatment as an ordinary English person'. The latter is the conclusion of Elizabeth Burney, the author of *Housing on Trial*.[47] A similar conclusion had been reached earlier by the P E P investigators of racial discrimination in Britain.

The designers of the PEP survey were aware of the widely held opinion which attributed the problems faced by coloured immigrants to their being immigrants rather than being coloured. Hence, for their tests of the housing (as well as the employment) situations, they used a set of three applicants – an Englishman, a white immigrant (a Hungarian), and a black immigrant (a West Indian).

Of the sixty applications made in response to advertisements for accommodation to let, which did not specify a colour bar, the West Indian was discriminated against forty-five times (that is seventy-five per cent); the Hungarian, three times (that is five per cent); and the Englishman not at all. In other words, only twenty-five per cent of the white landlords were prepared to give equal treatment to the coloured applicant. But since, according to the Milner-Holland Report, advertisements without a colour bar constituted only eleven per cent of the total accommodation vacancies, it meant that, in absolute terms, only three per cent of white landlords acted in a non-discriminatory manner.

47. *The Times*, 26 October 1967.

Follow-up interviews with the discriminating landlords produced comments such as:

Nobody wants this to become little Jamaica, do they?
I don't think it's good for the children ... to have them [coloured people] around.
My wife doesn't go for them much and anyway it would look bad with neighbours. And, come to think of it, give me a good reason why should we?[48]

An overwhelming number of accommodation agents were found to be discriminating, and they blamed the landlords. 'I'd like to fix them up,' said one agent. 'I make more money that way and it's no skin off my nose what colour they are ... [But] nine times out of ten you can't do a thing for them [coloured people].' Another agent stated, 'If you send a coloured person around, the landlords go berserk. The phone never stops ... They certainly never expect them.'[49]

In the case of house purchase, the discriminating estate agents, forming two-thirds of the sample, put forward a compounded reason. 'To begin with,' said one agent '[white] people are reluctant to sell to them [coloured people]. They are under pressure from their neighbours and so on. Secondly there are great difficulties in getting mortgages: either they are asked for higher deposits, or the interest rates are higher – or they aren't given loans at all. That's the way the building societies do it.'[50] And, since building societies finance three-quarters of all house mortgages in the country, their policies and attitudes in this matter are crucially important.

The building society officials, in turn, spelt out the criteria for granting mortgages: age, income and the reliability of the applicant with respect to the price, value and age of the house. They argued that if coloured immigrants fared badly it was because they failed these 'objective' criteria. But how objective was (or is) the rating of the applicant's reliability, particularly when it was stretched to include the reliability of his weekly wages as well? Very little. The fact that many coloured immigrants were able to obtain mortgages by bribing building society officials (directly or

48. P E P, *Racial Discrimination*, p. 71.
49. ibid., pp. 71–2.   50. ibid., p. 78.

through the agent) proved the subjectivity of the 'reliability rating'.[51]

Subjectivity also entered the judgment of most officials that the arrival of a coloured family into an all-white street leads to a depression in the values of property in general, and of the coloured house in particular.[52] Such a bias came to light when, for instance, some young white friends of Robert Moore (who studied housing conditions in Birmingham in the early 1960s) failed to obtain a mortgage 'purely on the grounds that coloured people were about to move into the area and would depress property values.'[53] A series of decisions like this by building societies and estate agents, coupled with their efforts to steer the socially mobile coloured settlers away from better residential areas, has led to *de facto* segregation in housing. The only chance in the future of breaking this pattern – which shows signs of developing along American lines – lies in the field of public housing. But the P E P findings in this sector are depressing.

In the six areas covered by the P E P, twenty-six per cent of the white residents rented accommodation from the local council, compared with one per cent of the blacks. This was the situation nearly two years after the 1965 White Paper on *Immigration from the Commonwealth* had sanguinely declared: 'Local authorities already have a wide range of powers, which, if judiciously used, can make a major contribution to this end [of relieving the immigrants' housing problems]'.[54]

In public housing, the demarcation of powers between local authorities and the national government is such that the latter can at best play a passive role. Local councils have the sole right to select their tenants, allocate them dwellings they consider suitable, and operate differential rent schemes. They also have a more or less free hand in demolishing buildings considered 'unfit for human habitation', and in enforcing public health rules.

51. From a 'purely' objective viewpoint, the mortgaged property, *not* the borrower, is the lender's primary security.
52. Present evidence, as described above (pp. 67–8), suggests that whatever be the temporary fluctuations in prices of houses, these eventually stabilize at higher levels than before.
53. Richard Hooper, edr, *Colour in Britain*, p. 59.
54. Cmnd 2739, p. 10.

Above all, they exercise sole authority over the allocation of funds, and over the administrative machinery that executes their redevelopment and housing policies.

Judicious use of this 'wide range of powers' (to relieve the immigrants' housing problems) implies that there was, among local councils, recognition that a problem existed. This was hardly the case. Because, as Elizabeth Burney points out, 'Most Labour councils make it a habit of resolutely ignoring the subject of immigration, to the extent of, wherever possible, ignoring the presence of the immigrants'.[55] In the major industrial conurbations, where most of the coloured settlers are to be found, local councils have been generally Labour-controlled.

In a few cases, such as Lambeth, the local council did take note of the inflow of black immigrants, but refrained from acting because it felt that 'any action it took would be regarded by the public as giving unfair priority to "coloured folk" '.[56] This was, and still is, a real dilemma for most civic leaders. For, as a governing institution, the local council is the nearest and most accessible to citizenry. As such, most councillors, like the leaders of many local trade union branches, find that they have little choice but to reflect the views and biases of the majority on this sensitive issue.[57] To act otherwise is to invite sharp and direct criticism from the white voters. Furthermore, there is the economic fact that, next to a slum house, a council dwelling provides a working-class family with the cheapest possible accommodation. In practically every town and city the waiting list for council accommodation is long, and the conditions for securing it often stiff.

Basic criteria for the allocation of council housing are: length

55. *Housing on Trial*, p. 188. By mid-1966, fifteen years after the first coloured families arrived in Wolverhampton, the Labour-controlled council had accommodated only 122 'non-European' families in public housing. They formed 0.3 per cent of the council's 38,400 tenants. The council owned nearly forty per cent of the total housing stock; and the coloured population of the city was then about six per cent. ibid., pp. 185, 190, 194.

56. E. J. B. Rose and Associates, *Colour and Citizenship*, p. 240.

57. 'In this sensitive area of housing,' wrote E. J. B. Rose, 'the local authority is very often too close to the voter to give parity of treatment to coloured citizens.' *The Times*, 15 May 1970.

of residence, period of waiting on the Housing Register, and the urgency of 'housing need'.

Residential qualification can range from a year to ten years and is, as the Town Halls repeatedly point out, equally applicable to everyone. Nevertheless, the *net* effect of this stipulation is to handicap coloured settlers. 'That may be so,' argue many City Fathers, 'but we certainly do not discriminate on racial grounds. How could we? We don't know whether the applicant is coloured or not.' But they do – if one is to believe the findings of an independent investigative body such as the P E P. Its report states:

> When someone was in the process of being housed by the council his colour was usually known. This may be a result of a discreet pencil remark in a margin subsequently rubbed out, something the sophisticated reader can tell from the housing visitor's report, or a straight record of 'country of origin'.[58]

'Country of origin' or 'Place of birth' often indicates the applicant's race – but not always. This was shown by a case in Birmingham. In September 1967, one Mrs Janet Ducille of Handsworth called at the city housing department for keys to a council house. One of the officials noticed her two-year-old son, and asked if her husband were coloured. He was. The official refused her the keys[59]. It so happened that Mr Ducille was born in Britain, but of West Indian parents. Hence, probably, the council's informal procedure of detecting coloured applicants failed. Of course, an Asian will never go unnoticed. Whether born in India, Pakistan, East Africa or Britain, he remains, by virtue of his *name*, identifiable and alien.

An incident such as this may anger a liberal journalist or lobbyist, but leaves most blacks unmoved. Awareness, and acceptance, of widespread discrimination makes them generally reluctant to apply for a council house. The P E P survey found that only ten per cent of the West Indians (and even fewer Asians) had registered for a council dwelling even though most of them belonged to the economic class in which such registration is

58. P E P, *Racial Discrimination*, p. 86. 'When we are interviewing we make a note that the family is a coloured one,' said a council official, ibid., p. 91.

59. The *Daily Mail*, 21 September 1967.

common. The majority of these applicants felt that their chance of securing council housing was 'poor' to 'non-existent' – a feeling that dovetails with Elizabeth Burney's observation that 'authorities were inclined to regard coloured tenants as an embarrassment'.[60]

There is, however, another route by which a coloured settler could, or should, become a council tenant: through slum-clearance or redevelopment plans. But this method is not as simple as it may seem at the outset.

First, a local council must decide which area is to be declared a slum-clearance/re-development area. Second, broad principles regarding who is to be rehoused must be laid down. Third, every household so qualified must be visited by a housing visitor. Finally, if recommended, a householder is to be offered one of the various types of council house or flat available. At each juncture of this elaborate procedure the dice are, or can be, subtly but definitely, loaded against black slum-dwellers.

The broad principle sacrosanct with local authorities that re-development should begin where there can be the highest gain in persons rehoused per unit of space redeveloped, is often translated as: areas of high-density population should be kept out of redevelopment plans. In practice, this means that areas with a high proportion of coloured residents tend to be by-passed.

As such decisions are taken *in camera*, hard evidence is difficult to produce. But, as shown in the chapter on employment practices, someone occasionally speaks his mind freely and reveals the facts. In August 1965, for instance, Professor John Rex and Robert Moore pointed out in the *Sunday Times* that, 'A few weeks ago a plan to re-develop part of Sparkbrook by the council was rejected by the council because, according to a member of the Public Works Committee, "six hundred immigrant families would have been rehoused".' It would probably be more accurate to attribute this statement by a councillor to a desire to reassure the white voters than to an unfortunate slip of discretion. In other words, in the ever-present conflict between according equal treatment to a disliked minority and reflecting the popular prejudices of the white majority, many local representatives opt

60. *The Times*, 26 October 1967.

for the latter course for popularity or sheer political survival.

Another example where popular prejudice overweighed moral considerations occurred in Lambeth. In 1958, the local council bought blocks of houses on the Geneva-Somerleyton Roads from the Church Commissioners with the intention of demolishing them, rehousing the occupants, and rebuilding. Seven years later (when the racial composition of these roads had changed from being partially-black to overwhelmingly-black) the council announced it would not do so. Explaining this decision, the leader of the ruling Labour group said, 'We'd still have a housing problem without coloured immigrants, but they've made it a damned sight worse'.[61] Earlier, however, Robert Mellish MP had been more explicit on the subject. Addressing the Labour Party conference in September, he had said that if the conference wanted him to ask Lambeth to give precedence over its 'own people' to coloured people, this would be 'asking Lambeth to create the most grievous racial disturbance we have ever seen in London'. He was wildly cheered by the delegates.

In deciding who is to be rehoused, the principal guidelines can be so formulated as to preclude a large majority of black residents. One Inner London borough has ruled that those living in furnished accommodation will not be rehoused. This automatically excludes a vast majority of its coloured residents. The housing manager of a large town told leaders of his local coloured community that 'Dirty people will not be rehoused'. He did not make this point to the leaders of the white community. Who is to decide who is 'dirty'? The council's housing visitors, who are qualified 'by experience'.

Which brings us to the third step of slum-clearance and rehousing procedures: the housing visitor's report. The function of a housing visitor is to collect 'objective' information, namely, household income, rents or rates paid; to pass 'subjective' judgement of cleanliness, furniture, and the general state of the household, and on the 'type' of applicant – good, fairly good, fair or unsuitable; to record the householder's preference regarding the location and type of accommodation desired; and, finally, to make his (or her) own recommendation.

61. The *Observer*, 5 December 1965.

Almost all housing visitors are white and quite unfamiliar with coloured settlers' cultural backgrounds. This fact alone puts most coloured residents at a disadvantage. Elizabeth Burney illustrates this when she writes:

There is, for example, the woman investigator who plainly gives higher marks for new highly polished furniture than for a well-cared-for baby in a shabby cot. There are others who are quite obviously biased, or baffled, or both, in dealing with coloured people, and therefore play safe by giving low marks. . . . When all the evidence showed a bright, spotless room . . . a good mark was sometimes justified with the comment 'Although she's coloured she does seem very clean'.[62]

Let us suppose that an ultra-clean, respectable coloured resident finds himself qualified for council housing. What kind of dwelling is he likely to be offered out of the large and varied bank of modern houses and flats; older houses and flats; and old, reclaimed houses? Most probably another run-down house with a further useful life of barely a decade or two, or, at best, a dwelling in an older, pre-war housing estate.

Wolverhampton is a case in point. In mid-1966, of the 122 non-European council tenants, four-fifths were accommodated in 'acquired houses' and 'pre-war housing estates'.[63] An official of an Outer London borough revealed to the P E P investigators that 'They [coloured tenants] have been housed in acquired properties which came on to the market in slum clearance areas and [which] the council buys'.[64] This is the fact as revealed privately by an 'insider'. But no spokesman for local councils would publicly admit that coloured tenants are being treated in a discriminatory way.

Local authorities explain the concentration of coloured tenants in old council properties on the following (non-racial) grounds: 'The immigrants themselves show such preference'; 'They have large families, and only old houses are large enough to accom-

62. *Housing on Trial*, p. 73.
63. ibid., p. 194. No breakdown of 'purely' non-European and 'interracial' families is given by Elizabeth Burney. But it is very likely that most of the families accommodated in 'post-war housing estates' have one white parent.
64. P E P,*Racial Discrimination*, p. 93.

modate them'; 'They like to live in areas where they find their "own people", they're happiest there'; and, 'In any case, it is our policy that those who have lived longest in the borough should get the best property'. But, characteristically, the real, and most important, reason remains publicly unstated. This is, that when coloured tenants are accommodated in old dwellings, 'they are not noticed as being housed by the council, which means that [white] people who do not qualify for housing do not nurse resentment against them'. This is what a councillor told the PEP researchers in private.[65] In other words, allotting new dwellings to coloured tenants is considered damaging to electoral popularity. No wonder then that the Birmingham Borough Labour conference in 1966 rejected a motion that the (Labour-controlled) council allot houses on new estates to coloured applicants; and that the Labour group in the council most exposed to the (white) electorate, opposed the motion.[66]

Those councils which have allotted new houses to coloured applicants have often done so begrudgingly. This is well illustrated by the case of a West Riding town which, in 1966–7, was 'rapidly getting to the position ... where people can come in wanting accommodation and have a key immediately'.[67] And yet, for the coloured residents involved in slum-clearance plans, the following procedure was adopted:

We leave them until last and they tend to find their own level and move out. They seem to move into the next bit of town before we get there. We give them time to get themselves sorted out. Out of the last block of two hundred houses we cleared, twelve or fifteen we knew had Pakistanis living in them. We eventually agreed to rehouse ... five families ... We try to keep them away from blocks of flats ... [and put them] on the edges of open estates – in cul-de-sacs ... Over the years we have rehoused perhaps a dozen or more coloured families.[68]

This is a town where coloured people began arriving in the mid-1950s, and now form four per cent of the total population of 56,000 which has remained static over the past thirty years. Due

65. PEP, *Racial Discrimination*, p. 93.
66. The *Birmingham Evening Mail*, 13 February 1966.
67. PEP, op. cit., p. 87   68. ibid., p. 91.

to lack of demand 120 council houses were lying vacant in March 1968. This case provides a text-book example of how, when caught in a cleft-stick of the moral wrong of racialism and the political expediency of reflecting white voters' racial bias, the councillors manage to wriggle out of it by manipulating administrative procedures and decisions effectively to keep black residents out of new public housing while simultaneously claiming a non-discriminatory policy. Not that policies *per se* are sacrosanct and fixed for all time.

If and when old policies seem to be favouring coloured residents these too can be changed. This happened in Slough, singled out by the PEP researchers as *the* progressive borough regarding public housing. It kept separate figures for coloured families rehoused, some of them in new flats. That was in 1966. A year later, following the local elections, Tories replaced Labour at the Town Hall. They discarded the old points system which considered the 'housing need' of the applicant, and replaced it with the 'First come, first served' system. Why? Because under the old system, by virtue of having a greater 'housing need' (due to larger families), many of the hundred coloured applicants (out of a total of five hundred) were rapidly earning points, moving up the scale, and becoming eligible for council houses. That had, somehow, to be prevented without barring the coloured immigrants on a racial basis. Councillor Huw Griffith, the leader of the ruling Tory group, however, argued that, 'The past system penalised Slough people, and we are putting the balance right'.[69] But the facts seem to provide evidence to the contrary.

Coloured settlers then formed twelve per cent of Slough's population, but occupied only two per cent of the council's seven thousand dwellings. It was they, not 'Slough people', who had been penalized. However, Councillor Griffith's statement has to be viewed in a wider context. For he also stated, 'The only people we consult with before putting in a major policy are the electorate.'[70] Two years later, Alderman Peter Farmer, chairman of the housing committee, Wolverhampton council, advanced a similar argument. Justifying the housing policy that discriminated between the immigrant and the native-born, he

69. The *Guardian*, 4 December 1967.   70. ibid.

said, 'We believe we have pursued a policy backed by the vast majority of people in Wolverhampton'.[71] His belief is well borne out by the research of Danny Lawrence, in 1967–68, in Nottingham: he found that sixty-two per cent of the white interviewees felt that (white) British families should be given preference in the allocation of council houses.[72]

This, and earlier surveys by Clifford S. Hill and Michael Banton regarding whites' reactions towards having coloured neighbours throw an interesting light on the contemporary white attitudes and practices.

71. *The Times*, 31 December 1969.
72. Danny Lawrence's letter, dated 3 December 1968, to the author.

6 CONTEMPORARY ATTITUDES AND PRACTICES

*I find myself resenting coloured people
driving cars and the bigger the car the greater
the resentment.*
A white correspondent[1]

*Well, I've never come across ... wealthy
negroes other than the brothel-keepers.*
Owner of a large garage[2]

*When three hundred fourth-year pupils
in a Birmingham comprehensive school
were asked in a questionnaire (filled in
anonymously), 'Are you prejudiced against
coloured people?' fifty-two per cent replied,
'Yes'.*
Tribune, 7 June 1968.

Through a survey in north London, in 1964, Clifford S. Hill discovered that forty-nine per cent of the respondents objected to having a coloured neighbour.[3] But, in 1955, in a national survey of white attitudes, Michael Banton had found that only ten per cent of his sample – spread over three English towns, one rural district and two Scottish towns – objected to having a coloured neighbour. The reason for this difference lay in that, in Banton's case, the question had an air of theoretical irrelevancy since, for most of the respondents, the possibility that coloured people might *actually* come to live next door was non-existent. In Hill's case, however, with a substantial number of coloured people living in north London, the question was visualized by the respondents in direct, personal terms.

Two conclusions can be drawn: (a) the settlement of coloured colonials in Britain has brought to the surface the submerged historical prejudices of the British; or (b) the influx of coloured

1. *The Birmingham Post*, 4 December 1965.
2. Cited in Richard Hooper, edr, *Colour in Britain*, p. 134.
3. *How Colour Prejudiced Is Britain?*, p. 56.

immigrants has *made* many white Britons racially prejudiced. If we bear in mind the historical background sketched earlier,[4] then the first conclusion seems valid; but, because of its simplicity, as well as superficiality, the second conclusion is more readily, and more widely, drawn and accepted. Moreover, it relieves most Britons of the stigma of being labelled racially prejudiced *per se*.

Although a substantial minority, probably twenty-five per cent, do not object to being labelled racially prejudiced,[5] the majority of white Britons regard racial prejudice as morally wrong. So they tend to rationalize their prejudice through ostensibly non-racialist arguments.

'I have nothing against coloured people but they suck the country's welfare system dry,' runs a popular rationalization.[6] Just how prevalent this feeling is was shown by a national survey, in 1966–7, by the Institute of Race Relations. Sixty-two per cent of those interviewed thought that the coloured immigrants took 'more out of the country than they put into it'.[7] The facts were to the contrary. A study by Mrs K. Jones shows that, in 1966, the total cost per head among immigrants was £48·7 compared with £62·4 per head for the total population, that is, about one-fifth less.[8]

According to this survey, ninety-one per cent of the whites considered that coloured immigrants took more out of the National Assistance services than they put into them; seventy per cent felt the same concerning the National Health service; and forty-five per cent regarding education.[9] The last finding was all the more ironic, because Mrs Jones's study showed that the cost per head among immigrants was fifteen per cent *higher* than the

4. See pp. ix–xxii.

5. Even by the very mild standards of judgement used by five 'social scientists', conducting a survey of whites' racial attitudes for the Institute of Race Relations, in 1966–7, some twenty-seven per cent were considered 'prejudiced or prejudiced-inclined'. E. J. B. Rose and Associates, *Colour and Citizenship*, p. 553.

6. The National Front, an extreme right-wing organization, produces much 'statistical' evidence to support this view.

7. E. J. B. Rose and Associates, op. cit., p. 571.

8. 'Immigrants and the Social Services', *The National Institute of Economic and Social Research Economic Review*, August 1967, pp. 28–40.

9. E. J. B. Rose and Associates, op. cit., p. 571.

national average for education. This was because many coloured children needed extra attention due to their lack of English: and this necessitated the appointment of extra teachers.

But the appointment of additional teachers in schools does not stand out in the minds of white adults as much as does the presence of coloured men, however few, at Employment Exchanges and offices of the National Assistance Board. However, facts belie impressions. Mrs Jones found that, nationally, immigrants made only fifty-five per cent of the average demand on National Insurance and Assistance benefits. This is so because the coloured community is younger,[10] and consequently more self-reliant, than the native population.

Also, being younger, and therefore generally healthier, than the native population, the coloured community makes less demand (five per cent less, to quote Mrs Jones's figures) on health services per head than the national average. However, because the proportion of persons in the twenty-five- to forty-four-year age bracket among coloured settlers is one and a half times that of the indigenous population, the coloured community makes proportionately higher demand on maternity wards.[11] The actual demand is higher than (the implied) fifty per cent because, percentage-wise, more coloured families live in overcrowded conditions than white; and therefore coloured women are more often advised to deliver babies in hospitals than white.

The 1966 census showed the following density of population in the London and West Midlands conurbations: under 0·6 persons per room for the indigenous population; over one person per room for coloured immigrants.[13] This overcrowding is not due to black settlers' own choice. It is, as shown in previous chapters, the end-result of racial discrimination in both housing and jobs.

Unfortunately, however, many whites seem to feel that blacks

10. According to the 1966 census, only eleven per cent among coloured settlers were above forty-five years in age, compared with thirty-eight per cent for the total population. Cited in E. J. B. Rose and Associates, op. cit., p. 111.

11. The exact percentages, according to the 1966 census, were: coloured settlers, forty-two; total population, twenty-five. ibid. p. 111.

13. ibid., p. 121.

are inclined, by nature, to live in overcrowded and filthy conditions. Such remarks as 'They live like pigs'; 'They live twenty-four to a room'; and 'They sleep in shifts', imply that coloured people wish to live like that. What was once true of a part of the coloured community has now become the prevalent truth about the whole community.

But then as black immigrants save, buy houses and spread out, many whites start complaining, 'They're taking over our streets,' or, 'One fine morning you wake up to find yourself living in Little Jamaica or Little Punjab.' This feeling is compounded by the growing presence of black citizens in streets, pubs and other public places. 'You go into the parks and you'll see that many turbans it looks like a field of bloody lilies,' said a white foundry worker in Wolverhampton.[14]

How prevalent this feeling of being 'swamped' by blacks is in the country was borne out by the I R R's survey in 1966–7, when racial feeling in the country was generally quiescent and the prospect of a 'flood' of Kenya Asians was nowhere on the horizon. Of those who guessed the number of coloured immigrants in Britain, nearly two thirds over-estimated it by a factor of three to seven-plus.[15]

Ours is a 'small and overcrowded' island is another remark which is repeated endlessly by many, including the national government.[16] And yet, in spite of this *general* overcrowding, the housing space occupied per head in the country has increased progressively as living standards have risen after the war. Also, over the past generation more people have left Britain to settle abroad than have entered. So immigrants could not have *caused*

14. The *Observer*, 14 July 1968.
15. That is, they estimated the coloured population to be two to five million, or more than five million. E. J. B. Rose and Associates, op. cit., p. 570. In contrast, the 1966 census revealed the following breakdown of immigrants, that is, people born outside the United Kingdom: from the New (coloured) Commonwealth, 730,000 (excluding an estimated 100,000 whites recorded as born in India, and a substantial number born in Africa); from the Irish Republic, 675,000; from foreign countries (mainly Europe and America), 840,000; and from the Old (white) Commonwealth, 113,000. In racial terms, therefore, the figures were: black immigrants, 730,000; white immigrants, 1,628,000.
16. Cmnd 2739, August 1965, p. 5.

the housing shortage that existed before the war and still persists in parts of the country.

It is worth noting that popular demands for control of immigration have not included white countries and continents such as Ireland, Europe and America. But then of course aversion towards immigrants manifests itself strongly only when they are coloured.

For historical reasons, dark pigmentation has become associated, in most white people's mind, with dirt, poverty, low social status, low intelligence, animal sexuality, primitiveness, violence and a general inferiority. Of these associations that of dark skin with dirt seems to be the strongest.

In Victorian times, soap manufacturers often advertised their product by showing a black boy turning white after he had used their soap. That such an idea still persists was underlined by a statement made by George Hall, the middle-aged secretary of the North Wolverhampton Working Men's Club, in 1968. 'My generation was always taught that black was dirty and white was clean,' he said.[17] Referring to a Somali worker under him, a white foreman told a (white) race relations researcher, 'He [the Somali] *knows* he's coloured. You can say to him: "Why don't you come in early one morning and we'll take a scrubbing brush and see if it will come off".[18] Coloured pupils in schools are often jeered by white classmates with 'You dirty wog' and 'Go, wash yourself'

Almost always it is the dirty, unkempt multi-occupancy house, where coloured lodgers or families live, that is considered typical of 'them' rather than the well-kept, brightly painted house, owned and occupied by one coloured family. A similar bias is shown by most whites in assigning social class to the coloured settlers. The coloured manual worker or bus-conductor is widely considered 'typical' of his community.

Despite the growth of coloured businesses in their areas of settlement and the impressive presence of coloured doctors and nurses in hospitals, only eight per cent of the whites, living within half an hour's walking distance of coloured people, thought that

17. The *Observer*, 14 July 1968.
18. Peter Wright, *The Coloured Worker in British Industry*, pp. 193–4.

coloured settlers could be middle class or skilled working class.[19] Many whites are prone to think of blacks belonging to a sub-class, much below the white working class. On the eve of his marriage to a West Indian ticket collector, a cockney labourer was asked by a close friend, 'Fred, aren't you marrying beneath yourself?' It is therefore not surprising to notice whites resenting the blacks displaying signs of material prosperity and social upgrading. This resentment is often complemented with a tendency to attribute a coloured person's material well-being to illegal and criminal activities such as 'drink rackets', 'gambling in the parks', 'drug rackets', 'having white prostitutes on the game', and 'income tax dodging'.

A white coalman in Wolverhampton was incensed by the fact that coloured people were 'even opening their own pubs ... even buying up businesses'.[20] The image of a coloured man as a publican or a businessman clashes with the post-slavery image of him as, at best, an agriculturist, a crooner, a boxer, or a sportsman, complemented by the contemporary image of a bus-conductor, mill-worker or a foundryman. None of these roles implies high intelligence or ingenuity.

Most whites consider blacks less intelligent than themselves. A survey of whites in Birmingham by John Darragh, in 1956, showed that sixty-four per cent of those interviewed thought coloured people intrinsically less intelligent than whites; only seventeen per cent considered them equal.[21] A decade later, a national survey by the I R R revealed that sixty-three per cent of those questioned considered the British 'superior' to the Africans or Asians; only nineteen per cent thought the British to be 'the same' as Africans or Asians.[22]

This notion of the general inferiority and low intelligence of coloured races goes hand in hand with a belief in their excessive

19. E. J. B. Rose and Associates, *Colour and Citizenship*, p. 569.
20. The *Observer*, 14 July 1968.
21. Cited in Paul Foot, *Immigration and Race in British Politics*, p. 128.
22. E. J. B. Rose and Associates, *Coloured and Citizenship*, p. 567. 'The attitude [of management] used to be: "You can't train them because they are Indians",' said the technical controller of Bradfield Foundry. 'I feel that they should be treated as intelligent children.' Cited in Peter Wright, *The Coloured Worker in British Industry*, p. 108.

sexuality and susceptibility to violence. That the negro is more virile, and that his penis is larger than the white's, is probably the most prevalent notion among whites. The roots of this theory can be traced back to the times of slavery in the Western World.

In 1799, at the zenith of the slave trade and slavery, Charles White, a surgeon in Manchester, claimed that the fact that the genitalia of the negroes were larger than those of whites had been demonstrated in every anatomical school in London.[23] This could hardly have been the case because, four years earlier, J. F. Blumenbach, a physical anthropologist, had stated that 'I have shown . . . on the weightiest testimony that this assertion [of the larger penis of the negro] is incorrect'.[24] Nonetheless, the idea persisted, and was reinforced by inductive logic. White planters and their assistants often indulged in the sexual exploitation of slave women. Compared with their own generally guilt-ridden, unresponsive women they found the negro women sexually uninhibited and responsive. Experiencing greater sexual pleasure with negro women, white men came to regard negroes, female and male, as sexually more vital than whites. Hence the image of male negro virility and the large penis.

At a subconscious level, excessive sexuality is associated with primitiveness. The primitiveness and violence of life in Africa used to be exaggerated and constantly reiterated by British merchants, planters and politicians in order to justify the slave trade and slavery. Later, as the British began to conquer lands in Asia and Africa, they tended further to downgrade the civilized and cultured aspects of the conquered people. In the skirmishes between the intruding British and the native rulers, it was always the inhuman behaviour of the 'natives' that was emphasized. It was important to make the people in Britain feel that the 'natives' were indeed savage, uncivilized and undisciplined, and needed to be subdued, civilized and enlightened by the nation whom Destiny has assigned this onerous, yet morally satisfying task. There is

23. Also, Charles White compared the measurements of anatomical features of over fifty negroes with those of whites, and concluded that the negro was nearer to the ape in 'bodily structure and economy' than was the European. Cited in Michael Banton, *Race Relations*, p. 20.
24. ibid., p. 157.

little doubt that this policy was successful, and that it has left deep marks on the psyche of many Britons. 'We were taught about the Black Hole of Calcutta, the Zulu war, and all the atrocities perpetrated by the coloured people,' said George Hall in Wolverhampton in 1968. 'That was what our education was about.'[25]

None of these 'atrocities' can match the cruelty of transporting twenty-four million Africans in overcrowded, rancid ships ('floating coffins', as James Pope-Hennessy called them) to the New World, and 'losing' nine million in transit. Yet it is very difficult for many white people to realize that the image of whites in the black man's mind is associated with chains, whips, branding irons, fetters, thumb-screws and mouth-openers, and with castration, mutilation and gallows; or that white people *still* strike fear among the blacks living in Britain and America. Describing his visits to coloured homes in present-day London, Clifford S. Hill writes:

The writer has more than once had the somewhat mortifying experience of calling at a house occupied by coloured people and having had the door opened by a small child who has immediately turned and run screaming back down the passageway shouting at the top of his voice, 'Mummy! It's a white man'.[26]

A study of the history of blacks in the Western World establishes them as a people with a remarkable degree of forbearance and a capacity to suffer silently. 'The Negro has loved even under severest punishment,' stated Marcus Garvey. 'In slavery the negro loved his master, he safeguarded his home even when he [the master] further planned to enslave him.'[27] Many blacks still show this trait. 'I'd much rather suffer than protest,' said a much respected West Indian leader in Luton.

It is as important to discuss fundamental attitudes and psychological undercurrents as it is to discuss whether or not black immigrants take out more from the social services funds than they put into them. There has been a deplorable absence of discussion in basic terms in contemporary Britain. Most of the debate in the

25. The *Observer*, 14 July 1968.
26. *How Colour Prejudiced is Britain?*, p. 89.
27. Cited in *Joffa*, March 1969, p. 8.

mass media, and even in serious journals, remains entangled in details, ignoring altogether the broader, more fundamental issues. 'We [British] have taken up the problem [of race relations] as it has appeared subjectively defined in our recent history,' writes Professor John Rex, 'or we have undertaken micro-sociological studies in abstraction from the real historical world.'[28]

The best explanation probably lies with the nature of British society, which is essentially reformist and pragmatic. The conscious or subconscious adoption of a reformist approach by the ruling group, since 1688, has enabled it to contain the periodic pressures exerted by the exploited or disaffected groups, thus successfully aborting the possibility of a violent, but radical, re-structuring of society. This approach has thus become an integral part of the British way of life. Therefore, almost always, the stress is on defining the symptoms of socio-political problems and on gradually reforming the system to redress particular grievances, rather than on carrying out a thoroughgoing investigation of basic causes which might suggest a radical change. This is a trait common to many liberal democracies; but it is probably most pronounced in Britain. Another allied feature of contemporary British society is the strong hold that middle-class values have on practically every facet of life, from accent to education to Parliament. Debate and reasearch on race relations have proved no exception.

Although a numerical minority, the middle class is over-represented in the seats of power and persuasion – in Parliament, civil service, communications media and the universities. A study made in the late 1950s revealed that whereas nearly seventy-five per cent of the population was working-class, less than ten per cent of the students at Oxford and Cambridge (which then pro-duced nearly one-quarter of all university graduates each year) had working-class backgrounds. Also, nearly forty per cent of all M Ps had Oxbridge degrees. Since then the situation has hardly changed. At present thirty-nine per cent of all M Ps have Oxbridge degrees. Of the 630 M Ps only 61 are 'mineworkers, engineers, railwaymen and other manual workers'; the remaining are 'barri-sters and solicitors (115), company directors (110), teachers and

28. *Race Today*, May 1969, p. 13.

lecturers (65), journalists (60), landowners (42), managers and administrators (41), businessmen (36) and other professionals'.[29]

Even the trade union movement, a citadel of the working class, has not remained immune from middle-class influences. The upper ranks of the movement tend to manifest middle-class mannerisms, styles and attitudes. Almost invariably, the attachment to middle-class values among the leadership of British institutions (no matter what the economic and class profile of the institution's members) is related directly to the level of leadership: the higher the rank, the greater the obeisance to middle-class mores. This explains the divergence that exists, for instance, between M Ps and local councillors, national and local trade-union leaders, and the editors of the national quality Press and the provincial and local papers.

A central characteristic of the British middle class is its preference for gentility, moderation, pragmatism, liberalism, subtlety and intellectualism over passion, radicalism, dogmatism, forthrightness and emotionalism. In short, the middle class aspires to remain 'civilized' to the point of blandness. It prefers to say, for instance, 'toilet' to 'lavatory', 'making love' to 'fucking'. Against this background, it is understandable why many M Ps, civil servants, academics and journalists are averse to saying 'coloured immigrants', 'coloured' or 'blacks' instead of 'immigrants', 'Commonwealth immigrants' or simply 'newcomers'.[30] Sometimes this evasiveness drives such moderate bodies as the Wolverhampton Association of Schoolmasters to blurt out in despair: 'Instead of talking about this problem as if it were something indecent (the kind of thing that must not be mentioned on a Department of Education and Science Course where there are only "nice,

29. *The Times*, 20 June 1970. The author feels certain that if a survey of racial attitudes of M Ps were conducted on the lines followed by Clifford S. Hill or the I R R, its results would differ dramatically from those found with respect to the British people as a whole.

30. As a middle-class organization, the Community Relations Commission is probably the most glaring example of this obliqueness. It keeps repeating the old clichés – 'host society', 'newcomers' – even produces new terms – 'ethnic groups', 'community relations', 'human relations' and so on. It uses all kinds of terms and phrases – except 'colour' or 'race'; the verv issue that led to its creation in the first place.

middle-class people" present) – present it to the profession and the nation as the major challenge of the 1970s'.[31]

Such appeals for frankness do not seem to weaken the middle-class belief that talking about a problem creates one. Besides, in this case, there is a painful realization among political leaders that there is no 'once-and-for-all' solution[32] to the problem, since race, like sex, is immutable; that the issue is highly inflammable and that its implications extend beyond national boundaries. This view is also widely shared by – what David Watt, the political editor of the *Financial Times*, calls – 'the political élite' consisting of 'political journalists, academics, and the listeners of the Third Programme', which transcends conventional party labels.

In most situations, this well-informed, vocal and articulate élite exerts a disproportionate pressure on the political leadership of the government and, more often than not, has its way. This is so mainly because, as David Watt points out, 'the British electorate is extraordinarily passive', a conclusion based on an extensive survey conducted by David Butler and Donald Stokes in the mid 1960s. Of those asked how much they felt the government paid attention to what people think, seventy-two per cent replied 'not much' or 'don't know'.

The passivity of British voters is blended with their almost total dependence on the government 'to drop everything in their mouths'; their feelings that 'the government is responsible for "good times" or "bad times" in general' and that 'the man in Whitehall knows best'; and a lack of confidence in their own personal judgement.

Under the circumstances it is not surprising that the liberal, well-educated élite has made the running in such issues as licensing hours, hanging, abortion, homosexuality, divorce law, defence policies and so on. However, on coloured immigration and race,

31. N A S, *Education and the Immigrants*, p. 44. The Wolverhampton teachers might as well shout at stone walls. Leaving aside 'the nation' they could hardly even expect to get their point across to the local Mayor who blithely told John Heilpern of the *Observer*, 'There isn't a colour problem in the racial sense'. This statement was made *after* Wolverhampton had witnessed three pro- and anti-Powell marches which had been reported at length by the local and national Press. The *Observer*, 14 July 1968.

32. As there is for, say, the death penalty or making hydrogen bombs.

it ran into popular opposition because the nature of these problems is different. The issue of capital punishment, for instance, does not directly affect 99.99 per cent of the population; nor does the fate of prospective unwed mothers, or the behaviour of homosexuals. But as residents in British conurbations, hundreds and thousands of whites are either already working with or living next to blacks, or stand a chance of finding themselves in such a situation. In short, the racial issue intrudes directly into the everyday experience of people. And when this happened to a large enough segment of white British society, many voters lost their passivity, became restive, and exposed what William Deedes calls, 'the most damaging division ... between Government and governed';[33] and, in successive moves, made the liberal political élite retreat.

However virulent and assertive, the popular response has been a reaction against a situation rather than a positive action. Although the expression of popular feelings effected changes in certain government policies, it did not alter the basic nature of British society, with its reasonably well-defined (and generally accepted) division of labour. Nor did, or could, this change the basic set-up of the government, civil service, trade unions, the communications media, or the universities. The day-to-day administration of those institutions remains, and will remain (because of their very nature), in the hands of a small minority. Whatever doubts arose in the minds of this liberal minority – as a result of illiberal events – soon disappeared as the old, embedded beliefs reasserted their hold.

It is not surprising then that the periodic public protest on this issue is almost always accompanied by an outcry that there has been a conspiracy to keep out the voice of 'the decent, ordinary Englishman', and that there has been a 'conspiracy of silence' among the political leaders.[34] There is, of course, no conspiracy in the formal sense of the word, but there certainly is a common inclination, shared by most of the upper and middle ranks of

33. William Deedes, *Race Without Rancour*, p. 32.
34. 'To talk of a conspiracy of silence among national and local leaders in unjust,' wrote William Deedes in August 1968. 'More accurately, there has been a ... shyness, a nervousness about the subject which has inhibited frank discussion.' *Race Without Rancour*, p. 21.

British institutions, towards keeping Britain 'civilized' in racial matters. In practice, it means barring (through subtle means), or whittling down to the absolute minimum, the airing of racialist views on most of the respectable public forums; and giving them no, or as little as possible, publicity through the means of communication. Until Enoch Powell's speech in April 1968, these views and practices were dominant, as is illustrated by the following examples.[35]

A television current affairs producer told the author in a private conversation, in March 1968, that, as a policy, they used stories on race 'to the minimum' and tried 'to play them down'. That this was the case 'for years' was disclosed publicly by Jeremy Isaacs, once the producer of BBC's *Panorama*, and now the Controller of Features Programmes for Thames Television. On 13 November 1968, the *Guardian* quoted him as saying:

> Television current affairs deliberately underplayed the strength of racist feelings for years, out of the misguided but honourable feeling that inflammatory utterances could only do damage. But the way feelings erupted after Enoch Powell's speech this year was evidence to me that the [racist] feeling has been under-represented on television, and other media.[36]

Let us consider the newspapers. Following a demonstration on the Vietnam War, in March 1968, a popular national daily invited its readers to send in letters on *any* subject they pleased. Of the nearly five thousand letters the newspaper received, more than two thirds concerned coloured immigrants, and were generally critical of them. Honesty demanded that the published

35. Not that this wariness has disappeared altogether. Here is an example that occurred in early 1970. 'Residents of Blackburn, recorded by Jeremy Seabrook for his continuing series on Radio Three, *City Close-Up*, talked so viciously about [coloured] immigrants that the B B C solicitors, as well as heads of department, had to clear the script of last Tuesday's programme,' wrote Paul Ferris, the radio critic of the *Observer*, 15 February 1970.

36. Three days later Enoch Powell, in his speech in Eastbourne, referred to 'a tiny minority, with almost a monopoly hold upon the channels of communication, who seem not to know the facts and not to face the realities and who will resort to any device or extremity to blind both themselves and others'.

letters reflect this proportion. And yet only one in ten of the published letters concerned coloured immigrants.

When, in the autumn of 1967, a quality Sunday paper published an article accurately describing the feelings of black youths in London, it was critized by the liberals for 'worsening race relations'. The author of the article was shaken by the experience. The following summer the same paper produced two long, painstakingly researched articles[37] describing the real feelings and attitudes of white and black residents of a Midlands city. The paper was then urged by the liberal lobby to 'balance' these articles by covering a Midlands city with 'good' race relations. This was done four months later. But the claim of 'good' race relations in this city, although carefully cultivated over the years, was found to be hollow. The *only* difference between the two cities was that in the latter case there was less verbal hostility towards blacks; the rest was almost identical.

This subservience to the liberal, middle-class value of 'not doing anything that might harm race relations' has led to some curious situations. Although two thirds of Britons feel that blacks draw more out of welfare services than they put in, very few of their elected representatives have said so – and that only at local level, not national. This is also the case with trade unions.

Although the subject continues to agitate the average trade unionist there has been practically no expression of anxiety from national platforms. The only exception was the statement by Sir William Carron, the President of the A E U, at the union's annual conference in 1967 that it would be 'interesting to have detailed figures of the grand total consumed in education grants, Health Services expenses and subsistence payments to the ever-growing number of individuals who are not born in this country and who have in no way contributed towards the setting up of the fund into which they so willingly dip their fingers'.[38] There has seldom been a fully-fledged discussion on race and coloured immigration

37. Two correspondents, one white, another black, were posted in this town for *four weeks* to study the situation thoroughly.

38. The *Guardian*, 25 April 1967. When the inevitable protest from the liberal lobby followed, Sir William cleverly pointed out that he had never used the word 'immigrant'. By carrying the art of subtlety further than his critics had done he successfully outwitted them.

at the annual conferences of major trade unions or the TUC.[39] That does not mean there is no concern or anxiety at the grass-roots level: there is. 'Every year the head office gets a lot of resolutions for the union's annual conference from branches all over the country which are strongly colour prejudiced,' said an (unnamed) ex-official of the TGWU in late April 1968. '[But] the senior officers ... see to it that none of them comes up for debate.'[40]

Even though this ex-official was sufficiently affected by the events that followed Enoch Powell's speech on 20 April 1968, to make this revelation, he *still* did not wish to be publicly named. This was all the more striking because he was no longer on the union's pay roll.

For the mass of British people, however, the situation was much simpler. Enoch Powell's speech, and the tremendous popular support it received, lifted, temporarily at least, the inhibition they had felt that it was morally wrong to be racially prejudiced. Indeed, more than moral inhibition was involved, as Enoch Powell, in his Birmingham speech, showed:

> What surprised and alarmed me was the high proportion of ordinary, decent, sensible people, writing a rational and often well-educated letter, who believed that they had to omit their address because it was dangerous to have committed themselves to paper to a Member of Parliament agreeing with the views I had expressed (in Walsall in February 1968), and that they would risk either penalties or reprisals if they were known to have done so.[41]

If, as a result of his speech, the British people lost their inhibition and fear, and spoke their mind freely, even if emotionally and inarticulately, he helped inject realism into race relations. He helped to remove the mask of hypocrisy and to reveal the feelings as they *actually* existed.[42] To that extent he did British society a

39. In spite of the well-reported work stoppages by workers in the country, the General Council of the TUC did *not* discuss Enoch Powell's Birmingham speech – or 'its industrial echoes'. The *Guardian*, 25 April 1968.

40. The *Observer*, 28 April 1968.   41. The *Observer*, 21 April 1968.

42. Commenting on Enoch Powell's speech and its aftermath, David Ennals said, 'These prejudices must have been there before. They were not created by Mr Powell. He took the lid off and we have seen what came out.' *The Times*, 27 April 1968.

service. Knowledge of social facts 'as are' is crucially important if lasting solutions are to be conceived and executed.

'It is the popular beliefs, and they alone, which enter directly into the causal mechanism of interracial relations,' writes Gunnar Myrdal, the author of *An American Dilemma*, a monumental study of race relations in America. 'The scientific facts of race and racial characteristics . . . are only of secondary and indirect importance . . . they are only virtual but not actual facts.'[43] Therefore the importance and discussion of the popular beliefs and attitudes can hardly be overstressed.

Enoch Powell's dramatic entry into the race relations field bewildered the liberal lobby and threw it into disarray. But that proved temporary. It quickly recovered from the initial shock, and remains committed, as strongly as before, to creating a racially 'integrated' society in Britain. It would like to see the generally sympathetic mass media help in this direction by (a) reporting more often, and at length, racially harmonious events or non-events; and (b) by 'educating' the 'unthinking masses'.

Before discussing (a) we must examine the general make-up of the news sections of the papers, and of newscasts on radio and television. Leaving aside the standard reporting of Parliamentary proceedings, the national conferences of political parties and trade unions, and the statements of prominent political and other figures, and the paraphrasing of important socio-political documents and surveys, the news sections consist of descriptions of natural disasters, accidents, scoops, rackets, scandals, violent or bizarre acts, dramatic political changes, and present or potential human conflicts such as strikes, lock-outs, marches, and demonstrations. This is particularly true of television. As Lord Aylestone, chairman of the Independent Television Authority points out, 'Television is essentially a reporting and dramatic medium: both subjects are about the unusual'.[44] So, the old cliché that 'Dog bites man is not news, but man bites dog is news,' is even more valid for television than for newspapers. In general, conflict makes news; harmony does not. And yet the liberal lobby advocates that in the case of race relations *in Britain* this general criterion be downgraded, and that such dull events as the appearance of a

43. Harper and Row, 1944, p. 110.   44. *The Times*, 3 December 1969.

nationally known politician at an elaborately arranged 'inter-racial' nursery, be dressed up as an item of 'news'. Its efforts do sometimes yield results.

Some television journalists and producers go out of their way to manipulate situations to show that happily integrated communities exist in the country. Often they get away with it[45] but sometimes their tactics prove too crude to go unnoticed. This happened, for instance, in Southall in early 1969, and was reported by the *Sunday Telegraph*:

The [BBC television] programme – prematurely entitled *Friendly Relations* – was planned to show how the Indian community in Southall had integrated with the white people shopping and talking in Indian shops. They chose a jeweller's and a confectionery shop ... When no white customers appeared they went out in the street to try to persuade people to come and make out they were shopping. So few would cooperate that they were forced to call off the production.[46]

Commenting on the incident, an official of the Southall Resident's Association said,

The two communities, Indian and white, do not integrate well. It is not right that the BBC should make out that they do ...[47]

They [the BBC producers] decide the type of programme they want to make, and then make the facts fit their case. Before Christmas they came to a school in Southall to film a programme on how the children mix. They had to buy ice creams for them to persuade them to stand together so that they could get the pictures they wanted.[48]

Knowing the situation, at first hand, in both public and com-

45. The author was a member of the studio audience (on a Thames Television programme on 19 December 1969) invited to comment on advertisements designed to improve race relations. The organizers of the show deliberately moved around the audience – who had, of their own choice seated themselves in a segregated pattern – to give an impression of racially integrated seating in the studio to the viewers.

46. 2 February 1969.

47. Lest the above comment be dismissed by liberals as biased, coming from an official of an 'extremist body', let us see how Martyn Grubb, the community relations officer for the area, describes the situation. In an interview with the *Evening Standard*, he expressed 'ultimate hope' that 'the separate communities in the area would merge into one, and that the key to harmony in Southall seemed to be the realization that the communities were equal but different'. 22 October 1969.

48. The *Sunday Telegraph*, 2 February 1969.

mercial television, the author cannot help but agree with this statement.

Then there is the suggestion, popular with the liberal lobby, that the mass media should educate the masses, and counter myths with facts and figures. They would, for example, like to see the popular belief in coloured people's low intelligence countered by the results of the following survey by the Inner London Education Authority:

The survey at Tulse Hill boys' school [in 1966] studied the educational performance of 294 immigrant children mostly coloured. Proportionately fewer managed the top stream (in the first year, only 21 per cent against 35 per cent for all the boys). But . . . almost 50 per cent of immigrant children who have received a full education [in Britain] qualified for the top stream.[49]

But it is doubtful if the presentation and re-presentation of such facts succeeds in dispelling white prejudice. 'You can go blue in the face pouring out statistics,' said a white employee of a local community relations council, 'but the average white man is not convinced. I've tried. It's a waste of time.' It is doubtful if this statistical approach works with even the majority of white teachers in multi-racial schools, whose attitudes are aptly summarized by a teacher in London:

The 'coloured boys' are often seriously . . . held responsible for the falling standards of the school. I tackled this view once in a heated staff-room argument, but it was earnestly defended. There is a frightening *emotional* logic about race prejudice, utterly irrational, and set inexorably deep.[50]

Here, then, is the key explanation underlying the problem: it is emotional.

More specifically, it is visual: black faces in a white society stand out. As such, only an arm-chair intellectual can seriously believe that he can contain the anxiety of 'being taken over by the blacks' felt by the whites in, say, Walsall, Gravesend or Luton by telling them that *nationally* blacks form only 2.5 of the population.

One is therefore driven to conclude that whatever the merit of

49. Cited in the *Sunday Times*, 28 April 1968.
50. *New Society*, 23 June 1966.

cataloguing facts and figures in *The Times* or *New Statesman*, Parliament or university debating-halls, this tactic is not proving effective in bringing about an emotional conversion of the white masses. If that be so, then the liberal leaders and opinion-formers may as well shift their ground to an emotional level, to the plank of Christian charity, love and compassion.[51] Understandably, this has been the approach of Church leaders; but, since the hold of the Church is minimal the net effect on the bulk of the population has been negligible.

It is perhaps best then to discard the overt sermonizing and, instead, resort to the technique of projecting simple, stark images – as is done by professional advertisers for such organizations as Oxfam and War on Want – to arouse sympathy and compassion among white viewers. However, when the projected image is that of a member of a racial 'out' group, it may create sympathy among the well-off liberal minority but it reinforces the unfavourable image that the illiberal majority already has about the 'out' group. Experiments in America have revealed that when exposed to certain images, viewers have remembered only those that have supported their *previous* convictions and beliefs.

Show a shot of a group of coloured people playing cards in a park in Coventry or Birmingham, and the liberal British will probably admire the coloured people for their sense of community, while the illiberal will most likely see 'wogs gambling in a park'. Show black slums in England or America, and you will have the well-off white liberals muttering 'These poor, poor people' and the illiberals cursing the blacks for 'degrading our towns'.

Besides the carefully arranged juxtaposition of pictures in the form of television documentaries, there is a steady stream of random images meant to convey news of events in Africa and Asia. Like all news, these images are centred around conflicts, tensions, political upheavals, wars and famines. Violent anarchy

51. It is worth noting that the North Wolverhampton Working Men's Club, which by the unanimous consent of its members, barred coloured people 'under any pretext, either as members, visitors, or visiting artists,' had, on its walls, the following motto (in July 1968): 'Honour All Men. Love The Brotherhood. Use Hospitality One To Another. Be Not Forgetful To Strangers.'

in the Congo, the raping of white nuns by African soldiers, civil war in Nigeria, a coup d'état in Ghana, near-revolution in Pakistan, starvation in Biafra and India – the list is endless, and will continue to be so for the simple statistical fact that Asia and Africa account for two thirds of the world population.

The few sophisticated liberals and radicals may view these convulsions as an essential part of the social and economic development of these continents recently freed from the yoke of European imperialism. But, for the many, these images provide continuing evidence that peoples of coloured races are, indeed, inherently anarchic, violent, and quite incapable of self-help and self-rule. The civil wars in the Congo and Nigeria shook the liberal beliefs of quite a few British intellectuals who seemed to forget that, historically, large, polyglot countries, such as Russia and America, have emerged as united nations only after undergoing bloody civil wars. But then, as Patrick Anderson points out, 'For most of us [British] the historical perspective is not acute, the sense of the past in the present even less vivid'.[52]

No wonder then that in the field of 'formal' education – which is expected to produce citizens for a harmonious multi-racial society – little attention has yet been paid to the inert and overt racialist bias of text-books. As early as 1963, this point of fundamental importance was raised by Sheila Patterson in *Dark Strangers*,[53] and again by a study group of the London Council of Social Service:

Some readers, text-books and curricula still reflect an insular, culturally exclusive attitude, the colour-class myths of a colonial past and occasionally the nineteenth-century pseudo-scientific racialism that helped to justify this past. Subjects of particular sensitivity in this respect are history, geography, English literature, biology and scripture.[54]

The following examples from a history book in use in British schools illustrate the racial bias of many text-books. In the chapter 'The British in India and America' of *Histories*, Book IV, the authors write six hundred words on Indian history from ancient times to 1600, when 'the famous' East India Company

52. The *Sunday Telegraph*, 12 November 1967.   53. pp. 210–11.
54. *Immigrants in London*, Sheila Patterson, edr, p. 39.

appeared on the scene. The period 1600–1763 takes up 1,500 words. Of these nearly 250 words are devoted to the Black Hole of Calcutta:

Clive had *still more* to do *for* India. In 1756 Suraja Dowlah, the Nabob ... a *violent* youth of nineteen ... marched against Calcutta at the head of *30,000* men. The European residents with fruitless *heroism* tried to defend Calcutta; but after three days they were *forced to surrender....*

A mixed company of men, women, and *children*, 146 in number, were driven into a narrow prison-cell of the fort, about eighteen by fifteen feet, with only two small barred windows to admit the air. Huddled together, and scarcely able to breathe, they had to endure the *intense heat* of a June night, from seven until six in the morning. Mad with *agony*, they *struggled* with one another.... At length the morning broke and the Nabob allowed the survivors to come forth. But there were only twenty-three of them, and it took some time to clear a passage through the *heaps of dead bodies* which barred the way.[55]

One may argue on purely technical grounds that it is impossible to pack 146 men, women and children in that limited space, or on historical grounds that the person responsible for whatever happened on that evening in 1756 was a *French* subaltern of the Nabob; but that is not really the point. The main question is: how important is this episode, real, imagined, or exaggerated, to the historical process of founding the British raj in India? Not at all.

On the other hand, a most significant event, Brigadier-General Dyer's massacre, in 1919, of unarmed Indians in a park at Amritsar – 379 killed and 1,200 wounded – which is widely recognized as marking the beginning of the end of British rule in India goes unmentioned in the book. Nor is there any indication that during the seventeenth and eighteenth centuries, Britain was heavily engaged in the slave trade and slavery. The mention of the slave trade by the British, which occurs towards the end of the book, opens with the statement, 'Soon after the beginning of the nineteenth century the Slave Trade was abolished'.[56] This is all the more ironic because the textile industry, which marked

55. Sir Henry Marten and E. H. Carter, revised edn, 1953, pp. 37–8. (Author's italics.)
56. ibid., p. 287.

the onset of the industrial revolution in Britain, was entirely dependent on the production of cotton by slave labour in the New World colonies, a point made by, among others, Karl Marx in the mid-nineteenth century. 'Without slavery, you have no cotton; without cotton, you have no modern industry,' he wrote in *The Poverty Of Philosophy*. 'It is slavery that has given the colonies their value; it is the colonies that have created world trade; and it is world trade that is the pre-condition of large-scale industry.'[57]

In modern times, Sir Winston Churchill made a similar point while addressing West Indian sugar barons just before the Second World War:

The West Indies, two hundred years ago, bulked very largely in the minds of all people who were making Britain and making the British Empire. Our possessions of the West Indies, like that of India – the colonial plantation and development, as they were then called – gave us the strength, the support, but specially the capital, the wealth, at a time when no other European nation possessed such a reserve, which enabled us to come through the great struggle of the Napoleonic Wars, the keen competition of the commerce of the eighteenth and nineteenth centuries, and enabled us not only to acquire this world-wide appendage of possessions we have, but also to lay the foundations of that commercial and financial leadership which, when the world was young, when everything outside Europe was undeveloped, enabled us to make our great position in the world.[58]

Compared with those who feel that 'Britain did a lot for the "natives"', how many feel that 'the "natives" did a lot, economically, for Britain', as stated by Sir Winston Churchill and Karl Marx? Very few. And yet it is important that the British acknowledge the debt they owe to their former coloured colonies, and that the authors of text-books on British history state it. Appeals

57. Cited in A. Chater, *Race Relations in Britain*, p. 14. This 'large-scale' textile industry in Britain and the world 'trade' played havoc with the hand-spinning and hand-weaving industry of British India. 'The (resulting) misery hardly finds a parallel in the history of commerce,' wrote the Governor-General of India in his annual report of 1834–5. 'The bones of the cotton weavers are bleaching the plains of India.' The population of Dacca, a leading centre of hand-weaving, for instance, fell from 150,000 in 1818 to 20,000 in 1836. ibid., p. 15.

58. Cited in Neville Maxwell, *The Power of Negro Action*, pp. 7–8.

to British fair-mindedness ought always to be accompanied by the acknowledgement that the ancestors of present-day coloured immigrants played a vital role in creating the affluence that the British are enjoying today. Future generations in Britain should be brought up on a balanced, not a grotesquely partisan, account of British history.

It is still not too late to add a historical perspective to present-day race relations in Britain. For the problem, or the challenge, of race relations will remain for at least the next few generations.[59]

Recent British history shows that neither bland postures nor naïve beliefs have 'solved' the racial problem. The initial policy of official 'colour blindness' proved a disastrous failure. The hope that 'integrated' schooling would usher in a racially harmonious society too has proved illusory. Nevertheless, many academic researchers and professional 'race workers' still persist in skirting reality by devising tortuous analyses and evaluations of the racial situation. For instance, some liberal 'social scientists', conducting an attitude survey (for the I R R) arrived, through an ingenious and highly subjective evalution of answers to their questionnaire, at the heartening conclusion that only ten per cent of white Britons are racially prejudiced, while seventy-three per cent are tolerant or tolerantly-inclined.[60] And the mass media, at once flattered and relieved, splashed these findings in bold headlines, conveniently forgetting that only two years earlier the P E P survey had produced evidence that there was much racial discrimination against black citizens. This was one more example of brushing aside the uncomfortable reality and exaggerating the comfortable analysis.

The I R R survey also stated that the youngest of the respondents (aged 21–34) were the least prejudiced. (Apparently, those under twenty-one were not interviewed.) One is therefore inclined to conclude that the future is hopeful. But the evidence regarding contemporary British teenagers belies this optimism. In his article

59. After all, the effects of African slavery in western societies, abolished during the period 1834–81, are still to be seen in both the ex-slaves and the ex-masters. (The Portuguese abolished slavery in 1881.)

60. E. J. B. Rose and Associates, *Colour and Citizenship*, p. 553. This survey is discussed further in the Appendix.

'Non-Swinging Youth', Bernard Davies shows, persuasively and conclusively, that contrary to the popular image of being liberal, permissive and 'swinging', the British teenagers remain, essentially, conservative and traditionalist.[61] He refers to a national poll, published in November 1967, which showed that thirty per cent of the interviewed teenagers wanted the coloured immigrants to be sent back home; and sixty-eight per cent wanted the death penalty restored.

The theory, current in liberal circles, that contact between youngsters breaks down stereotypes and negative images has yet to be proved. The contrary seems to be the case. Taysir Kawwa's study of ethnic attitudes among British adolescents revealed that children living in an area with a high percentage of immigrants showed more negative attitudes than children living in an area with a low percentage of immigrants.[62] Peter Figueroa's study of English and West Indian school leavers in north London, who went to the same schools, led to the following conclusion:

On the whole the English school-leavers were against immigrants coming to live and work in Britain. The English boys also expressed negative attitudes concerning the children of immigrants born in this country. On the whole, the English had negative stereotypes of the West Indians, while the West Indians had partly positive and partly negative stereotypes of the English.[63]

There is as yet another theory, widely prevalent, that young children are quite unconscious of colour or ethnic differences. Scientific evidence, however, counters this. 'Many studies have shown,' wrote Professor Henri Tajfel in 1965, 'that evaluation of groups other than their own exists at a very early age.'[64] Sociometric tests applied to children of different ethnic groups in three London schools (comprehensive in 1962, secondary in 1964, and primary in 1964) by Taysir Kawwa, revealed a significant preference for one's own group in the choice of associates.[65]

Keith Rowley made a study of 1,747 children, aged seven to

61. *New Society*, 3 July 1969.
62. Cited in *Race Relations Abstracts*, Spring 1969, p. 31.
63. *Race*, April 1969, p. 507.
64. Richard Hooper, edr, *Colour in Britain*, p. 136.
65. Cited in *Race Relations Abstracts*, Spring 1969, p. 31.

fifteen, in sixty classes in ten junior and five secondary modern schools in the West Midlands. Sixty-five per cent of the children were British; twenty-one per cent, Asian; and the remaining West Indian. Children were asked three questions: whom would you prefer to sit next to in class, to play with in the playground, and to invite home to tea or a party? He found that *at all ages* children preferred their own ethnic group: ninety per cent of the British, seventy-five per cent of the Asian and sixty per cent of the West Indian children did so.[66]

Gustav Jahoda, Thelma Veness and I. Pushkin studied 172 white children in three north London schools. In tests about social situations simulated through the use of dolls of different racial characteristics, thirty-one per cent of the children were rated consistently unfavourable to the negro dolls. For three-year-olds, this percentage was twenty-two; and for six-year-olds, it was sixty-five. In another test, twenty-five per cent chose very distant or distant houses for negro children. The choice patterns, deliberations and spontaneous comments of many white children indicated an awareness of physical attributes and of the inferior social status of the negro.[67]

These are studies of first-rate importance. They reveal the attitudes and behavioural patterns of children and adolescents in contemporary Britain, and are therefore indicative of race relations in the future. And yet they generally go unnoticed even in the 'quality' Press, probably because their conclusions are at odds with the comforting, middle-class beliefs.

In fact, often many influential whites and some coloured leaders tend to dismiss altogether certain facts and events simply because these are at odds with their own beliefs and complacent analysis. For instance, they have already concluded that Powellism is a spent force, and that the popular support he received was an aberration.[68] They have interpreted his speeches more as a tactic to win personal popularity and the Tory Party leadership than a reflection and articulation of popular feelings on race.

66. Cited in *New Society*, 2 May 1968.
67. Cited in Michael Banton, *Race Relations*, pp. 60–1.
68. The *New Statesman*, for example, reacted to Enoch Powell's Eastbourne speech with an editorial headlined: 'The Suicide of Powellism'. 22 November 1968.

But anyone speculating, in realistic terms, on the future of race relations in Britain must not only consider the implications of racial attitudes amongst white children but must also discuss, fully and frankly, the prospect of repatriation, voluntary and not-so-voluntary, particularly when Enoch Powell has called the issue (of race and coloured immigration) 'one of the greatest dangers facing the people of this country', and has said,

I shall continue to be concerned with it as long as it is necessary. I shall not give up. I shall not give in. It is no good sitting down and saying it is all a mistake we have made and there is no answer.[69]

These words cannot be dismissed lightly. For his views have been gaining increasing support among Tory ranks as Sir Cyril Osborne's did during the late 1950s. At the 1969 Tory conference, for instance, Powellite forces mustered 954 votes against the platform's motion on race and immigration, which they considered mild. Those supporting the motion numbered 1,349. It was one of the closest victories for Tory leadership which reiterated its commitment to the idea of 'helping' those coloured immigrants who wish to return home.

69. *The Times*, 30 August 1968.

7 SENDING THE BLACKS BACK HOME?[1]

> *A genuine fear of repatriation is growing (in the coloured community).*
> SARDUL SINGH GILL, a Labour councillor, Ealing.[2]

> *Here lies the crucial importance to you and me ... of that policy of assisted repatriation and resettlement, which Sir Alec Douglas-Home, when leader of the Party, adopted almost four years ago. [Applause] To proclaim that policy and, when we have the opportunity, to put it into effect ... is a duty which we owe to all, white and coloured. [Applause].*
> ENOCH POWELL at the 1968 Conservative Party conference.[3]

Enoch Powell mentioned 're-emigration' of immigrants in his April 1968 speech in these guarded terms:

It can be no part of any policy that existing families should be kept divided; but there are two directions in which families can be re-united, and if our former and present immigration laws have brought about the

1. It is worth recalling that the first order to repatriate the blacks was served during the days of Elizabeth I, and concerned 'divers blackamoors', slaves as well as free men, who had 'crept into the realme during the troubles between Her Highness and the King of Spain (in 1588).' The order issued by the Privy Council on 11 August 1596, read: 'Her Majesty understanding that there are of late divers blackamoors brought into this realme, of which kinde of people there are already too manie, consideringe howe God hath blessed this land with great increase of people of our owne nations ... those kinds of people should be sent forth of the lande'. Cited in Clifford S. Hill, *How Colour Prejudiced Is Britain?*, p. 22. Nearly two centuries later, a similar thing happened again. When the attention of the government was drawn to the plight of the slaves, freed during the 1770s and 1780s in London, it offered them free passage to 'the fertile land' of Africa and £12 per head as subsistence allowance. In 1786, 411 blacks and sixty-one white prostitutes were bundled off to Sierra Leone to found Freetown; and many more were shipped off to the West Indies as 'free labourers'.

2. The *Guardian*, 5 May 1969.   3. *The Times*, 11 October 1968.

division of families, we ought to be prepared to arrange for them to be re-united in their countries of origin.

And yet this was enough to make James Callaghan, the then Home Secretary, declare in a television interview that 'The Social Security Ministry will now repatriate *any* immigrant family that is unable to pay for itself and wants to return home.'[4] Subsequent enquiries at the Ministry of Social Security revealed that during 1965–7, 243 heads of families had been paid a total of £28,330 to help them return home (in most cases, to Jamaica). This was considered quite unimpressive by the Tory shadow Home Secretary, Quintin Hogg (now Lord Hailsham), generally considered 'liberal' on race and coloured immigration issues. He told a BBC radio interviewer: 'The Tories' plan for assisting the repatriation of immigrants would be far bigger than the government's "mouse of a scheme" . . . Theirs is for the dropouts.'[5]

The reaction of the Tory front benches, and even the Labour government, to the idea of 'assisted re-emigration' seemed sufficiently favourable to embolden Enoch Powell to state, in November 1968, 'What is meant is that we would cease to admit not only new settlers and their dependants, but the dependants of immigrants already here'. This call was to be picked up by Edward Heath two months later when he demanded that the government assume power to ban immigration altogether if necessary. Duncan Sandys was quick to point out that Edward Heath's proposal would require 'a simple amendment' to the latest Commonwealth Immigrants Act.[6]

In May 1969 the Labour government met this demand partially by imposing the requirement of entry certificates for all prospective Commonwealth immigrants, including dependants of those already in England. A month later Enoch Powell came out with an outline of a scheme for repatriating 600,000 to 700,000 immigrants over a period of 'ten years or more' at the total cost of £300 million. The Tory leadership probably saw little point in nagging

4. *The Times*, 30 April 1968.
5. The *Guardian*, 1 May 1968. As long as statements on repatriation do not specifically include *all* immigrants – from the Commonwealth, Ireland and Europe – these must surely be considered racialist.
6. *The Times*, 27 January 1969.

the Labour government further on this subject: it had made its stand abundantly clear.

The Tory manifesto for the June 1970 general election stated that 'We will give assistance to the Commonwealth immigrants who wish to return to their countries of origin, but will not tolerate any attempt to harass or compel them to go against their will.' In contrast, the Labour manifesto stated that 'the rate of immigration' was 'under firm control and much lower than in past years'.

Although in their emphasis and attitude the two manifestos were different, the issues of race and coloured immigration were not raised by national leaders of the major parties during the election campaign. Why? Because, as Richard Crossman 'let slip in a speech in his constituency', there existed 'a tacit understanding between two parties to smother a controversial debate on race'.[7]

But, as before, this did not deter Enoch Powell from raising the issue. On 1 June, in his campaign letter to his constituents, he listed Commonwealth immigration as the number one 'danger' facing Britain.[8] 'It [Commonwealth immigrant population] carries a threat of division, violence and bloodshed of American dimensions, and adds a powerful weapon to the armoury of anarchy,' he wrote. A few days later, Anthony Wedgwood Benn attacked Enoch Powell's views in these words:

The flag of racialism which has been hoisted in Wolverhampton is beginning to look like one that fluttered twenty-five years ago over Dachau and Belsen. If we do not speak up now against the filthy racialist propaganda under the imprint of the Conservative Central Office, the forces of hatred will mark their first success and mobilize for their next offensive.

He added that Enoch Powell, not Edward Heath, was the real hero of the Conservative Party.

From a moral point of view it was no doubt admirable of Mr

7. Nicholas Deakin and Jenny Bourne in *Race Today*, July 1970, p. 205.

8. Commenting on Enoch Powell's election letter, the *New Statesman* said, 'Alone, uninvited, unscripted, and magnetic, he [Enoch Powell] has walked on to the centre of the Tory stage . . . Mr Heath goes on desperately mouthing his lines, as though Mr Powell were not there – but there is no doubt whom the audience . . . want to hear.' 5 June 1970.

Benn to attack Mr Powell so strongly. But it seems that in terms of election tactics, his statement and the subsequent controversy on race and coloured immigration that continued until election day, proved a liability to the Labour Party, arguably causing its defeat at the polls.

There is strong evidence to suggest that Enoch Powell won over many traditional Labour voters to the Conservative column.[9] In the West Midlands, where he is particularly popular, the swing to the Conservatives was above the national average. In Wolverhampton North East, Dudley, Brierly Hill and Cannock, it was more than nine per cent.[10] In Wolverhampton South West, Enoch Powell more than doubled his majority, from 6,585 to 14,467.

'Labour [here] is convinced Powell lost them the election nationally,' wrote the Birmingham correspondent of *Race Today*. 'The Conservatives think he won it for them.'[11] They have good reason to think so because, of the sixty-six Conservative gains from Labour, nearly two thirds were in those constituencies which had a noticeable coloured population or were near to them, and/

9. Conversely, the vast majority of coloured electors voted for Labour. But then they had done so in the past as well. Most likely the *proportion* changed little. What happened was that (a) there were more coloured voters than in 1966, and (b) a greater percentage of them voted.

10. According to Woodrow Wyatt, formerly Labour M P for Bosworth, Leicestershire, 'Until then [the Powell-Benn confrontation] people had believed that there was nothing between the parties on the race issue, but Wedgwood Benn convinced them that a vote for the Tories would mean tougher action against immigration'. He stated that miners in the Midlands coal belt were infected by Powellism although there was no immigration locally. As a result he lost his seat. (*The Times*, 30 June 1970.) So did Jennie Lee, formerly Minister for the Arts, lose her seat in Cannock, Staffordshire. 'I blame it [my defeat] on Powellism,' she said. 'This is a different Cannock to the one I fought in 1966.' Her Tory opponent, Patrick Cormack, shared Enoch Powell's views on coloured immigration. (The *Observer*, 21 June 1970.) The reference to 1966 was pertinent. 'According to the authoritative book, *Political Change in Britain*, by David Butler and Donald Stokes, which is standard reading for party strategists, this [lack of electoral impact of the race issue in 1966] was because voters saw no difference on this issue between the two parties,' wrote Nora Beloff. 'If they had, the authors say, "the issue could have sharply altered the party balance".' (The *Observer*, 15 March 1970.)

11. July 1970, p. 208.

or had Powellite Tory candidates.[12] Given this and Enoch Powell's continuing popularity with the Tory rank and file, it is difficult to see how he can lose his influence over Tory policies on race and coloured immigration.

Already the Tory government has passed the Immigration Act 1971, which contains a provision for repatriation. This law authorizes the Secretary of State to 'make payments of such amount as may be determined to meet or provide for expenses of persons who are not patrial in leaving the United Kingdom for a country or territory where they intend to reside permanently, including travelling expenses for members of their families or households'.

When the Bill was first published in February, 1971, the Monday Club, a right-wing pressure group, called it 'a step in the right direction', its only regret being that 'the repatriation provision seems limited to the expenses of return. Unless that can include resettlement, the response may not be so large as it should be and the importance of that response cannot be overstated.'[13] During the final reading of the Bill in the Commons, Enoch Powell said that the clause providing financial help for immigrants wishing to return home did not perhaps provide as much assistance as might sometimes be desirable.[14] However, he believed that 'the scope [of this clause] is really substantial and the advantage of these powers being used on a substantial scale would be very considerable.'[15]

Indeed, in his speech in June 1969, Enoch Powell talked of the

12. These constituencies were: Bedford, Belper, Birmingham Perry Bar, Birmingham Yardley, Bolton East, Bolton West, Bradford West, Brighouse and Spenborough, Bristol North East, Bristol North West, Bristol West, Buckingham, Bury and Radcliffe, Cannock, Cardiff North, Chislehurst, Chorley, Clapham, Dartford, Epping, Gloucester Gravesend, Hampstead, Hornchurch, Ilford South, Ipswich, Keighley, Lewisham West, Lichfield and Tamworth, Luton, Middlesbrough West, Nottingham South, Oldbury and Halesowen, Oxford, Preston North, Preston South, Reading, Rochester and Chatham, Sheffield, Heeley, Stretford, Uxbridge, and the Wrekin.

13. The *Scotsman*, 25 February 1971. At its national conference in Nottingham, the Monday Club called for attractive resettlement grants to encourage repatriation of 'immigrants of alien races'. The *Guardian Journal*, 8 March 1971

14. *The Times*, 18 June 1971.   15. The *Guardian*, 18 June 1971.

repatriation of 600,000 to 700,000 coloured immigrants. Since neither his enthusiasm for, nor his commitment to, this idea is likely to wane in the near future, it becomes necessary, first of all, to examine the basis on which he has apparently based his estimate. This is the survey sponsored by the BBC's *Panorama* programme, and conducted by the Opinion Research Centre in November 1968. It concluded that thirty-eight per cent of the coloured immigrants would like to return to their country of origin if they received financial help. But the procedures employed to conduct this survey, as revealed by Humphrey Taylor of the Opinion Research Centre to the *Sunday Times*,[16] cast doubt on its reliability.

Although the ORC had a scientific sample of white adults selected to represent a cross-section of the white population at large, encompassing various age and economic brackets, it had no corresponding sample of coloured adults. So, it fell back on a crude technique of stopping coloured adults in the street to solicit their answers. 466 coloured people in ten cities with substantial coloured populations were questioned by white interviewers. As Humphrey Taylor himself pointed out, a number of coloured people refused to be interviewed. How many did so is not known. But that is a crucial figure, because it is fair to assume that those who refused to co-operate did not like the subject of the enquiry and would have most probably said so to a coloured pollster. It is also naïve of white interviewers to expect honest answers from coloured respondents on such an issue as repatriation.[17]

There are other flaws in the method employed. To be representative of the coloured population in Britain the sample had to have an almost equal number of West Indians and Asians. Among Asians there had to be an almost equal distribution of sexes. And to get accurate answers only Asian women must be employed to interview other Asian women in their native language. Even among Asian males, how many would grasp the meaning of a term such as 'financial help'? One must therefore

16. 22 June 1969.
17. In contemporary America, for instance, almost invariably, black interviewers are used to question blacks on racial issues.

not only agree with Humphrey Taylor that 'It was a straw poll', but must also conclude that it was a biased, unrepresentative poll, crudely conducted.[18]

There has been one more poll on the subject – by the *Sunday Telegraph* in the summer of 1968. It concluded that seventy-five per cent of the coloured immigrants interviewed had no wish to return home regardless of any financial help or inducement, while fifteen per cent would be willing to go if offered a financial incentive. It was not disclosed as to how the poll had been conducted or how many had been interviewed and by whom.

However, if an 'educated guess' has to be made regarding the proportion of coloured settlers who would re-emigrate 'voluntarily', it must remain nearer the fifteen per cent mark as given by the *Sunday Telegraph*. But expressing a willingness to return home, with or without financial assistance, is not the same as *actually* doing so. As U. Dhar, a Pakistani leader in Bradford, put it, 'Even those of us who have been here for thirty years have been *thinking* of going home all along. But it is something else altogether to start selling your property here, packing, buying the tickets, etc.'[19]

In the final analysis, who will go, or be 'persuaded to go'? Those who have not yet brought over their families; those nearing retirement age; those constantly out of work due to, say, ill-health; the professional class; and those who have saved enough capital here to be able to start something of their own in their country of origin. This means that 'Those [working-class] coloured people they want to get rid of, simply will not go,' as an Indian leader in Nottingham put it. What prospect awaits a returning mill-worker in the Indian sub-continent, or a returning bus-conductor in the West Indies? Another unskilled or semi-skilled job, if he can find one, at a fraction of the wages earned in Britain. There is massive unemployment in the Indian sub-continent. In Jamaica the present national unemployment rate is twenty per cent, that among teenagers is nearly sixty per cent.[20]

18. Quite simply, how representative are the people in the street of the *whole* population?

19. The *Observer*, 14 June 1969.

20. The *Observer*, 23 November 1969.

'To import expatriates [into the West Indies] from England, who have known better living standards would mean adding a disastrous element to the political situation there,' wrote a correspondent of the *Observer*.[21] Therefore the Caribbean, as well as Indian, Pakistani and Bangla Deshi governments will, out of political and economic considerations, resist such a back-flow of expatriates.

But if the pressure is still on in Britain, and if 'voluntary' repatriation is, by whatever subtle means (such as nationality laws allowing only British nationals to work permanently), transformed into 'not-so-voluntary', it will have ugly repercussions inside Britain,[22] and on British people, as well as investments, in the coloured Commonwealth countries. For instance, what is likely to happen when the repatriated West Indian has spent his £2,000 and has not found a job? He would notice, with bitterness, white bosses on sugar plantations and in most industrial concerns, living in luxury, while he was unemployed. What then? 'Certainly he's not going to let that white man stay,' says Eugene Griffin, a West Indian youth leader in Leeds.[23] Eugene Griffin should know the current economic and socio-psychological situation in the West Indies: he went back to his native St Kitts in 1967, but returned to Leeds after a few months, sobered by the experience.

The economic situation in the Indian sub-continent is even more grave. Pressure to send the Indian, Pakistani and Bangla Deshi settlers back home will lead to counter-pressure to oust British nationals from the Indian sub-continent and to take over British investments which run into hundreds of millions of pounds. 'There are ninety-eight tea plantations in [the then] East Pakistan, and almost all of these belong to the British,' said an East Pakistani leader in Birmingham in the summer of 1968. 'If we're sent back home, we'll make sure that these properties come into the hands of our own people.' That such contingencies have

21. 14 June 1969.
22. The chance of some militant blacks, and their white sympathizers, resorting to violent acts of sabotage and destruction of property, on the lines witnessed recently in Ulster, cannot be ruled out.
23. The *Observer*, 14 June 1969.

been imagined and counter-measures quite seriously conceived was brought home to the author when another Pakistani leader in Wolverhampton told him that 'an important Pakistani diplomatic official in London' had assured them that if Pakistanis were 'pushed out' from Britain they would be over-compensated for their losses through distribution of confiscated property of the British in Pakistan.

Demands were made both inside and outside the Indian Parliament to 'nationalize' British properties in retaliation against the passing of the 1968 Commonwealth Immigrants Act.[24] Certainly any attempt to thin out Indian settlers in Britain will lead to a rise in the anti-British feelings in India, making the take-over of British investments a distinct possibility. Also, the lives of the British in particular, and of whites in general, would be put in jeopardy, if we bear in mind the statements made by Sikh leaders in Delhi during the turban controversy in Wolverhampton.[25]

The complex issue of repatriation and its consequences was aptly summed up by Praful Patel, a Kenya Asian leader, and secretary of the Committee on British Citizenship:

Let us imagine that a quarter million immigrants in the Midlands are replaced by thousands of expatriate English businessmen who will be hounded out of various Afro-Asian countries by irate 'coloured' governments. What then of British commercial interests in her future markets? Mr Powell seems to forget that race is now an international problem and cannot be resolved in terms of 'little England'.[26]

It must therefore be realized by the Powellite, as well as the middle-of-the-road, Tories that the chance of thinning out the black population in Britain through repatriation is slim. Nor must they place too much hope in an economic recession flushing out the blacks. At an intellectual level this proposition seems

24. 'During a bitter anti-British debate in the Indian Parliament . . . Congress members supported opposition speakers who called for nationalization of British interests, penalties for British subjects in India and the severance of its ties with the United Kingdom and the Commonwealth,' wrote *The Times* correspondent in India. 'The proposal . . . was mooted by Mr Bhupesh Gupta, a Communist member, and supported by almost the entire house.' 29 February 1968.
25. See p. 129.   26. *The Times*, 23 November 1968.

valid: the availability of jobs brought the blacks in, so the lack of jobs will drive them out. But human life does not always follow logic.

Undoubtedly an economic recession will lead to an abrupt rise in Enoch Powell's popularity, and will sharpen anti-black feelings. But as economic recession in Britain, or in the Western world, will most likely be accompanied by an economic down-turn in the coloured Commonwealth countries as well, most black settlers here will choose to sit through the recession, on the dole, rather than face an even more hazardous existence in their countries of origin. This in turn will raise the chances of the use of force or harassment against black settlers in Britain. But it will induce a counter-force here as well as abroad, as happened in the case of Skinheads' violence against Asians in the spring of 1970. Asian leaders here threatened retaliation against the British in India and Pakistan.[27] 'Warnings of possible reprisal against British residents are already appearing in Pakistan's newspapers and have also been given by party speakers in the current election campaign there,' wrote a correspondent of the *Observer*.[28] The problem will therefore become international and hurt Britain's national and commercial interests in the Afro-Asian world.

Let us, however, put aside these fears of economic recession in the future, and assume that the steady economic prosperity experienced by Britain since the end of the war, will continue. This prosperity will no doubt be accompanied by a rise in productivity, the introduction of labour-saving devices and machinery in industry (in a word, automation), a greater demand for labour in service industries rather than in manufacturing, and the progressive dispersal of industrial concerns.[29] These developments will prove particularly detrimental to coloured settlers since they are employed predominantly in unskilled and semi-skilled jobs. As an economic class living mainly in areas with 'deprived' schools, the coloured settlers and their children will

27. *The Times*, 27 May 1970.

28. 31 May 1970. Earlier, on 2 May, the London-based *Mashriq* weekly had reported instances of assaults on British nationals 'in various parts of Pakistan'.

29. For example, Birmingham lost 60,000 jobs during 1963–8 as a result of the voluntary movement of industrial firms from the city.

suffer the effects of such changes more than the indigenous population. As a result, racial ill-feelings will sharpen, especially in firms with a multi-racial labour force, as has already happened.

In Luton, a plastic manufacturing firm decided to introduce new manning arrangements, and informed the local T G W U official. The change involved Pakistani workers. When management began moving them, they stopped working. They were threatened with dismissals. A strike ensued. The union declared an official lock-out; but white workers continued to work. In another case, as a result of a productivity agreement between a firm in Woolwich and the T G W U, management told operators in one department (manned by West Indians and Asians) to increase output by fifty per cent. The operators protested, and six of them were suspended. The rest walked out, and were later backed by the union which asked that the productivity agreement be suspended. Meanwhile white workers remained at their jobs.[30]

As the trend towards higher productivity and mechanization continues, such incidents will become more frequent, and will repeatedly highlight the following socio-political phenomenon: given a choice between class solidarity and racial alignment, most white workers choose the latter. Once again, this illustrates a physiological and psychological fact, that class is not so self-evident as colour. The white proletarian has to be continually reminded that he is being exploited by the capitalist and must feel antagonistic towards him. Such exhortations are unnecessary in the case of racial differences. The biological difference, aligned with the historical white antipathy towards blacks, provides a constant base which, given propitious circumstances, can easily be transformed into open hostility and violence against blacks.

30. *Race Today*, December 1969, p. 251 Analysing figures from selected employment exchanges in the West Midlands and Greater London areas for the period February 1970–November 1971, Barbara Omar discovered that the unemployed coloured adult males formed a very high percentage of the total unemployed 'If this is due to processes of automation and industrial change,' she concluded, 'we have to face the prospect of having created a chronically unemployed black population; if it is due to economic recession we have to recognize that black workers . . . are the first to be discarded when the economic situation worsens.' *Race Today*, March 1972, p. 94.

Let us, however, assume that these technological changes will be gradual and will be absorbed without causing much hardship among coloured settlers, and will, in the long run, like all such previous changes, prove economically beneficial. If so, coloured settlers, like the rest of society, will enjoy the fruits of this prosperity, and their living standards will rise correspondingly. They will, for example, buy more and better consumer goods. At least some among them will save enough to afford better housing. This does not necessarily mean that all such people will then move into predominantly white areas, even if an effective enforcement of the 1968 Race Relations Act accorded them equal access to housing. Nor does it mean that time and rising prosperity will automatically lead to the dispersal of coloured citizens in the near future. There are good reasons to temper an optimistic projection for the future.

Capital saving may enable the coloured man to buy a better house; but it does not attentuate his longing for the warmth and friendship of his fellow-countrymen. Nor does it dispel his fear or insecurity when in the midst of a sea of white faces. Five major outbreaks of violence against coloured people since 1958 are sufficient reminders to him that safety does lie in numbers. The feelings of coloured citizens of Leeds in the wake of a race riot in July 1969 illustrate this. Summing up the situation, the correspondents of the *Observer* wrote:

There are about 1,300 coloured immigrants – out of a total population of 17,000 – dispersed throughout the district [of Burley, where race riots occurred] . . . On the surface the ratio of immigrants to native would seem to conform to integrationist ideals, but the past week has demonstrated the practical realities. The Hassans and Rajas feel exposed and vulnerable in times of trouble. The situation contrasts sharply with the security of coloured immigrants in Chapeltown, the Leeds district with the highest proportion of coloured immigrants.[31] Two-thirds of all the city's coloured immigrants live there. They feel there is strength in their munbers. Mrs A. Malik (a Pakistani teacher), formerly an advocate of dispersal as the best means of achieving integration, said: 'I've learnt from this. I want my people to stay together now.'[32]

31. Forming about forty to fifty per cent of the district's total population.
32. 3 August 1969.

Recent violence in Northern Ireland illustrated this point even more dramatically. Catholics living in 'mixed' areas found themselves more vulnerable than those living in Catholic ghettoes, and vice versa. The rioting halted the slow, but definite, trend towards a 'mixed' residential pattern that was evident before. Inter-racial violence in Britain in the future will certainly lead to similar results. And only a rash man can off-handedly dismiss the possibility of future inter-racial strife in Britain, arising out of local, national or even international events.

Within the next generation, an element that had helped substantially to keep the racial temperature low – the general docility and diffidence of coloured immigrants – will disappear completely. Coloured children born and brought up in Britain will be self-confident and vocal, and will react sharply to any harassment or physical violence, to which they, or their parents, might be subjected. Counter-violence is therefore more likely to follow than has been the case hitherto.

In the international field, events in such countries as Rhodesia, South Africa and America, during the next generation or two, will have direct repercussions in Britain. Imagine for instance a civil war in Rhodesia in which blacks steadily gain an upper hand. Imagine, too, a quarter million white Rhodesians streaming into Britain. Under the circumstances, racial tranquillity in Britain will be almost impossible to maintain. The coloured minority here will become a target of white fury. But the black British will not take it lying down.

Or imagine a steady escalation of inter-racial strife in America and the detailed accounts of it in the British mass media. Both white and black citizens will feel involved, identifying with their counterparts in America. The feeling among white Britons that blacks are 'always a trouble' will be heightened, while the feeling of blacks that whites' violent hatred of them is incurable will be reinforced.

Let us, however, assume that racial peace in Britain will continue undisturbed, and that living standards will continue to rise. If so, the trend – at present nascent – among coloured settlers to disperse, through the private purchase of houses in predominantly white areas or through council housing, will develop. But then the question arises: is the present or potential rate of voluntary dispersal likely to outpace the rate of growth of the coloured population through immigration (mainly wives and dependants) and natural increase?[33] The answer is, no. The total yearly increase in coloured population is currently running in the region of 80,000 to 100,000 due to immigration (35,000 to 45,000),[34] and the excess of births over deaths (45,000 to 55,000).[35] This means simply that even if each year nearly 100,000 coloured citizens were to move to *predominantly white* areas, the situation with regard to coloured concentrations will remain the same as it is now.

Since this is not happening, or likely to happen, and since there is no decline in the 'propensity of white population to move out of mixed areas', as Enoch Powell puts it, one is led to conclude that concentrations of black residents in certain parts of cities and towns will increase. It is therefore realistic to predict that towards the end of the next generation, the residential pattern of the blacks in Britain will be midway between what it is now here and what it is now in America. By then, recent Irish arrivals and British old-age pensioners, who at present give areas of coloured settlement a 'multi-racial' appearance, will have left or died, and their houses will have been bought or occupied by the children of coloured immigrants.

The figures of births for March and April 1969 in Greater

33. More than four fifths of the present New Commonwealth immigrants are dependants. They will form the basis of future family units in Britain. The subsequent decline in the number of fresh immigrants, in the coming years, will be more than compensated by the rise in the number of coloured births.

34. Figures foɪ 1971 were: immigrants from the New Commonwealth 23,615; and the UK passport holders from East Africa 11,564; total, 35,179.

35. Figures released by the Registrar-General in March 1970 showed that for April–September 1969 the number of births in England and Wales where *both* parents were from the New Commonwealth was 23,500; and the number where *one* parent was from the New Commonwealth was nearly 6,000. This means an annual rate of 59,000. Excluding Malta, Cyprus and Gibraltar from the New Commonwealth, the annual rate was 57,000. From this one must subtract figures for annual deaths estimated at 5,000 (at the rate of 0.3 of one per cent of the estimated 1.5 million coloured population).

London and other cities that follow provide a statistical basis for this prediction. These figures also provide statistical proof of the *present* concentration of coloured settlers. For instance, in Greater London, most of them are to be found in only half of its thirty-three boroughs. There, the proportions of coloured births to the total births were:

Inner London Boroughs		*Outer London Boroughs*	
Lambeth	1 in 3	Brent	1 in 3
Hackney	1 in 3½	Ealing	1 in 4
Islington	1 in 4	Haringey	1 in 4
Wandsworth	1 in 5	Newham	1 in 5
Hammersmith	1 in 5	Waltham Forest	1 in 5
Southwark	1 in 6	Hounslow	1 in 7
Westminster	1 in 7	Croydon	1 in 11[36]
Kensington & Chelsea	1 in 7		
Camden	1 in 10		
Tower Hamlets	1 in 10		

Outside Greater London, the corresponding figures, as quoted by Enoch Powell in his speech on 18 July 1969, in Bradford, were:

Wolverhampton	1 in 4	Walsall	1 in 6
Huddersfield	1 in 4½	Leicester	1 in 6
Bradford	1 in 4½	Luton	1 in 9
Birmingham	1 in 5	West Riding	1 in 10
Slough	1 in 5	Reading	1 in 10

These are also the statistics which make Enoch Powell contemplate with a fear and foreboding (shared by 'thousands of my countrymen,' as he put it) a future when 'a fifth or a quarter of some of our major towns and cities, as well as smaller towns up and down the country, will be coloured '– a phenomenon which he quotes Lord Radcliffe describing as 'inserting into a fairly complex urban and industrial civilization a large alien wedge'.

When eminent persons such as Lord Radcliffe write about the 'fairly complex urban and industrial civilization', they ought to bear in mind that the nature of this civilization is undergoing

36. The *Evening Standard*, 12 November 1969.

continual change of the kind which can more clearly be seen in contemporary America. Large cities in America are losing population, as more and more people move out to the suburbs and commute daily to their workplaces which too are being increasingly relocated, or established, in suburban areas. This trend began modestly, but definitely, in Britain in the mid 1950s, and has continued since then. The population of Birmingham, for example, decreased between 1951 and 1961. Almost all those who have left, for whatever reason, the 'hearts' of British towns and cities, have benefited by this movement: they have found better, not worse, housing. However profound be the nostalgic regret of the old to see their family homes fall into the hands of blacks, most young Britons certainly do not share their sentiment. Furthermore, one must not underestimate the dulling effect that economic prosperity has on *all* socio-political conflicts; and race relations are no exception. Consequently, one is led to treat Enoch Powell's prediction that the English will not 'endure', what he calls, 'the transformation of whole areas which lie at the heart of it [England] into alien territory' with a realistic scepticism.

If, however, there is an economic recession, the national mood will certainly change; but then the primary concern will be with jobs, *not* housing patterns. A recession will not make the whites living in the suburbs trek back to the central zones of towns and cities. And, as stated earlier, if efforts are made forcibly to repatriate blacks, these will create national and international complications, injurious to the self-interest of Britain. The white British will find the price of putting back the racial clock much too high to pay, and will have to accept, bitterly perhaps, that their area of manoeuvre in this field is extremely limited, and that the best solution for all concerned is to follow the policy of peaceful co-existence – of 'live and let live'.

8 PEACEFUL CO-EXISTENCE: SOCIAL PLURALISM

There is no reason why cultural diversity should not be combined with loyalty to this country.
EDWARD HEATH[1]

My habits and way of life as an immigrant should be moulded not into a carbon copy of an Englishman, but into a part of the society. I should be able to keep my individuality and my culture.
SARDUL SINGH GILL, a Labour Councillor, Ealing.[2]

Future contingencies and speculative solutions apart, there are still the basic, much-reiterated themes of 'English identity' and 'the instinct to preserve that identity' to be considered. Enoch Powell has complemented these with his view that a West Indian or an Asian, by being born in England, does not become an Englishman.[3] How does the substantial presence of Afro-Asians threaten English identity? And what bars, for ever, the descendants of Afro-Asians from becoming Englishmen? Is it their racial stock, or cultural heritage, or both?

It cannot be their racial stock if one is to take seriously Enoch Powell's resentment at being called a 'racialist', that is, 'someone expressing either favourable or unfavourable bias [on racial grounds]'.[4] Then probably it is their cultural background. In that case, why does Enoch Powell bracket West Indians and Asians together, for the West Indians remain culturally nearer to the

1. In a letter to the Bexley community relations council, June 1970. *Race Relations Bulletin,* July 1970, p. 1.
2. The *Guardian,* 5 May 1969.
3. This runs contrary to the definition of an Englishman, in the *Pocket Oxford Dictionary* as 'someone English by birth, descent or naturalization'.
4. Webster's *New Collegiate Dictionary,* 1961, p. 696. According to this definition, therefore, one can, logically, term a person who, in discussing immigration or re-emigration, does not include *all* immigrants into Britain, as a racialist 'in that context'.

British than to their West African ancestors, which is not the case with Asians. Or perhaps Enoch Powell views the situation in terms of the size and concentration of the coloured community so that, for all practical purposes, it shields the Afro-Asian child from absorbing British culture?[5] After all, his plan for repatriation is not meant to eliminate the coloured community altogether but merely to reduce its size. Once that has happened, he feels, then 'the pressures towards integration which normally bear upon any small minority' will operate more effectively and lead to the 'integration' of the remaining Afro-Asians into British society; that is, help them become 'for all practical purposes indistinguishable from its other members'.

But the question is: has the smallness of the coloured communities living in such places as Cardiff and Liverpool for the past fifty years led to their integration into the local population and made them 'indistinguishable' from the rest? The answer is: no. And yet this historical evidence has apparently been ignored not only by Enoch Powell but also by such liberal sociologists as Sheila Patterson. In 1963, she concluded her study of Brixton (where a substantial number of West Indians settled during the 1950s) with the prediction that:

Over the next decades in Britain the West Indian migrants and their children will follow in the steps of the Irish; they will ... gradually ... fan out of the central areas of settlement ... [Their] adaptation and advancement will lead to closer relationships with the local population ... and to an at least partial biological absorption ... in the local population.[6]

Let us, for a moment, consider simply the immigrant-host relationship without regard to colour or race. The conventional relationship is dynamic and can be summarized thus. Initial contact and competition (for jobs and housing) are followed by accommodation and formal acceptance in structured situations (of work and education) whilst the immigrant is undergoing the process of acculturation. His acculturation is rewarded corres-

5. White Britons sharing Enoch Powell's views must not forget that a very high proportion among Afro-Asians, adults as well as children, watch *British* television and read *British* papers.
6. *Dark Strangers*, p. 343.

pondingly by social acceptance by the host community. In time, this leads to (biological) amalgamation whereby the immigrant loses his previous identity and is considered a fully-fledged member of the host society – that is, he is 'absorbed' by the receiving society. Many post-war Irish immigrants have already graduated from initial contact to an almost complete absorption into British society.

However, as we have seen in previous chapters, whatever their degree of anglicization or the length of stay in Britain, most of the West Indian and Asian immigrants, whether in Cardiff, Brixton or Southall, have not yet been rewarded with social acceptance by the receiving society. The primary reason for this is that they are racially different from the white British. 'Most recently it has begun to look as if the crude consideration of skin colour will matter most,' wrote Michael Banton, professor of sociology and the author of *Race Relations*, in 1967.

The evidence adduced in this book (especially in terms of the historical and contemporary attitudes of the white British) leads one to conclude that the relationship between Afro-Asians and white Britons will not, at least for the next generation or two, graduate beyond the stage of accommodation and formalized acceptance. Such a relationship is termed, by sociologists, 'social, or cultural, pluralism'.

Michael Banton defines 'social pluralism' as a system whereby 'members of different minorities enjoy equality in respect of civil rights and obligations, but keep themselves separate in marriage and mutual hospitality, while rivalling one another in other contexts – such as in political organizations.'[7] Sheila Patterson defines 'cultural pluralism' as 'a stage in which the incoming group as a whole, through its own organizations, adapts itself to permanent membership of the receiving society in certain major spheres of association, notably in economic and civic life. On its side, the receiving society accepts the group as a lasting entity, differing in certain spheres that do not directly affect the overall life of the society, such as religion, and cultural and family patterns, and sometimes even in the retention of a mother-tongue or second language or of secondary loyalties to a country

7. *New Society*, 9 November 1967.

of origin.'[8] Cultural pluralism has of course existed in Britain, with regard to the Jewish minority, for the last four generations.[9]

It seems that Sheila Patterson did not consider the possibility of such a relationship developing in the case of West Indian immigrants even though she was aware of the cultural differences between West Indians and the British, and described them at some length in *Dark Strangers*.[10] Instead of accepting these differences, and predicting that they could, or would, persist, albeit in an attentuated form, she wrote:

> If accommodation and ultimately assimilation are to be achieved, the West Indian migrants must face the fact that they have to make a thorough-going and sustained effort to adapt their behaviour and values in all major spheres of life.[11]

The schoolmasterly tone of this statement is a symptom of the egocentricity from which many British sociologists, as well as politicians, suffer. They consider British society to be stable, homogeneous and unitary, and feel strongly that all newcomers who have been allowed the 'privilege' of settling here must – regardless of how shabbily they are treated by the indigenous population – rapidly adjust and conform. Sheila Patterson's statement is also highly presumptive, as Neville Maxwell, a West Indian leader, pointed out. 'No West Indian, unless he is dreaming, now goes around piously seeking to be "accepted" by the native people as *Dark Strangers* all along conveyed,' he wrote. 'One must disabuse oneself of this generally accepted fallacy [among the British].'[12]

There are quite a few 'generally accepted fallacies' current even in the highest academic, political, and administrative circles. One of these is that in the past *all* immigrants to Britain have been 'assimilated'. This is certainly not true of the (white) Jews who first arrived in Britain in 1875 from Russia, and settled in small

8. *Dark Strangers*, pp. 21–2.

9. The fact that many British Jews went off to fight for Israel during the Middle-East conflict in 1967 highlighted their loyalty to Israel, a country of their *historic* origin. In case of a future conflict between Israel and Britain, highly unlikely but not impossible, British Jews will be caught in an agonizing dilemma.

10. pp. 200–206.   11. ibid., p. 353.

12. *The Power of Negro Action*, p. 12.

numbers (120,000 over a period of forty years). Dr Ernest Krausz's recent study of the Jewish community in Edgware, which he considers typical of the Jewish minority in Britain, reveals the following facts.[13]

Eighty per cent are affiliated to synagogues. Seventy-one per cent of the Jews with one or more children under fifteen bring up their children 'very strictly' or 'fairly strictly' (in religious terms). Thirty-five per cent belong to a Jewish organization or club and another forty per cent belonged, in the past, to a similar organization; whereas only nineteen per cent belong to a non-Jewish organization or club. Nearly two thirds feel more 'at home' in a Jewish district than elsewhere; and the same proportion consider Edgware as 'a predominantly Jewish' district (whereas it is only forty per cent so).

In spite of the fact that many Jews in Dr Krausz's sample do not work for Jewish firms (and thus come in contact daily with non-Jews), and have a 'liberal' attitude towards social mixing with non-Jews, in reality there is little social mixing between Jews and non-Jews.[14] When mixing takes place it is often circumscribed.[15] The important reason for this social distance between Jews and non-Jews, writes Dr Krausz, is 'the difference between the cultural background of the two groups'.

If this is the case with an immigrant minority which is visually indistinguishable from the majority, and which first appeared in Britain *almost a hundred years ago*, what chance is there for the 'assimilationist' dream of many white liberals with regard to Asians and West Indians, whose cultural differences are compounded by physical distinctions? To be fair, outside the academic and specialist circles, the word 'assimilation' is rarely used. The magic word, popularized by the mass media, is 'integration'.

13. Ernest Krausz, 'Jews In Britain: Integrated Or Apart?' A paper presented to the Fourth Annual Conference of the Institute of Race Relations, 19 September 1969.

14. 'The results show unmistakably that Jews in Edgware are on friendly terms mostly with other Jews and that their close friendships are almost exclusively recruited from within Jewish ranks,' states Dr Krausz.

15. Only twenty-nine per cent of the Jews do *not* have strong objection to inter-marriage with non-Jews.

Its present currency is derived from its extensive use in reporting events in America (beginning in the mid 1950s) concerning school segregation in the southern states. In the American context, integration is used as an antonym for (*de facto* or *de jure*) segregation meaning, more specifically, discontinuation of *de jure* segregation. In Britain, however, various meanings and interpretations have been attributed to the term.

'To integrate,' says Webster's *New Collegiate Dictionary*, is 'to form into a whole; to unite or become united as to form a complete or perfect whole.' 'To integrate,' writes Lord Elton, quoting Fowler's *Modern English Usage*, is 'to combine components into a single congurous whole'. Fowler adds that the public have now borrowed the verb from psychologists with such freedom that it has become a vogue word, habitually preferred to less stylish but more suitable words such as 'merge, fuse, consolidate'.[16] Then we have Enoch Powell stating that 'To be integrated into a population means to become for all practical purposes indistinguishable from its other members':[17] clearly he is thinking of assimilation while he is talking of integration. According to Fowler's definition, however, these two words are not far apart. And yet Roy Jenkins stated in May 1966 that, 'I define integration not as a flattening process of assimilation but as equal opportunity, accompanied by cultural diversity, in an atmosphere of mutual tolerance.' This is a highly subjective definition which has no relationship with *either* the common understanding of the word *or* its dictionary meaning.

Yet the intellectual liberals, following their Burkian tradition, continually attempt to dispel 'common ignorance' and dispense 'special wisdom' to whomsoever will take heed. The Race Relations Board has even incorporated this very subjective definition into one of its reports.[18] The Community Relations

16. *The Times*, 20 March 1969.

17. If we accept this definition then we must interpret the use of bleaching creams and hair-straighteners by the Afro-Caribbeans and the discarding of turbans by Sikhs as steps towards 'integration'.

18. *Report Of The Race Relations Board for 1966–7*, para. 44, pp. 16–17. This paragraph also states that 'They [West Indians, Indians and Pakistanis] are identifiable and will remain indentifiable, unless they are wholly assimilated into the native population. But assimilation . . . is not the

Commission never tires of it. Every liberal speaker or spokesman or publication, at one point or another, quotes Mr Jenkins's definition. Even then, present evidence suggests that there are few takers.

Let us leave aside the 'common people' who, in this age of sociological surveys and questionnaires, have not yet been polled to find out what they think 'integration' means. Let us, instead, concentrate on professional and semi-professional 'race workers', those who feel dedicated to creating a 'racially harmonious society in Britain'. A study of active members of local community relations councils by a sociologist, in 1969, showed that only ten per cent thought of integration in Jenkins's terms, whereas twenty-five per cent defined it in 'assimilationist' terms. But, most significantly, over fifty per cent could produce no definition of integration at all.[19] But why blame them? Even the drafters of the 1965 White Paper devoted exclusively to immigration from the Commonwealth, while crowning its Part III 'Integration', left the term undefined.[20]

However, despite the lack of a precise definition, or a plethora of subjective definitions and interpretations, a strong attachment to the ideal of integration remains. This sentimental attachment is often coupled with an almost instinctive presumption that whoever as much as questions the term is an advocate of 'segregation' or 'separate development'. And the dreaded, emotive word 'segregation' brings with it an agglomeration of images associated with America and South Africa. No attempt is made even by otherwise well-informed people, such as British journalists, to distinguish between the 'Separate and Unequal' concept as enforced by *law* in South Africa; the 'Separate but Equal' philosophy as widely practised by *custom* in present-day America; and the 'Separate and Equal' concept as practised, through *voluntary*

policy of Her Majesty's Government.' It must be noted that assimilation could not *possibly* be the government's policy. Because to be 'wholly assimilated' into the native population, coloured citizens will have either to get their skins bleached or be married, *on a massive scale*, to white citizens.

19. As described by the researcher to the author in September 1969.

20. Or, perhaps, like all self-evident truths such as 'The United Kingdom is already a multi-racial society' (a statement made in the above document), 'integration' does not need an official definition or explanation.

separation, by, say, the Asians in Bradford or the Jews in Edgware. The separate life-style, as lived by the Jewish minority, for instance, is not, and need not, be underlined by rigid belief, on racial lines, in the philosophy of inferiority /superiority. This tendency for voluntary separation may be regarded as 'transient' if only to soothe the British liberal conscience. However, to be realistic, the transient phase must be visualized in terms of *decades*, not years.

A realist will find it hard to share the trepidation of the British liberals at having to lower their sights from 'assimilation' to 'integration' and now to what is being called 'pluralistic integration'.[21] The simple fact remains that, with the possible exception of post-revolutionary Cuba, nowhere else in the white Western world, is there yet a just, harmoniously assimilated, interracial society. The case of Brazil is often cited as the ideal. A close examination of modern Brazilian society by sociologists has, however, revealed that the race relations there are far from ideal.

Summing up the situation in contemporary Brazil, Colin Legum writes:

Roger Bastide, who carried out research for UNESCO in Brazil, concluded that it is 'a country in which prejudice is based not on race but on colour, where discrimination varies in direct proportion to the blackness of the skin'. A Brazilian professor, Florestan Fernandes, has shown that the historico-social transformations that have taken place since the 1800s have benefited only the white population. 'Legally the caste system was abolished; in practice the Negro and mulatto population did not rise above the social situation they have known earlier. Instead of entering *en masse* into the social classes that were in the process of formation and differentiation, they found themselves incorporated into the "plebs"' ... His researches in Sao Paulo – Brazil's most industrially developed city – showed that the traditional social systems 'assure that white supremacy and Negro inferiority would survive intact.'

In fact ... the cruel reality about Brazil is that it is a social pyramid in which the whitest are at the pinnacle and the blackest are at the base. The process of dark people rising in this pyramid is spoken of as 'whitening' themselves.[22]

21. This proves the liberals' continued attachment to the word 'integration'. 'Pluralistic integration' is really a misnomer for 'social pluralism'.
22. The *Observer*, 10 March 1968.

In other words, Brazilian society is indeed biased in favour of whites. And the policy of racial equality, often proclaimed by official agencies,[23] co-exists with the practice of discrimination by white citizens towards those who are not 'one hundred per cent' white. For historical reasons, there has been much inter-racial breeding – between Europeans, Africans and American-Indians– in Brazil; and yet the 'white bias' of society has remained un-altered. This is worth noting because many British liberals regard inter-racial marriage (which, in the popular parlance, is called miscegenation) as a crucially important element in the creation of a racially harmonious and just society.

No doubt biological amalgamation helps assimilate the racial minority. But one has to assess the situation in Britain (or else-where) quantitatively. The sexually imbalanced composition of the early West Indian migrants created amongst them a pressure to court white women. In those days the incidence of inter-racial marriage or co-habitation was substantial, probably fifteen per cent. Since then the situation has changed. As the West Indian, and later Asian, communities have become more sexually balanced, and larger in size, this pressure has considerably lessened. Consequently, the *incidence* of inter-racial marriage has steadily declined. However, due to the larger size of the coloured population at present, as compared with the late 1950s, the actual *number* of inter-racial marriages taking place each year now is probably the same as it was then.

Amongst whites, dislike of inter-racial marriage remains high: between seventy and ninety per cent disapprove; only seven to thirteen per cent approve.[24] The author's research in this field

23. For instance, the author was told by the Brazilian Embassy in Washington D C that the government did not categorize the population on a racial basis and it was not known how many people were 'non-white'. However, the *Encyclopedia Britannica* states that twenty-seven per cent of the population is coloured.

24. Figures vary with the wording of the question. The Gallup poll in 1961, for instance, asked, 'Do you think that marriage between a white person and a coloured person is, or is not, advisable?' In contrast, Clifford S. Hill, a few years later asked, 'Would you approve of your sister, or your daughter, marrying a coloured person?' *How Colour Prejudiced is Britain?* p. 39. Characteristically enough, no national poll of coloured people has yet been taken on the subject.

shows that although middle-class inter-racial couples and their children experience few social or psychological problems, this is not the case with working-class homes. In most cases, the white spouse, female or male, has to forego social contacts with white friends and acquaintances, and even sometimes family ties. Their children, too, experience considerable psychological problems. The two-category classification prevalent in the Anglo-Saxon world (of Britain and America) terms inter-racial children 'coloured', not 'mulatto' or 'half-white'.

Under the circumstances, children of mixed marriages, with a working-class background, often socialize, and identify themselves, with coloured children. When they reach adulthood they tend either to choose coloured or inter-racial partners for marriage because (a) their social contacts with whites are minimal, and (b) they wish to save *their* children the distasteful experience of the psychological ambivalence they themselves underwent during childhood and adolescence. Hence one cannot visualize the past or present incidence or inter-racial marriage steadily rising and thus leading us to the ideal of a racially amalgamated society in the near future.

It appears, therefore, that we must accept the proposition that the relationship of 'social pluralism' – which, in fact, *now* exists – is most likely to persist over the next few generations. Already there are signs that after years of myopia and fantasy-mongering, realism is steadily creeping into the sociological, administrative and political circles. The change in official thinking is well illustrated by the difference in the tone of the following statements. In its report, *Immigrants And The Youth Service*, in 1967, the Committee of the Youth Service Development Council wrote:

> The demand for separate provision is, then, real enough, for the young immigrants ... We, as a Committee, recognize that young immigrants may genuinely feel more at home among other people with a similar background ... At the same time, we cannot lose sight of the fact that an over-emphasis on distinctiveness, rather than on shared values and attitudes, can widen, rather than narrow, the gap.[25]

In contrast stands the statement in *The Problems Of Coloured School-Leavers*, a report by the House of Commons Select

25. Department of Education and Science, p. 13.

Committee on Race Relations and Immigration, in 1969. After referring to a multi-racial club in Ealing, and to 'mainly coloured clubs in Wolverhampton and Huddersfield, and all-coloured clubs in Liverpool and Hackney', the Committee stated:

> It is pointless to dogmatize about what type of club is best. Each has to develop naturally in response to the wishes of the local population, both white and coloured. If this means that some clubs become all-white or all-coloured, no one need object as long as the club does not actively seek to bar entry to one race or another.[26]

Here, at last, is a statement from a body of legislators which is at once honest and undogmatic and which, above all, recognizes reality as it exists *without* the customary liberal guilt or moralizing, or the exhortations about multi-racialism and 'integration'. The realization is finally being reached by the national as well as local leadership level that neither sermonizing nor breast-beating will lead to the millennium of a socially integrated multi-racial society in Britain. Edward Heath, for instance, said, in September 1967, that, 'We must do everything in our power to enable these immigrants and their families to live *their* lives in the community'.[27] Realism was also shown by Edward Short, the then Minister of Education, when, in early 1969, he said:

> In my view the concept of the neighbourhood school should not be lightly abandoned. But to impose dispersal by legislation or by regulation in the centre regardless of local circumstances would probably create far more discord than harmony .. there will inevitably be schools with a very high proportion of immigrant children on the roll.[28]

Indeed there already are scores of schools in the country with more than sixty per cent coloured pupils.[29] But these schools, like the rest, must be judged by their scholastic and other achievements, not by their racial composition. Also, these schools must

26. Vol. I, July 1969, p. 56.

27. Edward Heath expanded this idea in his letter to the Bexley community relations council in June 1970 when he said, 'This [playing a full part in public life] does not mean that the immigrant must feel obliged to abandon his own culture'. Cited in *Race Relations Bulletin*, July 1970, p. 1. This statement runs parallel to the definition of 'social pluralism' given by Michael Banton. (See p. 320.)

28. N A S, *Education and the Immigrants*, p. 22.

29. In 1969, in Birmingham alone, sixteen schools had more than sixty per cent coloured children. *Race Today*, May 1969, p. 25.

begin to reflect the backgrounds and feelings of the pupils; and these must be recognized, even encouraged, by local authorities. Some councils are already beginning to do so. 'Members of the council feel that it would be a pity if the Indian children were to lose their own culture,' said a spokesman of the Ealing borough council in July 1969. The council decided to arrange for the CSE examination to be taken in Punjabi.[30] In short, the idea of social pluralism is already being subconsciously accepted by those in power. What is missing is a conscious understanding of it and formal commitment to it.

As a national policy social pluralism is preferable to social integration for the following reasons. It is realizable in the very near future: indeed it has been, more or less, achieved in the case of Afro-Asian immigrants. All that is needed now is a formal recognition of this fact in official circles, and a greater popular awareness that this is the kind of relationship that has existed between (white) Christians and the Jews in Britain for a long time. This in turn will relieve the frustration that a society feels when it continually fails to reach a social goal it has been conditioned to think desirable, namely, social integration.

More specifically, this model of relationship will exorcize the small, but influential, liberal segment of British society of their guilt and anxiety regarding coloured fellow-citizens which often leads it to be either artificially polite or patronizing towards blacks. The white liberals need no longer invite coloured people to tea or, in any other way, self-consciously strive to bring about 'integration'.

At the popular level this conscious effort, which implies a certain initiative, has been totally missing. The attitude has generally been 'Live and let live'. This fits the model of social pluralism perfectly since it means leaving a minority well alone in cultural and social areas.

Finally, this relationship whereby people of different racial stocks 'mix but do not combine' will reassure those white Britons who, for good or evil, do not wish to see their culture or racial stock adulterated with the Afro-Asian. This is an important factor and deserves serious consideration. Shifting the stress from

30. The *Evening Standard*, 1 July 1969.

'integration' to mere acceptance, in a neutral sense of the word, will relieve the anxiety and fear of most white Britons. For, the word 'integration' generally seems to imply inter-racial sex and marriage.[31] The much-detested prospect that 'Britain will soon become a coffee-coloured nation' has been an important element in engendering antipathy towards coloured immigrants. Reiterating social pluralism, instead of social integration, as a national policy will help dispel, at least partially, this anxiety about 'our nation'.

Nevertheless, some *basic* questions ought to be raised and discussed regarding 'our nation', namely, 'What is a nation?'; 'What does "being an Englishman" mean?'; 'What is British identity?'. Furthermore, 'Is the concept of British identity static or regressive?'; or 'Is it, or should it be, a flexible, dynamic and forward-looking concept?'. Are we to remain prisoners of the past, insisting on a *unitary* image of a Briton as a person who is white, Christian, clean-shaven, wearing a suit or skirt; or should we start conceiving a pluralistic image of being a Briton, possibly black or brown, Hindu or Muslim, wearing a turban or a toga or a sari? These are the sort of questions which should be raised, and debated at length, at both the popular and élitist levels.

After all, it is not for the Afro-Asian immigrants alone to adapt to British society. The latter too, if it is dynamic and ingenious, should accept the challenges implicit in the newly-risen situation, absorb new experiences, and evolve enriched and somewhat transformed. We, in the western world, are living in a period of rapid technological changes. It is therefore not unrealistic, or high-handed, to suggest that a vital industrial nation, such as Britain, should adapt to an altered national circumstance at a fraction of the speed that technological changes demand. 'Ethnic pluralism,' writes Banton, 'may prove well adapted to the circumstance of an automated society.'[32] If so, then let British society face automation as well as socio-racial change with confidence and realism.

31. Many of the author's conversations with (generally liberal) British journalists on race relations in Britain end with a resigned statement by them: 'We'll all be coffee-coloured in fifty years' time'.
32. *New Society*, 9 November 1967.

APPENDIX
THE INSTITUTE OF RACE
RELATIONS' SURVEY
OF WHITE ADULTS'
ATTITUDES TOWARDS
COLOURED PEOPLE

During December 1966–January 1967 a team of five social scientists, led by Dr Mark Abrams, conducted, for the Institute of Race Relations, a survey of white adults' attitudes towards coloured people. The survey involved interviewing 2,500 white adults in five boroughs in England with a fifty-item questionnaire. The findings were included in *Colour and Citizenship*, a Report on British Race Relations, published in July 1969. The main conclusion was that 35 per cent of the whites were 'tolerant'; 38 per cent were 'tolerant-inclined'; 17 per cent were 'prejudice-inclined'; and only 10 per cent were 'prejudiced'.[1]

The Report and especially the findings of the attitudes survey received an almost unprecedented publicity and comment in the mass media. Typical of this reaction was the *Daily Mirror* editorial on 10 July 1969, which began: 'The most interesting and encouraging finding in today's impressive report by the Institute of Race Relations is this: Only ten per cent of the people of this country could be described as highly prejudiced about coloured immigrants ... That must mean that the vast majority of people – 90 per cent – are ready, or can be persuaded, to make a success of race relations in Britain.'

In view of that statement, this survey needs to be examined carefully. One of the persons who has done so is Danny Lawrence, a sociologist with the University of Nottingham. His critique is so cogent that it deserves to be quoted at length:

The main body of his [Dr Abrams's] findings are presented in the form of a prejudice-tolerance scale. It is not clear whether or not his questionnaire was constructed with this scale in mind. Certainly he offers no explanation for presenting his findings in this way, nor does he make any claims for the reliability or validity of the scale.

1. Chapter 28, p. 553.

Respondents were placed in one of the following four categories: prejudiced, prejudice-inclined, tolerant-inclined and tolerant. But the procedures by which respondents were placed in these categories is not made clear by Dr Abrams. He explains that fourteen questions in his questionnaire were used in the construction of the prejudice-tolerance scale. Four of these items are quoted in full. The reader is referred to the Institute of Race Relations Library for full details of the other ten. Those included do, however, form the main basis of the scale. An unconditionally prejudiced reply to any of these four 'key' items was given a score of *fifteen* points. Hence, a respondent who gave very prejudiced replies to all four key questions was awarded a score of sixty points. A prejudiced reply on any of the ten unnamed items was given only *one* point.[2]

Based on the answers to these four questions, Dr Abrams divided the respondents into four categories:

Tolerant: no hostile answer at all;
Tolerant-inclined: one hostile answer;
Prejudice-inclined: two hostile answers;
Prejudiced: three or four hostile answers.[3]

What about the answers to ten supplementary questions? Only an oblique reference is made to that: 'In each of the four groups there could, of course, be people who had expressed unfavourable attitudes to coloured people on one or more of the supplementary questions,' wrote Dr Abrams.[4] But, in any case, the weighting of supplementary questions to key items was 15:1. So that even if a respondent gave hostile answers to *all* the supplementary questions he could only score 10 points, five less than his score on giving a hostile answer to *one* key question!

The crucial point here is: why did Dr Abrams give such massive weighting to key questions? Because, 'the [four] key items produced a smaller proportion of hostile replies than some of the other ten items,' explained Danny Lawrence.[5] This explanation seems all the more satisfactory when we examine the content of the four key questions. *Three* of these concern housing.[6]

2. *Race Today*, October 1969, p. 175.
3. *Colour and Citizenship*, p. 552.   4. ibid., p. 552.
5. *Race Today*, October 1969, p. 175.   6. *Colour and Citizenship*, p. 552.

In his *Colour, Citizenship and British Society*, an abridged version of *Colour and Citizenship*, Nicholas Deakin used a different interpretation of the results. The two interpretations were as follows:

Dr Mark Abrams's terms		*Nicholas Deakin's terms*
Tolerant: ⎰35 per cent	:	Tolerant
Tolerant-inclined: ⎱38 per cent	:	⎰Mildly Prejudiced
Prejudice-inclined: 17 per cent	:	⎰Prejudiced
Prejudiced[7]: 10 per cent	:	⎱Intensely Prejudiced[8]

So, according to Dr Mark Abrams, 73 per cent of the whites were 'tolerant' or 'tolerantly-inclined'; whereas, according to Nicholas Deakin, 65 per cent were 'midly prejudiced', or 'prejudiced', or 'intensely prejudiced'!

Next to be considered is the wording of the questions. The three questions concerning housing were: 'If you had any choice would you particularly avoid having neighbours from any of these places – West Indies, India, or Pakistan?'; 'Do you think the authorities should let or refuse to let a Council house or flat to a family born in the West Indies, India, or Pakistan?'; 'Do you think a private landlord should let or refuse to let accommodation to a family born in the West Indies, India, or Pakistan?' Only the first question is worded in personal terms because it needs to be. The second question should have been worded as 'Do you think your family should or should not be treated on par with a family born in ...?' And the third as, 'If you had a room or a house to let, would you ...?'

In the case of the fourth question, 'Do you think the majority of coloured people in Britain are superior, equal, or inferior to you?'*only* those who said that coloured people are inferior and added that this was because of their colour were given a prejudice score of fifteen. Only five per cent of those who considered coloured people inferior gave 'skin colour' as their reason; forty-four per cent said 'lack of education'; and thirty-eight per cent said 'general cultural differences'.[9]

7. ibid., p. 553.
8. *Colour, Citizenship and British Society*, Panther Books, 1970, pp. 318–19.
9. *Colour and Citizenship*, p. 567.

It should be interesting to conduct a similar survey among the whites in South Africa, Rhodesia and the southern states of America to find out whether a large majority of them too give 'reason' other than 'skin colour' for their belief in the inferiority of blacks.

For some explanation of the nature of this survey one must refer to Professor John Rex's analysis that 'A great deal of what is going on (in sociological and historical research in British race relations) is insular and policy-oriented.'[10] *Colour and Citizenship* seems to fit that category exactly. Indeed, before presenting their recommendations, which run into eighty pages, the authors state:

> From our survey of British attitudes to colour, we have evidence that, contrary to the general view, the majority of the population are tolerantly inclined . . . We are therefore encouraged by these findings to put forward our recommendations, since they seem to us to provide solid ground for expecting a favourable response to positive policies.[11]

But this 'general view' was well supported by another survey – on the extent of racial discrimination against coloured people – by the P E P. It is interesting to note that this survey was conducted at about *the same time* as the above survey. Put together the two surveys were saying this: there is a massive discrimination against coloured people by whites, 73 per cent of whom are 'tolerant' or 'tolerant-inclined'!

10. *New Society*, 6 April 1970.
11. pp. 675–6. The decision to advance the publication of this report by a year was in itself a *political* decision, a reaction to Enoch Powell's speech in April 1968. In essence, it was a case of subjugating sociological research to serve a political purpose.

SELECT BIBLIOGRAPHY

BANTON, MICHAEL, *Race Relations*, Tavistock, 1967.

BEETHAM, DAVID, *Immigrant School Leavers and the Youth Employment Service in Birmingham*, Institute of Race Relations, Special Series, 1968.

BRAITHWAITE, E. R., *Paid Servant*, Bodley Head, 1962.

BURNEY, ELIZABETH, *Housing on Trial*, Oxford University Press for the Institute of Race Relations, 1967.

BUTTERWORTH, ERIC, *A Muslim Community in Britain*, Church Information Service for The Church Assembly Board For Social Responsibility, 1967.

CALLEY, MALCOLM J. C., *God's People*, Oxford University Press for the Institute of Race Relations, 1965.

CARMICHAEL, STOKELY, and HAMILTON, CHARLES V., *Black Power*, Jonathan Cape, 1968.

CHATER, A., *Race Relations in Britain*, Lawrence and Wishart, 1966.

COX, OLIVER CROMWELL, *Caste, Class & Race*, New York, Monthly Review Press, 1959.

DANIEL, W. W., *Racial Discrimination in England*, Penguin Books, 1968.

DAVISON, R. B., *Black British*, Oxford University Press for the Institute of Race Relations, 1966.
West Indian Migrants, Oxford University Press for the Institute of Race Relations, 1962.

DEAKIN, NICHOLAS, *Colour, Citizenship and British Society*, Panther Books, 1970.

DEEDES, WILLIAM, *Race Without Rancour*, Conservative Political Centre, 1968.

DESAI, RASHMI, *Indian Immigrants in Britain*, Oxford University Press for the Institute of Race Relations, 1963.

FITZHERBERT, KATRIN, *West Indian Children In London*, G. Bell & Sons, 1967.

FOOT, PAUL, *Immigration and Race in British Politics*, Penguin Books, 1965.

GLASS, RUTH, *Newcomers*, Allen & Unwin for Centre for Urban Studies, 1960.

GRIER, WILLIAM H., and COBBS, PRICE M., *Black Rage*, Jonathan Cape, 1969.

GRIFFITHS, PETER, *A Quest.on of Colour?*, Leslie Frewin, 1966.

GRIGG, MARY, *The White Question*, Secker & Warburg, 1967.

HASHMI, FARRUKH, *The Pakistani Family in Britain*, Community Relations Commission, 1969.

HEPPLE, BOB, *Race, Jobs and the Law in Britain*, Allen Lane The Penguin Press, 1968.

HILL, CLIFFORD S., *How Colour Prejudiced Is Britain?*, Gollancz, 1965.

West Indian Migrants and the London Churches, Oxford University Press for the Institute of Race Relations, 1963.

HINDS, DONALD, *Journey to an Illusion*, Heinemann, 1966.

HIRO, DILIP, *The Indian Family in Britain*, Community Relations Commission. 1969.

HOOPER, RICHARD, edr, *Colour in Britain*, British Broadcasting Corporation, 1965.

House of Commons Select Committee on Race Relations and Immigration, *The Problems of Coloured School-Leavers*, Volume I, Her Majesty's Stationery Office, 1969.

JEPHCOTT, PEARL, *A Troubled Area: Notes on Notting Hill*, Faber & Faber, 1964.

KIERNAN, V. G., *The Lords of Human Kind*, Weidenfeld and Nicolson, 1969.

LITTLE, K. L., *Negroes in Britain*, Kegan Paul, 1947.

MAXWELL, NEVILLE, *The Power of Negro Action*, The Author, 1965.

NAIPAUL, V. S., *The Middle Passage*, André Deutsch, 1962.

National Association of Schoolmasters, *Education and the Immigrants*, Educare for the National Association of Schoolmasters, 1969.

New Society Social Studies Reader, *Race and Immigration*, IPC Magazines, 1970.

NORRIS, KATRIN, *Jamaica: The Search For An Identity*, Oxford University Press for the Institute of Race Relations, 1962.

OTTLEY, ROI, *No Green Pastures*, John Murray, 1952.

PATTERSON, SHEILA, *Dark Strangers*, Tavistock, 1963.

Immigration and Race Relations in Britain, 1960–1967, Oxford University Press for the Institute of Race Relations, 1969.

edr, *Immigrants In London*, The London Council of Social Service, 1963.

PEACH, CERI, *West Indian Migration to Britain*, Oxford University Press for the Institute of Race Relations, 1968.

Political and Economic Planning Ltd, *Racial Discrimination*, PEP, 1967.

POPE-HENNESSY, JAMES, *Sins of the Fathers*, Weidenfeld & Nicolson, 1967.

POWER, JOHN, *Immigrants in School*, Councils and Education Press, 1967

REX, JOHN and MOORE, ROBERT, *Race, Community and Conflict: a study of Sparkbrook*, Oxford University Press for the Institute of Race Relations, 1967.

ROSE, E. J. B., and Associates, *Colour and Citizenship*, Oxford University Press for the Institute of Race Relations, 1969.

WICKENDEN, JAMES, *Colour in Britain*, Oxford University Press for the Institute of Race Relations, 1958.

WILLIAMS, ERIC, *Capitalism and Slavery*, André Deutsch, 1964.

WOOD, WILFRED, and DOWNING, JOHN, *Vicious Circle*, SPCK, 1968.

WRIGHT, PETER, *The Coloured Worker in British Industry*, Oxford University Press for the Institute of Race Relations, 1968.

YOUNG, GEORGE K., *Who Goes Home?*, The Monday Club, 1969.

INDEX

Rowley, Keith, study of Midlands children, 299

St Kitts, 4, 27
St Lucia, 29
St Vincent, 27, 29
Sandys, Duncan, 218, 226, 303; Kenya Asians, 206–7, 208n., 209
Sawh, Roy, 52–3
Schools, immigrant children in, 68, 69–71, 79–80, 236–40, 278, 293, 299–300, 328–9; difference between West Indians and Asians, 71–3; special problems of Asians, 123–4, 160–2, 173–5
Sekyi, Kobina, xviii
Separatism and segregation, 27, 79–80, 81–4, 113, 165, 235–7, 239–40
Seventh Day Adventist Church, 32
Sexual character and customs of West Indians, 18–19, 326; of Asians, 153; fallacious views on negroes, 282
Shearer, Hugh, 89
Short, Edward, 328
Shromani Akali Dal (SAD), 129 and n.
Sikh religion and customs, 125–8, 132, 150–54, 155–7, 163–4
Sikhs in India, willingness to emigrate, 103, 104–5
Sikhs' insistence on the turban, in Manchester, 128, 163; in Wolverhampton, 128–30, 147, 163, 310
Simey, Lord, 252
Singh, Baba Udham, assassinates Sir Michael O'Dwyer, 139–40
Singh, Guru Gobind, 125, 128
Singh, Jathedar Santokh, 129n.
Singh, Sant Fateh, 127–8
Skinheads, 39n., 56n., 175, 176n., 311
Slavery, historical outline of, ix–xiv, 3, 10, 296–7; and Christianity, 28–9; effect on West Indian way of life, 14–20, 73
Slough, Anguillans in, 27; Asians in, 178–9; housing policy in 274
Smethwick, local politics before 1964, 141–2, 195–6, 1964 election,

50, 142, 197, 205n., its aftermath, 56; 1966 election, 205; Sikhs in, 127
Social welfare, 227, 228–33
Society of Labour Lawyers, 58
Somersett, James, xi
Soskice, Sir Frank, 185, 204–5
Southall, disturbances in, 41, 177; demand for segregation in schools, 68, 69–70, 236–7; Asians in, 120, 127, 142–3, 262, 292
Standing Committee of Leaders of Organizations Concerned with West Indians in Britain, 45
Stephenson, Paul, 43, 49–50, 71n.
Stevenson, Dennis and Wallis, Peter, survey of West Indian youths in London, 15n., 16n., 77n.
Stonham, Lord, 248

Taylor, Humphrey, 307–8
Television, coverage of race relations, 288–85 *passim*
Thomas, J. J., work on the creole language, 14n.
Tipton, strike of Asian workers, 262–3
Tomney, Frank, 191
Trades Union Congress, 200, 217, 260–61, 289–90
Trade unionism, 141, 260–64, 285, 289–90
Trinidad, early history, 4; national economy, 6–7, 8; Roman Catholics in, 29–31; influence of Black Power, 62, 90; creole language, 14n.; effect of Powellism in, 84
Trollope, Anthony, on the West Indian negro, xiii, 85–6
Ulster, *see* Ireland, Northern
Universal Coloured People's Association (UCPA), 59–60, 91

Watson, Peter, 83n.
Watt, David, 286
Weekes, George, on Black Power, 62
Wenham, Brian, 210n.
West Indian Development Council, in Bristol, 49
West Indian Gazette, 43, 44